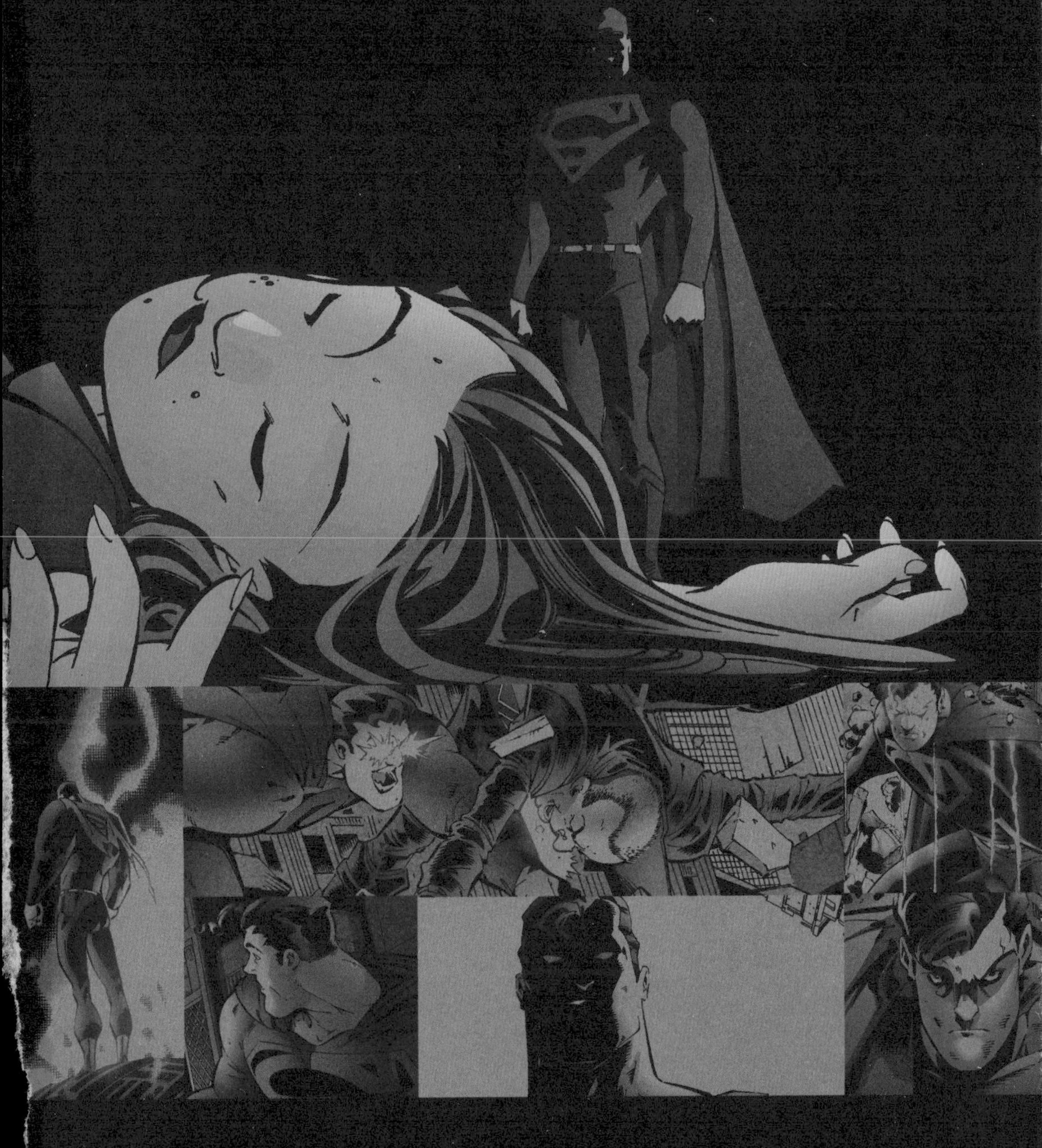

UPERMAN **ENDING BATTLE**

DAN DIDIO Senior VP-Executive Editor EDDIE BERGANZA Editor-original series TOM PALMER JR. Associate Editor-original series SEAN MACKIEWICZ Editor-collected edition

ROBBIN BROSTERMAN Senior Art Director PAUL LEVITZ President & Publisher GEORG BREWER VP-Design & DC Direct Creative RICHARD BRUNING Senior VP-Creative Director

PATRICK CALDON Executive VP-Finance & Operations CHRIS CARAMALIS VP-Finance JOHN CUNNINGHAM VP-Marketing TERRI CUNNINGHAM VP-Managing Editor

AMY GENKINS Senior VP-Business & Legal Affairs ALISON GILL VP-Manufacturing DAVID HYDE VP-Publicity HANK KANALZ VP-General Manager, WildStorm

JIM LEE Editorial Director-WildStorm GREGORY NOVECK Senior VP-Creative Affairs SUE POHJA VP-Book Trade Sales STEVE ROTTERDAM Senior VP-Sales & Marketing

CHERYL RUBIN Senior VP-Brand Management ALYSSE SOLL VP-Advertising & Custom Publishing JEFF TROJAN VP-Business Development, DC Direct BOB WAYNE VP-Sales

SUPERMAN CREATED BY JERRY SIEGEL & JOE SHUSTER

COVER BY CARLOS PACHECO AND JESUS MERINO

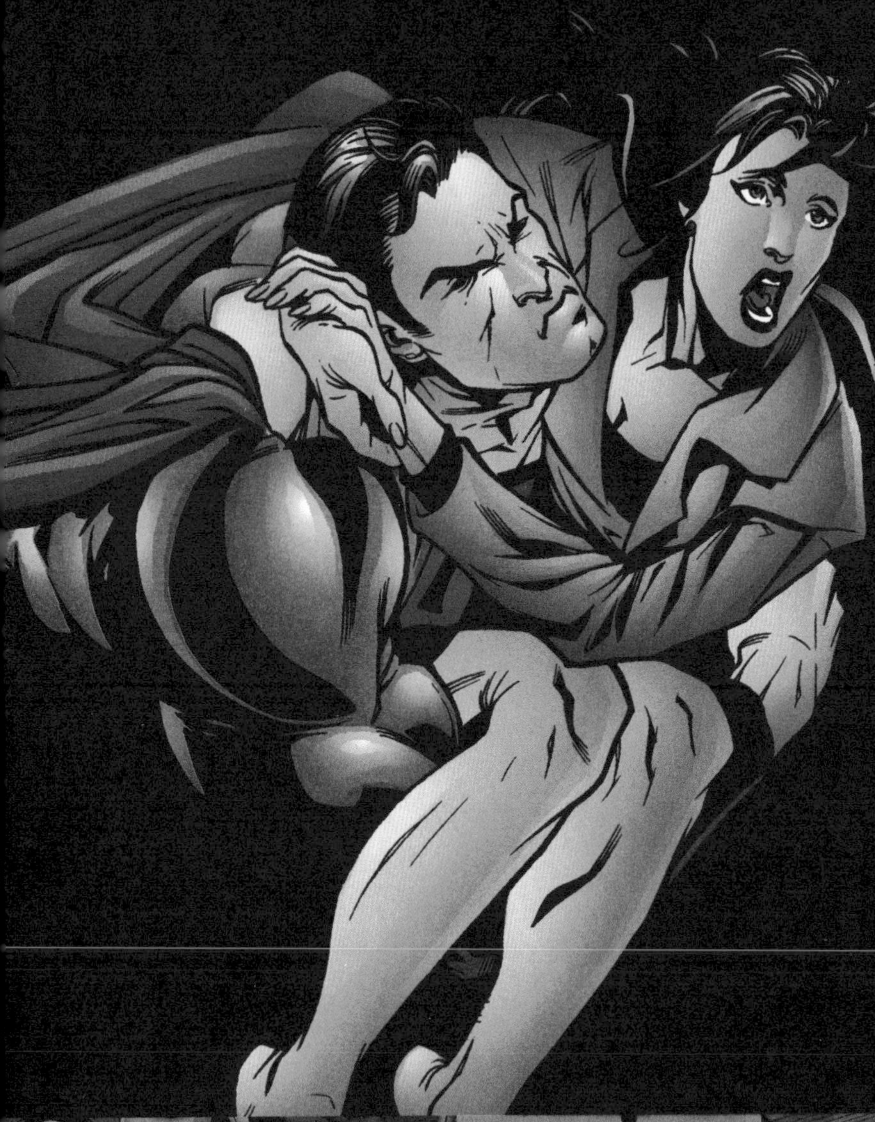

Joe Casey
Geoff Johns
Joe Kelly
Mark Schultz
WRITERS

Derec Aucoin
Brandon Badeaux
Pascual Ferry
Duncan Rouleau
PENCILLERS

Marlo Alquiza
Derec Aucoin
Mark Farmer
Mark Morales
Cam Smith
INKERS

Comicraft
Ken Lopez
Richard Starkings
LETTERERS

Tanya & Richard Horie
Rob Ro & Alex Bleyaert
Moose Baumann
COLORISTS

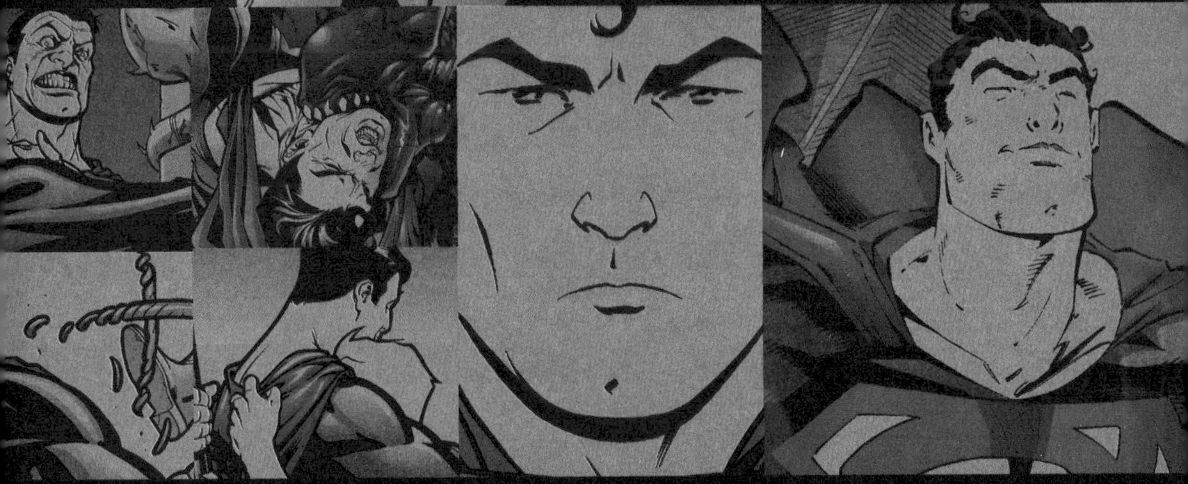

SUPERMAN **ENDING BATTLE**

Cover art by PASCUAL FERRY & CAM SMITH

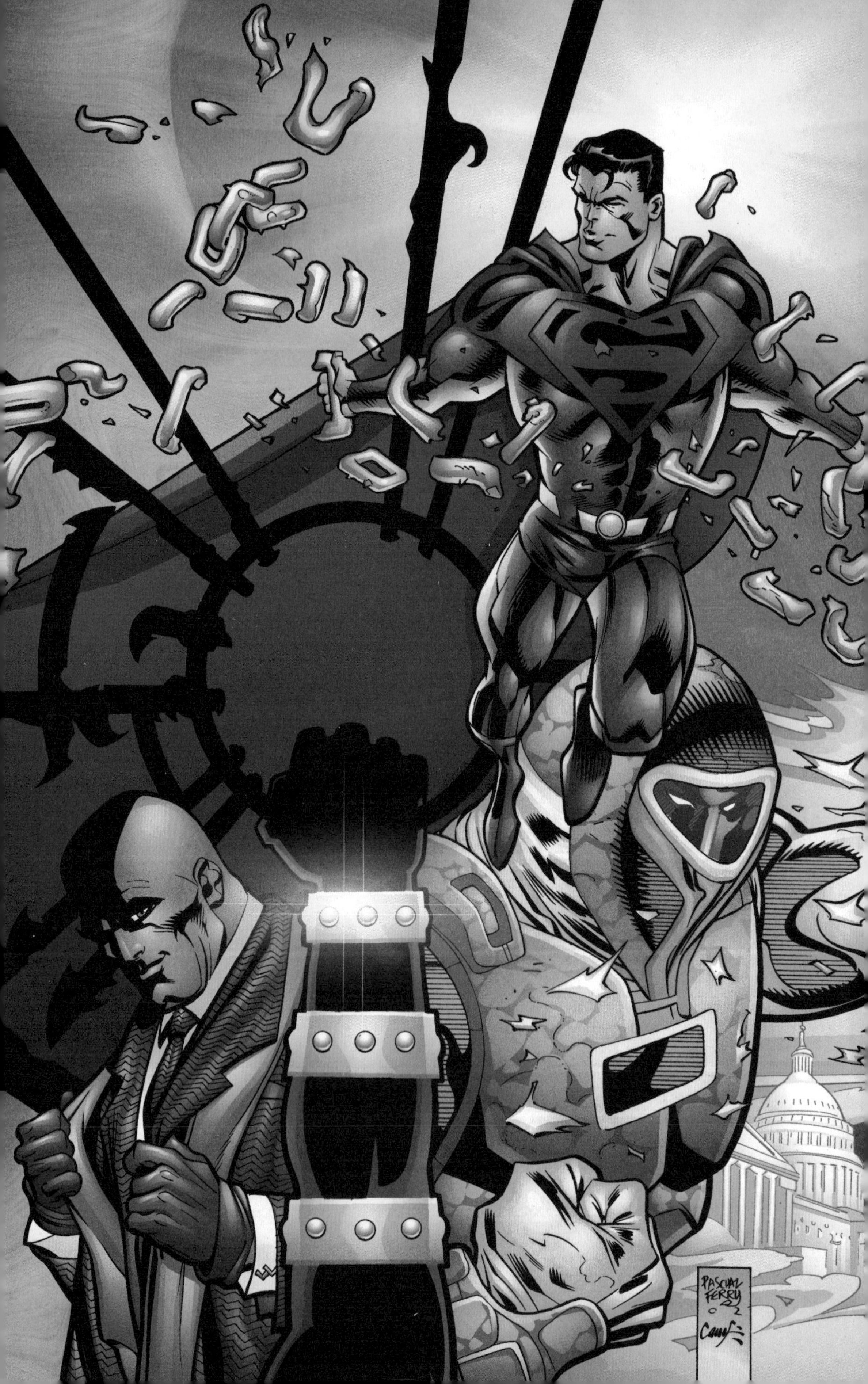
PASCUAL FERRY
02
Cam

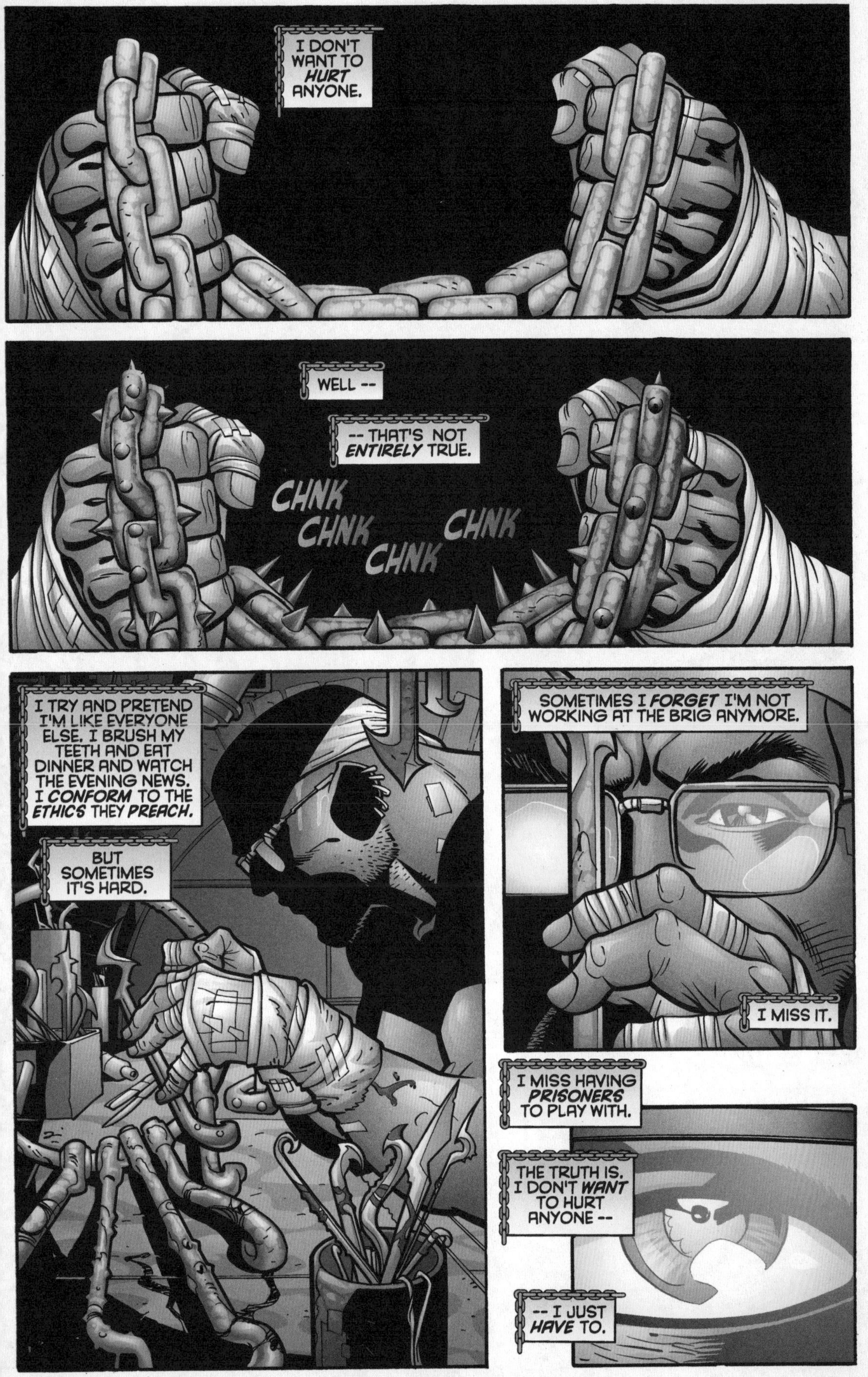
I DON'T WANT TO *HURT* ANYONE.
WELL --
-- THAT'S NOT *ENTIRELY* TRUE.
CHNK
CHNK
CHNK
CHNK
I TRY AND PRETEND I'M LIKE EVERYONE ELSE. I BRUSH MY TEETH AND EAT DINNER AND WATCH THE EVENING NEWS. I *CONFORM* TO THE *ETHICS* THEY *PREACH.*
BUT SOMETIMES IT'S HARD.
SOMETIMES I *FORGET* I'M NOT WORKING AT THE BRIG ANYMORE.
I MISS IT.
I MISS HAVING *PRISONERS* TO PLAY WITH.
THE TRUTH IS. I DON'T *WANT* TO HURT ANYONE --
-- I JUST *HAVE* TO.

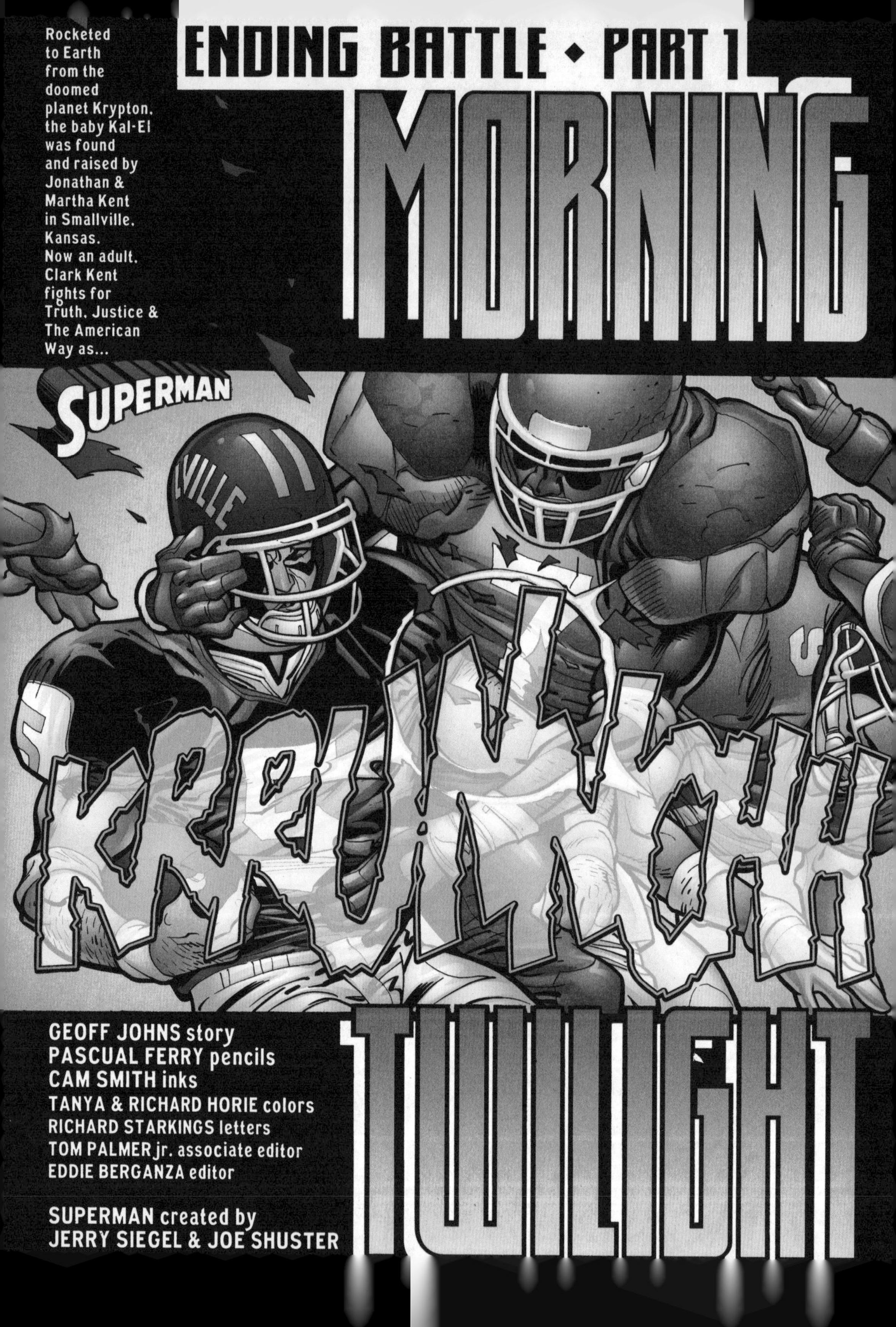
ENDING BATTLE • PART 1
MORNING
Rocketed to Earth from the doomed planet Krypton, the baby Kal-El was found and raised by Jonathan & Martha Kent in Smallville, Kansas. Now an adult, Clark Kent fights for Truth, Justice & The American Way as...
SUPERMAN
VILLE
KRRUNNCH!
TWILIGHT
GEOFF JOHNS story
PASCUAL FERRY pencils
CAM SMITH inks
TANYA & RICHARD HORIE colors
RICHARD STARKINGS letters
TOM PALMER jr. associate editor
EDDIE BERGANZA editor
SUPERMAN created by
JERRY SIEGEL & JOE SHUSTER

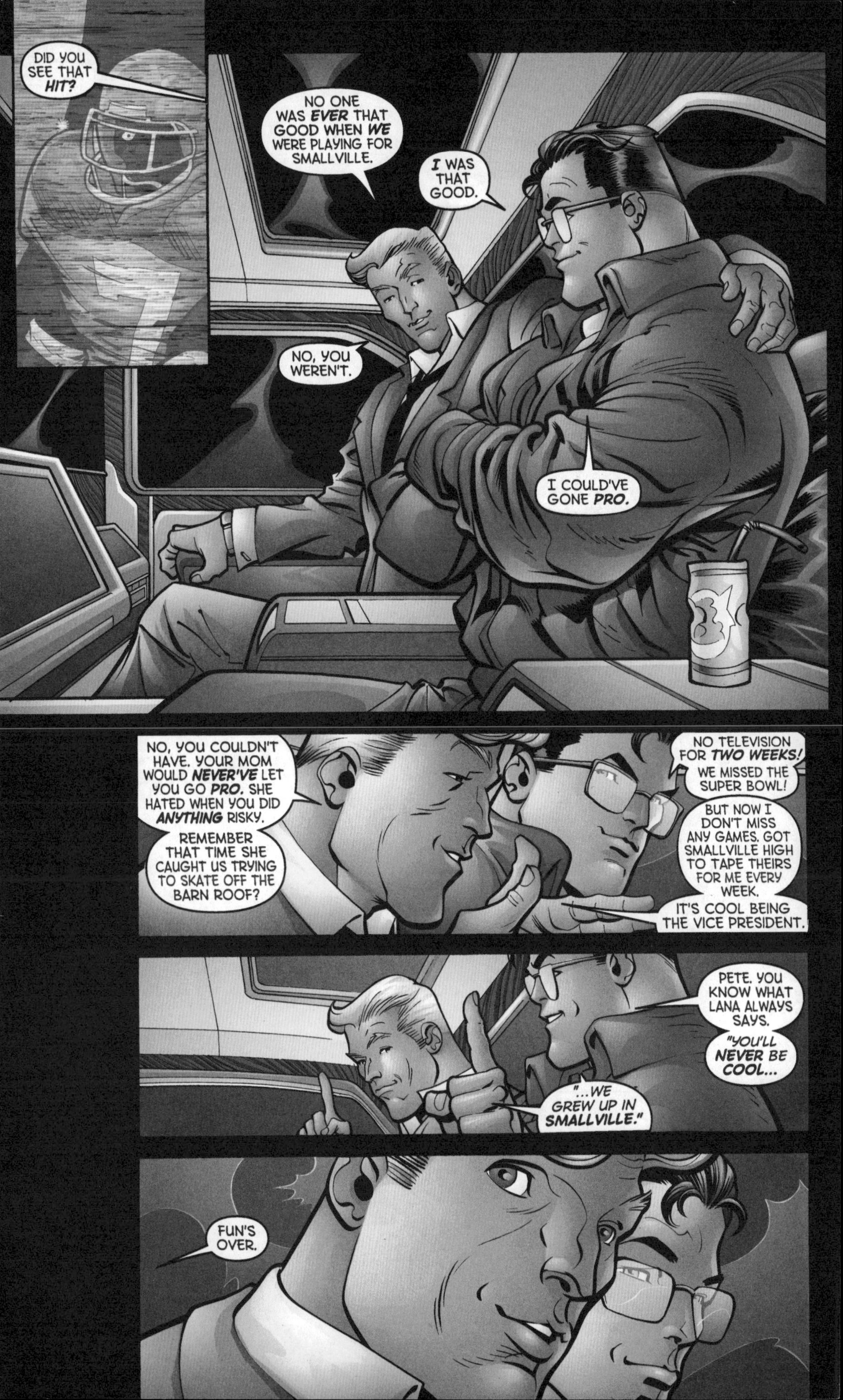
DID YOU SEE THAT HIT?
NO ONE WAS EVER THAT GOOD WHEN WE WERE PLAYING FOR SMALLVILLE.
I WAS THAT GOOD.
NO, YOU WEREN'T.
I COULD'VE GONE PRO.
NO, YOU COULDN'T HAVE. YOUR MOM WOULD NEVER'VE LET YOU GO PRO. SHE HATED WHEN YOU DID ANYTHING RISKY.
REMEMBER THAT TIME SHE CAUGHT US TRYING TO SKATE OFF THE BARN ROOF?
NO TELEVISION FOR TWO WEEKS! WE MISSED THE SUPER BOWL!
BUT NOW I DON'T MISS ANY GAMES. GOT SMALLVILLE HIGH TO TAPE THEIRS FOR ME EVERY WEEK.
IT'S COOL BEING THE VICE PRESIDENT.
PETE. YOU KNOW WHAT LANA ALWAYS SAYS.
"YOU'LL NEVER BE COOL...
"...WE GREW UP IN SMALLVILLE."
FUN'S OVER.

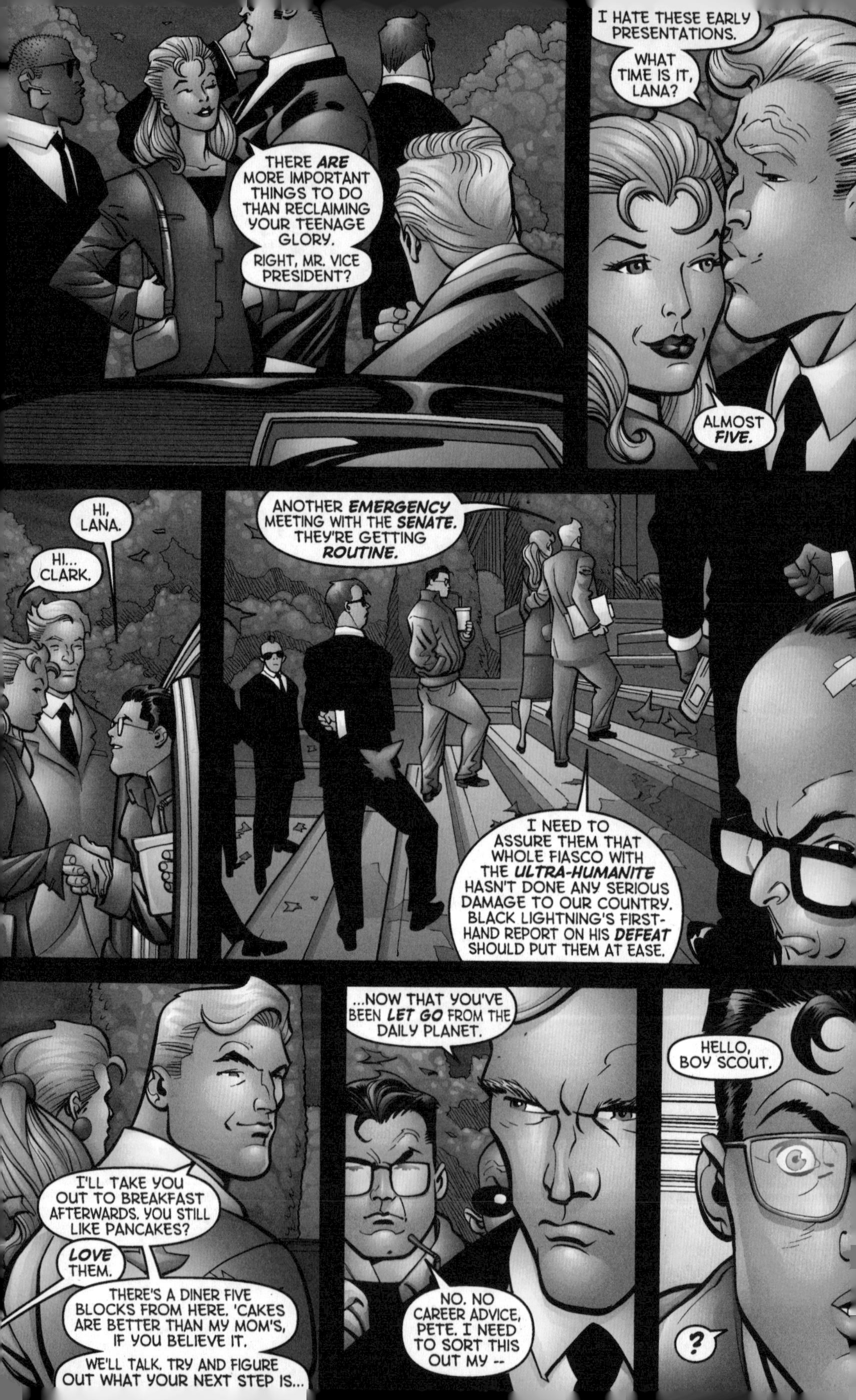
THERE ARE MORE IMPORTANT THINGS TO DO THAN RECLAIMING YOUR TEENAGE GLORY.
RIGHT, MR. VICE PRESIDENT?
I HATE THESE EARLY PRESENTATIONS.
WHAT TIME IS IT, LANA?
ALMOST FIVE.
HI, LANA.
HI... CLARK.
ANOTHER EMERGENCY MEETING WITH THE SENATE. THEY'RE GETTING ROUTINE.
I NEED TO ASSURE THEM THAT WHOLE FIASCO WITH THE ULTRA-HUMANITE HASN'T DONE ANY SERIOUS DAMAGE TO OUR COUNTRY. BLACK LIGHTNING'S FIRST-HAND REPORT ON HIS DEFEAT SHOULD PUT THEM AT EASE.
I'LL TAKE YOU OUT TO BREAKFAST AFTERWARDS. YOU STILL LIKE PANCAKES?
LOVE THEM.
THERE'S A DINER FIVE BLOCKS FROM HERE. 'CAKES ARE BETTER THAN MY MOM'S, IF YOU BELIEVE IT.
WE'LL TALK. TRY AND FIGURE OUT WHAT YOUR NEXT STEP IS...
...NOW THAT YOU'VE BEEN LET GO FROM THE DAILY PLANET.
NO. NO CAREER ADVICE, PETE. I NEED TO SORT THIS OUT MY --
HELLO, BOY SCOUT.
?

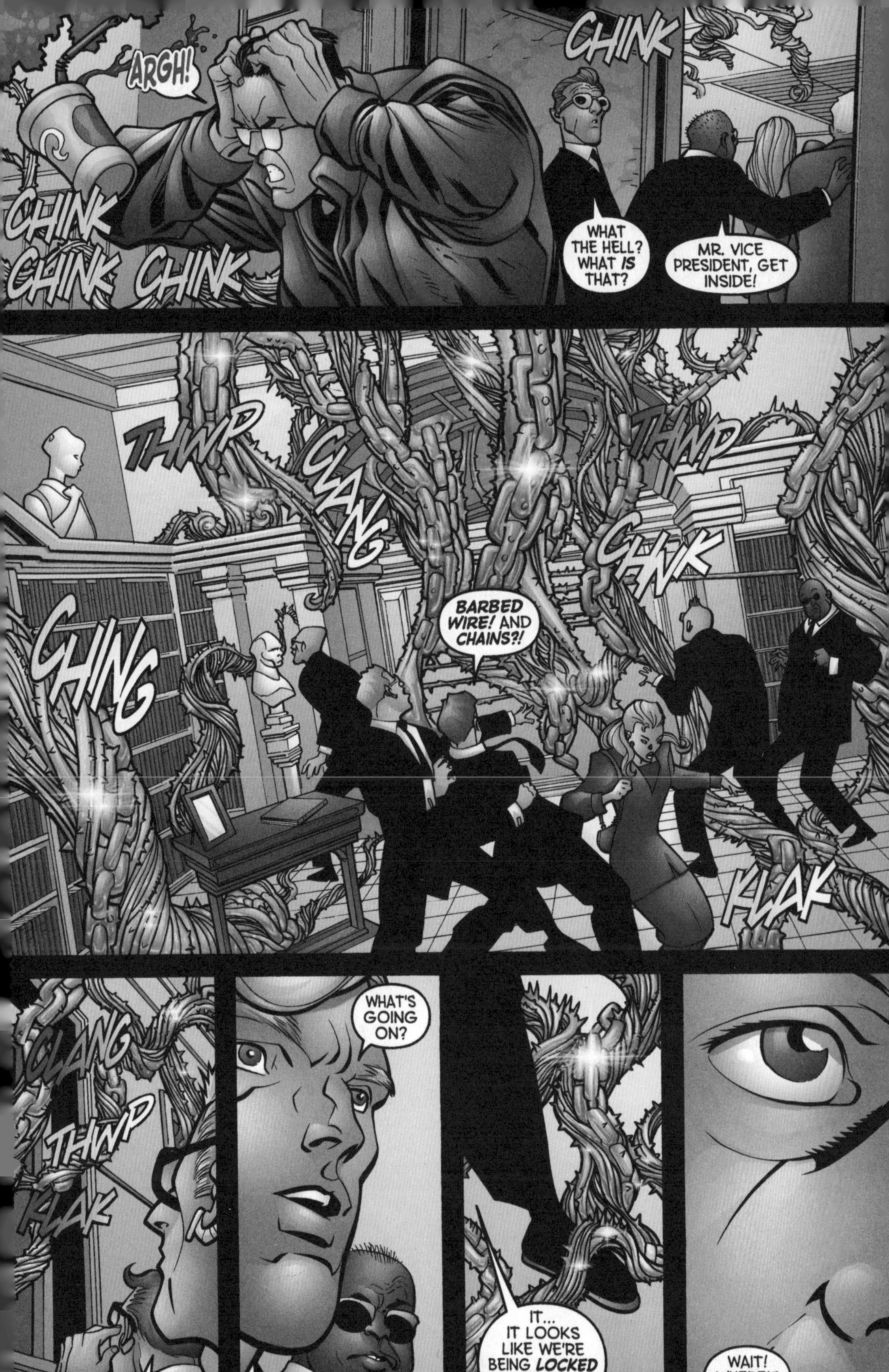
ARGH!
CHINK
CHINK CHINK CHINK
CHINK
WHAT THE HELL? WHAT IS THAT?
MR. VICE PRESIDENT, GET INSIDE!
THWP
CLANG
THWP
CHNK
CHING
BARBED WIRE! AND CHAINS?!
KLAK
CLANG
THWP
KLAK
BARS ARE FORMING OVER THE WINDOWS.
WHAT'S GOING ON?
IT... IT LOOKS LIKE WE'RE BEING LOCKED IN, MR. VICE PRESIDENT!
WAIT! WHERE'S CLARK?!

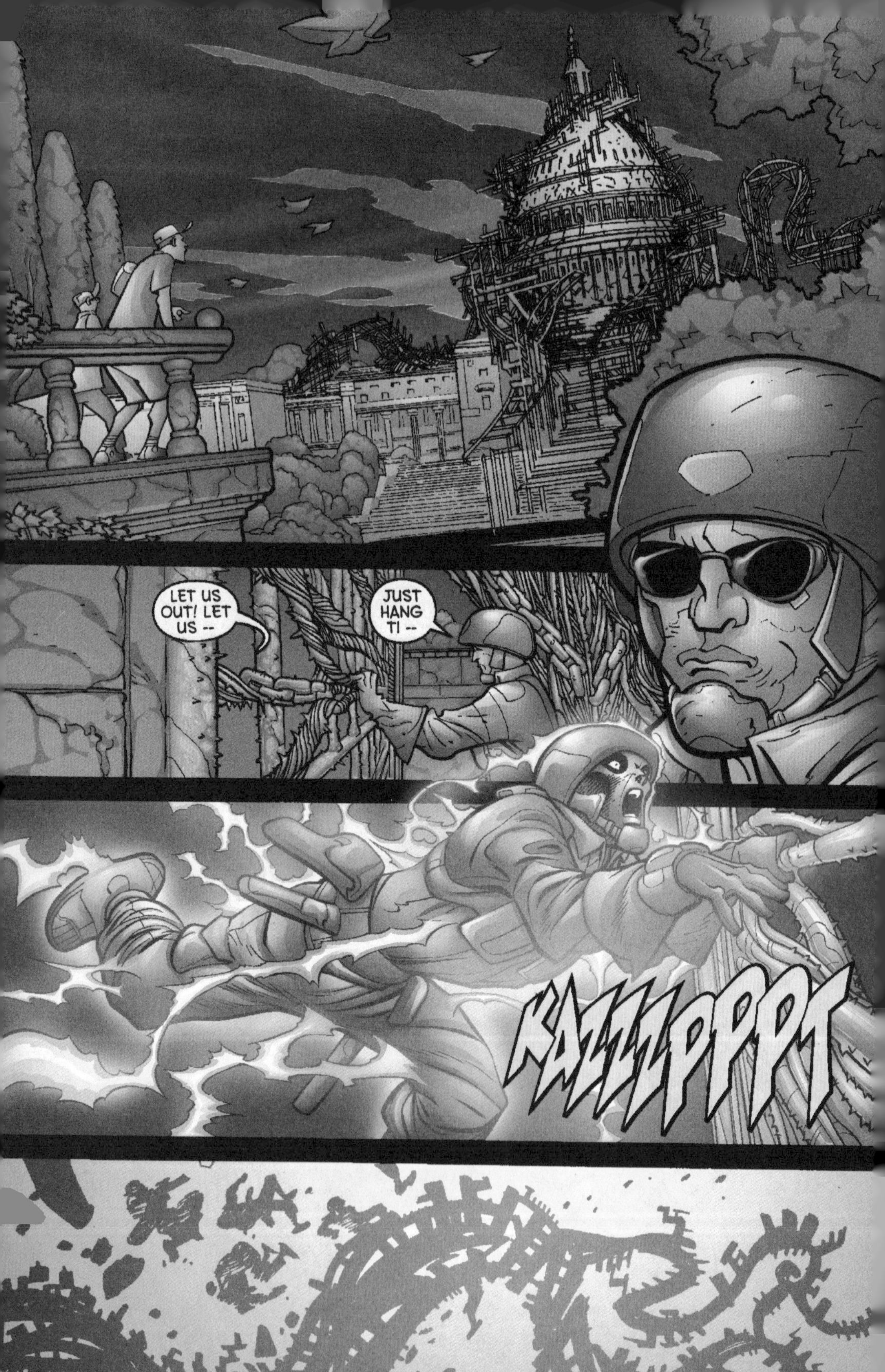
LET US OUT! LET US --
JUST HANG TI --
KAZZZPPPT

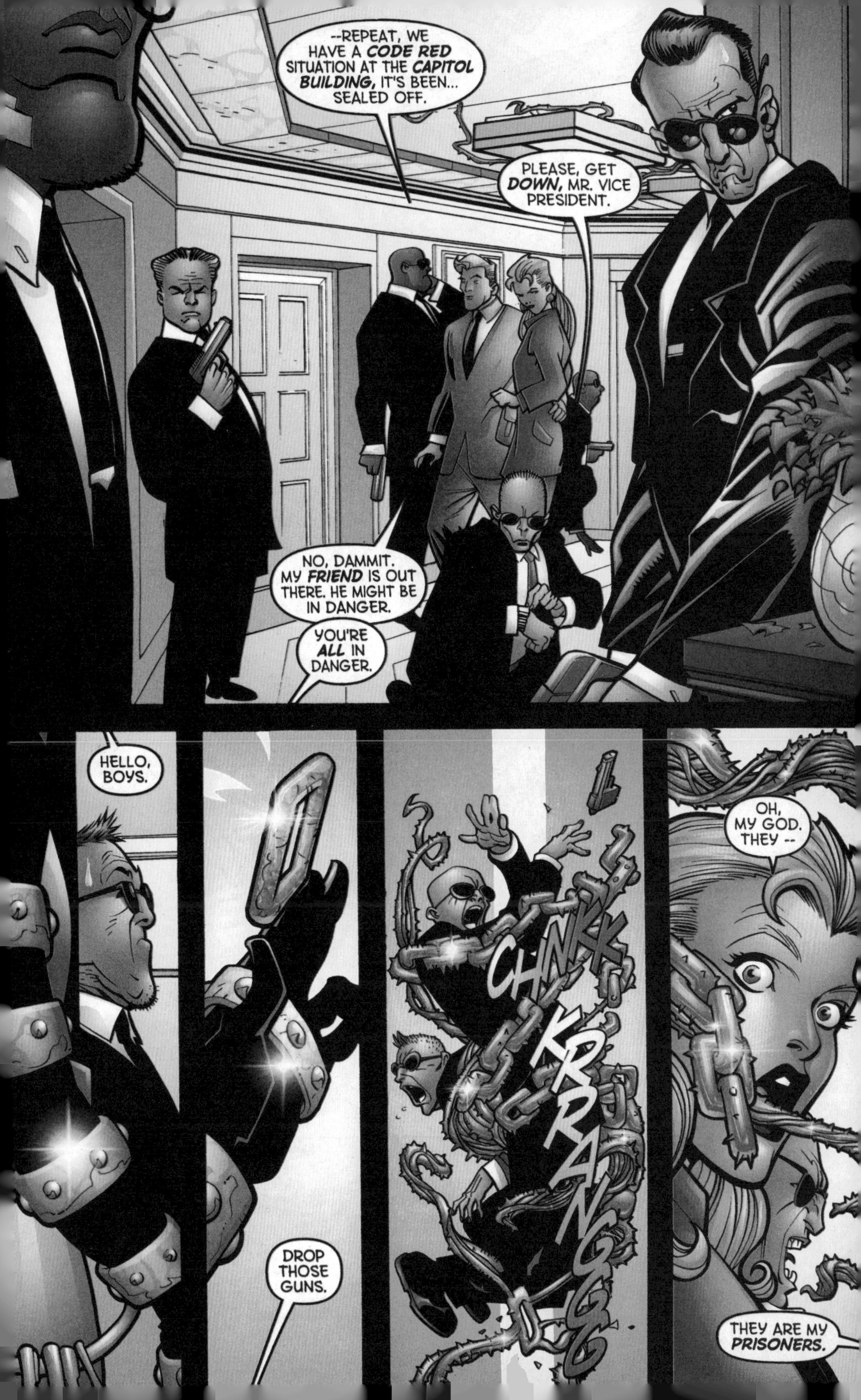
--REPEAT, WE HAVE A CODE RED SITUATION AT THE CAPITOL BUILDING, IT'S BEEN... SEALED OFF.
PLEASE, GET DOWN, MR. VICE PRESIDENT.
NO, DAMMIT. MY FRIEND IS OUT THERE. HE MIGHT BE IN DANGER.
YOU'RE ALL IN DANGER.
HELLO, BOYS.
DROP THOSE GUNS.
CHINKK
KRRANGGG
OH, MY GOD. THEY --
THEY ARE MY PRISONERS.

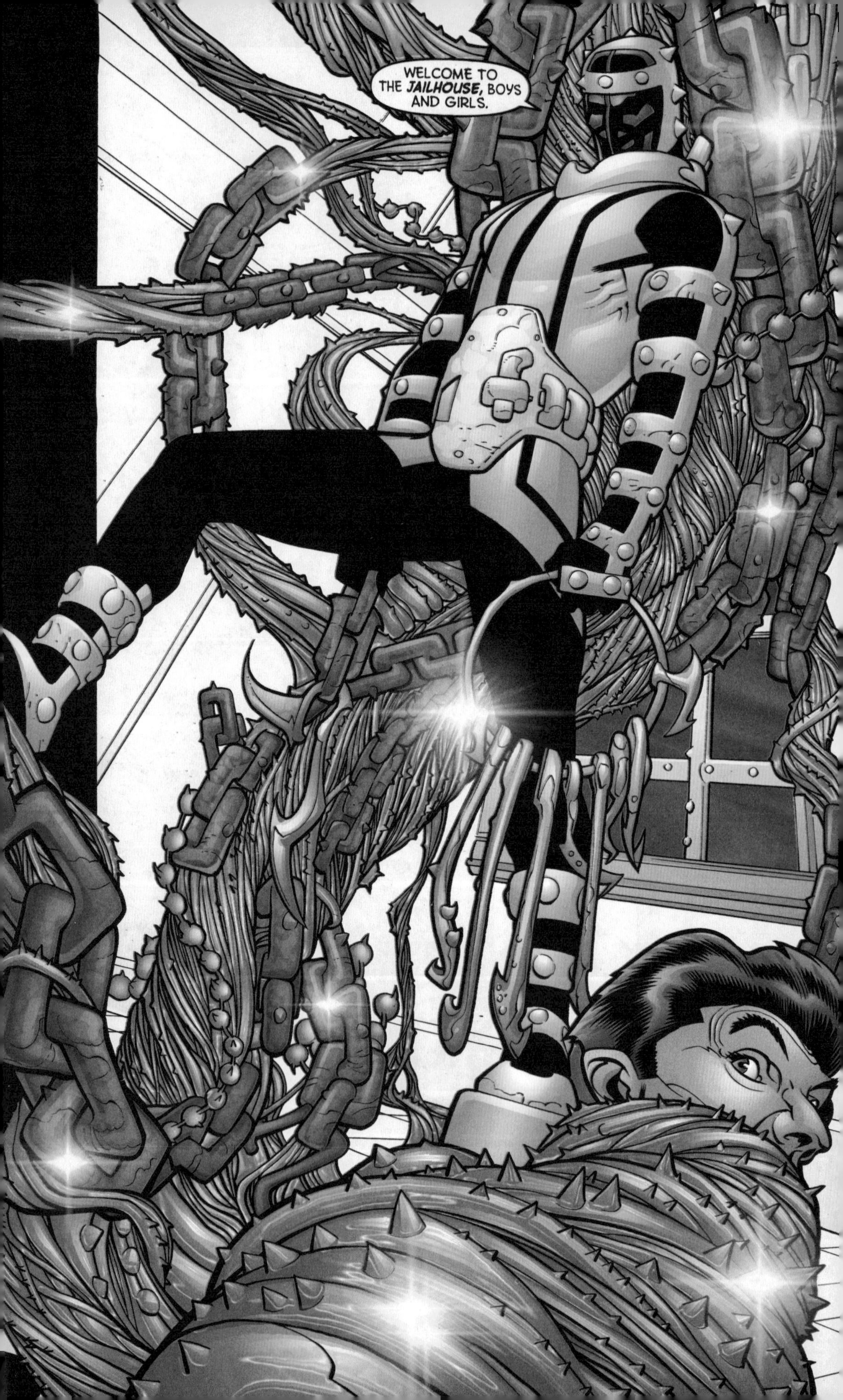
WELCOME TO THE JAILHOUSE, BOYS AND GIRLS.

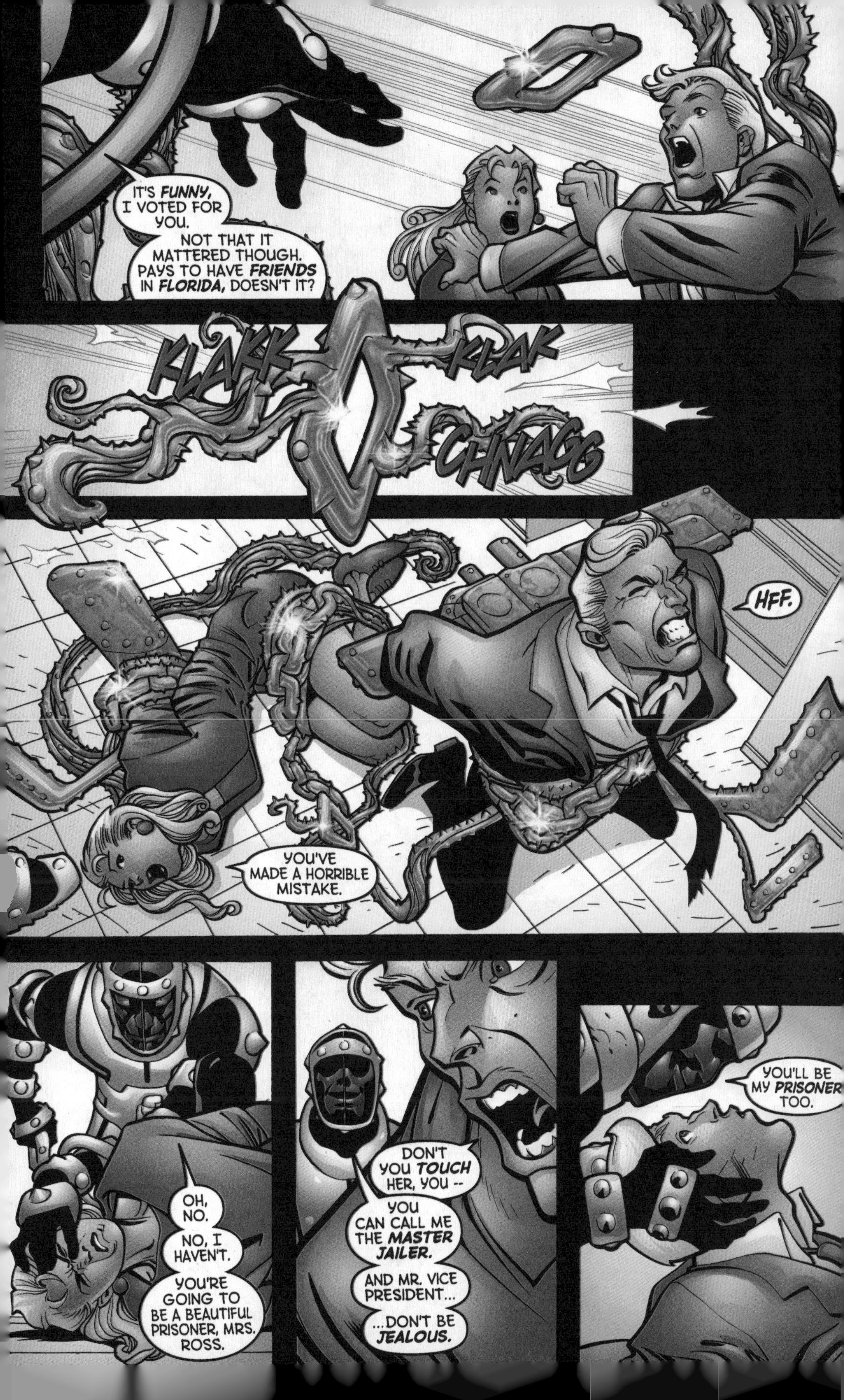
IT'S FUNNY, I VOTED FOR YOU.
NOT THAT IT MATTERED THOUGH. PAYS TO HAVE FRIENDS IN FLORIDA, DOESN'T IT?
KLAKK
KLAK
CHNAGG
HFF.
YOU'VE MADE A HORRIBLE MISTAKE.
OH, NO.
NO, I HAVEN'T.
YOU'RE GOING TO BE A BEAUTIFUL PRISONER, MRS. ROSS.
DON'T YOU TOUCH HER, YOU --
YOU CAN CALL ME THE MASTER JAILER.
AND MR. VICE PRESIDENT...
...DON'T BE JEALOUS.
YOU'LL BE MY PRISONER TOO.

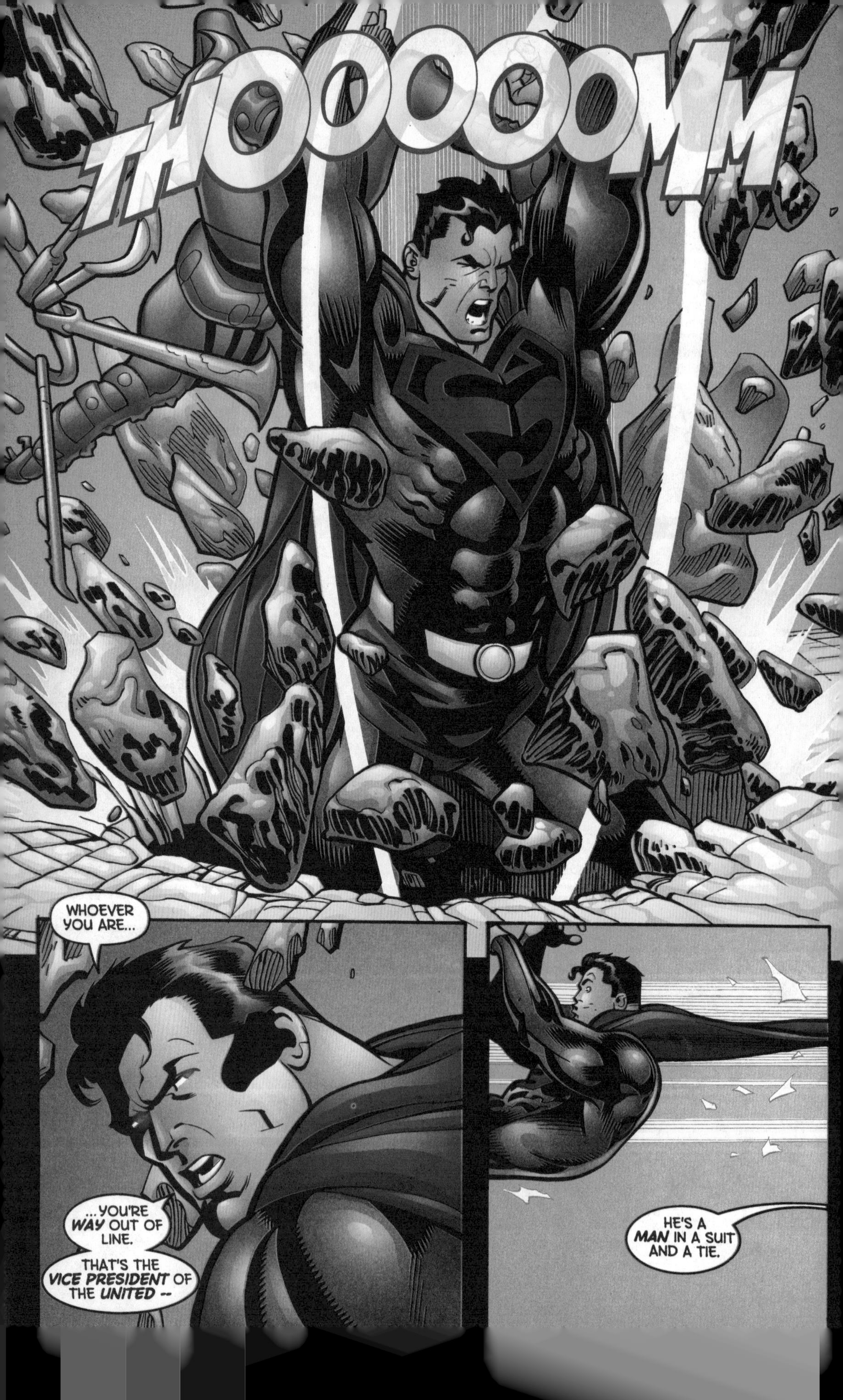
THOOOOOMM
WHOEVER YOU ARE...
...YOU'RE WAY OUT OF LINE.
THAT'S THE VICE PRESIDENT OF THE UNITED --
HE'S A MAN IN A SUIT AND A TIE.

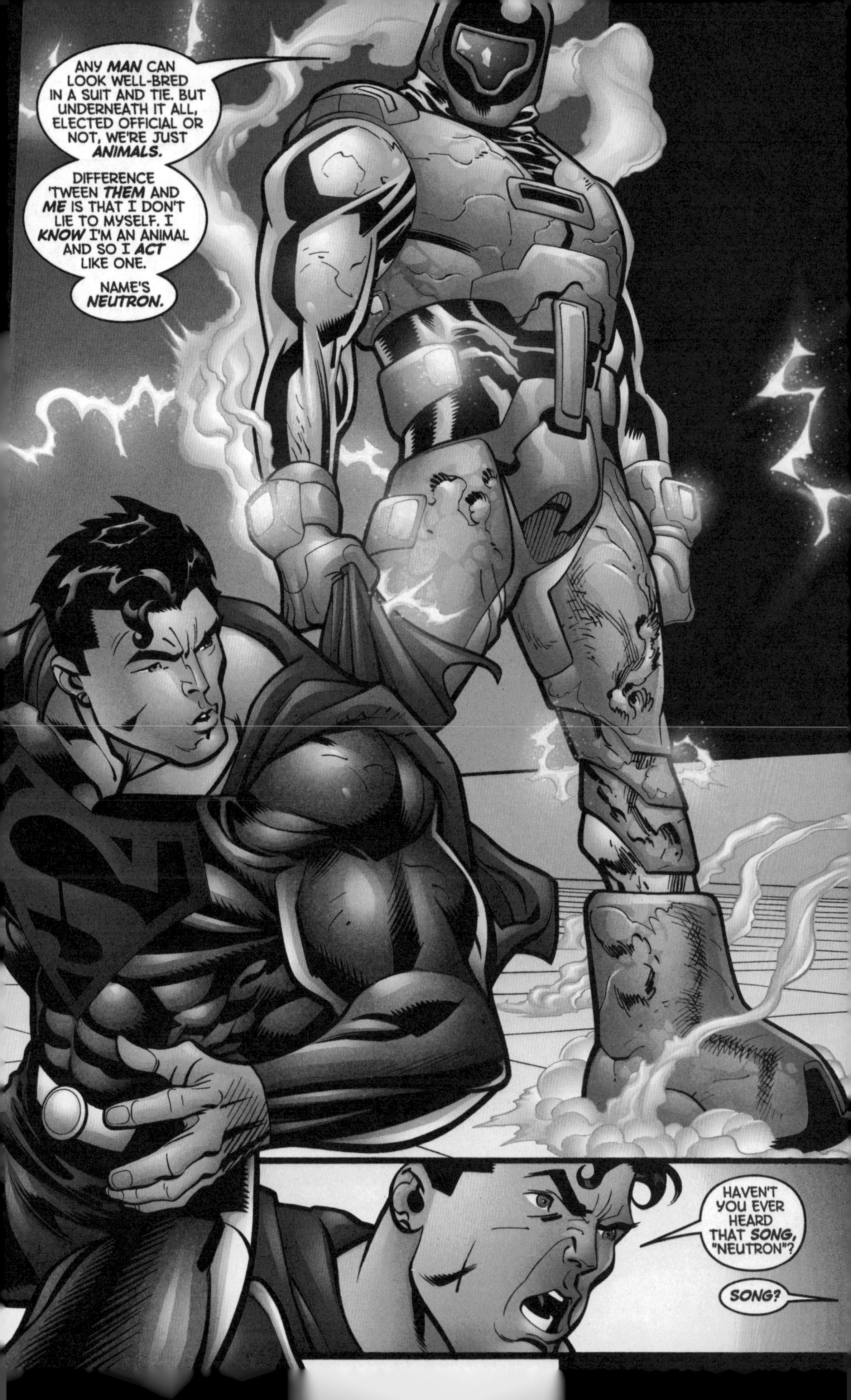
ANY *MAN* CAN LOOK WELL-BRED IN A SUIT AND TIE. BUT UNDERNEATH IT ALL, ELECTED OFFICIAL OR NOT, WE'RE JUST *ANIMALS.*
DIFFERENCE 'TWEEN *THEM* AND *ME* IS THAT I DON'T LIE TO MYSELF. I *KNOW* I'M AN ANIMAL AND SO I *ACT* LIKE ONE.
NAME'S *NEUTRON.*
HAVEN'T YOU EVER HEARD THAT *SONG,* "NEUTRON"?
SONG?

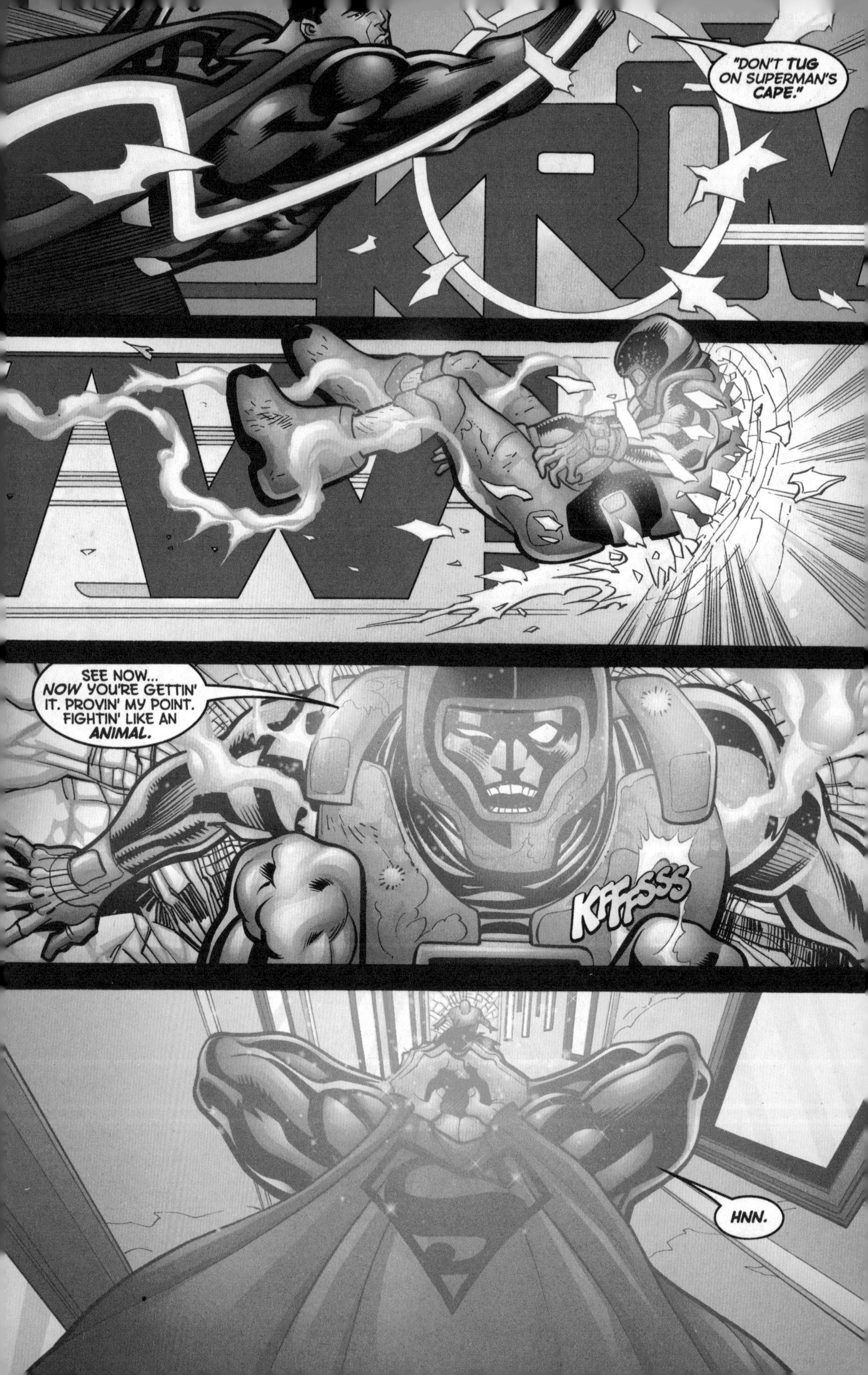

"DON'T TUG ON SUPERMAN'S CAPE."
SEE NOW... NOW YOU'RE GETTIN' IT. PROVIN' MY POINT. FIGHTIN' LIKE AN ANIMAL.
KFF-SSS
HNN.

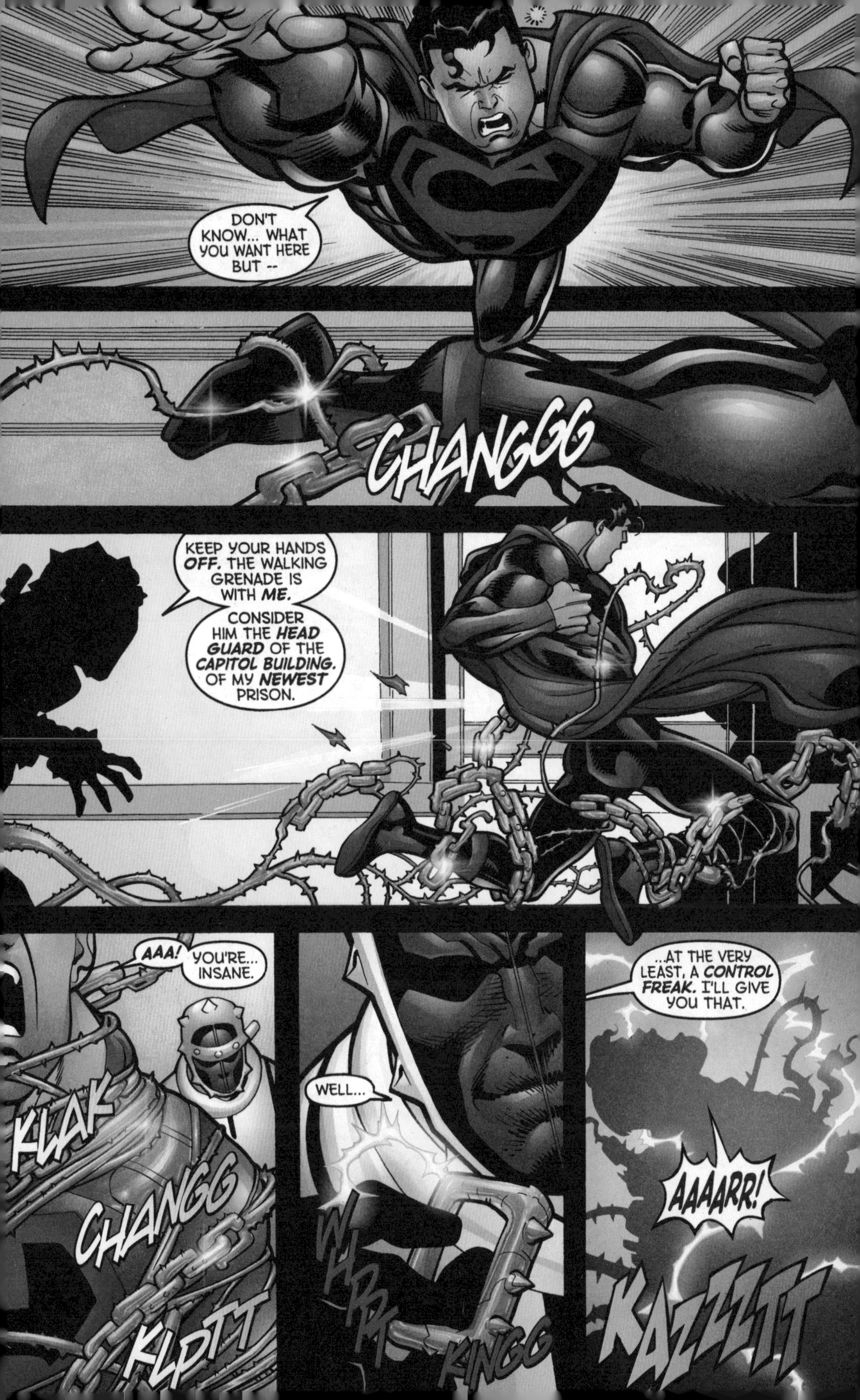
DON'T KNOW... WHAT YOU WANT HERE BUT --
CHANGGG
KEEP YOUR HANDS OFF. THE WALKING GRENADE IS WITH ME.
CONSIDER HIM THE HEAD GUARD OF THE CAPITOL BUILDING. OF MY NEWEST PRISON.
AAA!
YOU'RE... INSANE.
KLAK
CHANGG
KLPTT
WELL...
WHPPK
KINGG
...AT THE VERY LEAST, A CONTROL FREAK. I'LL GIVE YOU THAT.
AAAARR!
KAZZZTT

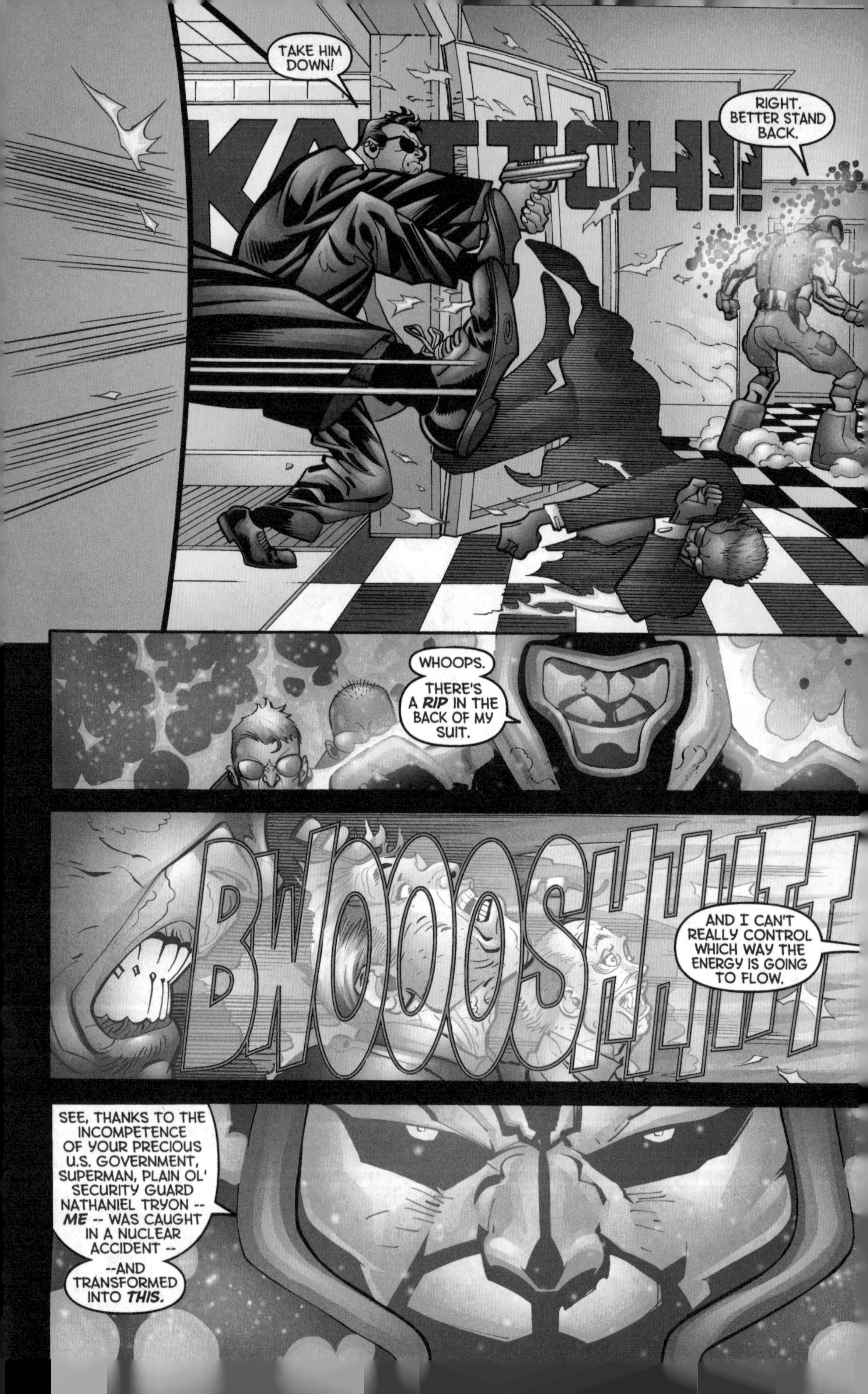
TAKE HIM DOWN!
KATTTCH!!
RIGHT. BETTER STAND BACK.
WHOOPS.
THERE'S A RIP IN THE BACK OF MY SUIT.
BWOOOSHHHT
AND I CAN'T REALLY CONTROL WHICH WAY THE ENERGY IS GOING TO FLOW.
SEE, THANKS TO THE INCOMPETENCE OF YOUR PRECIOUS U.S. GOVERNMENT, SUPERMAN, PLAIN OL' SECURITY GUARD NATHANIEL TRYON -- ME -- WAS CAUGHT IN A NUCLEAR ACCIDENT --
--AND TRANSFORMED INTO THIS.

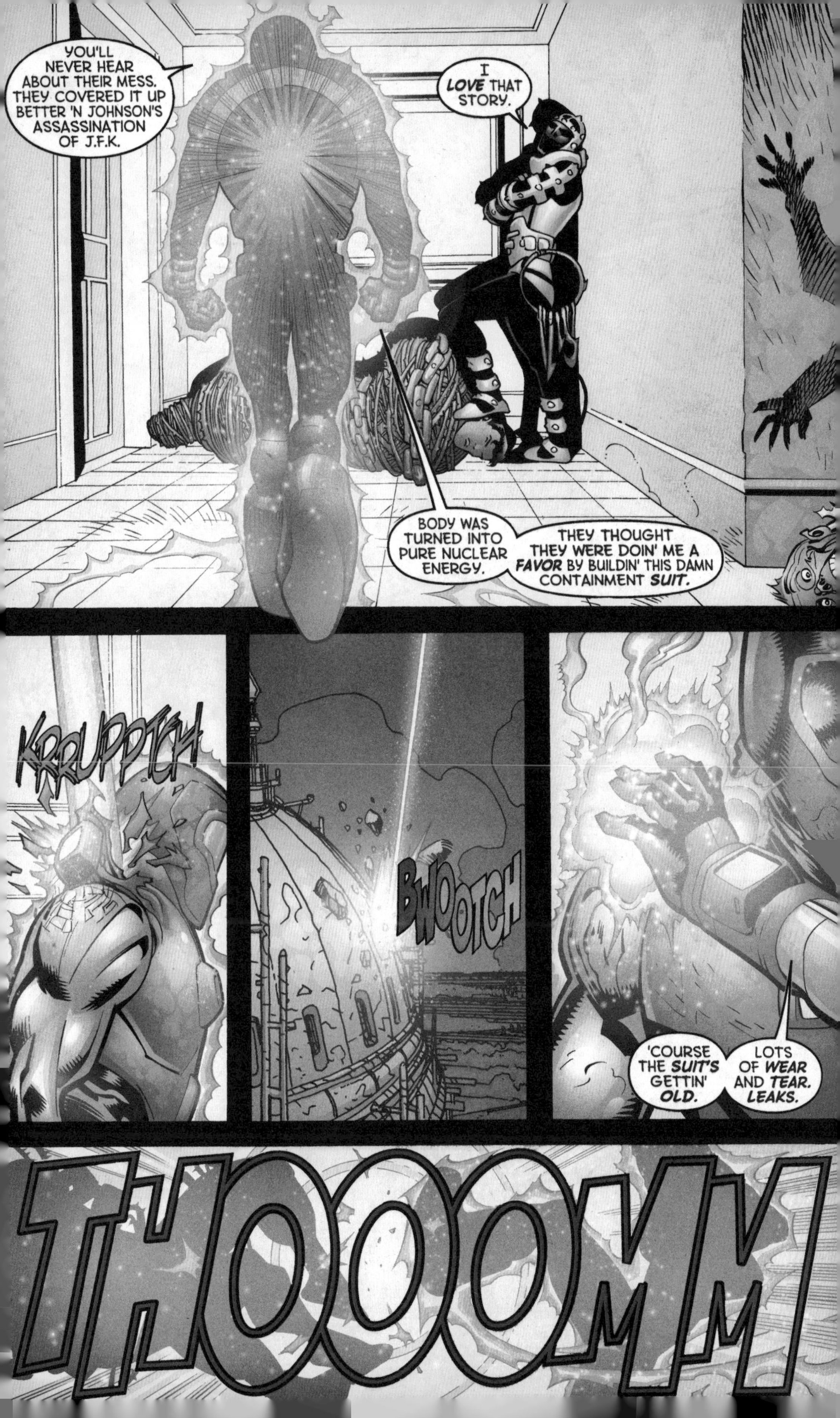
YOU'LL NEVER HEAR ABOUT THEIR MESS. THEY COVERED IT UP BETTER 'N JOHNSON'S ASSASSINATION OF J.F.K.
I LOVE THAT STORY.
BODY WAS TURNED INTO PURE NUCLEAR ENERGY.
THEY THOUGHT THEY WERE DOIN' ME A FAVOR BY BUILDIN' THIS DAMN CONTAINMENT SUIT.
KRRUPPTCH
BWOOTCH
'COURSE THE SUIT'S GETTIN' OLD.
LOTS OF WEAR AND TEAR. LEAKS.
THOOOMM

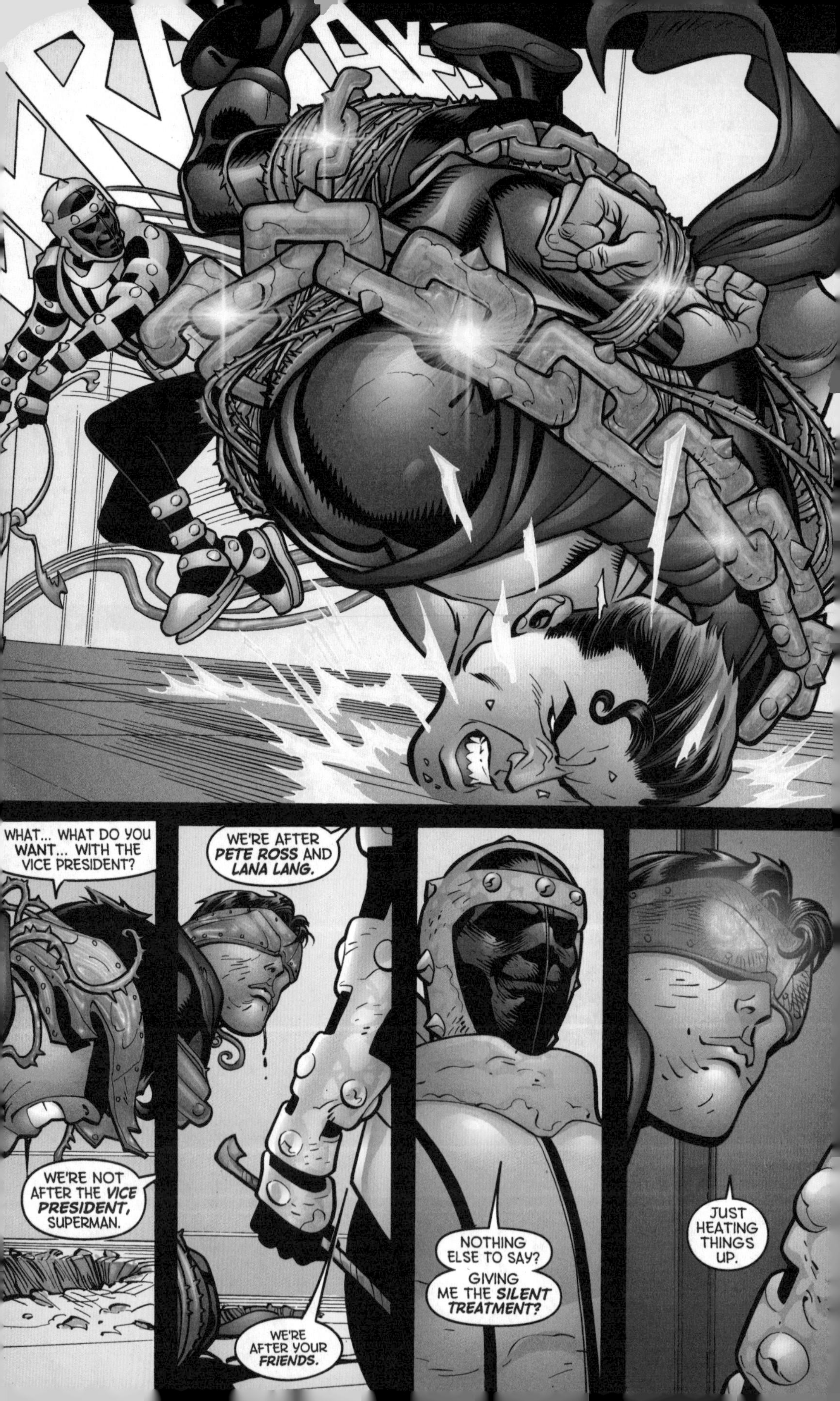
WHAT... WHAT DO YOU WANT... WITH THE VICE PRESIDENT?
WE'RE NOT AFTER THE VICE PRESIDENT, SUPERMAN.
WE'RE AFTER PETE ROSS AND LANA LANG.
WE'RE AFTER YOUR FRIENDS.
NOTHING ELSE TO SAY? GIVING ME THE SILENT TREATMENT?
JUST HEATING THINGS UP.

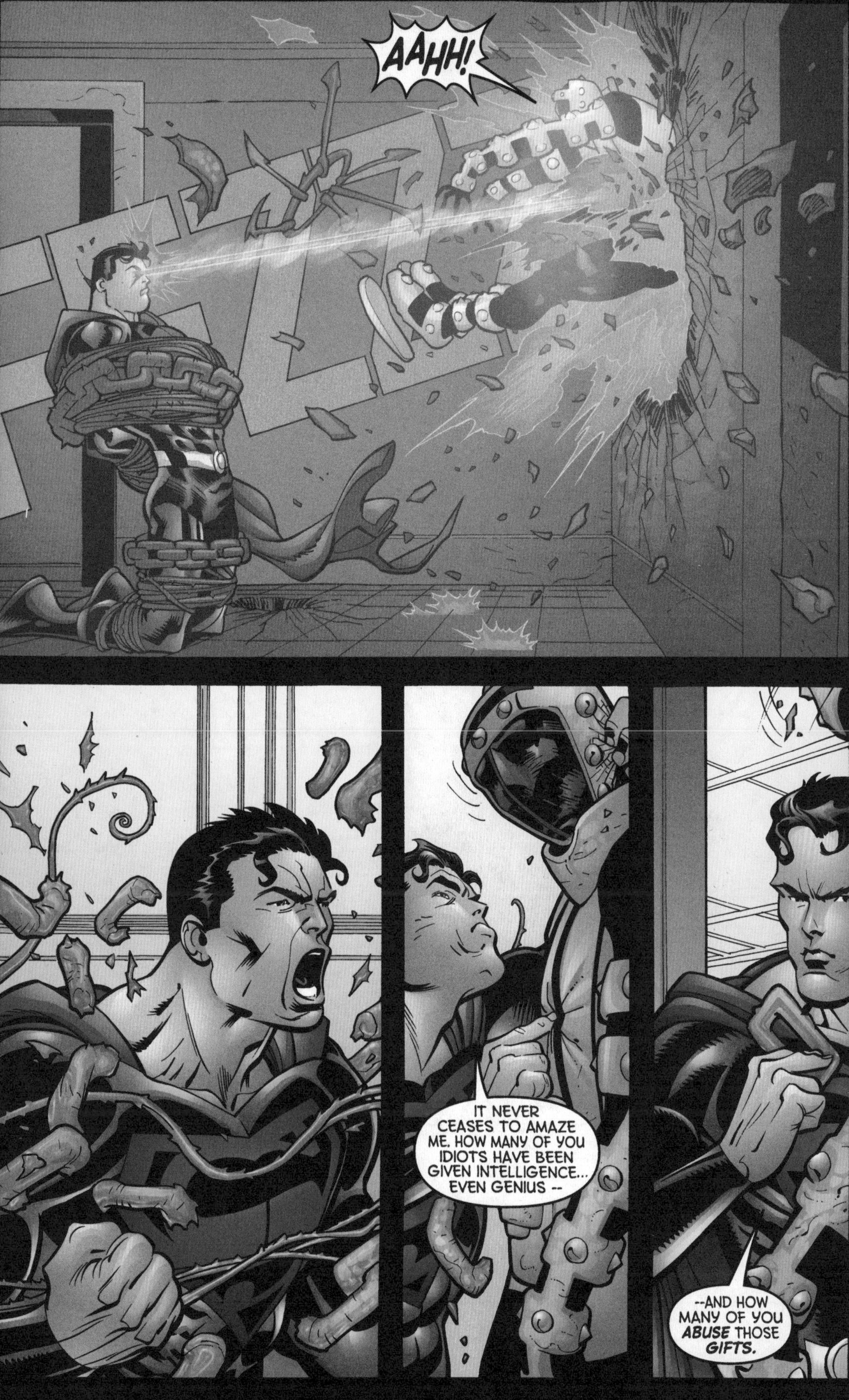
AAHH!
IT NEVER CEASES TO AMAZE ME. HOW MANY OF YOU IDIOTS HAVE BEEN GIVEN INTELLIGENCE... EVEN GENIUS --
--AND HOW MANY OF YOU ABUSE THOSE GIFTS.

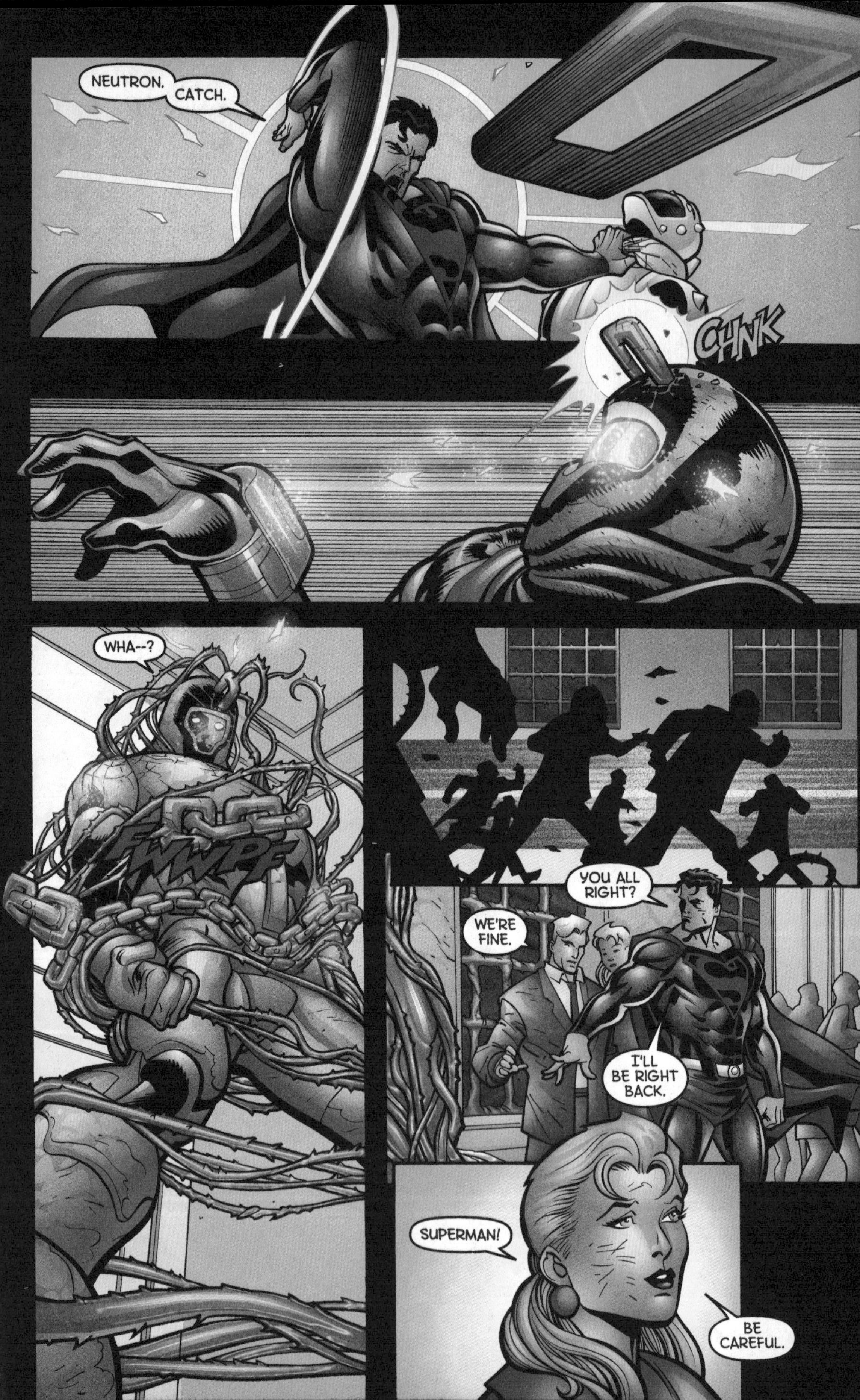
NEUTRON.
CATCH.
CHNK
WHA--?
FWWPF
YOU ALL RIGHT?
WE'RE FINE.
I'LL BE RIGHT BACK.
SUPERMAN!
BE CAREFUL.

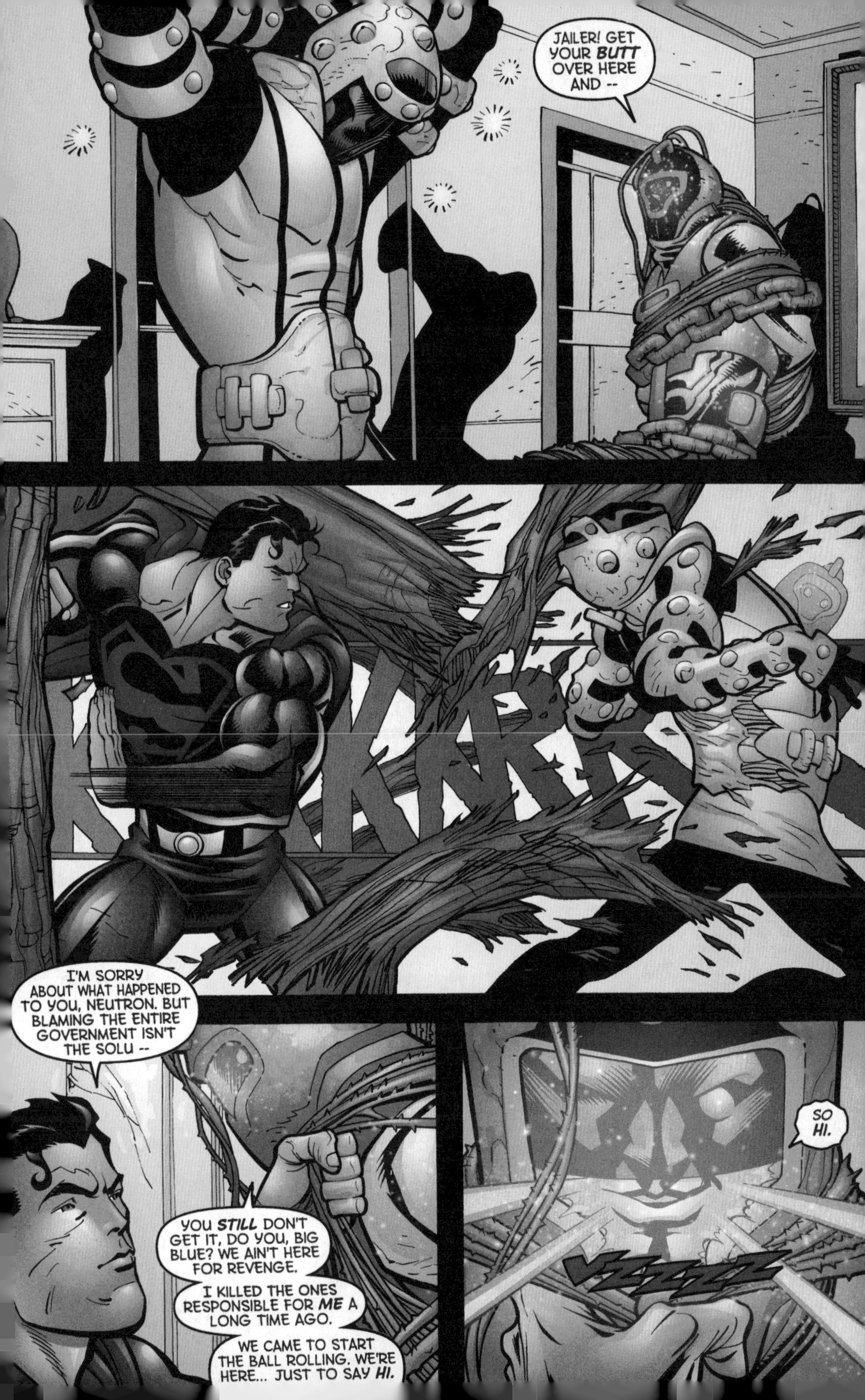
JAILER! GET YOUR BUTT OVER HERE AND --
KKRRT
I'M SORRY ABOUT WHAT HAPPENED TO YOU, NEUTRON. BUT BLAMING THE ENTIRE GOVERNMENT ISN'T THE SOLU --
YOU STILL DON'T GET IT, DO YOU, BIG BLUE? WE AIN'T HERE FOR REVENGE.
I KILLED THE ONES RESPONSIBLE FOR ME A LONG TIME AGO.
WE CAME TO START THE BALL ROLLING. WE'RE HERE... JUST TO SAY HI.
SO HI.

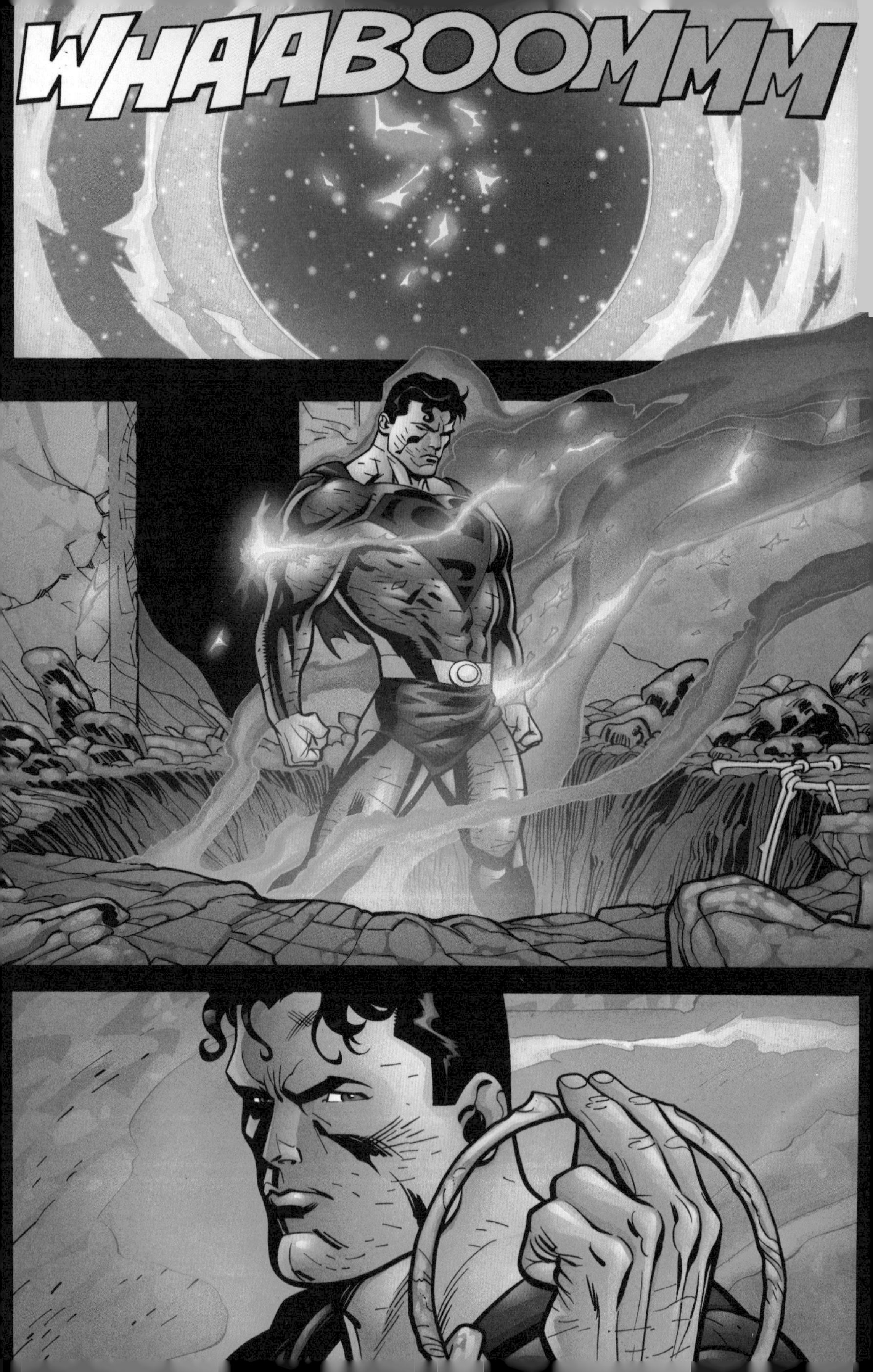
WHAABOOMMM

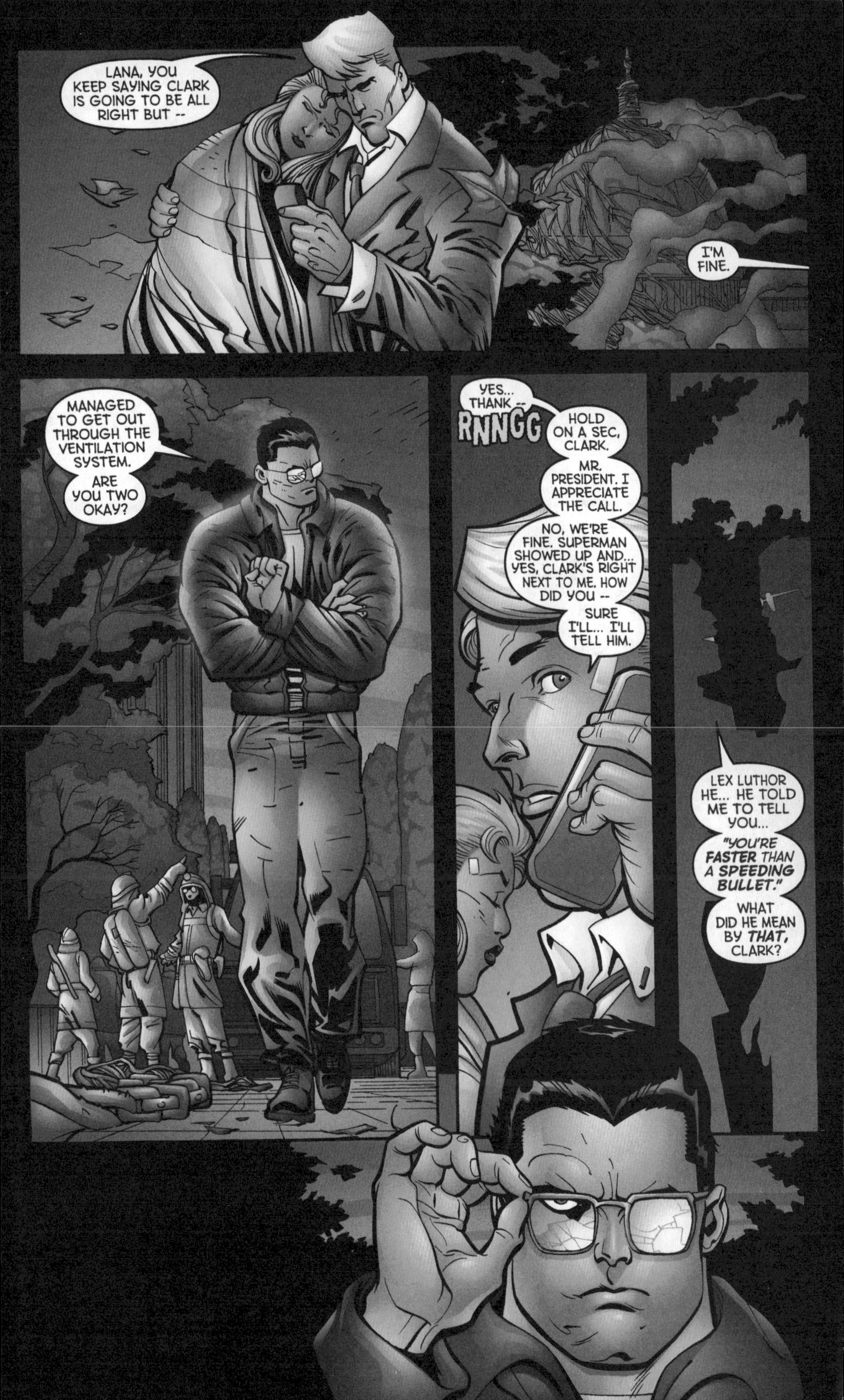
LANA, YOU KEEP SAYING CLARK IS GOING TO BE ALL RIGHT BUT --
I'M FINE.
MANAGED TO GET OUT THROUGH THE VENTILATION SYSTEM.
ARE YOU TWO OKAY?
YES... THANK --
RNNGG
HOLD ON A SEC, CLARK.
MR. PRESIDENT. I APPRECIATE THE CALL.
NO, WE'RE FINE. SUPERMAN SHOWED UP AND... YES, CLARK'S RIGHT NEXT TO ME. HOW DID YOU --
SURE I'LL... I'LL TELL HIM.
LEX LUTHOR HE... HE TOLD ME TO TELL YOU...
"YOU'RE FASTER THAN A SPEEDING BULLET."
WHAT DID HE MEAN BY THAT, CLARK?

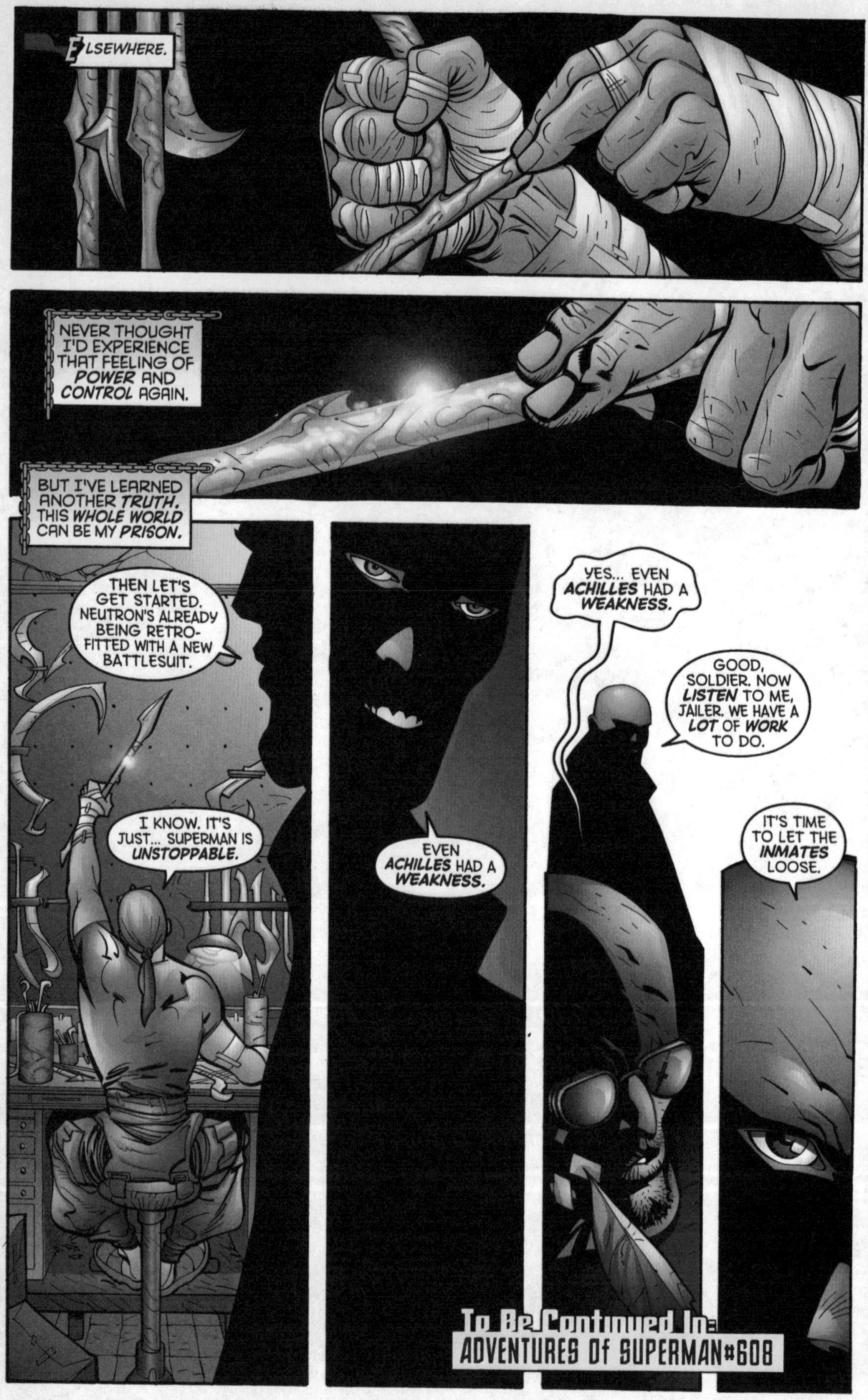
ELSEWHERE.
NEVER THOUGHT I'D EXPERIENCE THAT FEELING OF POWER AND CONTROL AGAIN.
BUT I'VE LEARNED ANOTHER TRUTH. THIS WHOLE WORLD CAN BE MY PRISON.
THEN LET'S GET STARTED. NEUTRON'S ALREADY BEING RETRO-FITTED WITH A NEW BATTLESUIT.
I KNOW. IT'S JUST... SUPERMAN IS UNSTOPPABLE.
EVEN ACHILLES HAD A WEAKNESS.
YES... EVEN ACHILLES HAD A WEAKNESS.
GOOD, SOLDIER. NOW LISTEN TO ME, JAILER. WE HAVE A LOT OF WORK TO DO.
IT'S TIME TO LET THE INMATES LOOSE.
To Be Continued In:
ADVENTURES Of SUPERMAN #608

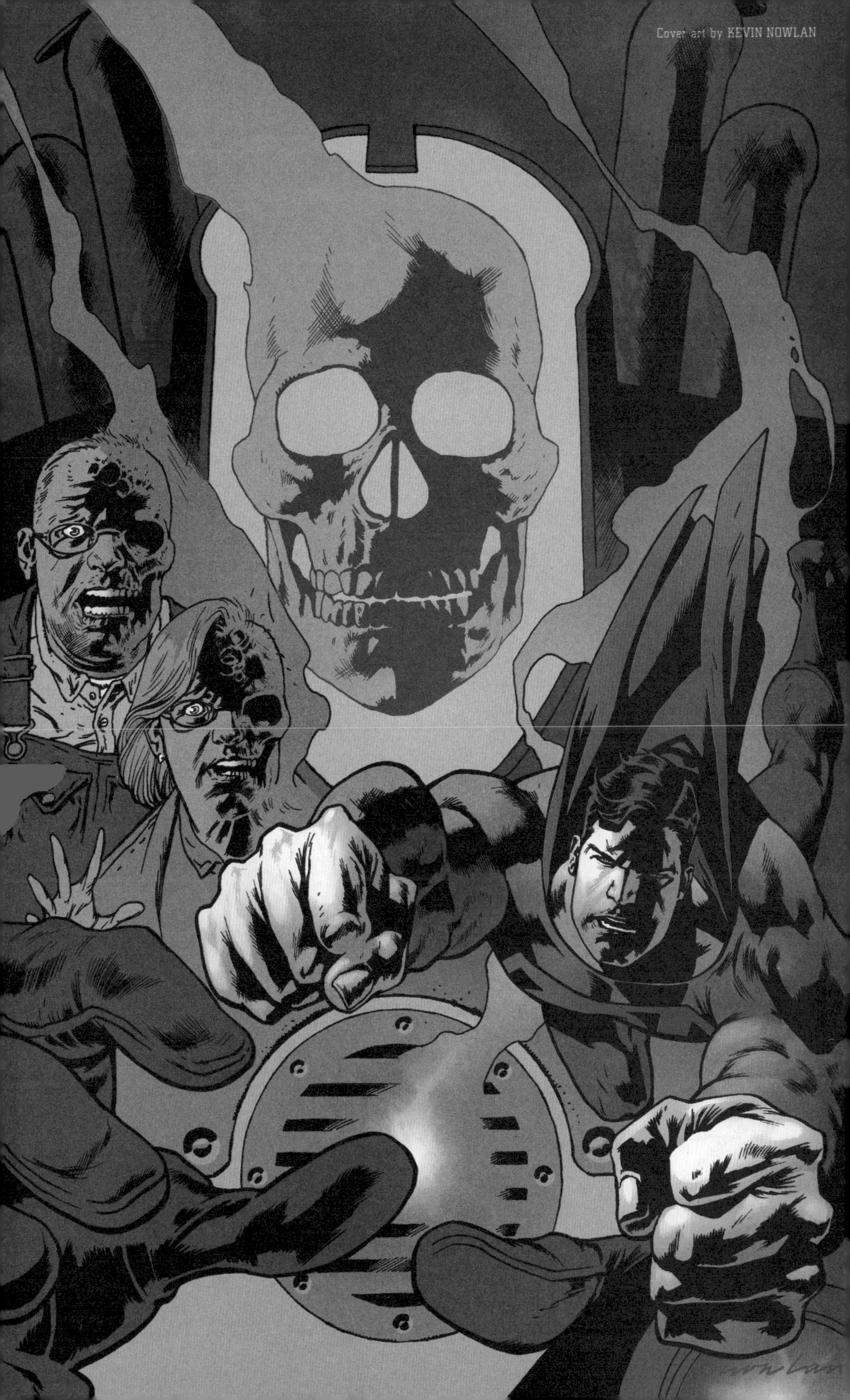

Cover art by KEVIN NOWLAN

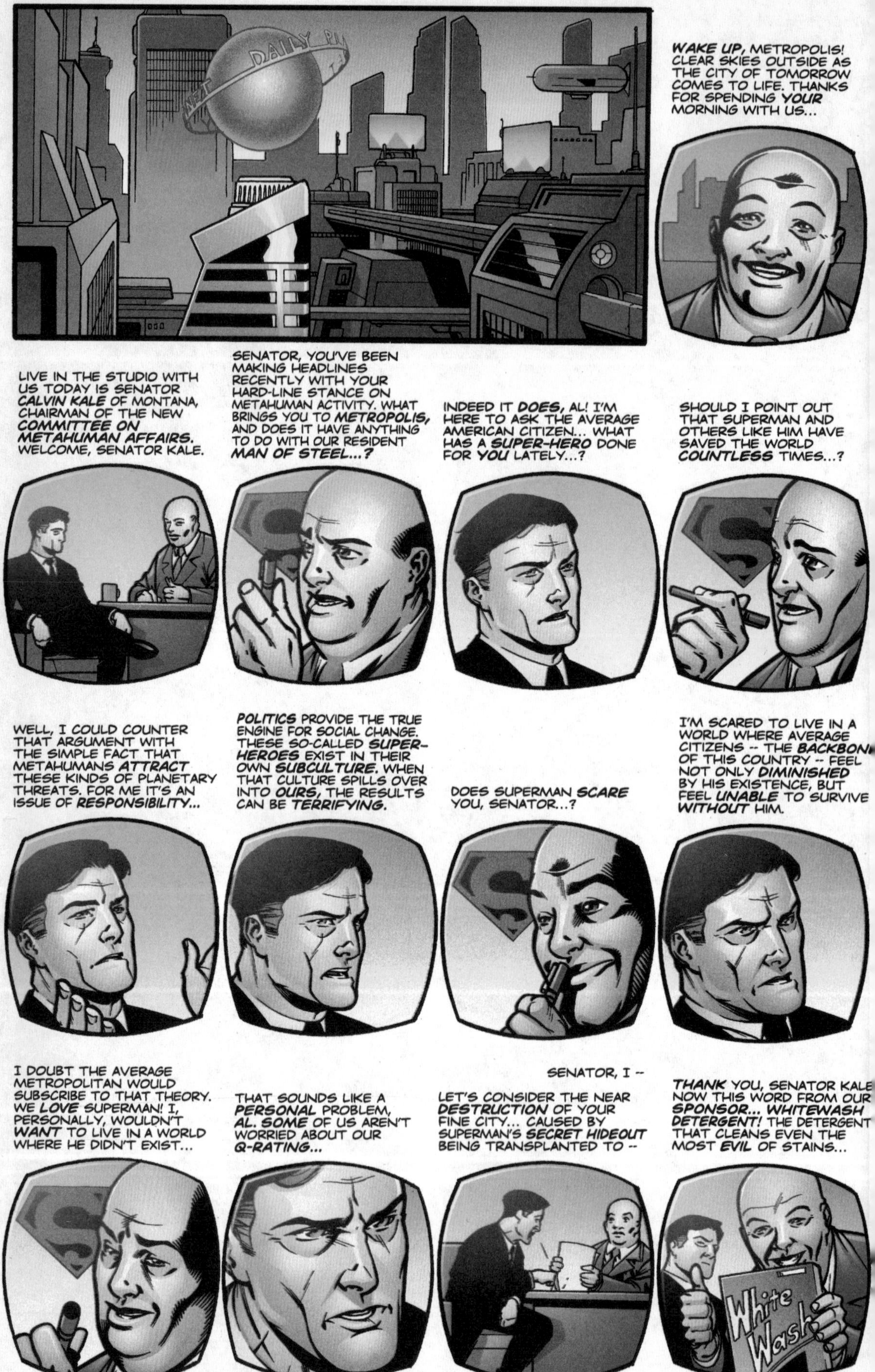
DAILY PLANET
WAKE UP, METROPOLIS! CLEAR SKIES OUTSIDE AS THE CITY OF TOMORROW COMES TO LIFE. THANKS FOR SPENDING YOUR MORNING WITH US...
LIVE IN THE STUDIO WITH US TODAY IS SENATOR CALVIN KALE OF MONTANA, CHAIRMAN OF THE NEW COMMITTEE ON METAHUMAN AFFAIRS. WELCOME, SENATOR KALE.
SENATOR, YOU'VE BEEN MAKING HEADLINES RECENTLY WITH YOUR HARD-LINE STANCE ON METAHUMAN ACTIVITY. WHAT BRINGS YOU TO METROPOLIS, AND DOES IT HAVE ANYTHING TO DO WITH OUR RESIDENT MAN OF STEEL...?
INDEED IT DOES, AL! I'M HERE TO ASK THE AVERAGE AMERICAN CITIZEN... WHAT HAS A SUPER-HERO DONE FOR YOU LATELY...?
SHOULD I POINT OUT THAT SUPERMAN AND OTHERS LIKE HIM HAVE SAVED THE WORLD COUNTLESS TIMES...?
WELL, I COULD COUNTER THAT ARGUMENT WITH THE SIMPLE FACT THAT METAHUMANS ATTRACT THESE KINDS OF PLANETARY THREATS. FOR ME IT'S AN ISSUE OF RESPONSIBILITY...
POLITICS PROVIDE THE TRUE ENGINE FOR SOCIAL CHANGE. THESE SO-CALLED SUPER-HEROES EXIST IN THEIR OWN SUBCULTURE. WHEN THAT CULTURE SPILLS OVER INTO OURS, THE RESULTS CAN BE TERRIFYING.
DOES SUPERMAN SCARE YOU, SENATOR...?
I'M SCARED TO LIVE IN A WORLD WHERE AVERAGE CITIZENS -- THE BACKBONE OF THIS COUNTRY -- FEEL NOT ONLY DIMINISHED BY HIS EXISTENCE, BUT FEEL UNABLE TO SURVIVE WITHOUT HIM.
I DOUBT THE AVERAGE METROPOLITAN WOULD SUBSCRIBE TO THAT THEORY. WE LOVE SUPERMAN! I, PERSONALLY, WOULDN'T WANT TO LIVE IN A WORLD WHERE HE DIDN'T EXIST...
THAT SOUNDS LIKE A PERSONAL PROBLEM, AL. SOME OF US AREN'T WORRIED ABOUT OUR Q-RATING...
SENATOR, I --
LET'S CONSIDER THE NEAR DESTRUCTION OF YOUR FINE CITY... CAUSED BY SUPERMAN'S SECRET HIDEOUT BEING TRANSPLANTED TO --
THANK YOU, SENATOR KALE. NOW THIS WORD FROM OUR SPONSOR... WHITEWASH DETERGENT! THE DETERGENT THAT CLEANS EVEN THE MOST EVIL OF STAINS...
White Wash

JOE CASEY WRITER DEREC AUCOIN ART
ROB RO & ALEX BLEYAERT COLORS COMICRAFT LETTERS
TOM PALMER JR. ASSOCIATE EDITOR EDDIE BERGANZA EDITOR

ENDING BATTLE PART 2

SUPERMAN CREATED BY JERRY SIEGEL & JOE SHUSTER

Dawn's Early Light

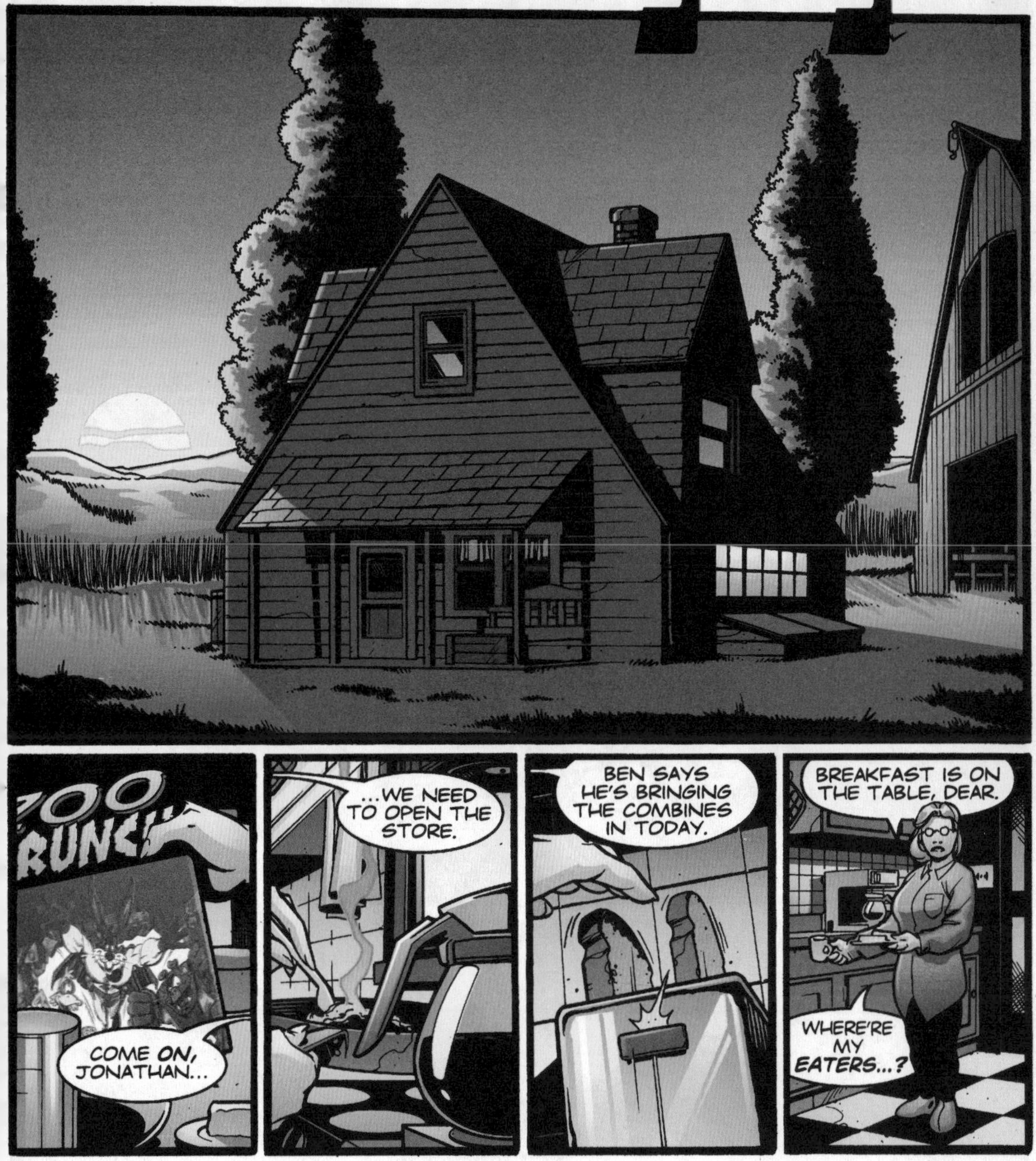
COME ON, JONATHAN...
...WE NEED TO OPEN THE STORE.
BEN SAYS HE'S BRINGING THE COMBINES IN TODAY.
BREAKFAST IS ON THE TABLE, DEAR.
WHERE'RE MY EATERS...?

LORD **KNOWS** WHERE THAT BOY IS...

WHERE'S THE **PAPER**?

CHECK THE FRONT PORCH, DEAR.

EVERY MORNING...

MARTHA KENT...

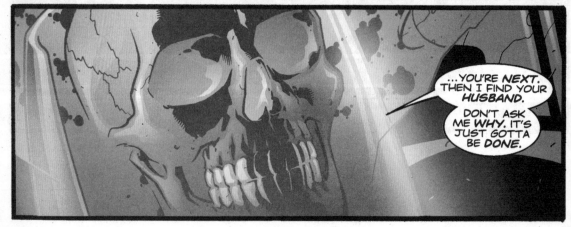

...YOU'RE **NEXT**. THEN I FIND YOUR **HUSBAND**.

DON'T ASK ME **WHY**. IT'S JUST GOTTA BE **DONE**.

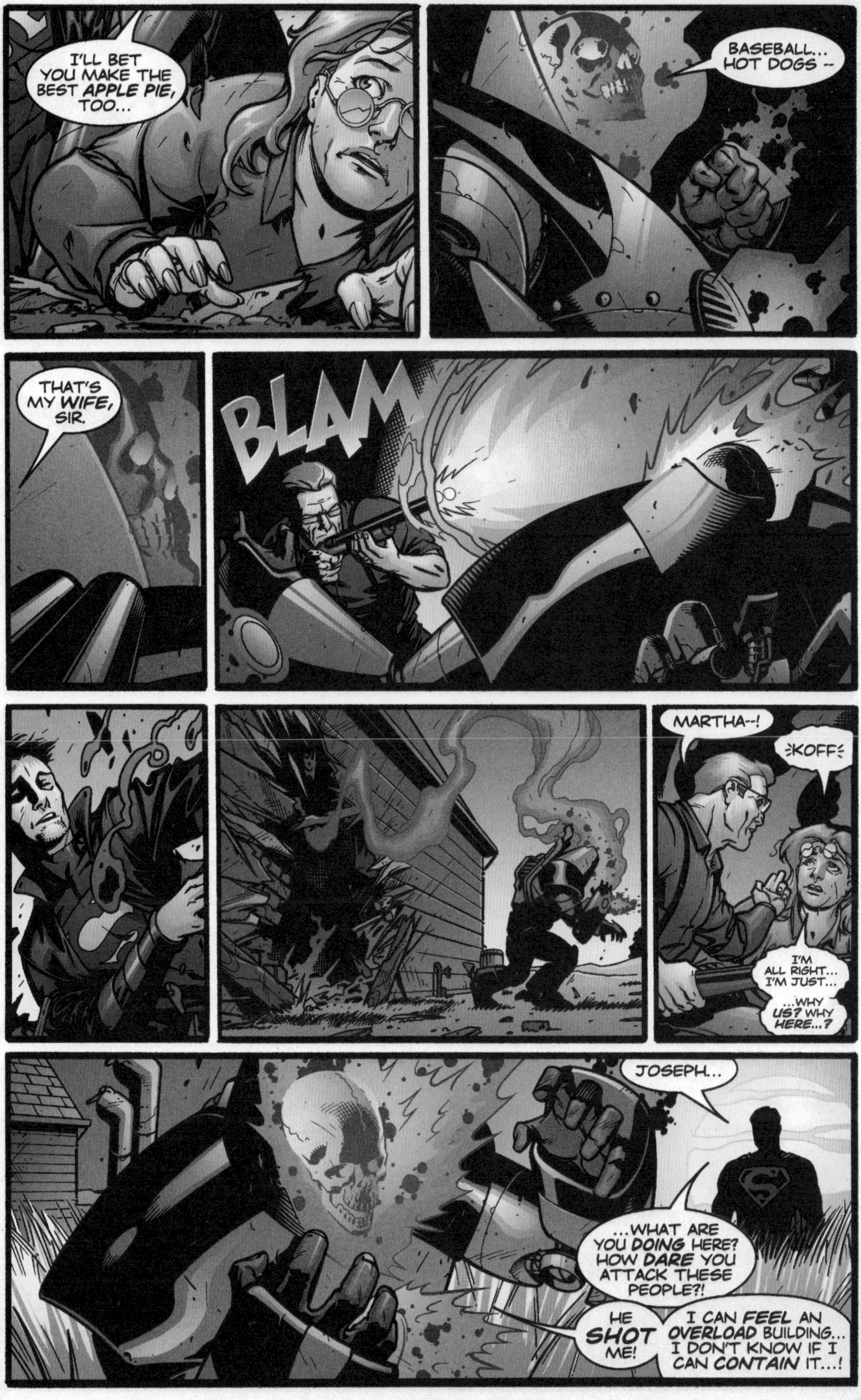
I'LL BET YOU MAKE THE BEST APPLE PIE, TOO...
BASEBALL... HOT DOGS --
THAT'S MY WIFE, SIR.
BLAM
MARTHA--!
KOFF
I'M ALL RIGHT... I'M JUST...
...WHY US? WHY HERE...?
JOSEPH...
...WHAT ARE YOU DOING HERE? HOW DARE YOU ATTACK THESE PEOPLE?!
HE SHOT ME!
I CAN FEEL AN OVERLOAD BUILDING... I DON'T KNOW IF I CAN CONTAIN IT...!

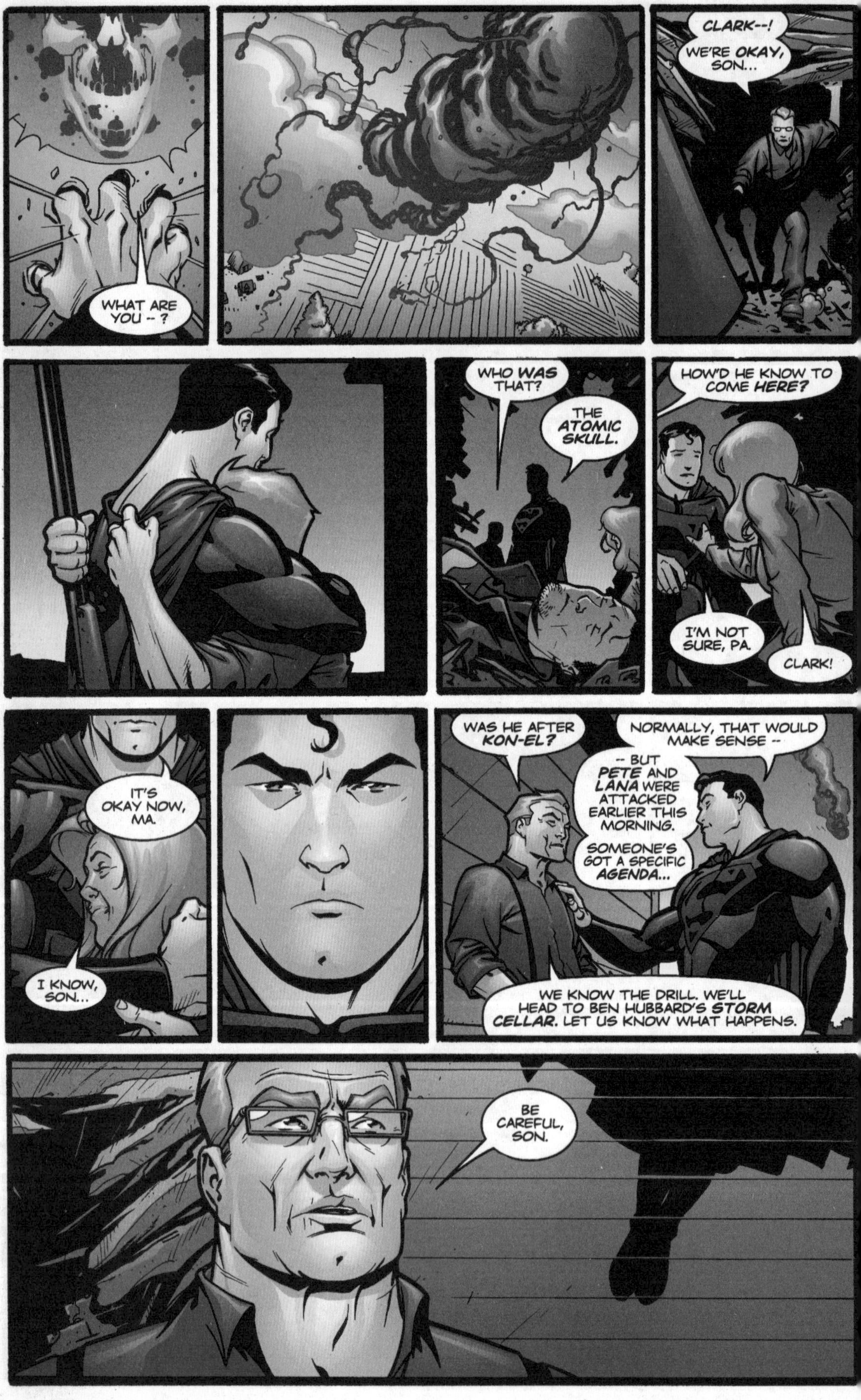
WHAT ARE YOU -- ?
CLARK--!
WE'RE OKAY, SON...
WHO WAS THAT?
THE ATOMIC SKULL.
HOW'D HE KNOW TO COME HERE?
I'M NOT SURE, PA.
CLARK!
IT'S OKAY NOW, MA.
I KNOW, SON...
WAS HE AFTER KON-EL?
NORMALLY, THAT WOULD MAKE SENSE --
-- BUT PETE AND LANA WERE ATTACKED EARLIER THIS MORNING.
SOMEONE'S GOT A SPECIFIC AGENDA...
WE KNOW THE DRILL. WE'LL HEAD TO BEN HUBBARD'S STORM CELLAR. LET US KNOW WHAT HAPPENS.
BE CAREFUL, SON.

HE'S WORN IT TO EVERY GAME FOR EIGHTEEN YEARS. FIVE STATE PLAYOFFS. TWO CHAMPIONSHIPS...

...HIS LUCKY CAP.

WALT ANDREWS HAS BEEN THE SMALLVILLE HIGH SCHOOL COACH FOR NEARLY TWENTY YEARS.

HE'S SEEN SOME TRULY GIFTED ATHLETES PLAY ON THIS FIELD. SOME MORE THAN OTHERS.

ONE, IN PARTICULAR, WAS BY FAR THE MOST NATURAL COMPETITOR HE'D EVER SEEN. HAD HE NOT GIVEN UP THE GAME HALFWAY THROUGH HIS SENIOR YEAR, HE COULD'VE GONE ALL THE WAY...

THE THINGS YOU REMEMBER WHEN SOMEONE WANTS TO KILL YOU...

HE PICTURES HIS WIFE AND TWO SONS...

...COLLEGE ALL-STARS.

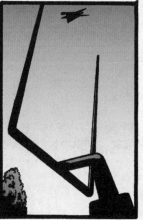

HE'S NOT READY TO DIE.

HERE YOU GO, COACH...

SORRY ABOUT THAT. THEY WON'T BOTHER YOU AGAIN.

GOOD LUCK IN THE PLAYOFFS.

THE PATTERN IS BECOMING ALL TOO OBVIOUS.

THE QUESTION IS... WHO'S NEXT?

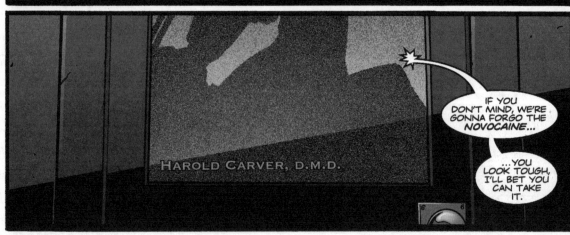
HAROLD CARVER, D.M.D.

IF YOU DON'T MIND, WE'RE GONNA FORGO THE NOVOCAINE...

...YOU LOOK TOUGH, I'LL BET YOU CAN TAKE IT.

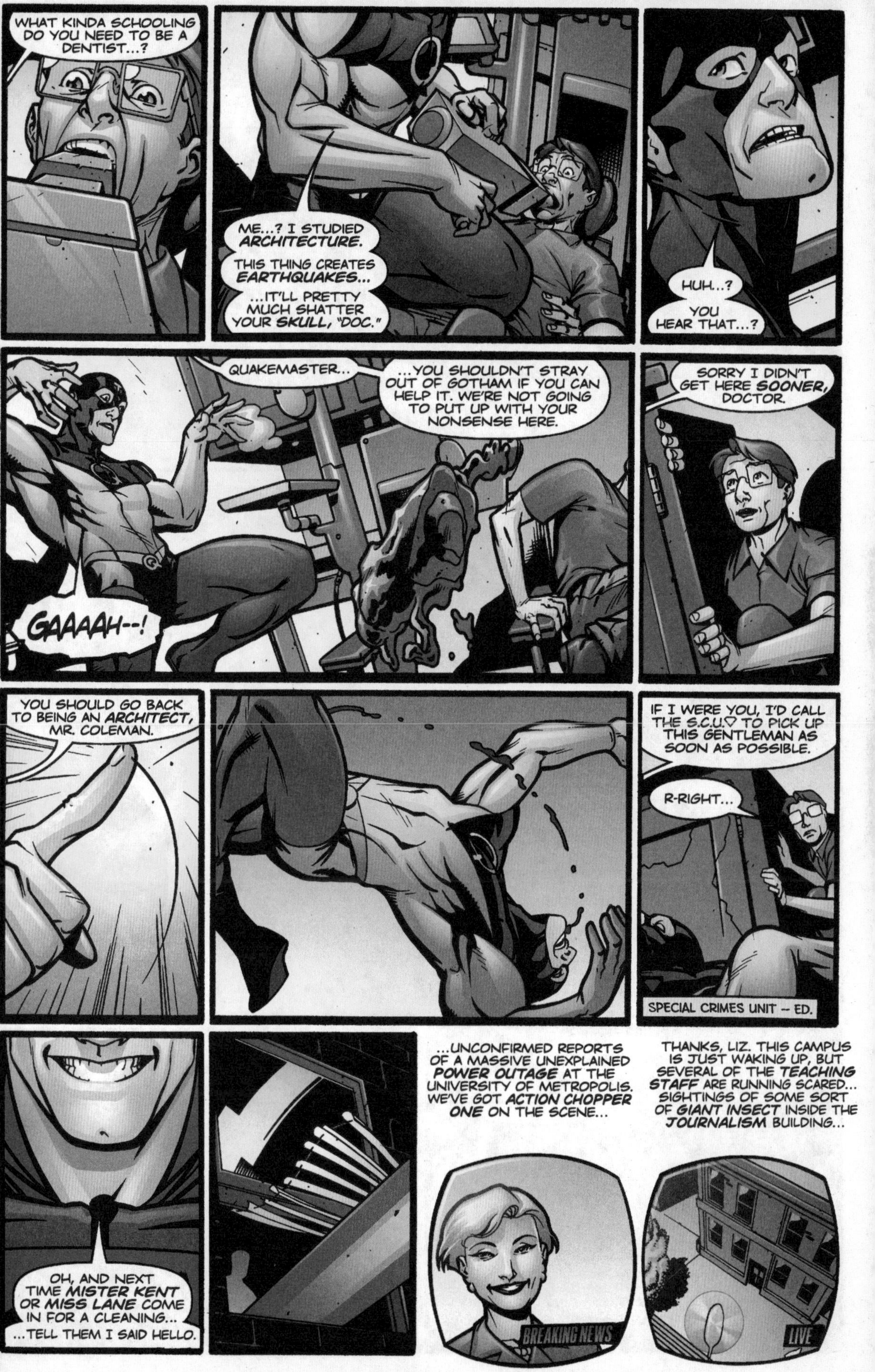
WHAT KINDA SCHOOLING DO YOU NEED TO BE A DENTIST...?
ME...? I STUDIED ARCHITECTURE.
THIS THING CREATES EARTHQUAKES...
...IT'LL PRETTY MUCH SHATTER YOUR SKULL, "DOC."
HUH...?
YOU HEAR THAT...?
QUAKEMASTER...
...YOU SHOULDN'T STRAY OUT OF GOTHAM IF YOU CAN HELP IT. WE'RE NOT GOING TO PUT UP WITH YOUR NONSENSE HERE.
GAAAAH--!
SORRY I DIDN'T GET HERE SOONER, DOCTOR.
YOU SHOULD GO BACK TO BEING AN ARCHITECT, MR. COLEMAN.
IF I WERE YOU, I'D CALL THE S.C.U.♡ TO PICK UP THIS GENTLEMAN AS SOON AS POSSIBLE.
R-RIGHT...
SPECIAL CRIMES UNIT -- ED.
OH, AND NEXT TIME MISTER KENT OR MISS LANE COME IN FOR A CLEANING...
...TELL THEM I SAID HELLO.
...UNCONFIRMED REPORTS OF A MASSIVE UNEXPLAINED POWER OUTAGE AT THE UNIVERSITY OF METROPOLIS. WE'VE GOT ACTION CHOPPER ONE ON THE SCENE...
THANKS, LIZ. THIS CAMPUS IS JUST WAKING UP, BUT SEVERAL OF THE TEACHING STAFF ARE RUNNING SCARED... SIGHTINGS OF SOME SORT OF GIANT INSECT INSIDE THE JOURNALISM BUILDING...
BREAKING NEWS
LIVE

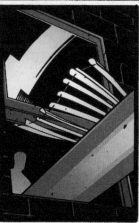

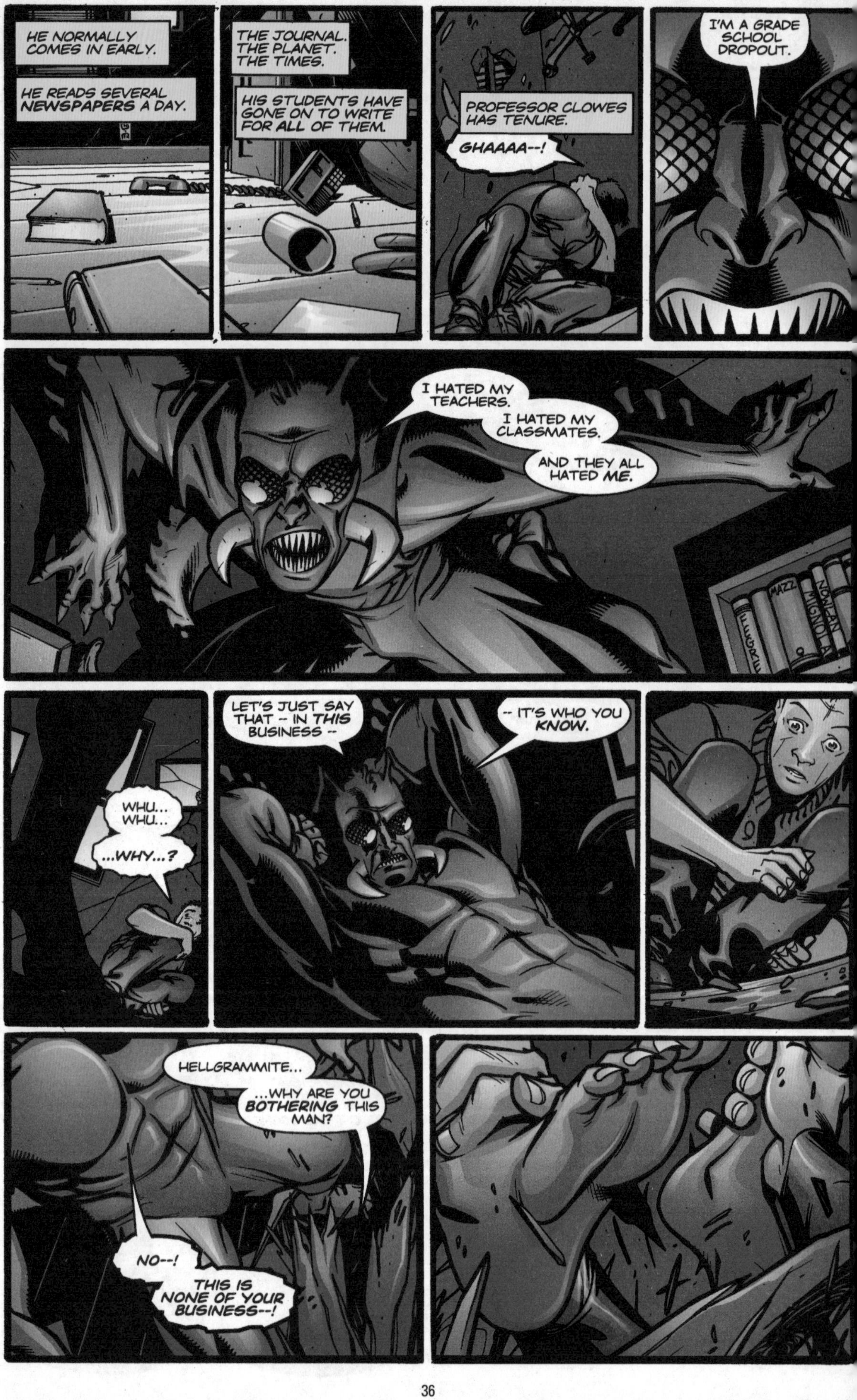
HE NORMALLY COMES IN EARLY.
HE READS SEVERAL NEWSPAPERS A DAY.
THE JOURNAL. THE PLANET. THE TIMES.
HIS STUDENTS HAVE GONE ON TO WRITE FOR ALL OF THEM.
PROFESSOR CLOWES HAS TENURE.
GHAAAA--!
I'M A GRADE SCHOOL DROPOUT.
I HATED MY TEACHERS.
I HATED MY CLASSMATES.
AND THEY ALL HATED ME.
MAZZ
NOWLAN
MIGNOLA
WHU... WHU...
...WHY...?
LET'S JUST SAY THAT -- IN THIS BUSINESS --
-- IT'S WHO YOU KNOW.
HELLGRAMMITE...
...WHY ARE YOU BOTHERING THIS MAN?
NO--!
THIS IS NONE OF YOUR BUSINESS--!

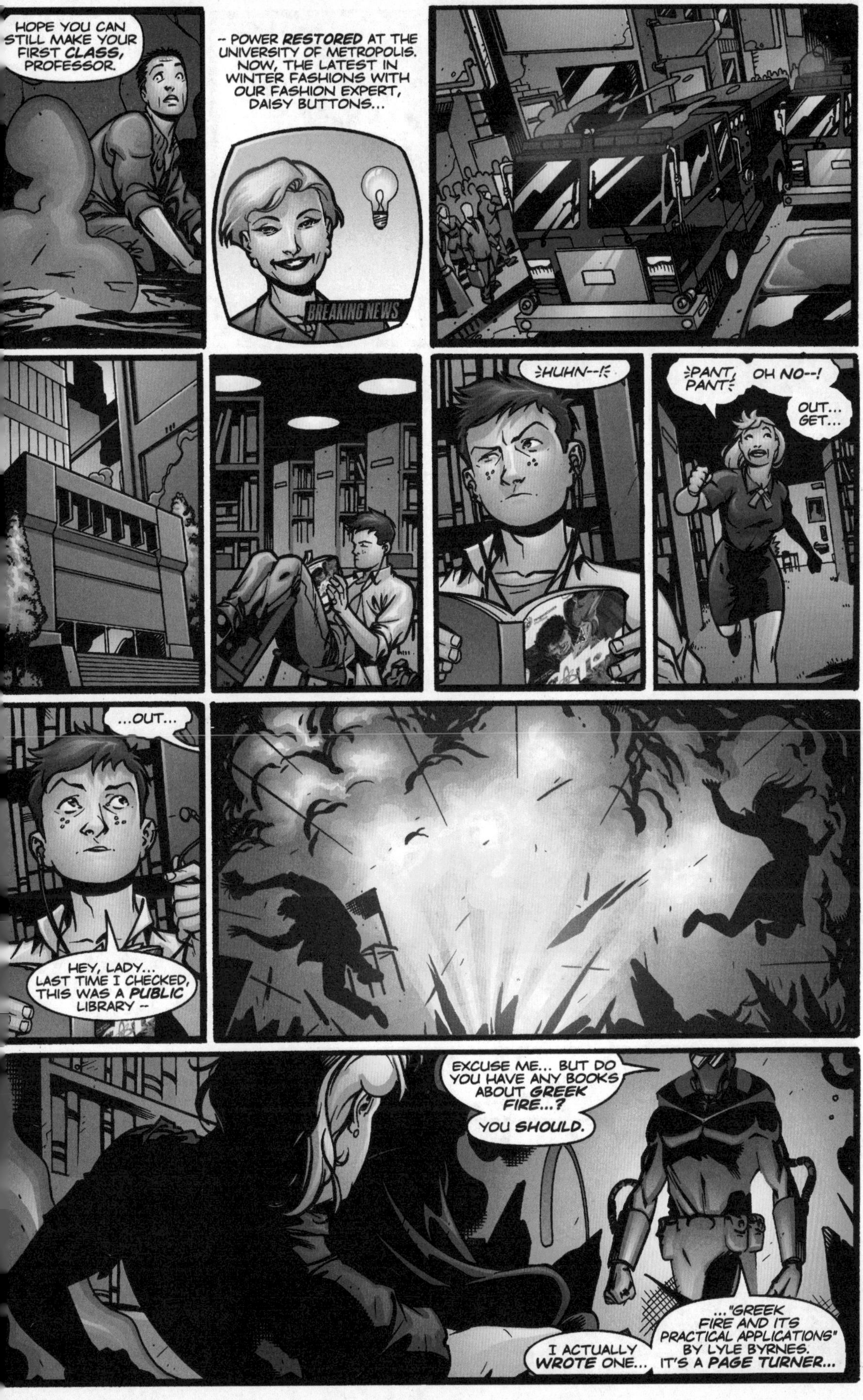
HOPE YOU CAN STILL MAKE YOUR FIRST CLASS, PROFESSOR.
-- POWER RESTORED AT THE UNIVERSITY OF METROPOLIS. NOW, THE LATEST IN WINTER FASHIONS WITH OUR FASHION EXPERT, DAISY BUTTONS...
BREAKING NEWS
HUHN--!
PANT, PANT
OH NO--!
OUT... GET...
...OUT...
HEY, LADY... LAST TIME I CHECKED, THIS WAS A PUBLIC LIBRARY --
EXCUSE ME... BUT DO YOU HAVE ANY BOOKS ABOUT GREEK FIRE...?
YOU SHOULD.
I ACTUALLY WROTE ONE...
..."GREEK FIRE AND ITS PRACTICAL APPLICATIONS" BY LYLE BYRNES. IT'S A PAGE TURNER...

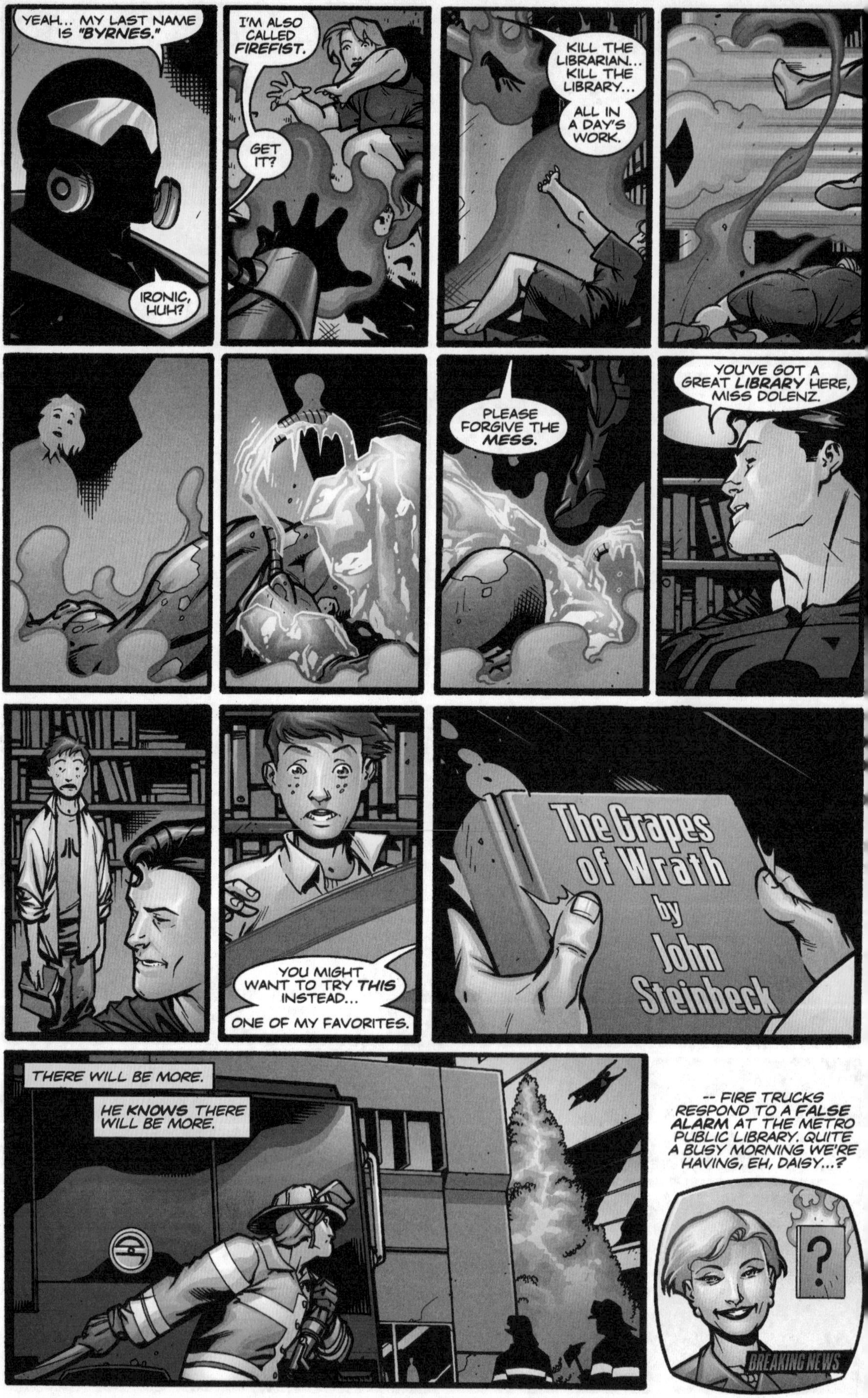

YEAH... MY LAST NAME IS "BYRNES."
IRONIC, HUH?
I'M ALSO CALLED FIREFIST.
GET IT?
KILL THE LIBRARIAN... KILL THE LIBRARY...
ALL IN A DAY'S WORK.
PLEASE FORGIVE THE MESS.
YOU'VE GOT A GREAT LIBRARY HERE, MISS DOLENZ.
YOU MIGHT WANT TO TRY THIS INSTEAD...
ONE OF MY FAVORITES.
The Grapes of Wrath by John Steinbeck
THERE WILL BE MORE.
HE KNOWS THERE WILL BE MORE.
-- FIRE TRUCKS RESPOND TO A FALSE ALARM AT THE METRO PUBLIC LIBRARY. QUITE A BUSY MORNING WE'RE HAVING, EH, DAISY...?
BREAKING NEWS

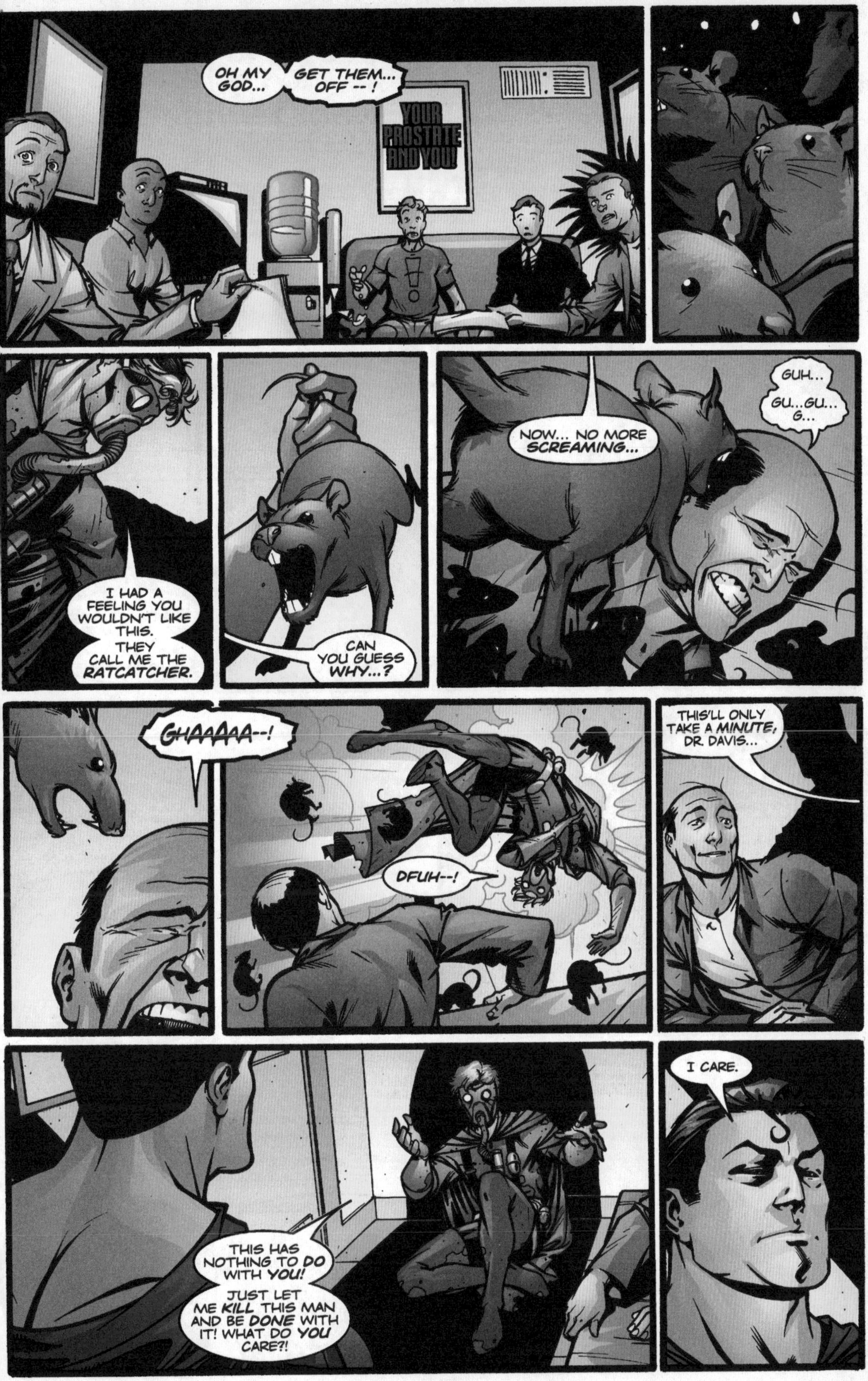
OH MY GOD...
GET THEM... OFF -- !
YOUR PROSTATE AND YOU!
I HAD A FEELING YOU WOULDN'T LIKE THIS. THEY CALL ME THE RATCATCHER.
CAN YOU GUESS WHY...?
NOW... NO MORE SCREAMING...
GUH...
GU...GU... G...
GHAAAAA--!
DFUH--!
THIS'LL ONLY TAKE A MINUTE, DR. DAVIS...
THIS HAS NOTHING TO DO WITH YOU!
JUST LET ME KILL THIS MAN AND BE DONE WITH IT! WHAT DO YOU CARE?!
I CARE.

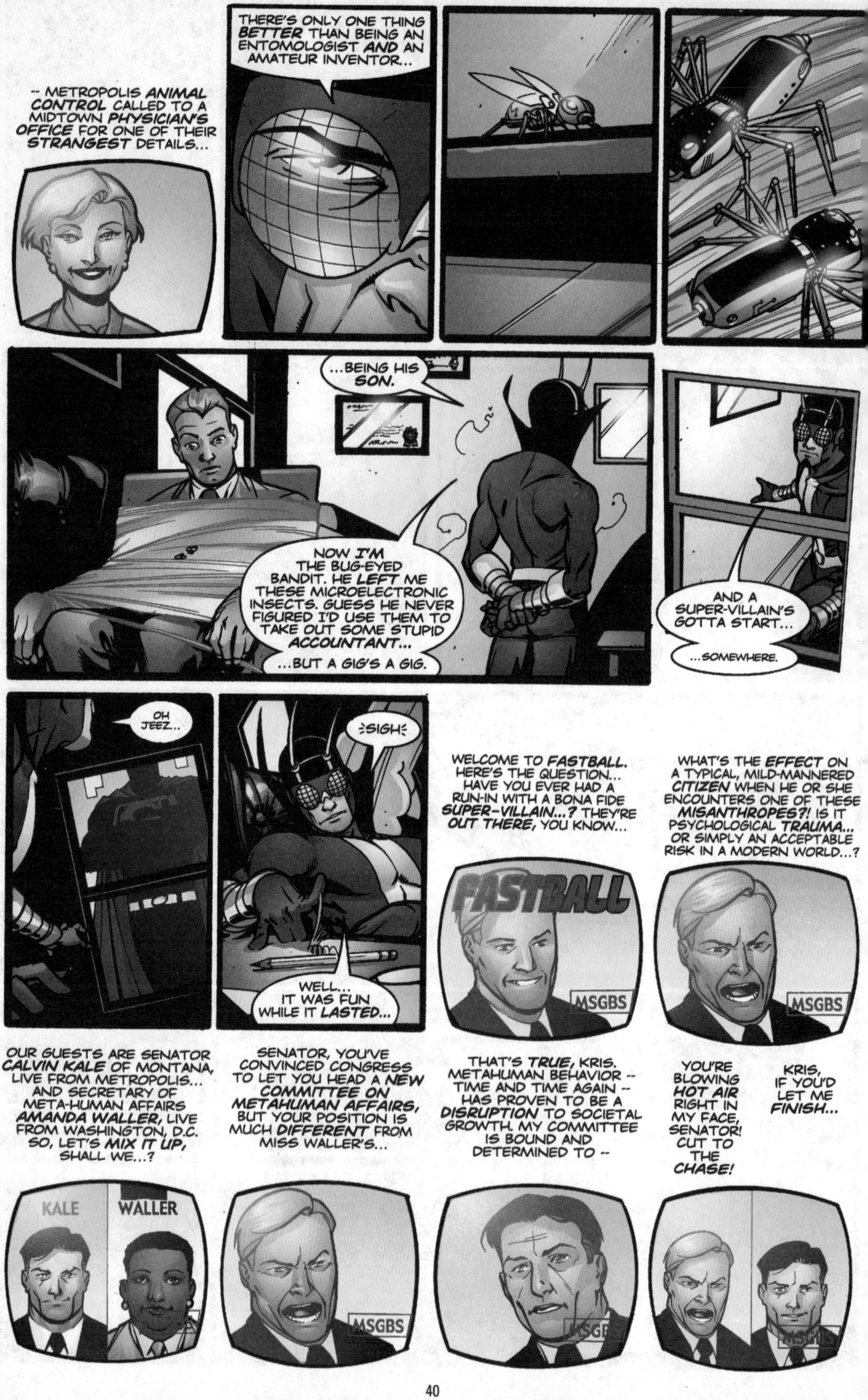
-- METROPOLIS ANIMAL CONTROL CALLED TO A MIDTOWN PHYSICIAN'S OFFICE FOR ONE OF THEIR STRANGEST DETAILS...
THERE'S ONLY ONE THING BETTER THAN BEING AN ENTOMOLOGIST AND AN AMATEUR INVENTOR...
...BEING HIS SON.
NOW I'M THE BUG-EYED BANDIT. HE LEFT ME THESE MICROELECTRONIC INSECTS. GUESS HE NEVER FIGURED I'D USE THEM TO TAKE OUT SOME STUPID ACCOUNTANT...
...BUT A GIG'S A GIG.
AND A SUPER-VILLAIN'S GOTTA START...
...SOMEWHERE.
OH JEEZ...
SIGH
WELL... IT WAS FUN WHILE IT LASTED...
WELCOME TO FASTBALL. HERE'S THE QUESTION... HAVE YOU EVER HAD A RUN-IN WITH A BONA FIDE SUPER-VILLAIN...? THEY'RE OUT THERE, YOU KNOW...
FASTBALL
MSGBS
WHAT'S THE EFFECT ON A TYPICAL, MILD-MANNERED CITIZEN WHEN HE OR SHE ENCOUNTERS ONE OF THESE MISANTHROPES?! IS IT PSYCHOLOGICAL TRAUMA... OR SIMPLY AN ACCEPTABLE RISK IN A MODERN WORLD...?
MSGBS
OUR GUESTS ARE SENATOR CALVIN KALE OF MONTANA, LIVE FROM METROPOLIS... AND SECRETARY OF META-HUMAN AFFAIRS AMANDA WALLER, LIVE FROM WASHINGTON, D.C. SO, LET'S MIX IT UP, SHALL WE...?
KALE
WALLER
SENATOR, YOU'VE CONVINCED CONGRESS TO LET YOU HEAD A NEW COMMITTEE ON METAHUMAN AFFAIRS, BUT YOUR POSITION IS MUCH DIFFERENT FROM MISS WALLER'S...
MSGBS
THAT'S TRUE, KRIS. METAHUMAN BEHAVIOR -- TIME AND TIME AGAIN -- HAS PROVEN TO BE A DISRUPTION TO SOCIETAL GROWTH. MY COMMITTEE IS BOUND AND DETERMINED TO --
YOU'RE BLOWING HOT AIR RIGHT IN MY FACE, SENATOR! CUT TO THE CHASE!
KRIS, IF YOU'D LET ME FINISH...

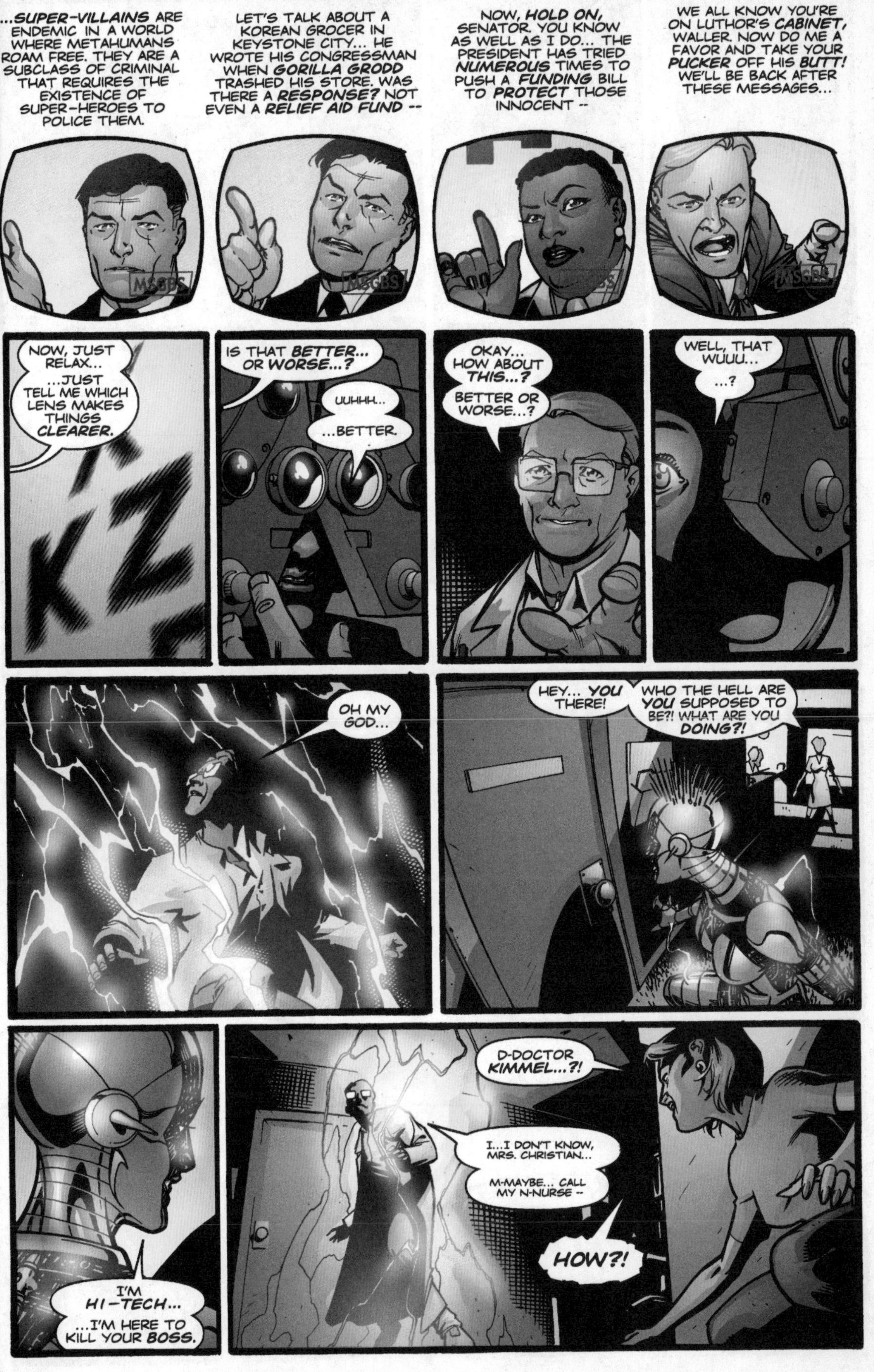
...SUPER-VILLAINS ARE ENDEMIC IN A WORLD WHERE METAHUMANS ROAM FREE. THEY ARE A SUBCLASS OF CRIMINAL THAT REQUIRES THE EXISTENCE OF SUPER-HEROES TO POLICE THEM.
MSGBS
LET'S TALK ABOUT A KOREAN GROCER IN KEYSTONE CITY... HE WROTE HIS CONGRESSMAN WHEN GORILLA GRODD TRASHED HIS STORE. WAS THERE A RESPONSE? NOT EVEN A RELIEF AID FUND --
MSGBS
NOW, HOLD ON, SENATOR. YOU KNOW AS WELL AS I DO... THE PRESIDENT HAS TRIED NUMEROUS TIMES TO PUSH A FUNDING BILL TO PROTECT THOSE INNOCENT --
WE ALL KNOW YOU'RE ON LUTHOR'S CABINET, WALLER. NOW DO ME A FAVOR AND TAKE YOUR PUCKER OFF HIS BUTT! WE'LL BE BACK AFTER THESE MESSAGES...
MSGBS
NOW, JUST RELAX...
...JUST TELL ME WHICH LENS MAKES THINGS CLEARER.
KZZ
IS THAT BETTER... OR WORSE...?
UUHHH...
...BETTER.
OKAY... HOW ABOUT THIS...?
BETTER OR WORSE...?
WELL, THAT WUUU...
...?
OH MY GOD...
HEY... YOU THERE!
WHO THE HELL ARE YOU SUPPOSED TO BE?! WHAT ARE YOU DOING?!
I'M HI-TECH...
...I'M HERE TO KILL YOUR BOSS.
D-DOCTOR KIMMEL...?!
I...I DON'T KNOW, MRS. CHRISTIAN...
M-MAYBE... CALL MY N-NURSE --
HOW?!

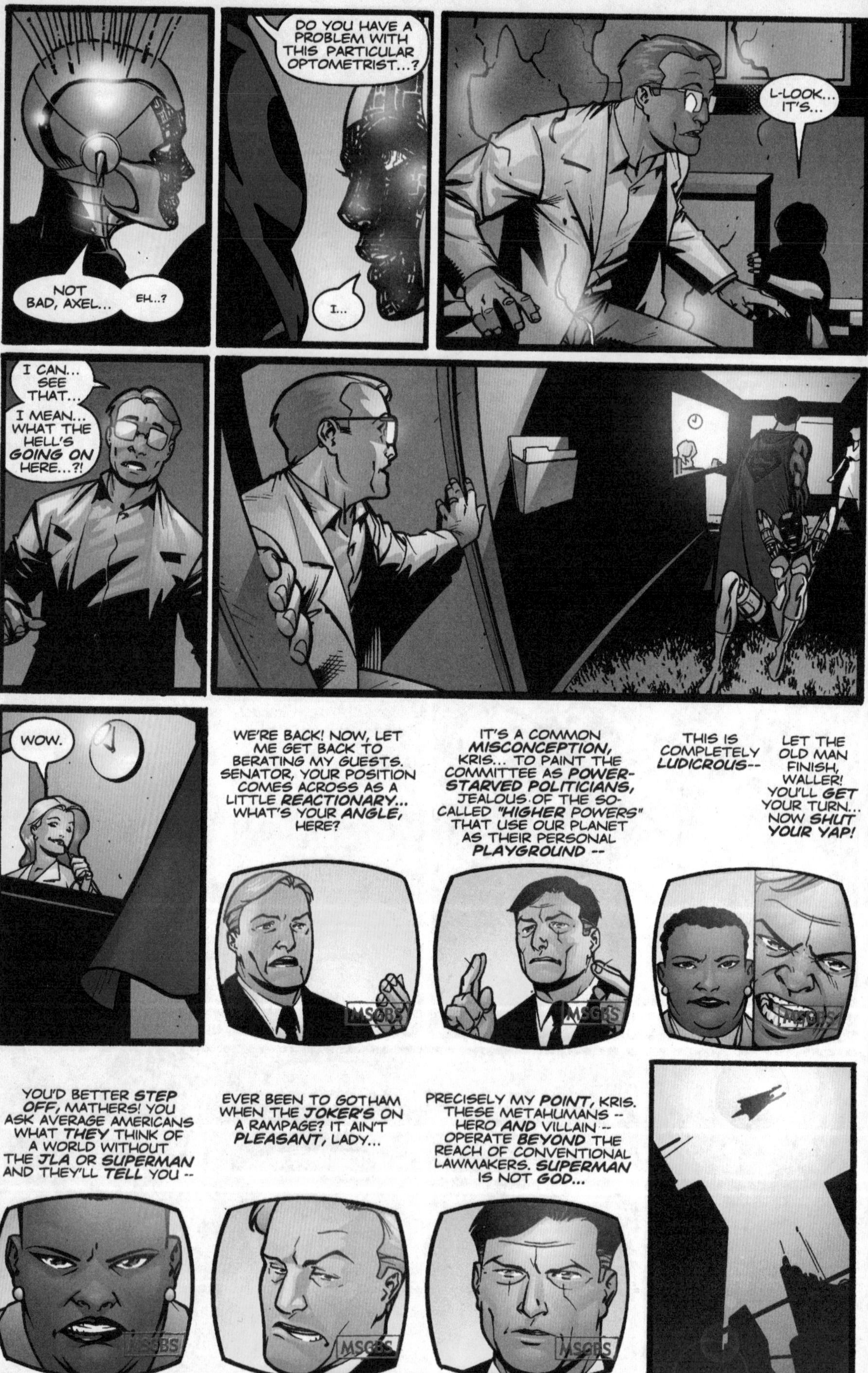
NOT BAD, AXEL...
EH..?
DO YOU HAVE A PROBLEM WITH THIS PARTICULAR OPTOMETRIST...?
I...
L-LOOK... IT'S...
I CAN... SEE THAT...
I MEAN... WHAT THE HELL'S GOING ON HERE...?!
WOW.
WE'RE BACK! NOW, LET ME GET BACK TO BERATING MY GUESTS. SENATOR, YOUR POSITION COMES ACROSS AS A LITTLE REACTIONARY... WHAT'S YOUR ANGLE, HERE?
MSGBS
IT'S A COMMON MISCONCEPTION, KRIS... TO PAINT THE COMMITTEE AS POWER-STARVED POLITICIANS, JEALOUS OF THE SO-CALLED "HIGHER POWERS" THAT USE OUR PLANET AS THEIR PERSONAL PLAYGROUND --
MSGBS
THIS IS COMPLETELY LUDICROUS--
LET THE OLD MAN FINISH, WALLER! YOU'LL GET YOUR TURN... NOW SHUT YOUR YAP!
MSGBS
YOU'D BETTER STEP OFF, MATHERS! YOU ASK AVERAGE AMERICANS WHAT THEY THINK OF A WORLD WITHOUT THE JLA OR SUPERMAN AND THEY'LL TELL YOU --
MSGBS
EVER BEEN TO GOTHAM WHEN THE JOKER'S ON A RAMPAGE? IT AIN'T PLEASANT, LADY...
MSGBS
PRECISELY MY POINT, KRIS. THESE METAHUMANS -- HERO AND VILLAIN -- OPERATE BEYOND THE REACH OF CONVENTIONAL LAWMAKERS. SUPERMAN IS NOT GOD...
MSGBS

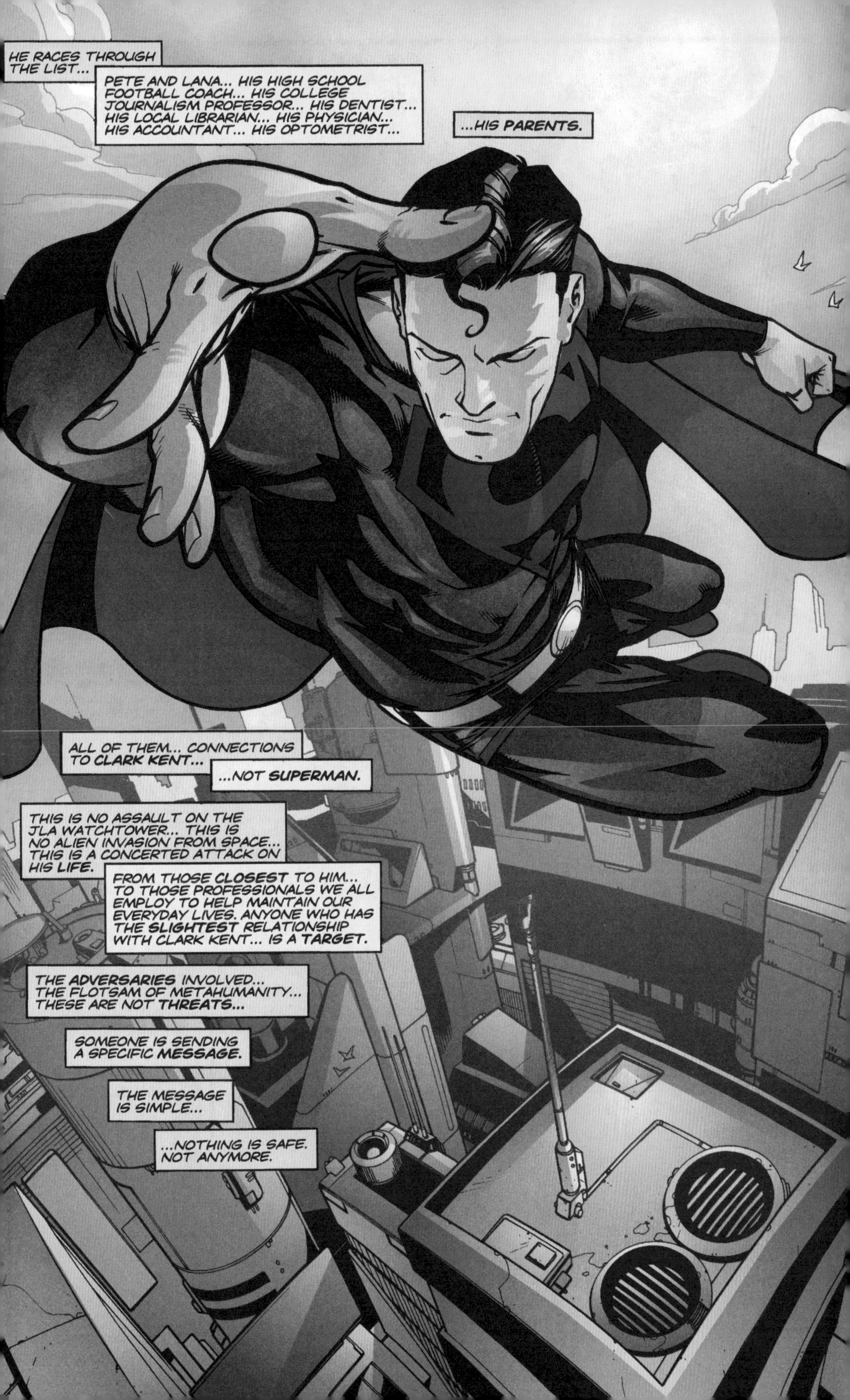
HE RACES THROUGH THE LIST...
PETE AND LANA... HIS HIGH SCHOOL FOOTBALL COACH... HIS COLLEGE JOURNALISM PROFESSOR... HIS DENTIST... HIS LOCAL LIBRARIAN... HIS PHYSICIAN... HIS ACCOUNTANT... HIS OPTOMETRIST...
...HIS PARENTS.
ALL OF THEM... CONNECTIONS TO CLARK KENT...
...NOT SUPERMAN.
THIS IS NO ASSAULT ON THE JLA WATCHTOWER... THIS IS NO ALIEN INVASION FROM SPACE... THIS IS A CONCERTED ATTACK ON HIS LIFE.
FROM THOSE CLOSEST TO HIM... TO THOSE PROFESSIONALS WE ALL EMPLOY TO HELP MAINTAIN OUR EVERYDAY LIVES. ANYONE WHO HAS THE SLIGHTEST RELATIONSHIP WITH CLARK KENT... IS A TARGET.
THE ADVERSARIES INVOLVED... THE FLOTSAM OF METAHUMANITY... THESE ARE NOT THREATS...
SOMEONE IS SENDING A SPECIFIC MESSAGE.
THE MESSAGE IS SIMPLE...
...NOTHING IS SAFE. NOT ANYMORE.

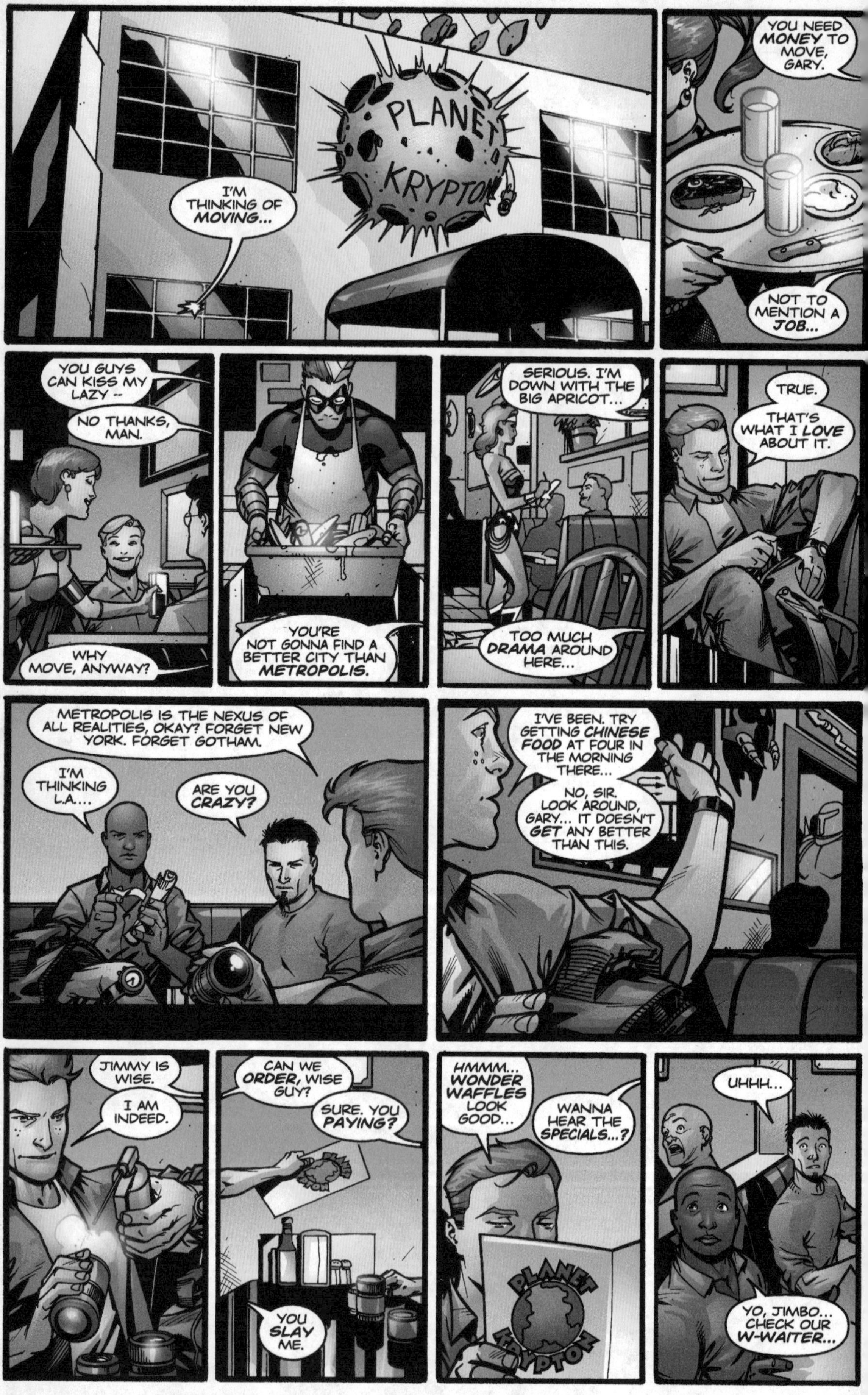
PLANET KRYPTON
I'M THINKING OF MOVING...
YOU NEED MONEY TO MOVE, GARY.
NOT TO MENTION A JOB...
YOU GUYS CAN KISS MY LAZY --
NO THANKS, MAN.
WHY MOVE, ANYWAY?
YOU'RE NOT GONNA FIND A BETTER CITY THAN METROPOLIS.
SERIOUS. I'M DOWN WITH THE BIG APRICOT...
TOO MUCH DRAMA AROUND HERE...
TRUE.
THAT'S WHAT I LOVE ABOUT IT.
METROPOLIS IS THE NEXUS OF ALL REALITIES, OKAY? FORGET NEW YORK. FORGET GOTHAM.
I'M THINKING L.A....
ARE YOU CRAZY?
I'VE BEEN. TRY GETTING CHINESE FOOD AT FOUR IN THE MORNING THERE...
NO, SIR. LOOK AROUND, GARY... IT DOESN'T GET ANY BETTER THAN THIS.
JIMMY IS WISE.
I AM INDEED.
CAN WE ORDER, WISE GUY?
SURE. YOU PAYING?
YOU SLAY ME.
HMMM... WONDER WAFFLES LOOK GOOD...
WANNA HEAR THE SPECIALS...?
PLANET KRYPTON
UHHH...
YO, JIMBO... CHECK OUR W-WAITER...

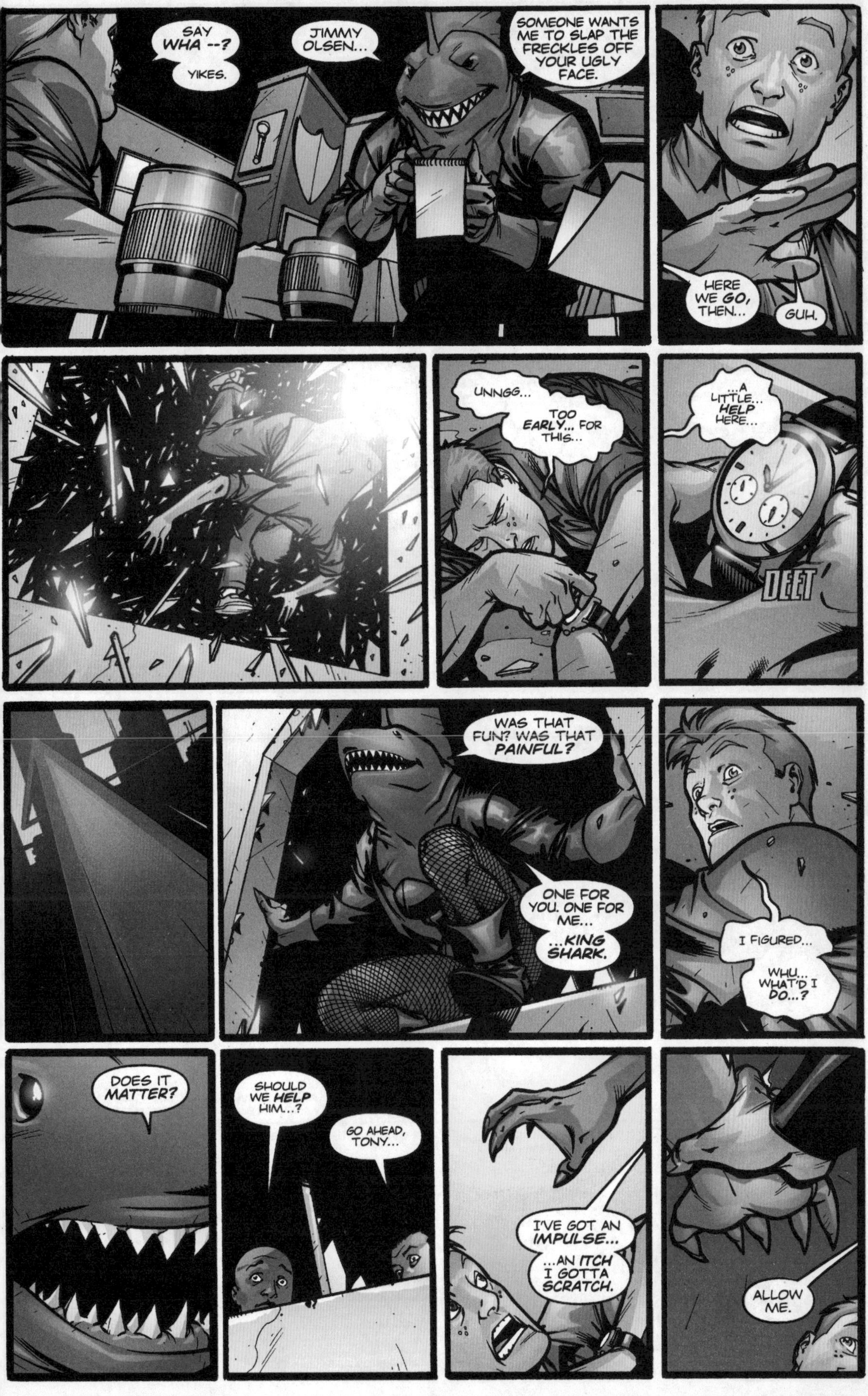
SAY WHA --?
YIKES.
JIMMY OLSEN...
SOMEONE WANTS ME TO SLAP THE FRECKLES OFF YOUR UGLY FACE.
HERE WE GO, THEN...
GUH.
UNNGG...
TOO EARLY... FOR THIS...
...A LITTLE... HELP HERE...
DEET
WAS THAT FUN? WAS THAT PAINFUL?
ONE FOR YOU. ONE FOR ME...
...KING SHARK.
I FIGURED...
WHU... WHAT'D I DO...?
DOES IT MATTER?
SHOULD WE HELP HIM...?
GO AHEAD, TONY...
I'VE GOT AN IMPULSE...
...AN ITCH I GOTTA SCRATCH.
ALLOW ME.

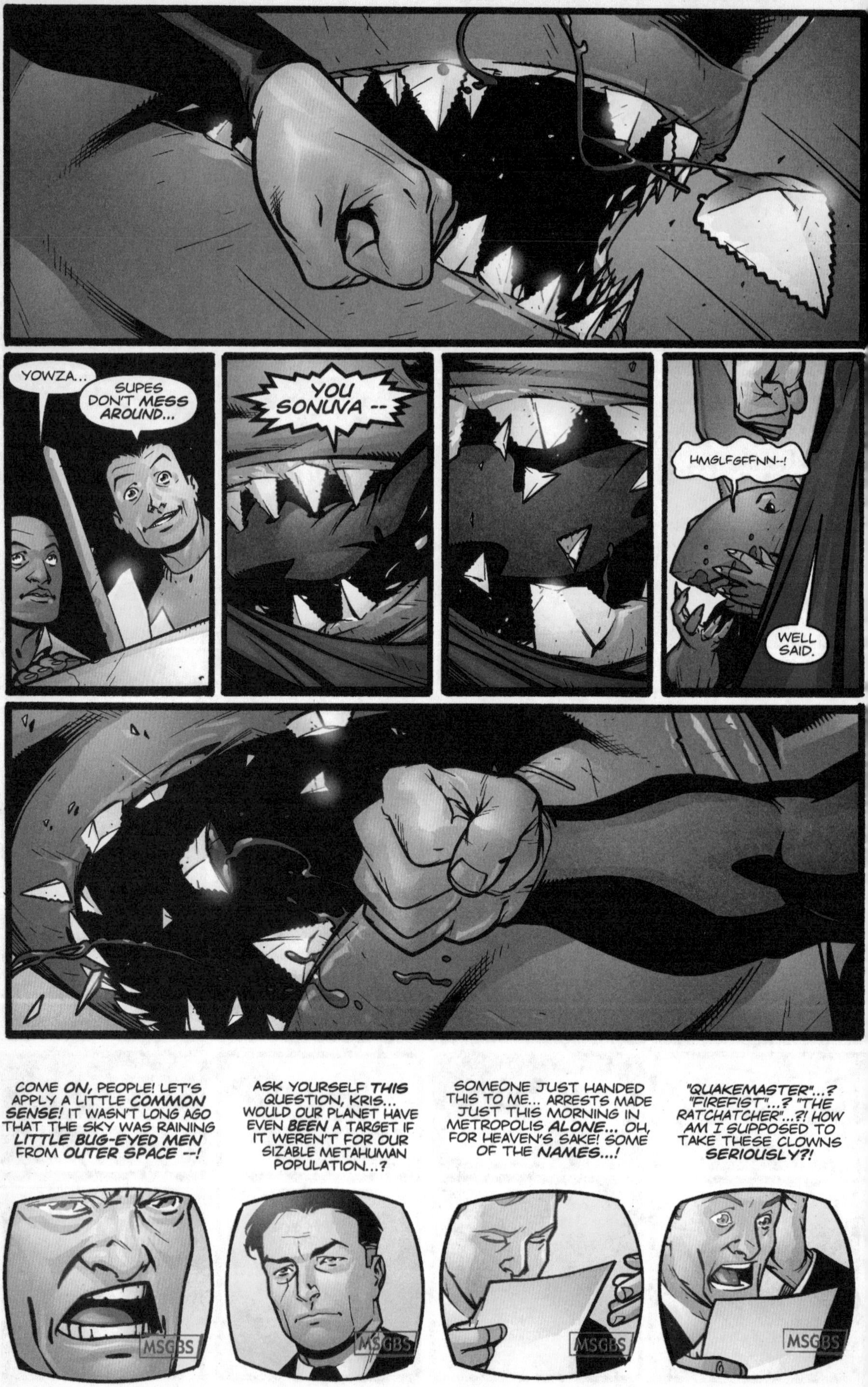
YOWZA...
SUPES DON'T MESS AROUND...
YOU SONUVA --
HMGLFGFFNN--!
WELL SAID.
COME ON, PEOPLE! LET'S APPLY A LITTLE COMMON SENSE! IT WASN'T LONG AGO THAT THE SKY WAS RAINING LITTLE BUG-EYED MEN FROM OUTER SPACE --!
ASK YOURSELF THIS QUESTION, KRIS... WOULD OUR PLANET HAVE EVEN BEEN A TARGET IF IT WEREN'T FOR OUR SIZABLE METAHUMAN POPULATION...?
SOMEONE JUST HANDED THIS TO ME... ARRESTS MADE JUST THIS MORNING IN METROPOLIS ALONE... OH, FOR HEAVEN'S SAKE! SOME OF THE NAMES...!
"QUAKEMASTER"...? "FIREFIST"...? "THE RATCHATCHER"...?! HOW AM I SUPPOSED TO TAKE THESE CLOWNS SERIOUSLY?!
MSGBS
MSGBS
MSGBS
MSGBS

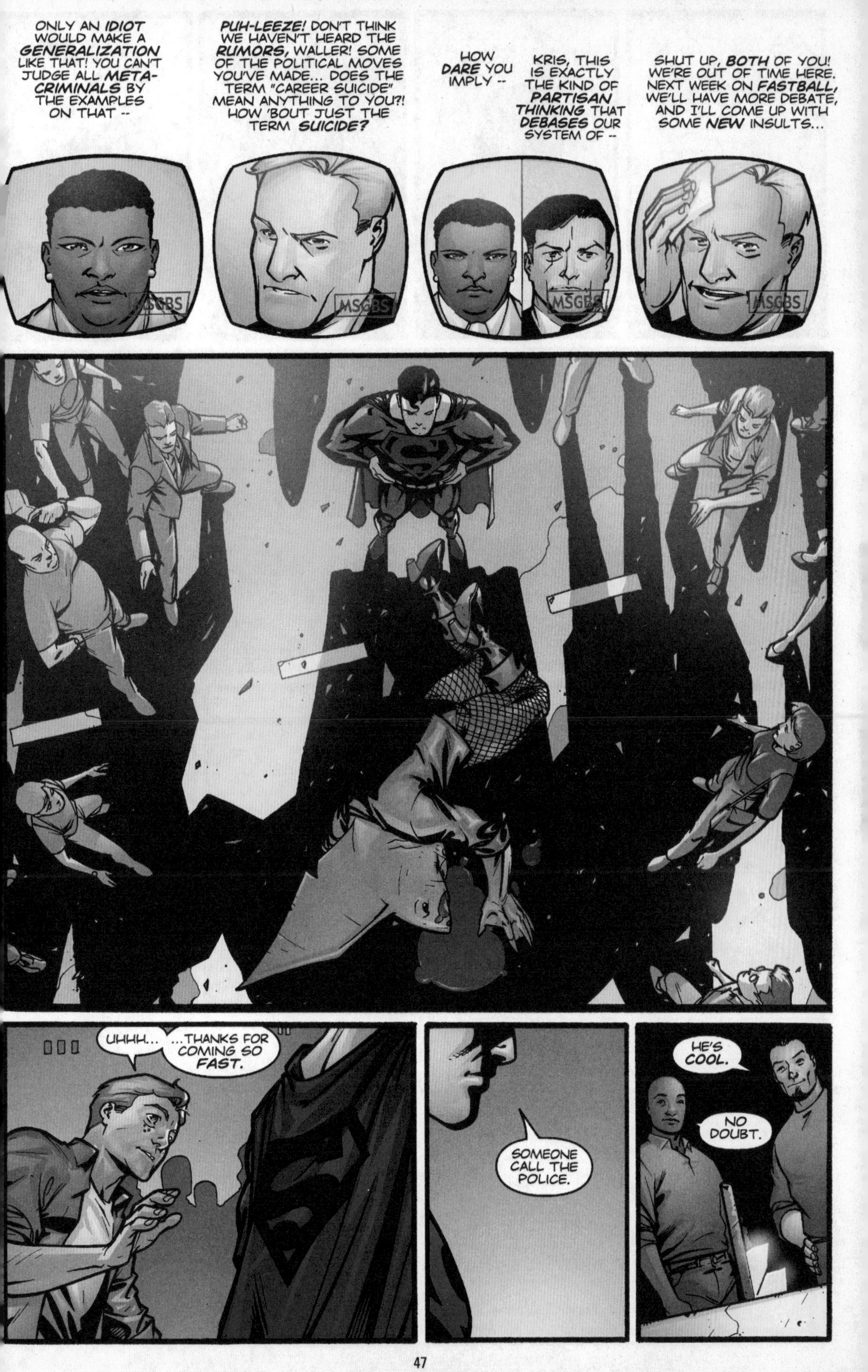
ONLY AN IDIOT WOULD MAKE A GENERALIZATION LIKE THAT! YOU CAN'T JUDGE ALL META-CRIMINALS BY THE EXAMPLES ON THAT --
PUH-LEEZE! DON'T THINK WE HAVEN'T HEARD THE RUMORS, WALLER! SOME OF THE POLITICAL MOVES YOU'VE MADE... DOES THE TERM "CAREER SUICIDE" MEAN ANYTHING TO YOU?! HOW 'BOUT JUST THE TERM SUICIDE?
HOW DARE YOU IMPLY --
KRIS, THIS IS EXACTLY THE KIND OF PARTISAN THINKING THAT DEBASES OUR SYSTEM OF --
SHUT UP, BOTH OF YOU! WE'RE OUT OF TIME HERE. NEXT WEEK ON FASTBALL, WE'LL HAVE MORE DEBATE, AND I'LL COME UP WITH SOME NEW INSULTS...
MSGBS
MSGBS
MSGBS
MSGBS
UHHH...
...THANKS FOR COMING SO FAST.
SOMEONE CALL THE POLICE.
HE'S COOL.
NO DOUBT.

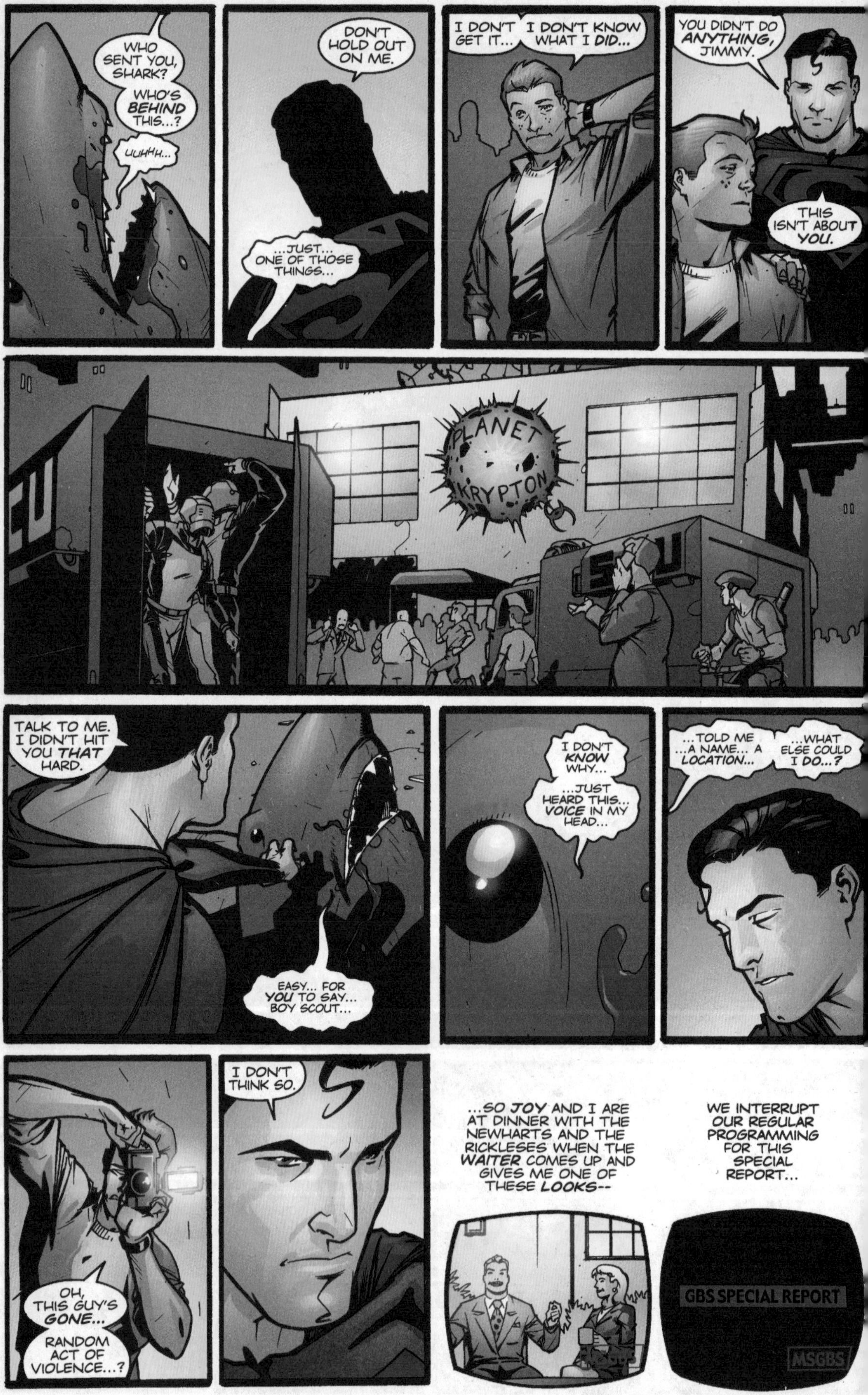
WHO SENT YOU, SHARK?
WHO'S BEHIND THIS...?
UUHHH...
DON'T HOLD OUT ON ME.
...JUST... ONE OF THOSE THINGS...
I DON'T GET IT...
I DON'T KNOW WHAT I DID...
YOU DIDN'T DO ANYTHING, JIMMY.
THIS ISN'T ABOUT YOU.
PLANET KRYPTON
TALK TO ME. I DIDN'T HIT YOU THAT HARD.
EASY... FOR YOU TO SAY... BOY SCOUT...
I DON'T KNOW WHY...
...JUST HEARD THIS... VOICE IN MY HEAD...
...TOLD ME ...A NAME... A LOCATION...
...WHAT ELSE COULD I DO...?
OH, THIS GUY'S GONE...
RANDOM ACT OF VIOLENCE...?
I DON'T THINK SO.
...SO JOY AND I ARE AT DINNER WITH THE NEWHARTS AND THE RICKLESES WHEN THE WAITER COMES UP AND GIVES ME ONE OF THESE LOOKS--
WE INTERRUPT OUR REGULAR PROGRAMMING FOR THIS SPECIAL REPORT...
GBS SPECIAL REPORT
MSGBS

WE'VE GOT REPORTS OF A *FIRE* IN MIDTOWN METROPOLIS. ACTION CHOPPER ONE IS IN THE AIR AND ON THE SCENE. WES...?

THESE WERE NEW THREADS--

HOLD ON...

--LOOKS LIKE THE *EDITORIAL FLOORS,* MARTY! HEAVY SMOKE... I CAN'T REALLY MAKE OUT EXACTLY *WHICH* FLOORS ARE AFFECTED...

LIVE

WHOA--!

UP UNTIL *NOW,* IT HAD ALMOST BEEN A GAME TO HIM.

ALMOST.

TOO MANY TIMES, HE'S BEEN SWEPT UP IN THESE CAT-AND-MOUSE SCENARIOS.

AND, ONCE AGAIN, EVERYONE WAS SAVED. NO ONE WAS KILLED. THE GOOD GUYS WON.

BUT NOW...

...THE GAME IS UP.

LOIS.

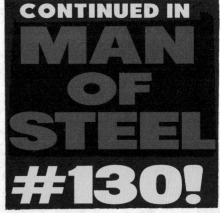

CONTINUED IN

MAN OF STEEL #130!

49

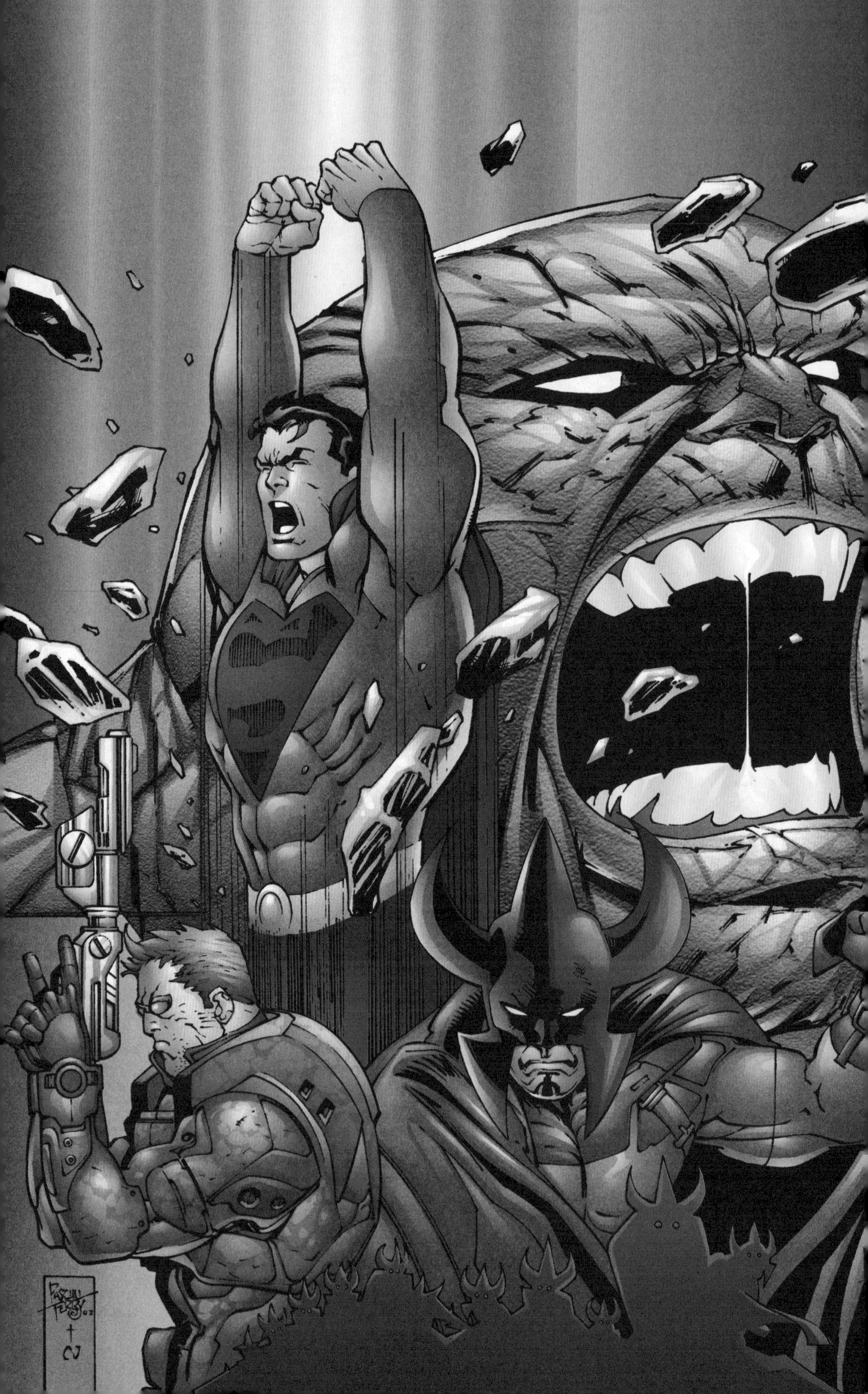

Cover art by PASCUAL FERRY & PAUL NEARY

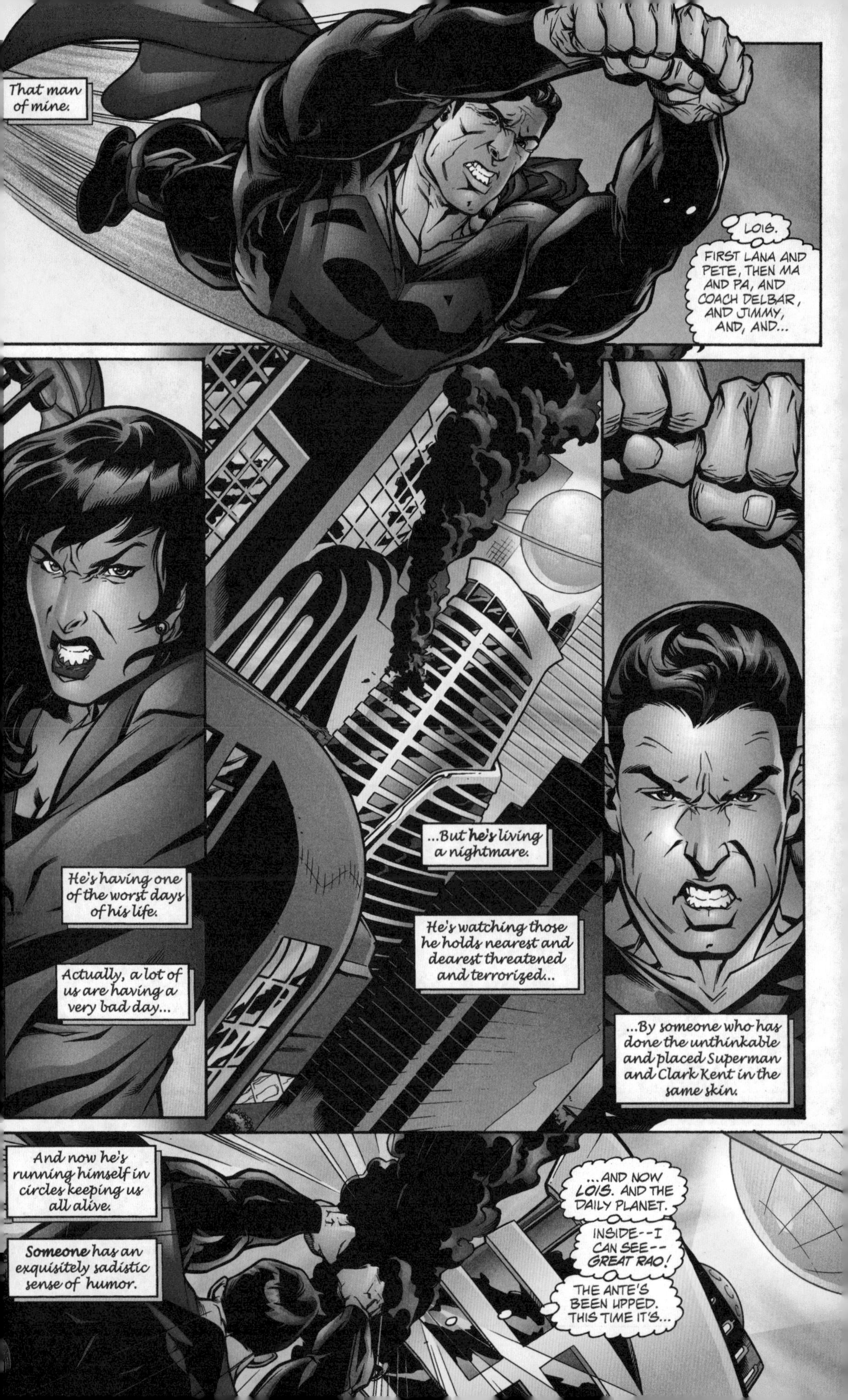
That man of mine.
LOIS.
FIRST LANA AND PETE, THEN MA AND PA, AND COACH DELBAR, AND JIMMY, AND, AND...
He's having one of the worst days of his life.
Actually, a lot of us are having a very bad day...
...But he's living a nightmare.
He's watching those he holds nearest and dearest threatened and terrorized...
...By someone who has done the unthinkable and placed Superman and Clark Kent in the same skin.
And now he's running himself in circles keeping us all alive.
Someone has an exquisitely sadistic sense of humor.
...AND NOW LOIS. AND THE DAILY PLANET.
INSIDE--I CAN SEE--GREAT RAO!
THE ANTE'S BEEN UPPED. THIS TIME IT'S...

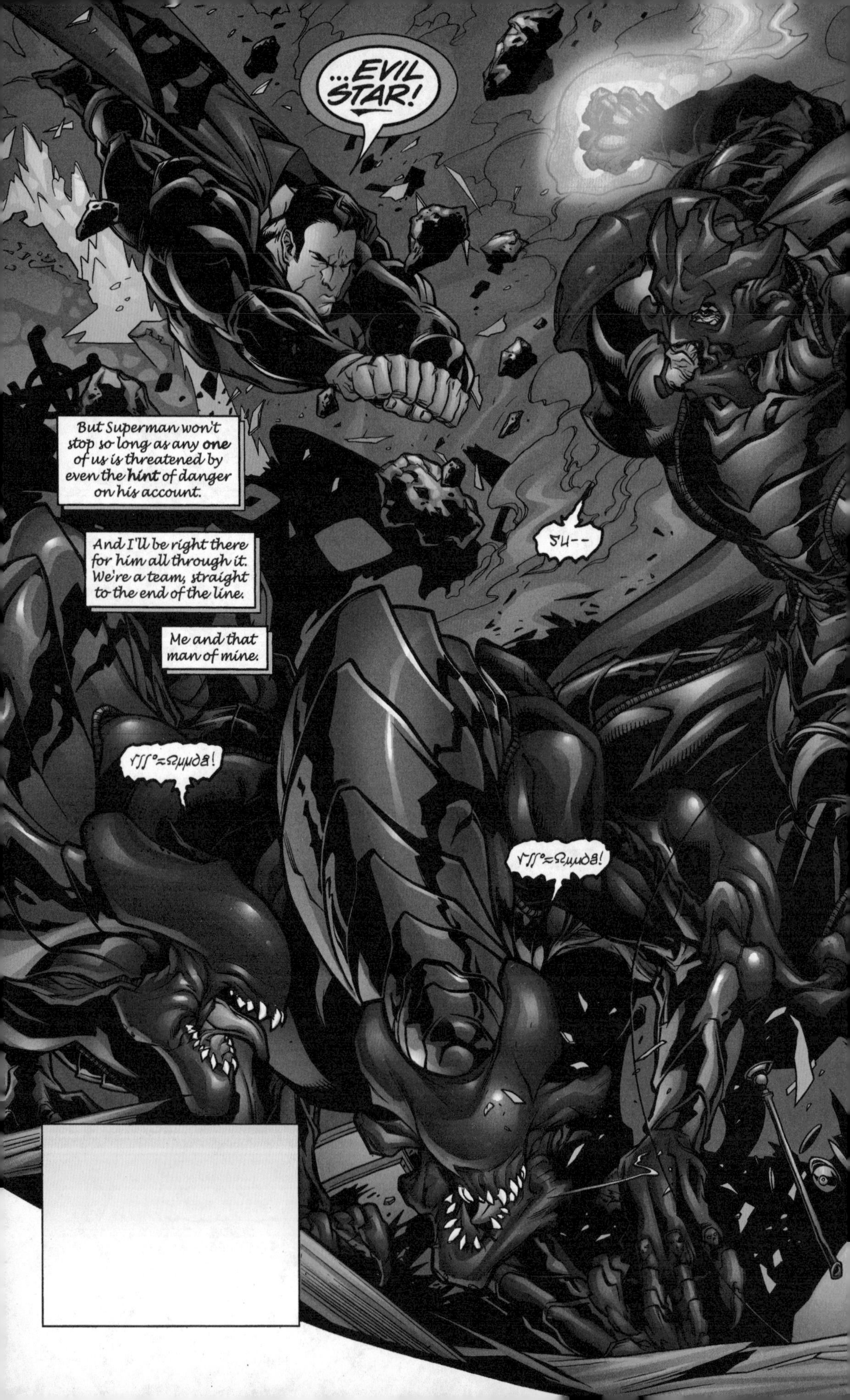
...EVIL STAR!
But Superman won't stop so long as any one of us is threatened by even the hint of danger on his account.
And I'll be right there for him all through it. We're a team, straight to the end of the line.
Me and that man of mine.

ENDING BATTLE PART 9
IN THE DARK OF THE NOON DAY SUN

MARK SCHULTZ	BRANDON BADEAUX	MARK MORALES	TANYA & RICHARD HORIE	KEN LOPEZ	TOM PALMER, JR.	EDDIE BERGANZA
writer	penciller	inker	colors and seps	letterer	associate editor	editor

SUPERMAN CREATED BY
JERRY SIEGEL AND JOE SHUSTER

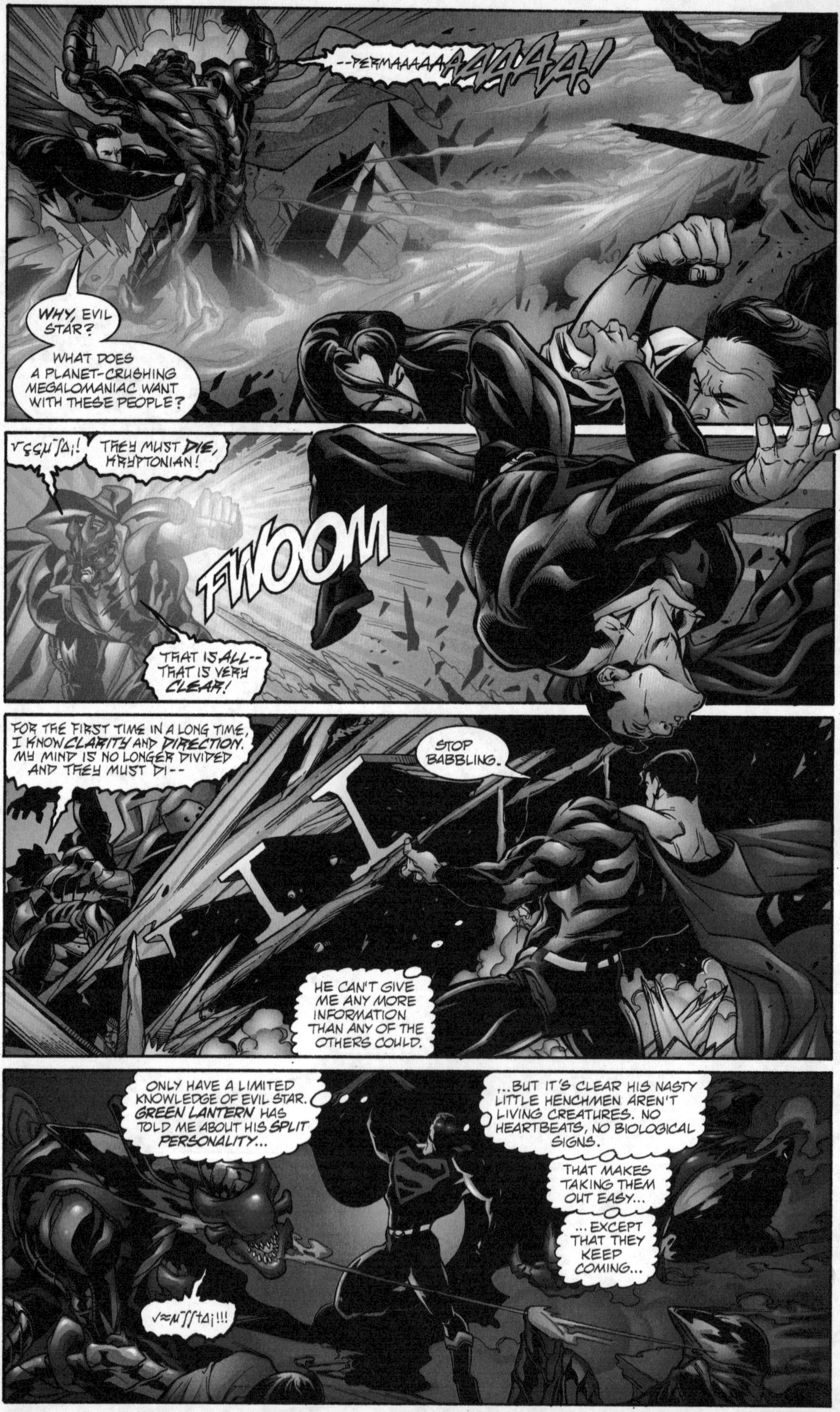
--PERMAAAAAAAAAAA!
WHY, EVIL STAR?
WHAT DOES A PLANET-CRUSHING MEGALOMANIAC WANT WITH THESE PEOPLE?
THEY MUST DIE, KRYPTONIAN!
FWOOM
THAT IS ALL-- THAT IS VERY CLEAR!
FOR THE FIRST TIME IN A LONG TIME, I KNOW CLARITY AND DIRECTION. MY MIND IS NO LONGER DIVIDED AND THEY MUST DI--
STOP BABBLING.
HE CAN'T GIVE ME ANY MORE INFORMATION THAN ANY OF THE OTHERS COULD.
ONLY HAVE A LIMITED KNOWLEDGE OF EVIL STAR. GREEN LANTERN HAS TOLD ME ABOUT HIS SPLIT PERSONALITY...
...BUT IT'S CLEAR HIS NASTY LITTLE HENCHMEN AREN'T LIVING CREATURES. NO HEARTBEATS, NO BIOLOGICAL SIGNS.
THAT MAKES TAKING THEM OUT EASY...
...EXCEPT THAT THEY KEEP COMING...

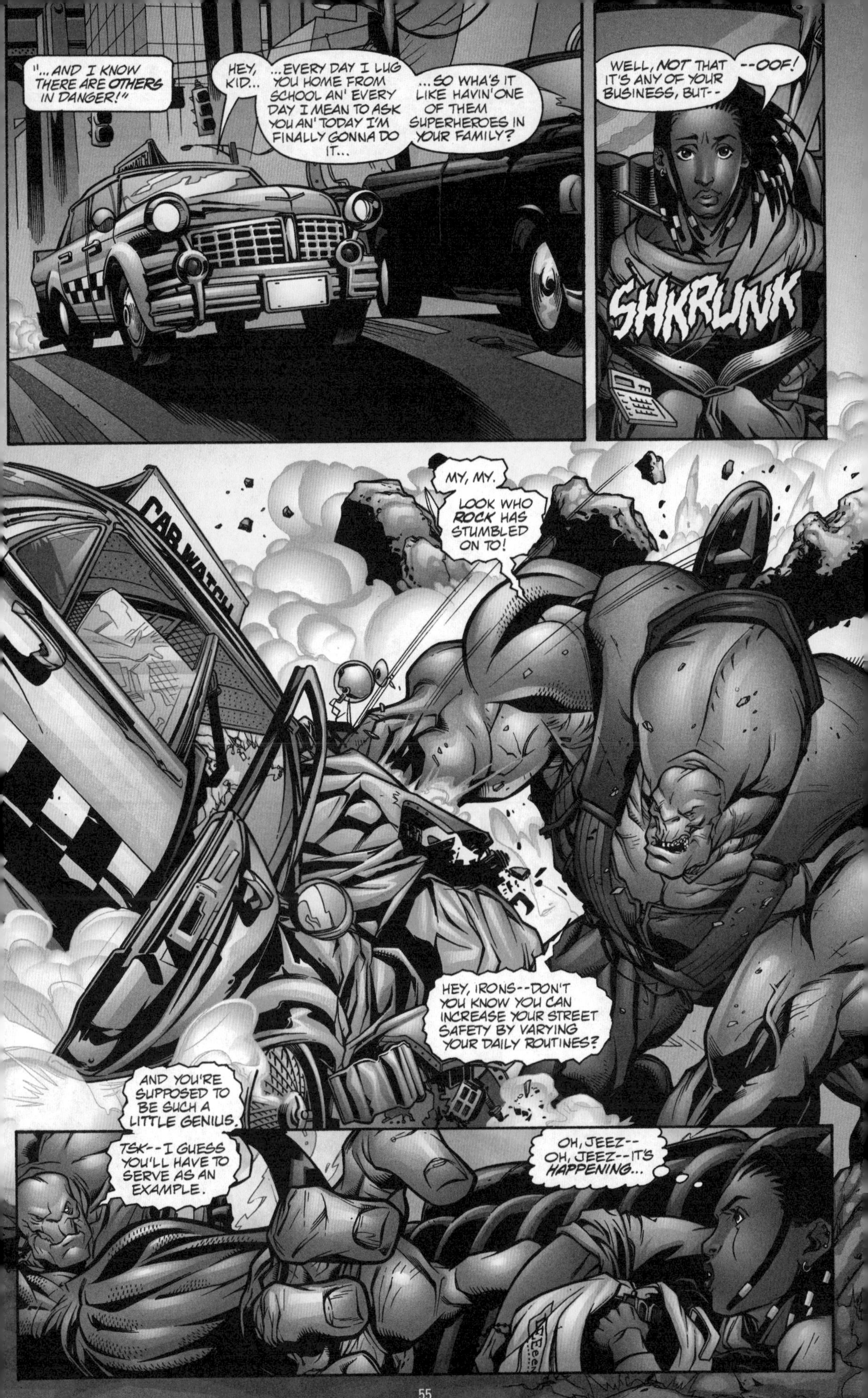
"...AND I KNOW THERE ARE OTHERS IN DANGER!"
HEY, KID...
...EVERY DAY I LUG YOU HOME FROM SCHOOL AN' EVERY DAY I MEAN TO ASK YOU AN' TODAY I'M FINALLY GONNA DO IT...
...SO WHA'S IT LIKE HAVIN' ONE OF THEM SUPERHEROES IN YOUR FAMILY?
WELL, NOT THAT IT'S ANY OF YOUR BUSINESS, BUT--
--OOF!
SHKRUNK
CAB WATCH
MY, MY.
LOOK WHO ROCK HAS STUMBLED ON TO!
HEY, IRONS--DON'T YOU KNOW YOU CAN INCREASE YOUR STREET SAFETY BY VARYING YOUR DAILY ROUTINES?
AND YOU'RE SUPPOSED TO BE SUCH A LITTLE GENIUS.
TSK--I GUESS YOU'LL HAVE TO SERVE AS AN EXAMPLE.
OH, JEEZ-- OH, JEEZ--IT'S HAPPENING...

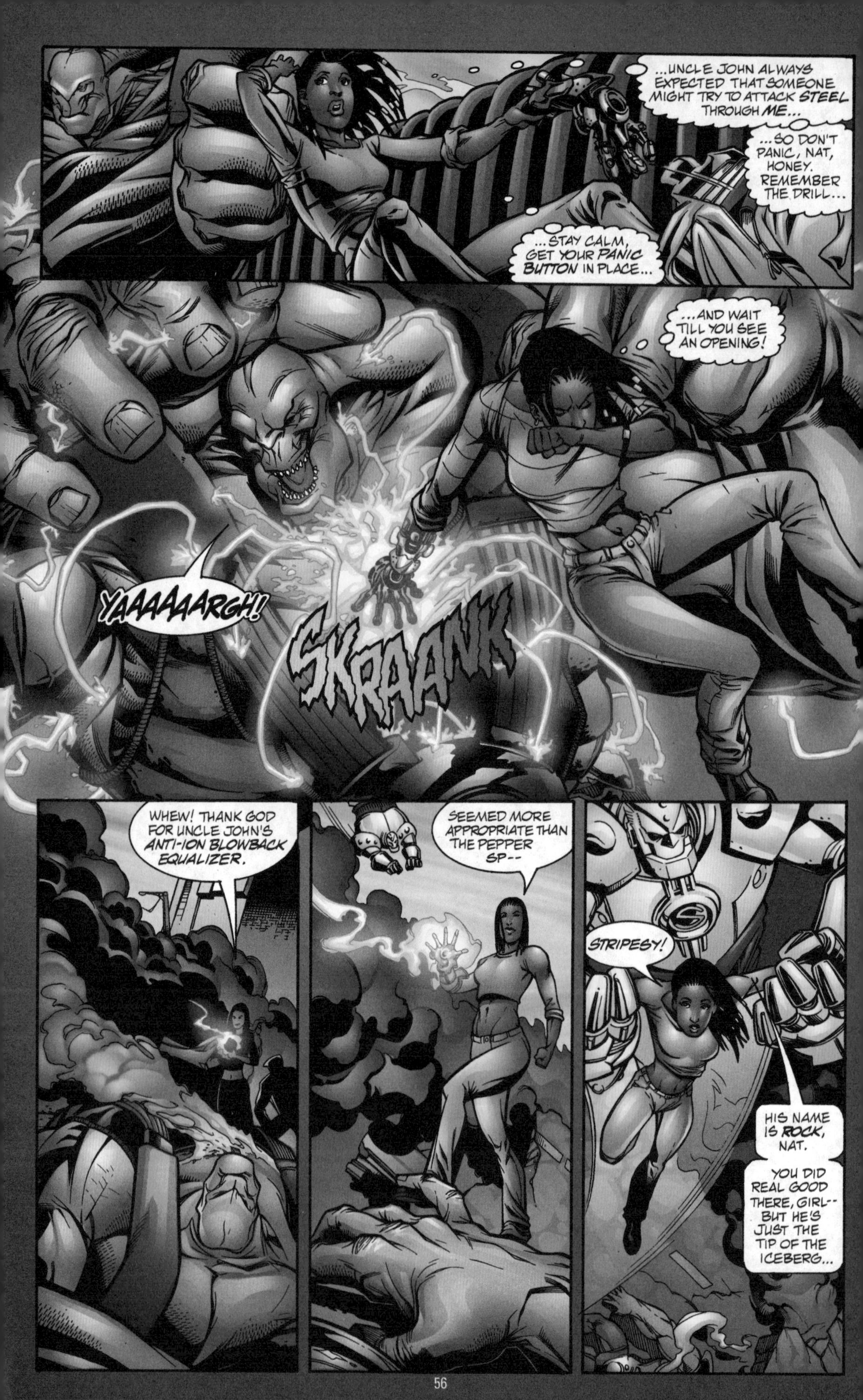
...UNCLE JOHN ALWAYS EXPECTED THAT SOMEONE MIGHT TRY TO ATTACK STEEL THROUGH ME...
...SO DON'T PANIC, NAT, HONEY. REMEMBER THE DRILL...
...STAY CALM, GET YOUR PANIC BUTTON IN PLACE...
...AND WAIT TILL YOU SEE AN OPENING!
YAAAAAARGH!
SKRAANK
WHEW! THANK GOD FOR UNCLE JOHN'S ANTI-ION BLOWBACK EQUALIZER.
SEEMED MORE APPROPRIATE THAN THE PEPPER SP--
STRIPESY!
HIS NAME IS ROCK, NAT.
YOU DID REAL GOOD THERE, GIRL-- BUT HE'S JUST THE TIP OF THE ICEBERG...

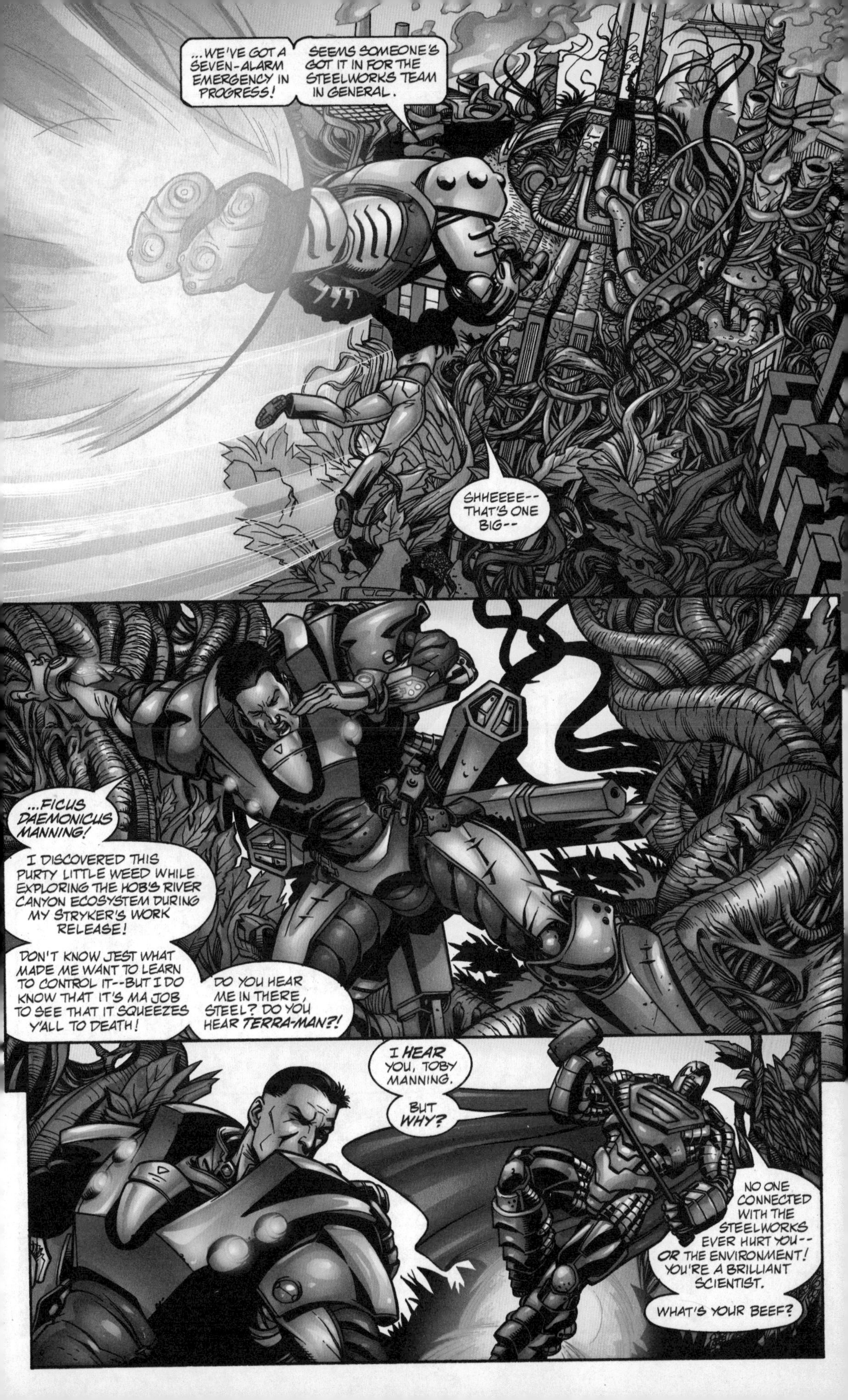
...WE'VE GOT A SEVEN-ALARM EMERGENCY IN PROGRESS!
SEEMS SOMEONE'S GOT IT IN FOR THE STEELWORKS TEAM IN GENERAL.
SHHEEEE--THAT'S ONE BIG--
...FICUS DAEMONICUS MANNING!
I DISCOVERED THIS PURTY LITTLE WEED WHILE EXPLORING THE HOB'S RIVER CANYON ECOSYSTEM DURING MY STRYKER'S WORK RELEASE!
DON'T KNOW JEST WHAT MADE ME WANT TO LEARN TO CONTROL IT--BUT I DO KNOW THAT IT'S MA JOB TO SEE THAT IT SQUEEZES Y'ALL TO DEATH!
DO YOU HEAR ME IN THERE, STEEL? DO YOU HEAR TERRA-MAN?!
I HEAR YOU, TOBY MANNING.
BUT WHY?
NO ONE CONNECTED WITH THE STEELWORKS EVER HURT YOU--OR THE ENVIRONMENT! YOU'RE A BRILLIANT SCIENTIST.
WHAT'S YOUR BEEF?

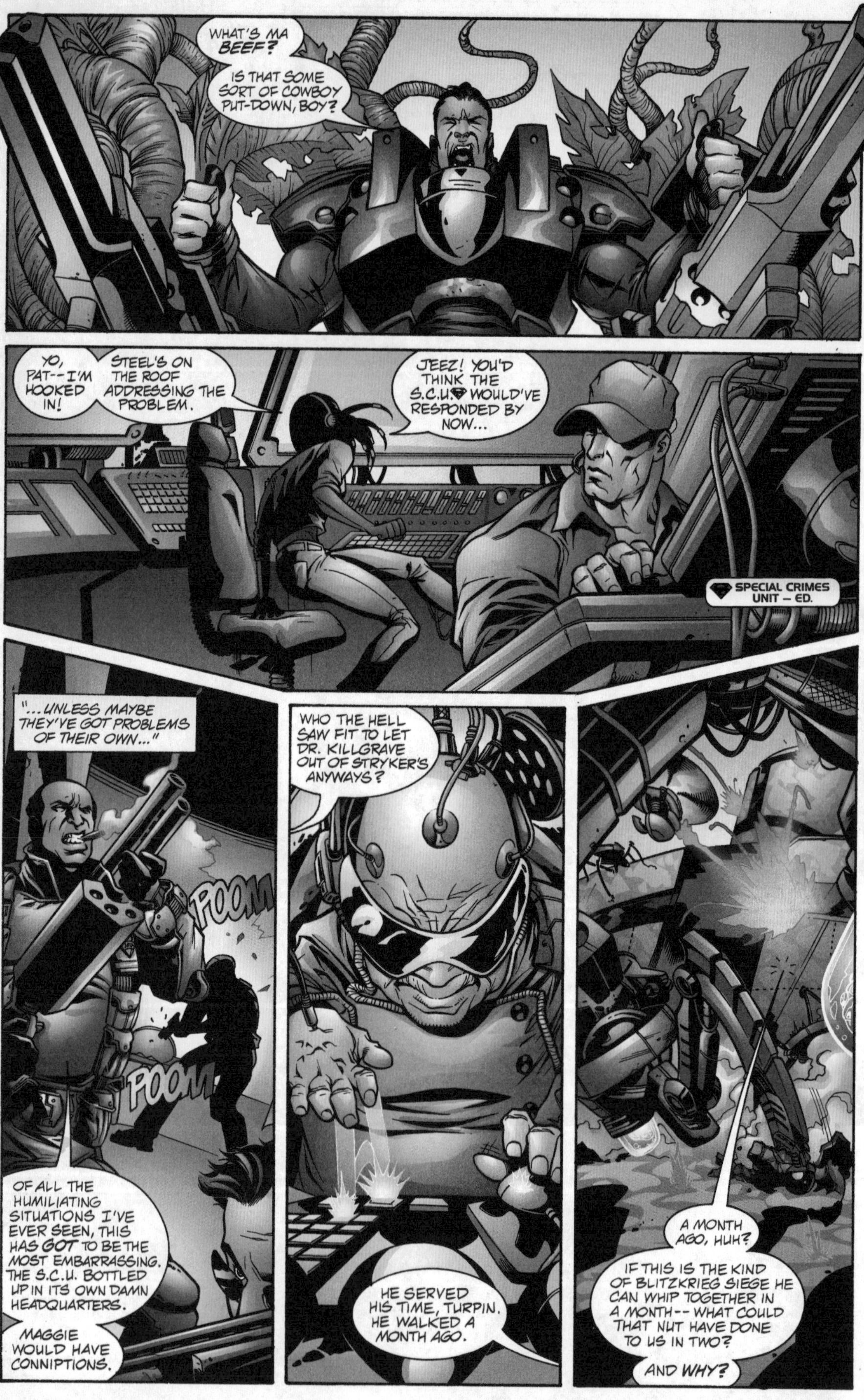
WHAT'S MA BEEF?
IS THAT SOME SORT OF COWBOY PUT-DOWN, BOY?
YO, PAT--I'M HOOKED IN!
STEEL'S ON THE ROOF ADDRESSING THE PROBLEM.
JEEZ! YOU'D THINK THE S.C.U. WOULD'VE RESPONDED BY NOW...
SPECIAL CRIMES UNIT – ED.
"...UNLESS MAYBE THEY'VE GOT PROBLEMS OF THEIR OWN..."
POOM
POOM
OF ALL THE HUMILIATING SITUATIONS I'VE EVER SEEN, THIS HAS GOT TO BE THE MOST EMBARRASSING. THE S.C.U. BOTTLED UP IN ITS OWN DAMN HEADQUARTERS.
MAGGIE WOULD HAVE CONNIPTIONS.
WHO THE HELL SAW FIT TO LET DR. KILLGRAVE OUT OF STRYKER'S ANYWAYS?
HE SERVED HIS TIME, TURPIN. HE WALKED A MONTH AGO.
A MONTH AGO, HUH?
IF THIS IS THE KIND OF BLITZKRIEG SIEGE HE CAN WHIP TOGETHER IN A MONTH-- WHAT COULD THAT NUT HAVE DONE TO US IN TWO?
AND WHY?

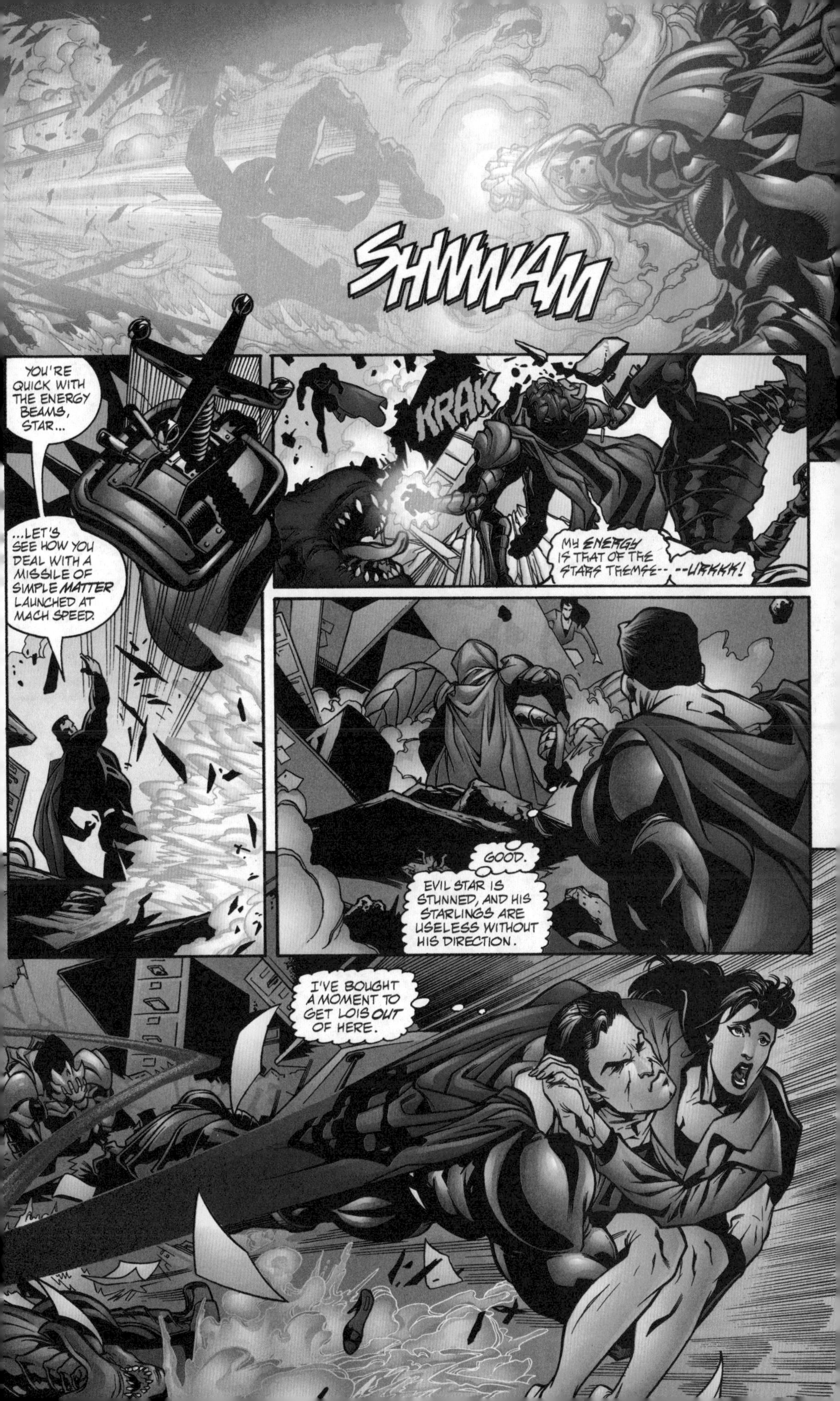
SHWWAM
YOU'RE QUICK WITH THE ENERGY BEAMS, STAR...
...LET'S SEE HOW YOU DEAL WITH A MISSILE OF SIMPLE MATTER LAUNCHED AT MACH SPEED.
KRAK
MY ENERGY IS THAT OF THE STARS THEMSE--
--URKKK!
GOOD.
EVIL STAR IS STUNNED, AND HIS STARLINGS ARE USELESS WITHOUT HIS DIRECTION.
I'VE BOUGHT A MOMENT TO GET LOIS OUT OF HERE.

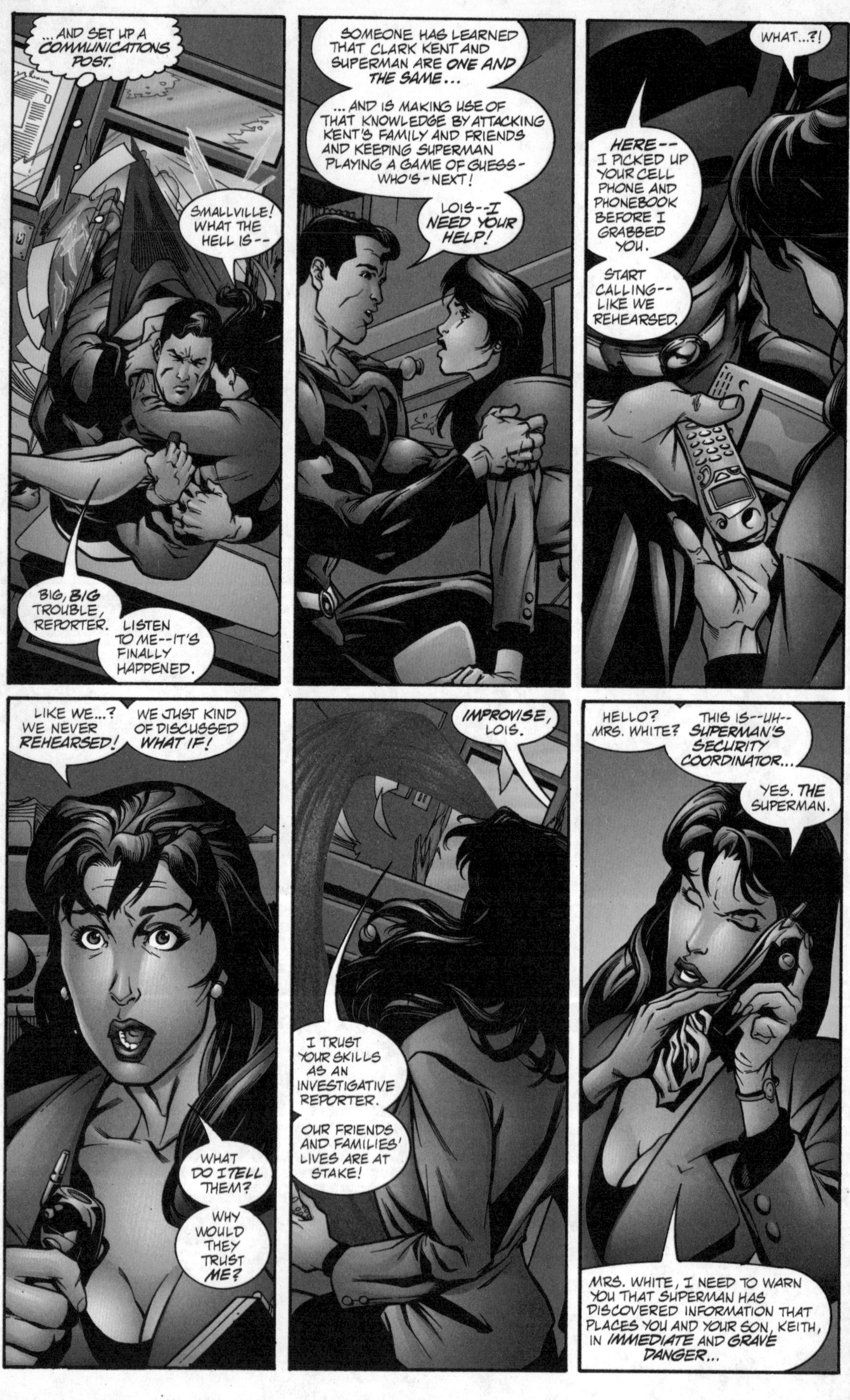

...AND SET UP A COMMUNICATIONS POST.
SMALLVILLE! WHAT THE HELL IS--
BIG, BIG TROUBLE, REPORTER.
LISTEN TO ME--IT'S FINALLY HAPPENED.
SOMEONE HAS LEARNED THAT CLARK KENT AND SUPERMAN ARE ONE AND THE SAME...
...AND IS MAKING USE OF THAT KNOWLEDGE BY ATTACKING KENT'S FAMILY AND FRIENDS AND KEEPING SUPERMAN PLAYING A GAME OF GUESS-WHO'S-NEXT!
LOIS--I NEED YOUR HELP!
WHAT...?!
HERE-- I PICKED UP YOUR CELL PHONE AND PHONEBOOK BEFORE I GRABBED YOU.
START CALLING-- LIKE WE REHEARSED.
LIKE WE...? WE NEVER REHEARSED!
WE JUST KIND OF DISCUSSED WHAT IF!
WHAT DO I TELL THEM?
WHY WOULD THEY TRUST ME?
IMPROVISE, LOIS.
I TRUST YOUR SKILLS AS AN INVESTIGATIVE REPORTER.
OUR FRIENDS AND FAMILIES' LIVES ARE AT STAKE!
HELLO? MRS. WHITE?
THIS IS--UH-- SUPERMAN'S SECURITY COORDINATOR...
YES. THE SUPERMAN.
MRS. WHITE, I NEED TO WARN YOU THAT SUPERMAN HAS DISCOVERED INFORMATION THAT PLACES YOU AND YOUR SON, KEITH, IN IMMEDIATE AND GRAVE DANGER...

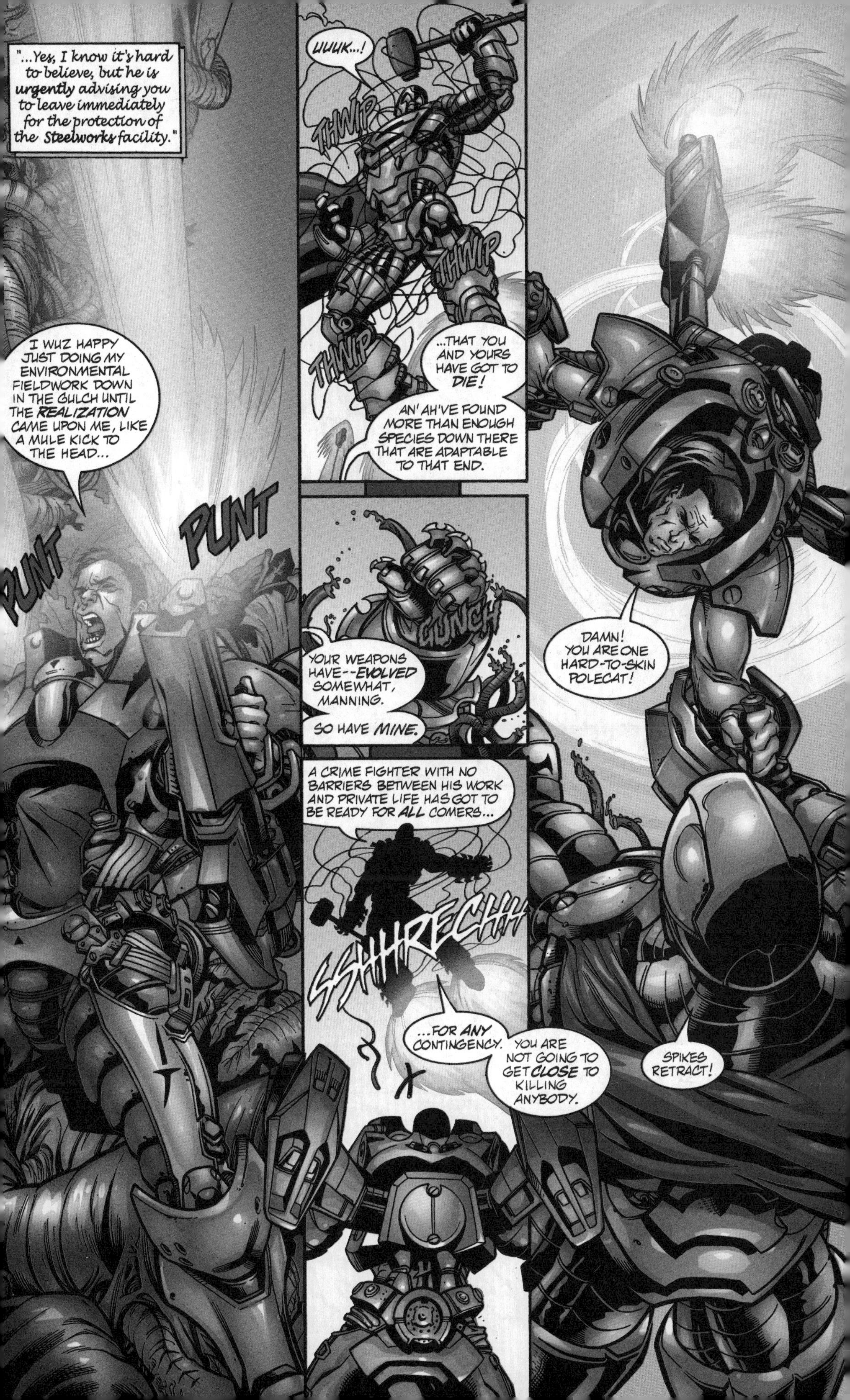
"...Yes, I know it's hard to believe, but he is urgently advising you to leave immediately for the protection of the Steelworks facility."
I WUZ HAPPY JUST DOING MY ENVIRONMENTAL FIELDWORK DOWN IN THE GULCH UNTIL THE REALIZATION CAME UPON ME, LIKE A MULE KICK TO THE HEAD...
PUNT
PUNT
UUUK...!
THWIP
THWIP
THWIP
...THAT YOU AND YOURS HAVE GOT TO DIE!
AN' AH'VE FOUND MORE THAN ENOUGH SPECIES DOWN THERE THAT ARE ADAPTABLE TO THAT END.
GUNCH
YOUR WEAPONS HAVE--EVOLVED SOMEWHAT, MANNING.
SO HAVE MINE.
A CRIME FIGHTER WITH NO BARRIERS BETWEEN HIS WORK AND PRIVATE LIFE HAS GOT TO BE READY FOR ALL COMERS...
SSHHRECHH
...FOR ANY CONTINGENCY.
YOU ARE NOT GOING TO GET CLOSE TO KILLING ANYBODY.
DAMN! YOU ARE ONE HARD-TO-SKIN POLECAT!
SPIKES RETRACT!

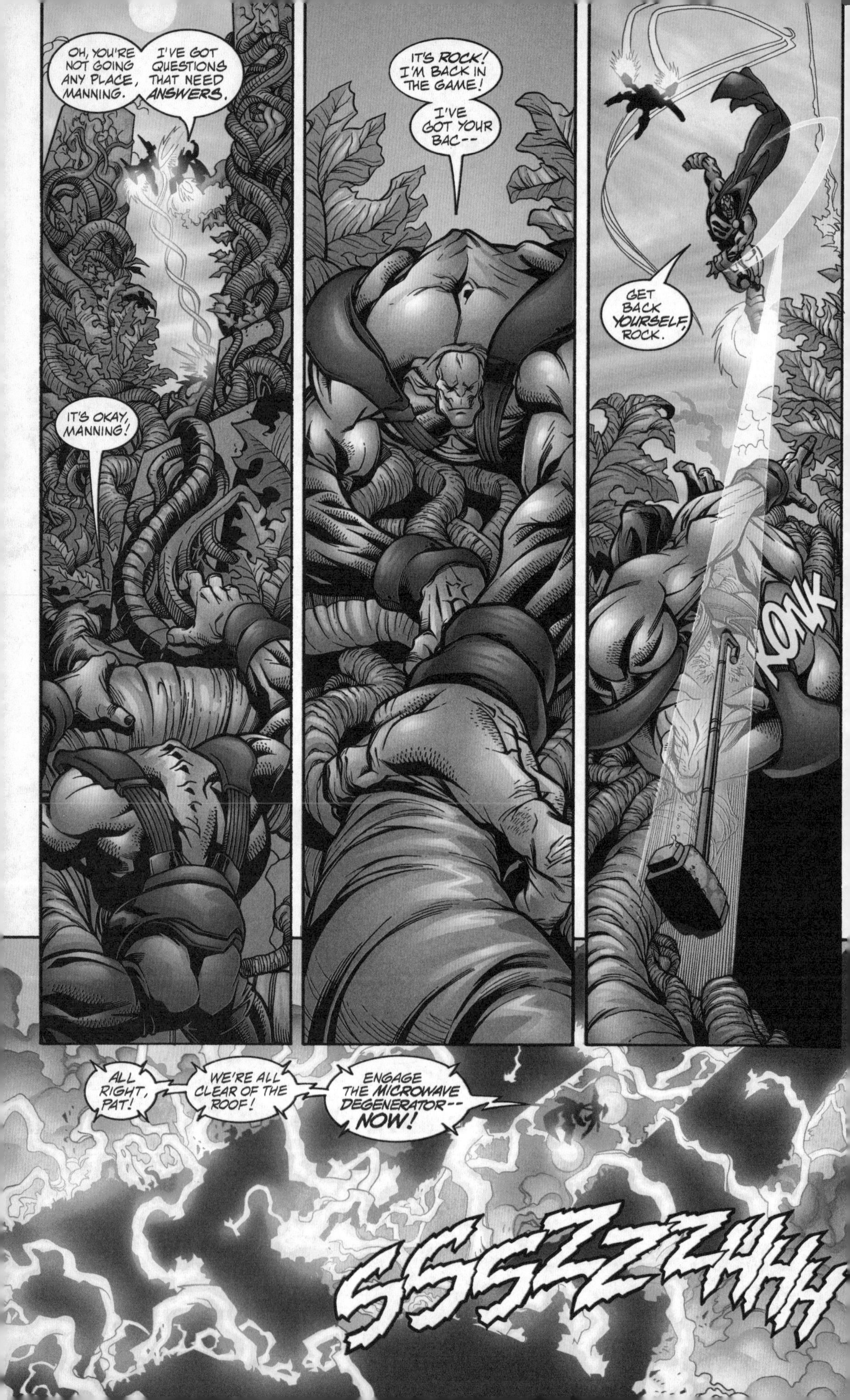
OH, YOU'RE NOT GOING ANY PLACE, MANNING.
I'VE GOT QUESTIONS THAT NEED ANSWERS.
IT'S OKAY, MANNING!
IT'S ROCK! I'M BACK IN THE GAME!
I'VE GOT YOUR BAC--
GET BACK YOURSELF, ROCK.
KONK
ALL RIGHT, PAT!
WE'RE ALL CLEAR OF THE ROOF!
ENGAGE THE MICROWAVE DEGENERATOR-- NOW!
SSSZZZHHH

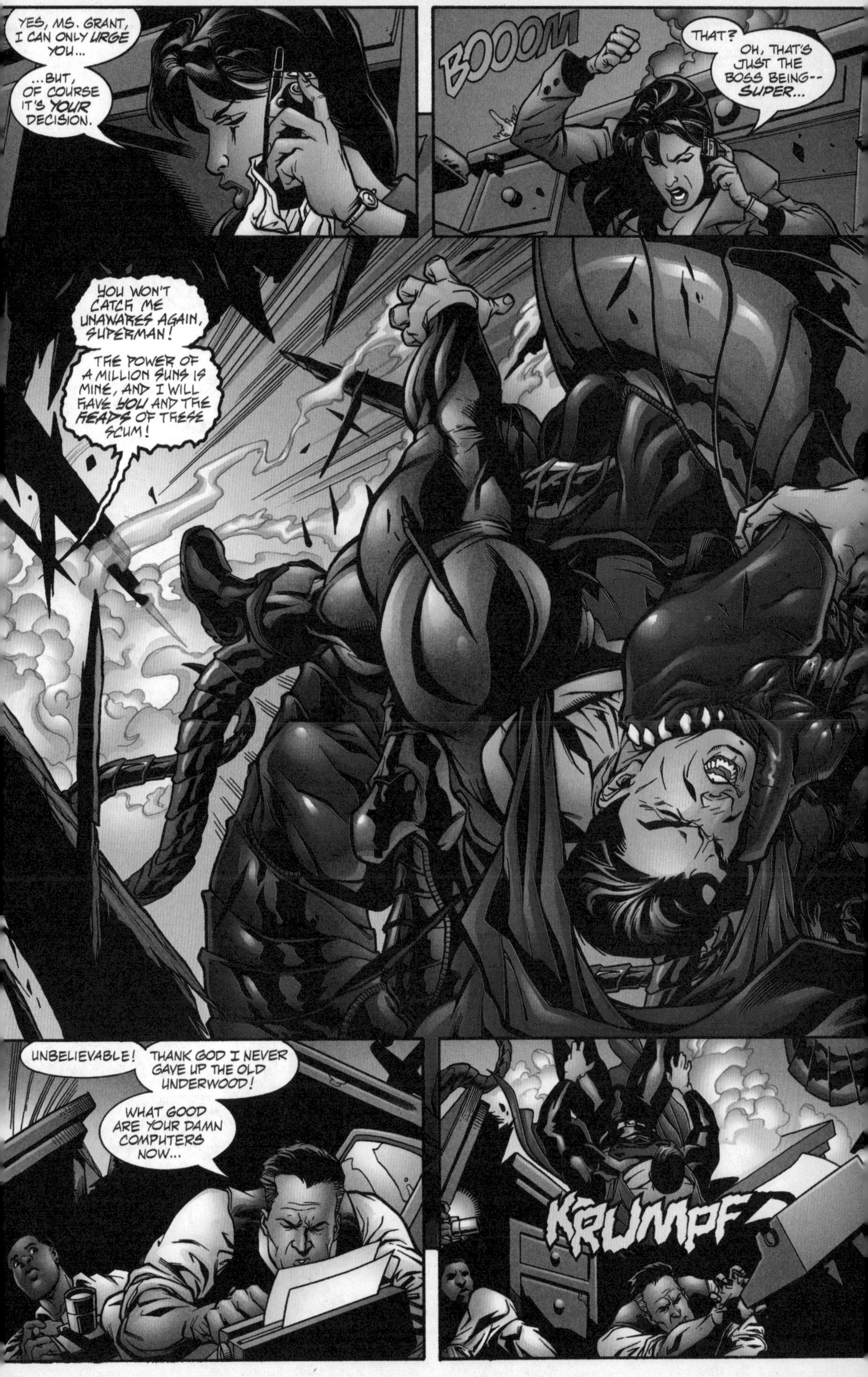
YES, MS. GRANT, I CAN ONLY URGE YOU...
...BUT, OF COURSE IT'S YOUR DECISION.
BOOOM
THAT? OH, THAT'S JUST THE BOSS BEING-- SUPER...
YOU WON'T CATCH ME UNAWARES AGAIN, SUPERMAN!
THE POWER OF A MILLION SUNS IS MINE, AND I WILL HAVE YOU AND THE HEADS OF THESE SCUM!
UNBELIEVABLE!
THANK GOD I NEVER GAVE UP THE OLD UNDERWOOD!
WHAT GOOD ARE YOUR DAMN COMPUTERS NOW...
KRUMPF

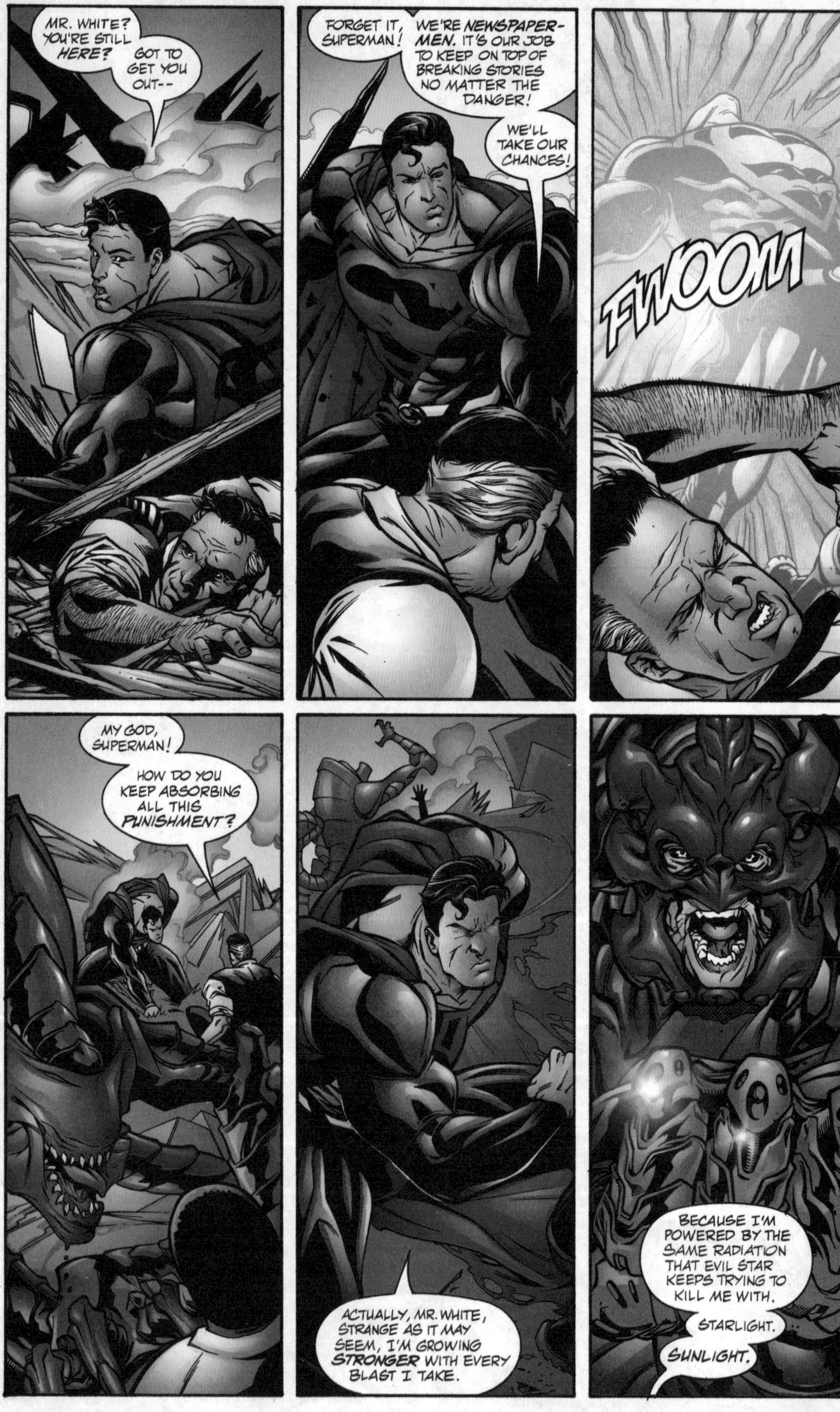
MR. WHITE? YOU'RE STILL HERE?
GOT TO GET YOU OUT--
FORGET IT, SUPERMAN!
WE'RE NEWSPAPER-MEN. IT'S OUR JOB TO KEEP ON TOP OF BREAKING STORIES NO MATTER THE DANGER!
WE'LL TAKE OUR CHANCES!
FWOOM
MY GOD, SUPERMAN!
HOW DO YOU KEEP ABSORBING ALL THIS PUNISHMENT?
ACTUALLY, MR. WHITE, STRANGE AS IT MAY SEEM, I'M GROWING STRONGER WITH EVERY BLAST I TAKE.
BECAUSE I'M POWERED BY THE SAME RADIATION THAT EVIL STAR KEEPS TRYING TO KILL ME WITH.
STARLIGHT.
SUNLIGHT.

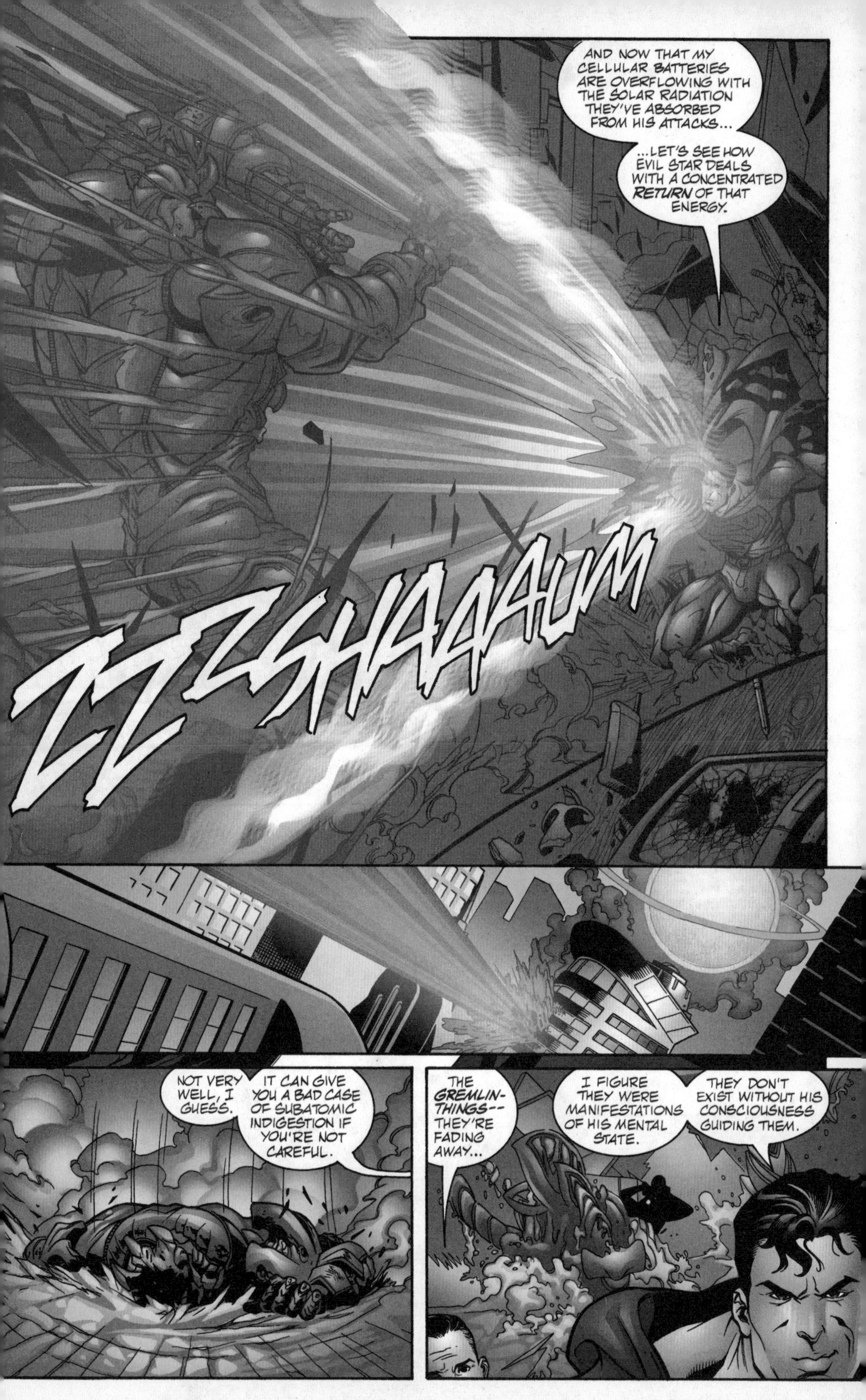
AND NOW THAT MY CELLULAR BATTERIES ARE OVERFLOWING WITH THE SOLAR RADIATION THEY'VE ABSORBED FROM HIS ATTACKS...
...LET'S SEE HOW EVIL STAR DEALS WITH A CONCENTRATED *RETURN* OF THAT ENERGY.
ZZZSHAAAAUM
NOT VERY WELL, I GUESS.
IT CAN GIVE YOU A BAD CASE OF SUBATOMIC INDIGESTION IF YOU'RE NOT CAREFUL.
THE *GREMLIN-THINGS*-- THEY'RE FADING AWAY...
I FIGURE THEY WERE MANIFESTATIONS OF HIS MENTAL STATE.
THEY DON'T EXIST WITHOUT HIS CONSCIOUSNESS GUIDING THEM.

"NOW PLEASE EXCUSE ME, MR. WHITE--THERE ARE OTHERS WHO NEED ME..."

OH, SO THE HOTSHOT META THOUGHT WE COULDN'T SAVE OUR *OWN* SORRY BUTTS...

YOU--YOU JUST *FRIED* MA FICUS DAEMONICUS...

...*WITHOUT* DAMAGING YOUR FACILITY...?

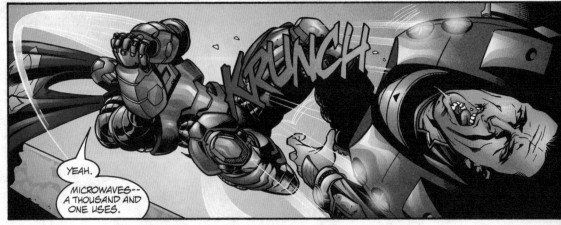

KRUNCH

YEAH. MICROWAVES-- A THOUSAND AND ONE USES.

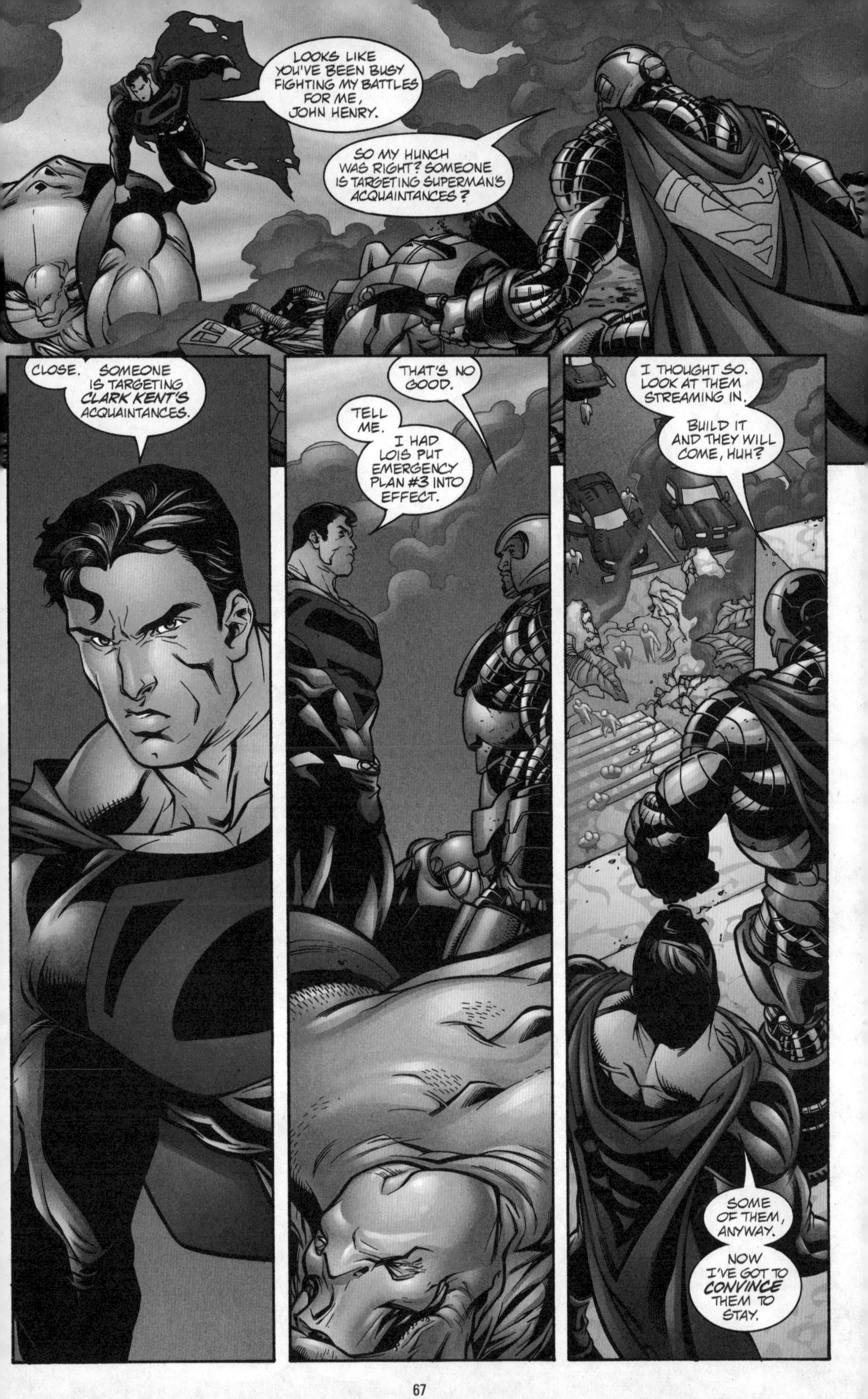
LOOKS LIKE YOU'VE BEEN BUSY FIGHTING MY BATTLES FOR ME, JOHN HENRY.
SO MY HUNCH WAS RIGHT? SOMEONE IS TARGETING SUPERMAN'S ACQUAINTANCES?
CLOSE. SOMEONE IS TARGETING CLARK KENT'S ACQUAINTANCES.
THAT'S NO GOOD.
TELL ME.
I HAD LOIS PUT EMERGENCY PLAN #3 INTO EFFECT.
I THOUGHT SO. LOOK AT THEM STREAMING IN.
BUILD IT AND THEY WILL COME, HUH?
SOME OF THEM, ANYWAY.
NOW I'VE GOT TO CONVINCE THEM TO STAY.

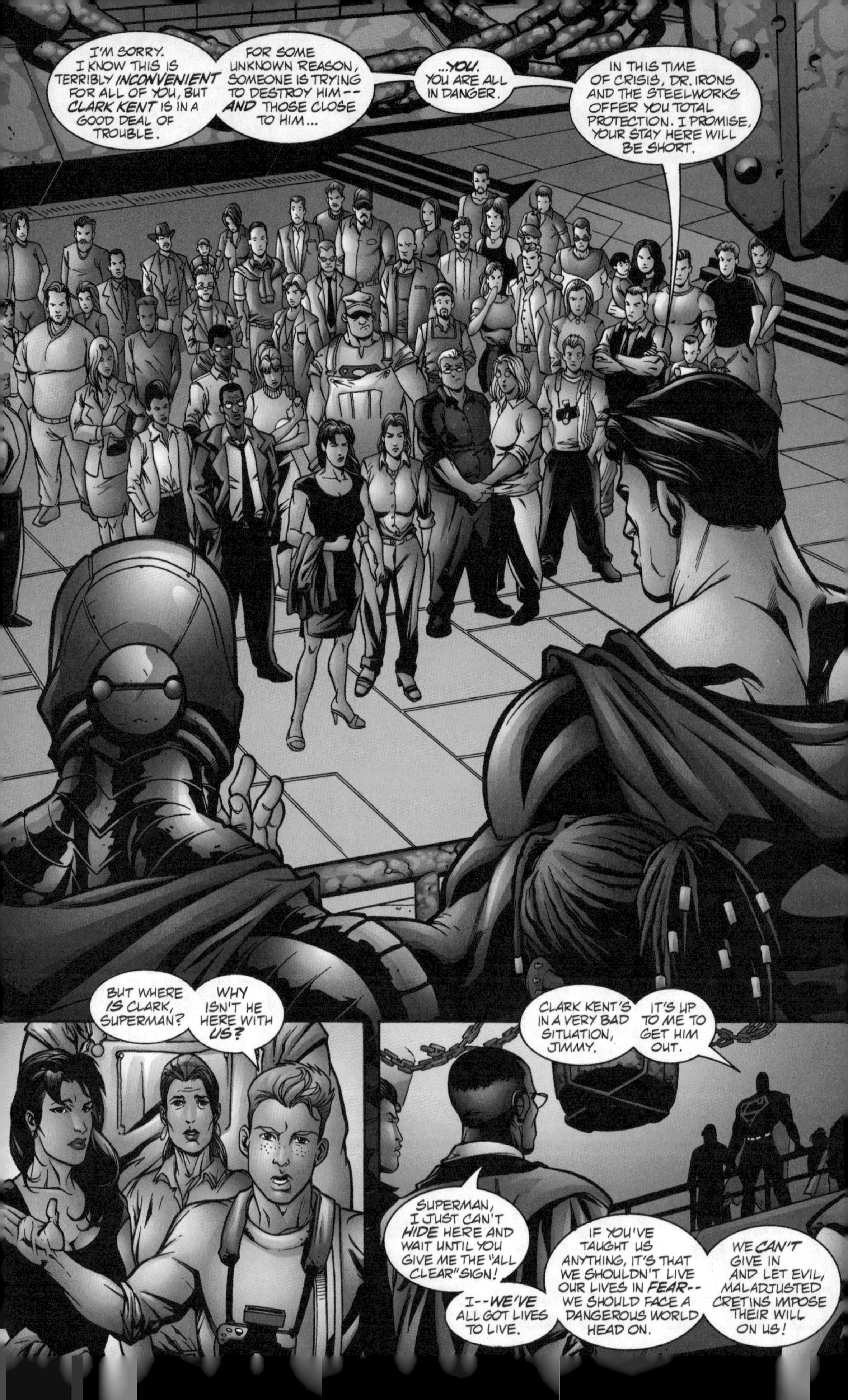
I'M SORRY. I KNOW THIS IS TERRIBLY INCONVENIENT FOR ALL OF YOU, BUT CLARK KENT IS IN A GOOD DEAL OF TROUBLE.
FOR SOME UNKNOWN REASON, SOMEONE IS TRYING TO DESTROY HIM--AND THOSE CLOSE TO HIM...
...YOU. YOU ARE ALL IN DANGER.
IN THIS TIME OF CRISIS, DR. IRONS AND THE STEELWORKS OFFER YOU TOTAL PROTECTION. I PROMISE, YOUR STAY HERE WILL BE SHORT.
BUT WHERE IS CLARK, SUPERMAN?
WHY ISN'T HE HERE WITH US?
CLARK KENT'S IN A VERY BAD SITUATION, JIMMY.
IT'S UP TO ME TO GET HIM OUT.
SUPERMAN, I JUST CAN'T HIDE HERE AND WAIT UNTIL YOU GIVE ME THE "ALL CLEAR" SIGN!
I--WE'VE ALL GOT LIVES TO LIVE.
IF YOU'VE TAUGHT US ANYTHING, IT'S THAT WE SHOULDN'T LIVE OUR LIVES IN FEAR--WE SHOULD FACE A DANGEROUS WORLD HEAD ON.
WE CAN'T GIVE IN AND LET EVIL, MALADJUSTED CRETINS IMPOSE THEIR WILL ON US!

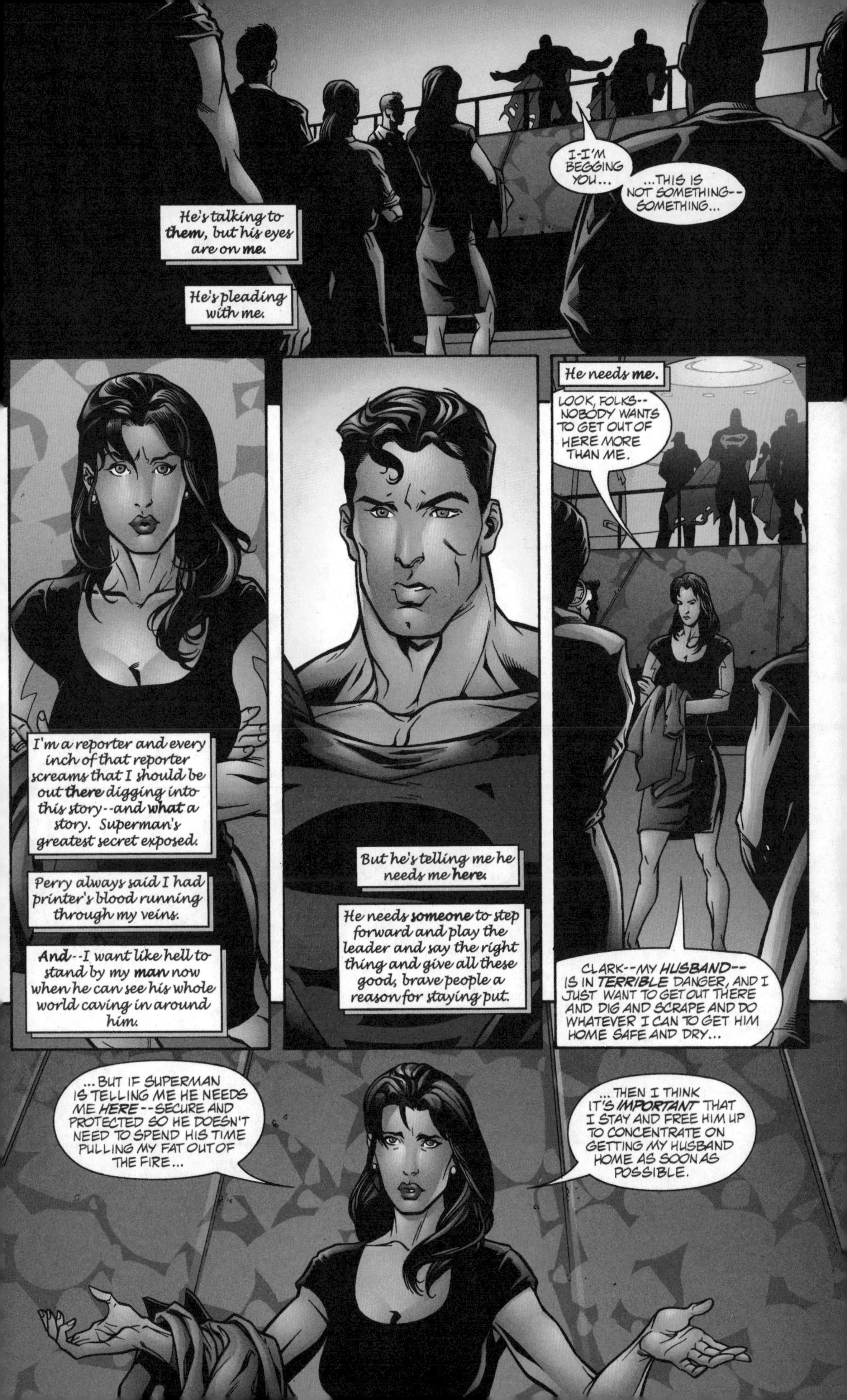
I-I'M BEGGING YOU...
...THIS IS NOT SOMETHING-- SOMETHING...
He's talking to them, but his eyes are on me.
He's pleading with me.
I'm a reporter and every inch of that reporter screams that I should be out there digging into this story--and what a story. Superman's greatest secret exposed.
Perry always said I had printer's blood running through my veins.
And--I want like hell to stand by my man now when he can see his whole world caving in around him.
But he's telling me he needs me here.
He needs someone to step forward and play the leader and say the right thing and give all these good, brave people a reason for staying put.
He needs me.
LOOK, FOLKS-- NOBODY WANTS TO GET OUT OF HERE MORE THAN ME.
CLARK--MY HUSBAND-- IS IN TERRIBLE DANGER, AND I JUST WANT TO GET OUT THERE AND DIG AND SCRAPE AND DO WHATEVER I CAN TO GET HIM HOME SAFE AND DRY...
...BUT IF SUPERMAN IS TELLING ME HE NEEDS ME HERE--SECURE AND PROTECTED SO HE DOESN'T NEED TO SPEND HIS TIME PULLING MY FAT OUT OF THE FIRE...
...THEN I THINK IT'S IMPORTANT THAT I STAY AND FREE HIM UP TO CONCENTRATE ON GETTING MY HUSBAND HOME AS SOON AS POSSIBLE.

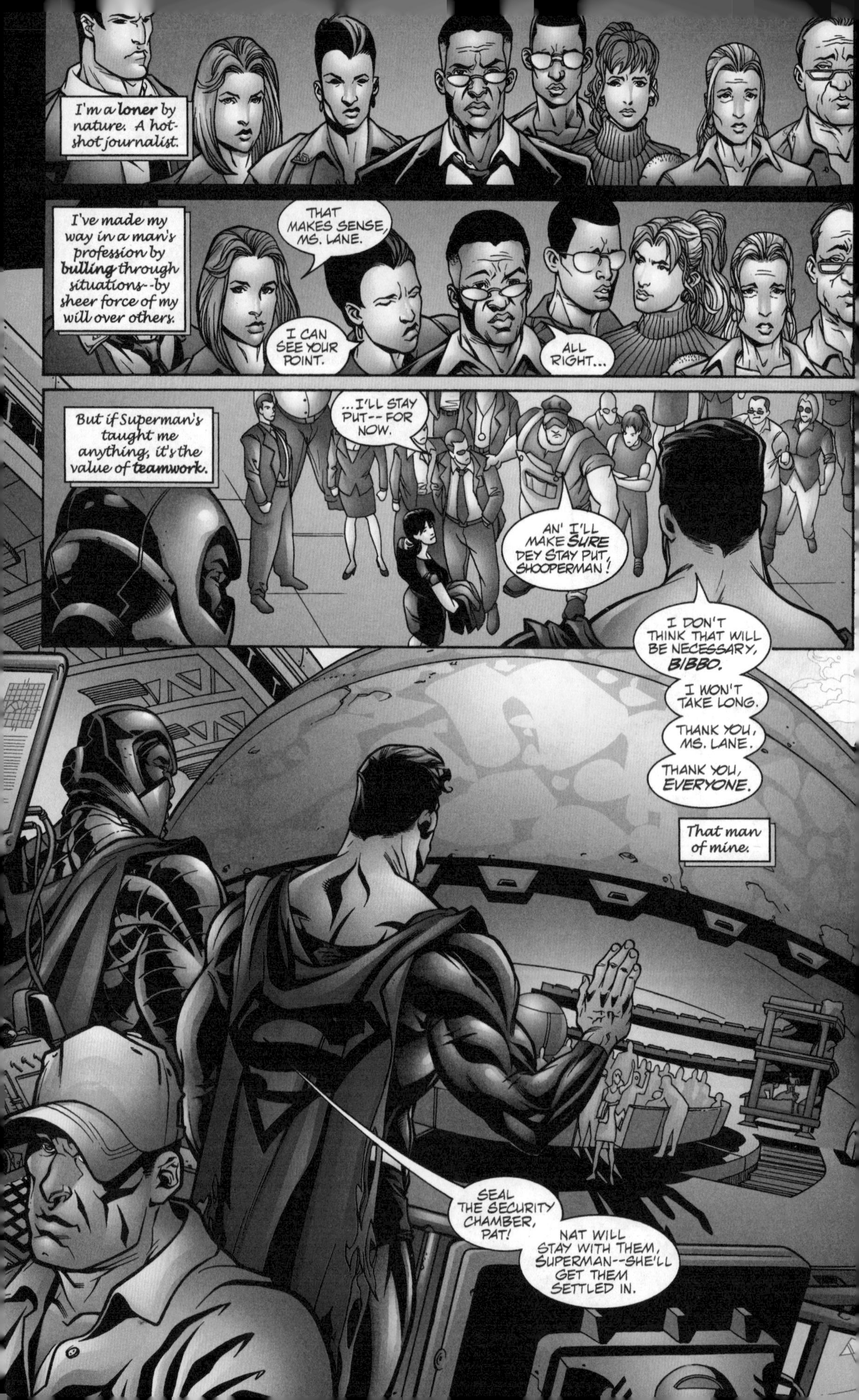
I'm a loner by nature. A hot-shot journalist.
I've made my way in a man's profession by bulling through situations--by sheer force of my will over others.
THAT MAKES SENSE, MS. LANE.
I CAN SEE YOUR POINT.
ALL RIGHT...
But if Superman's taught me anything, it's the value of teamwork.
...I'LL STAY PUT-- FOR NOW.
AN' I'LL MAKE SURE DEY STAY PUT, SHOOPERMAN!
I DON'T THINK THAT WILL BE NECESSARY, BIBBO.
I WON'T TAKE LONG.
THANK YOU, MS. LANE.
THANK YOU, EVERYONE.
That man of mine.
SEAL THE SECURITY CHAMBER, PAT!
NAT WILL STAY WITH THEM, SUPERMAN--SHE'LL GET THEM SETTLED IN.

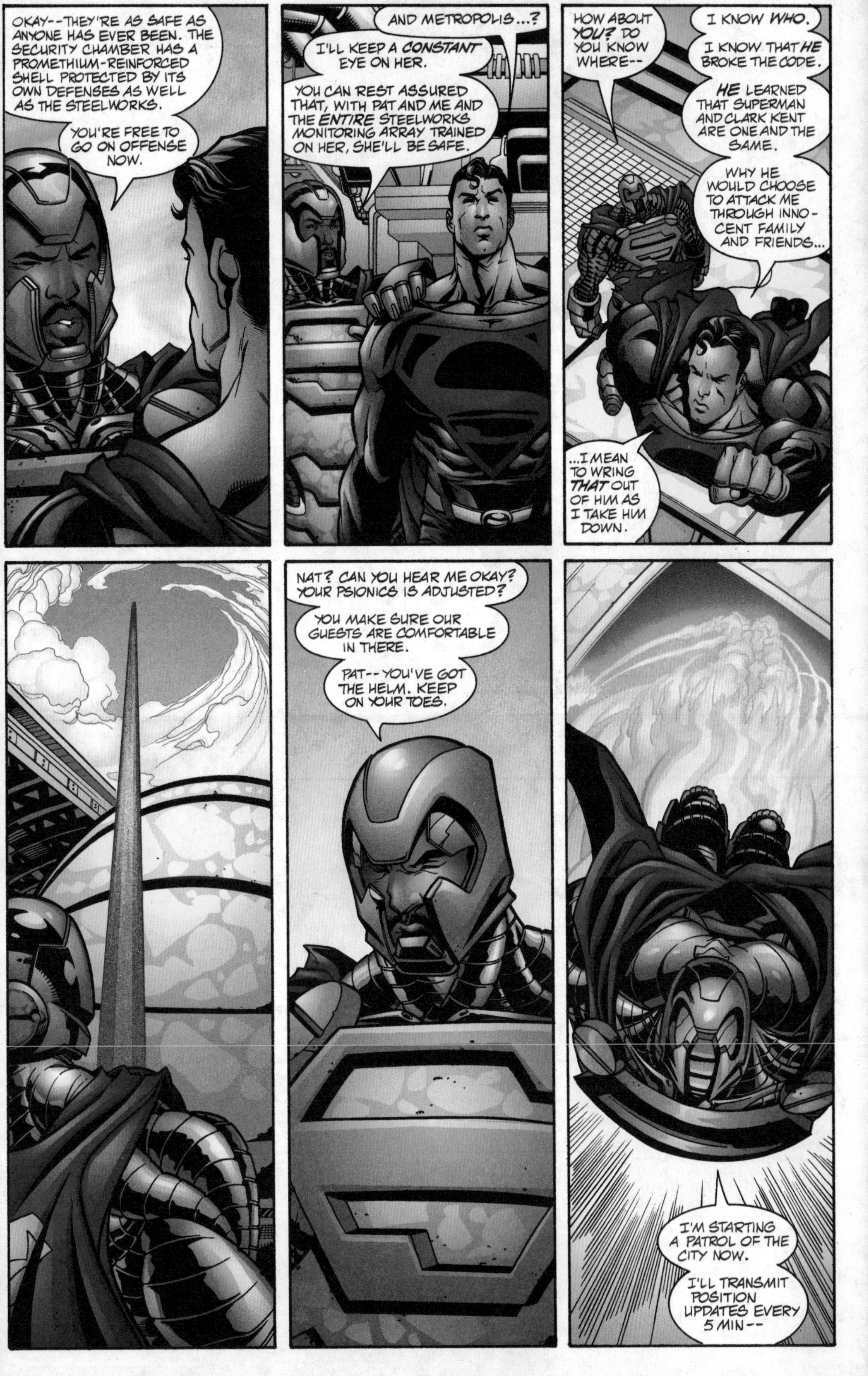
OKAY--THEY'RE AS SAFE AS ANYONE HAS EVER BEEN. THE SECURITY CHAMBER HAS A PROMETHIUM-REINFORCED SHELL PROTECTED BY ITS OWN DEFENSES AS WELL AS THE STEELWORKS.
YOU'RE FREE TO GO ON OFFENSE NOW.
AND METROPOLIS ...?
I'LL KEEP A CONSTANT EYE ON HER.
YOU CAN REST ASSURED THAT, WITH PAT AND ME AND THE ENTIRE STEELWORKS MONITORING ARRAY TRAINED ON HER, SHE'LL BE SAFE.
HOW ABOUT YOU? DO YOU KNOW WHERE--
I KNOW WHO.
I KNOW THAT HE BROKE THE CODE.
HE LEARNED THAT SUPERMAN AND CLARK KENT ARE ONE AND THE SAME.
WHY HE WOULD CHOOSE TO ATTACK ME THROUGH INNO-CENT FAMILY AND FRIENDS...
...I MEAN TO WRING THAT OUT OF HIM AS I TAKE HIM DOWN.
NAT? CAN YOU HEAR ME OKAY? YOUR PSIONICS IS ADJUSTED?
YOU MAKE SURE OUR GUESTS ARE COMFORTABLE IN THERE.
PAT--YOU'VE GOT THE HELM. KEEP ON YOUR TOES.
I'M STARTING A PATROL OF THE CITY NOW.
I'LL TRANSMIT POSITION UPDATES EVERY 5 MIN--

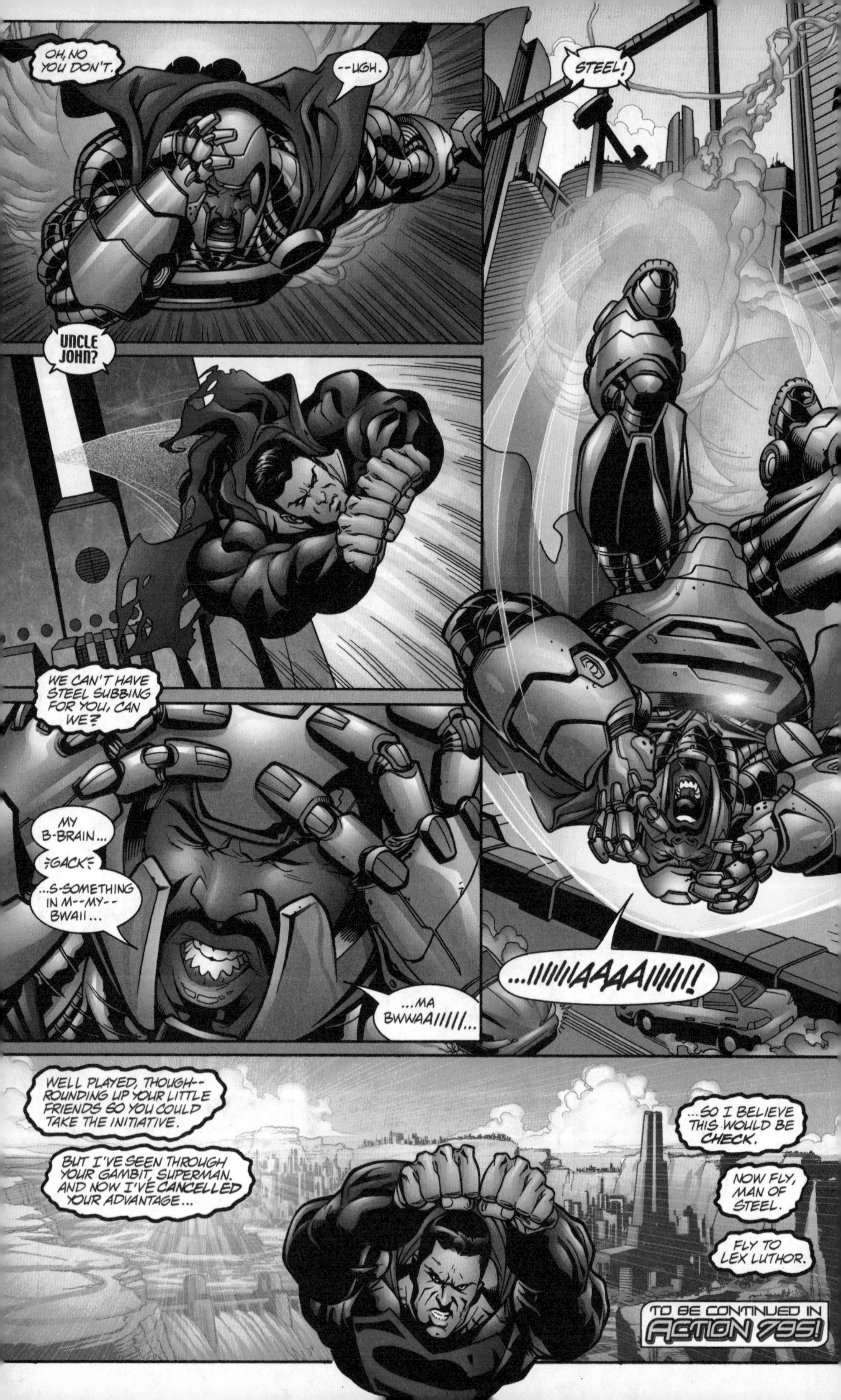

OH, NO YOU DON'T.
--UGH.
STEEL!
UNCLE JOHN?
WE CAN'T HAVE STEEL SUBBING FOR YOU, CAN WE?
MY B-BRAIN...
GACK
...S-SOMETHING IN M--MY--BWAII...
...MA BWWAAIIIII...
...IIIIIIAAAAIIIIII!
WELL PLAYED, THOUGH--ROUNDING UP YOUR LITTLE FRIENDS SO YOU COULD TAKE THE INITIATIVE.
BUT I'VE SEEN THROUGH YOUR GAMBIT, SUPERMAN. AND NOW I'VE CANCELLED YOUR ADVANTAGE...
...SO I BELIEVE THIS WOULD BE CHECK.
NOW FLY, MAN OF STEEL.
FLY TO LEX LUTHOR.
TO BE CONTINUED IN ACTION 795!

Cover art by KEVIN NOWLAN

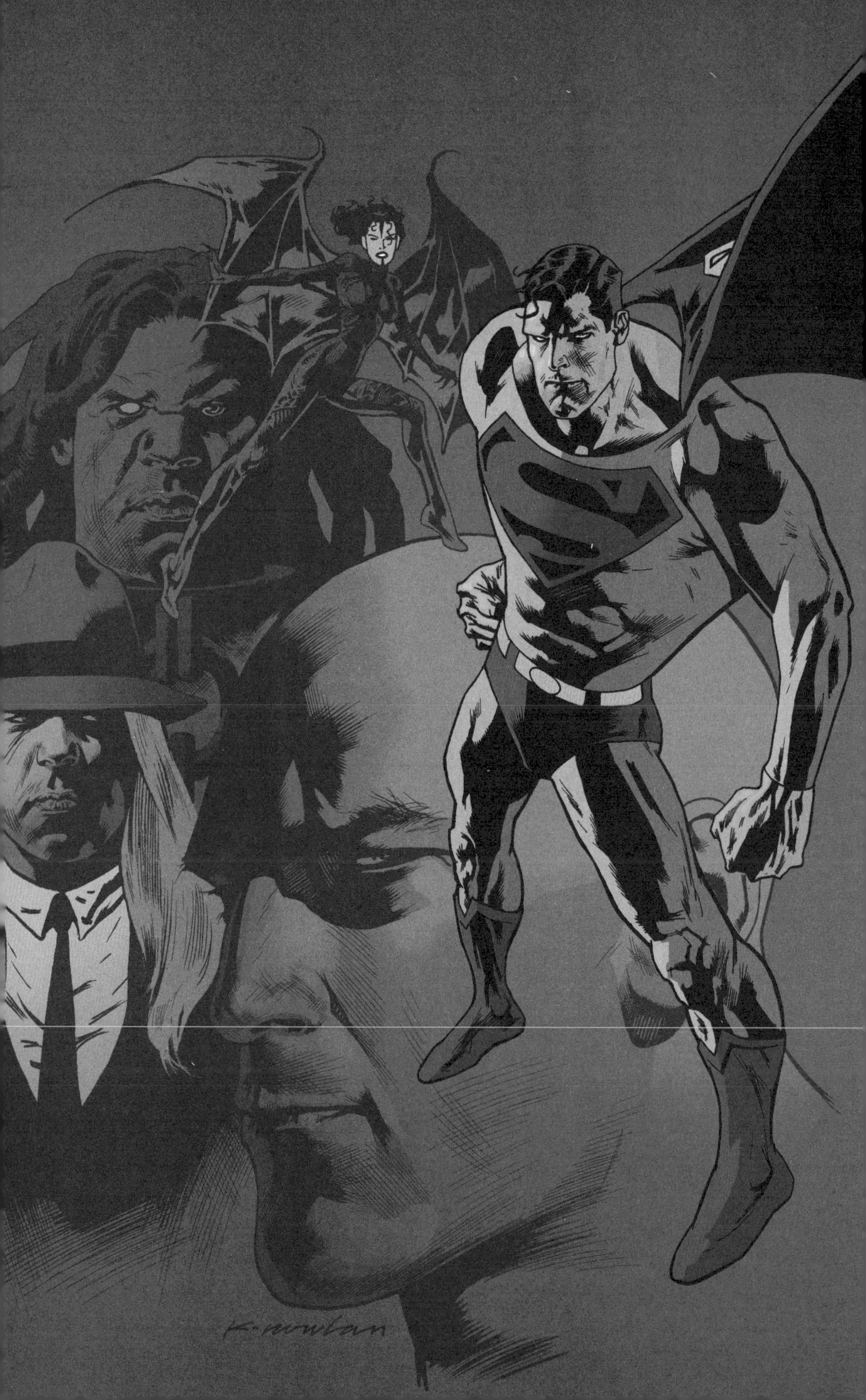

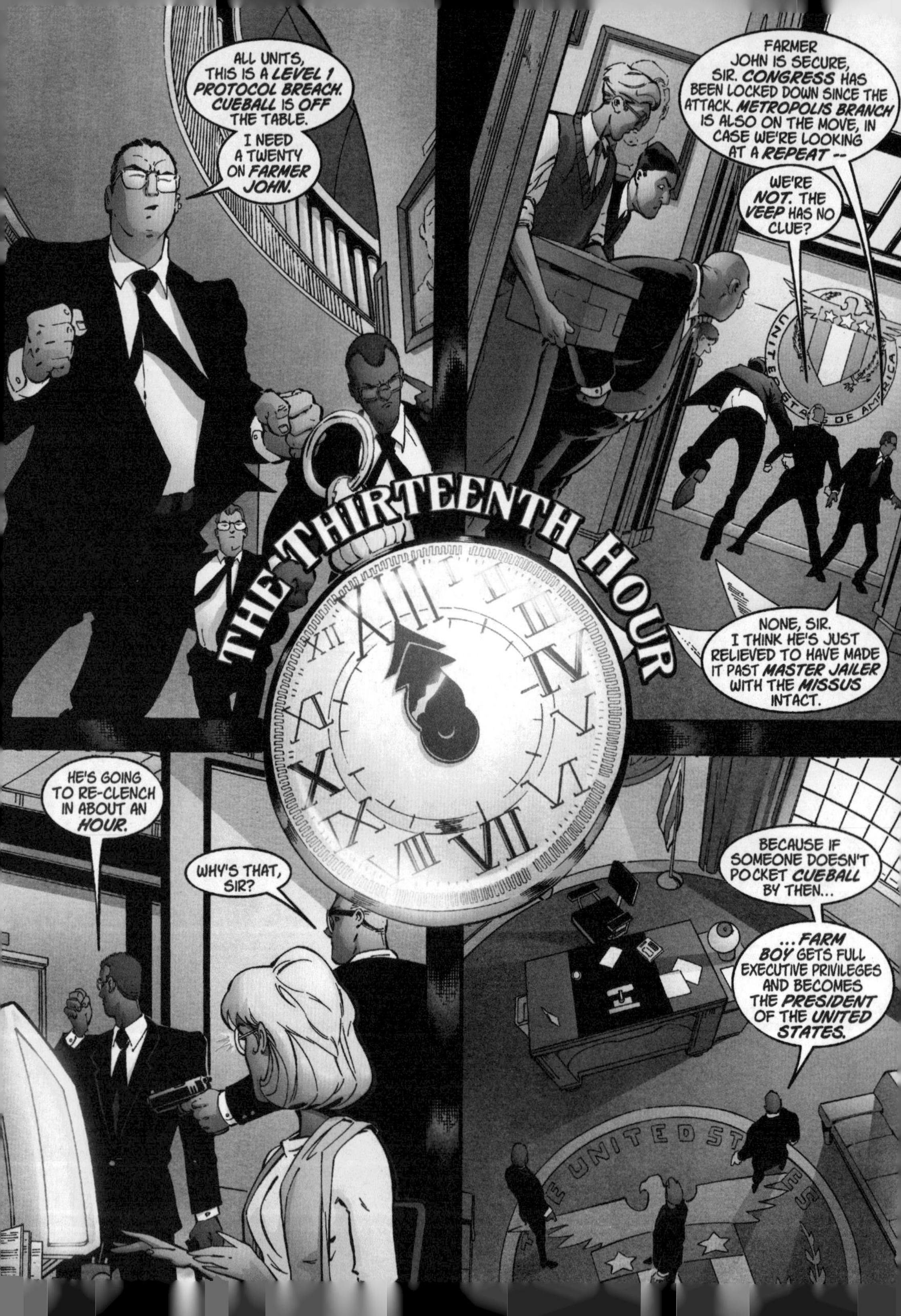

ALL UNITS, THIS IS A LEVEL 1 PROTOCOL BREACH. CUEBALL IS OFF THE TABLE.
I NEED A TWENTY ON FARMER JOHN.
FARMER JOHN IS SECURE, SIR. CONGRESS HAS BEEN LOCKED DOWN SINCE THE ATTACK. METROPOLIS BRANCH IS ALSO ON THE MOVE, IN CASE WE'RE LOOKING AT A REPEAT --
WE'RE NOT. THE VEEP HAS NO CLUE?
NONE, SIR. I THINK HE'S JUST RELIEVED TO HAVE MADE IT PAST MASTER JAILER WITH THE MISSUS INTACT.
THE THIRTEENTH HOUR
HE'S GOING TO RE-CLENCH IN ABOUT AN HOUR.
WHY'S THAT, SIR?
BECAUSE IF SOMEONE DOESN'T POCKET CUEBALL BY THEN...
...FARM BOY GETS FULL EXECUTIVE PRIVILEGES AND BECOMES THE PRESIDENT OF THE UNITED STATES.

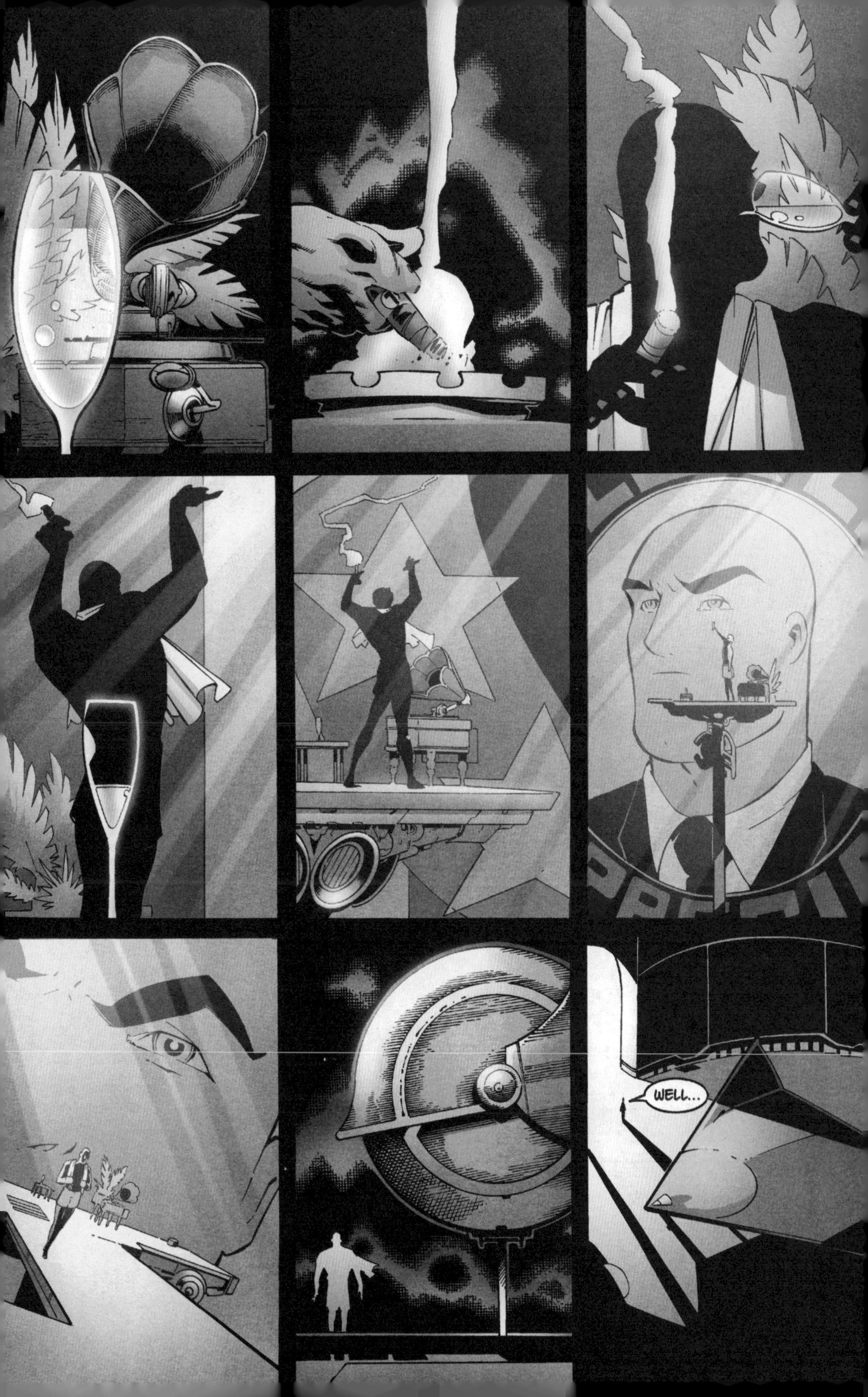
WELL...

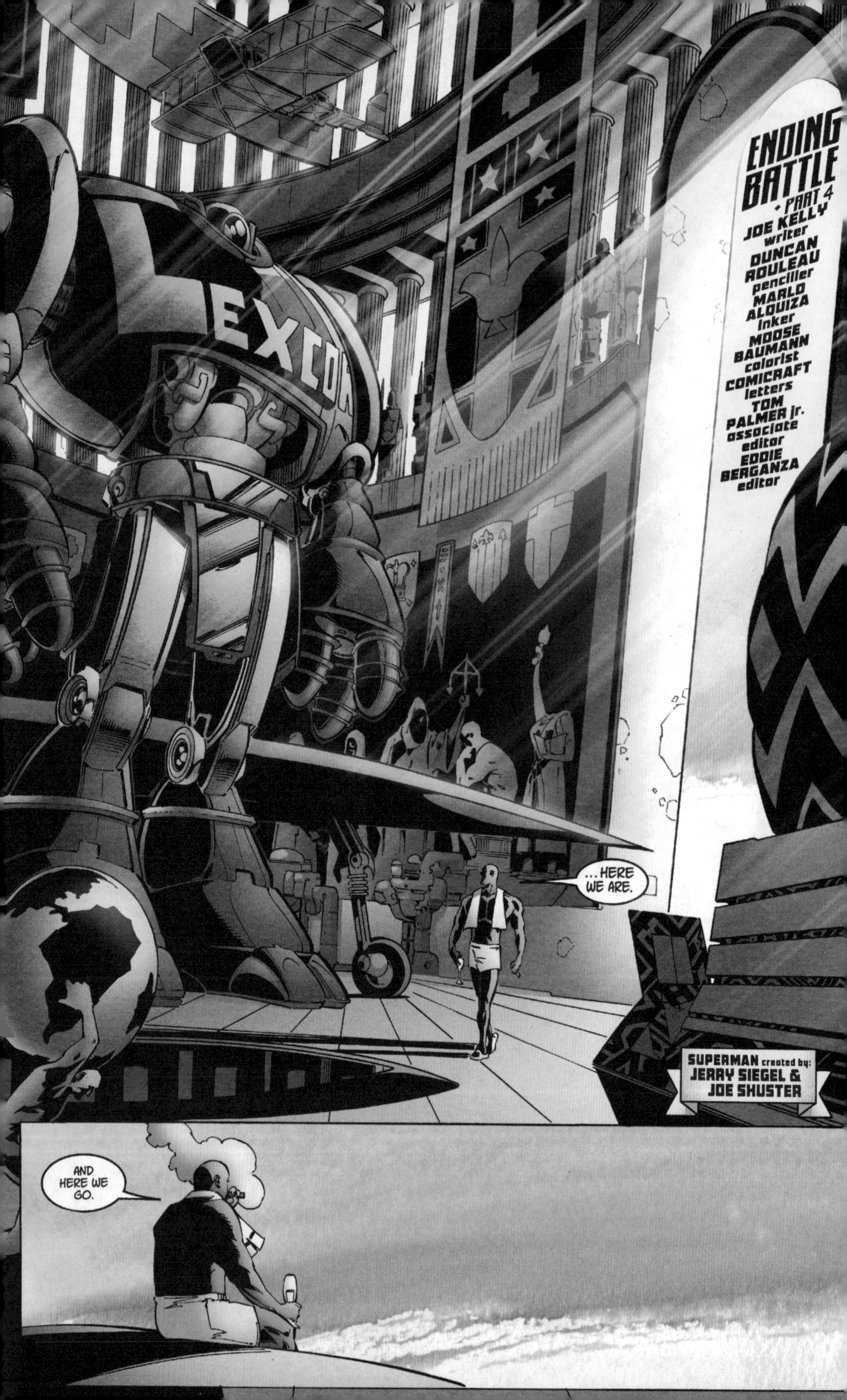
ENDING BATTLE
PART 4
JOE KELLY writer
DUNCAN ROULEAU penciller
MARLO ALQUIZA inker
MOOSE BAUMANN colorist
COMICRAFT letters
TOM PALMER jr. associate editor
EDDIE BERGANZA editor
EXCO
...HERE WE ARE.
SUPERMAN created by: JERRY SIEGEL & JOE SHUSTER
AND HERE WE GO.

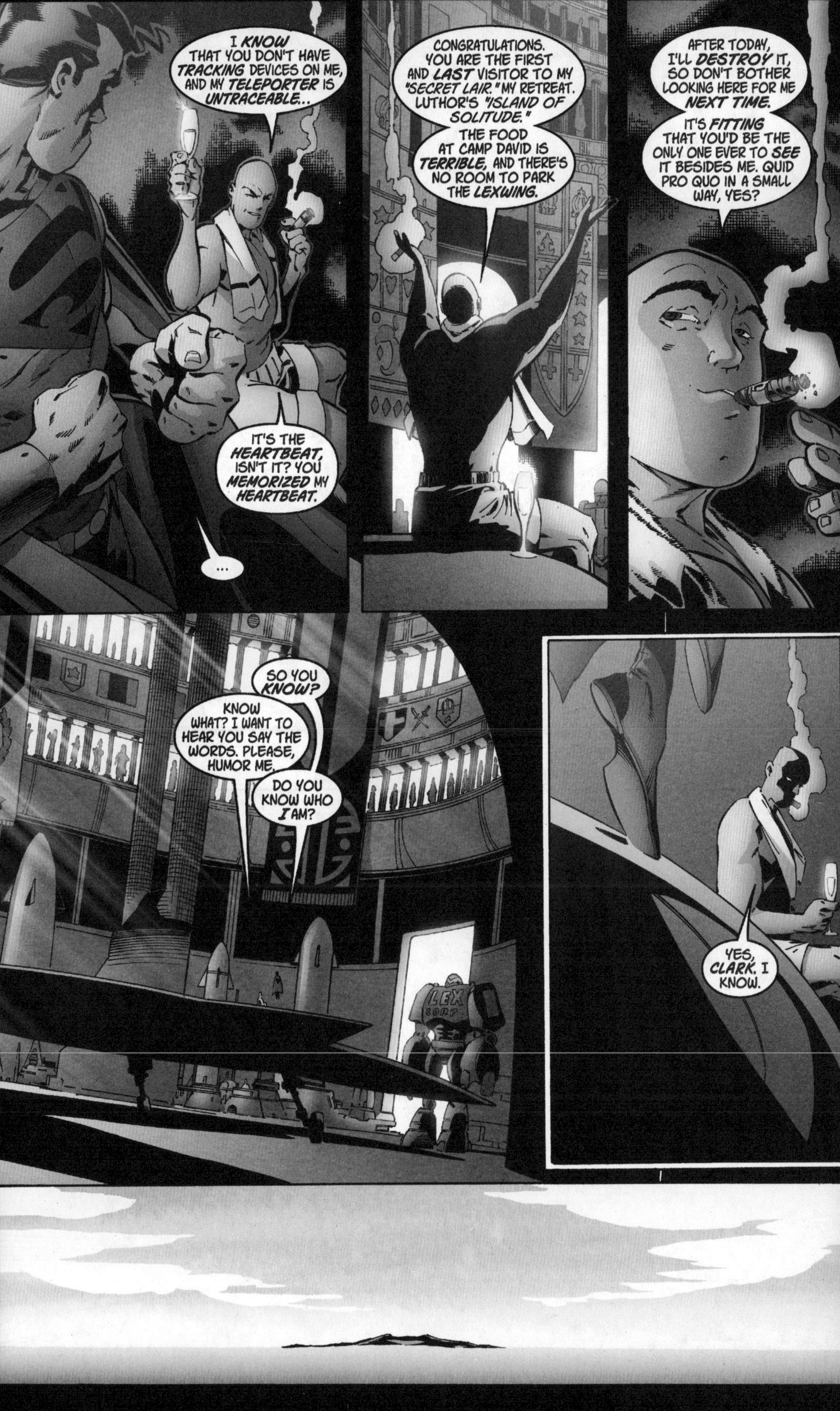
I KNOW THAT YOU DON'T HAVE TRACKING DEVICES ON ME, AND MY TELEPORTER IS UNTRACEABLE...
IT'S THE HEARTBEAT, ISN'T IT? YOU MEMORIZED MY HEARTBEAT.
...
CONGRATULATIONS. YOU ARE THE FIRST AND LAST VISITOR TO MY "SECRET LAIR." MY RETREAT. LUTHOR'S "ISLAND OF SOLITUDE."
THE FOOD AT CAMP DAVID IS TERRIBLE, AND THERE'S NO ROOM TO PARK THE LEXWING.
AFTER TODAY, I'LL DESTROY IT, SO DON'T BOTHER LOOKING HERE FOR ME NEXT TIME.
IT'S FITTING THAT YOU'D BE THE ONLY ONE EVER TO SEE IT BESIDES ME. QUID PRO QUO IN A SMALL WAY, YES?
SO YOU KNOW?
KNOW WHAT? I WANT TO HEAR YOU SAY THE WORDS. PLEASE, HUMOR ME.
DO YOU KNOW WHO I AM?
LEX CORP
YES, CLARK. I KNOW.

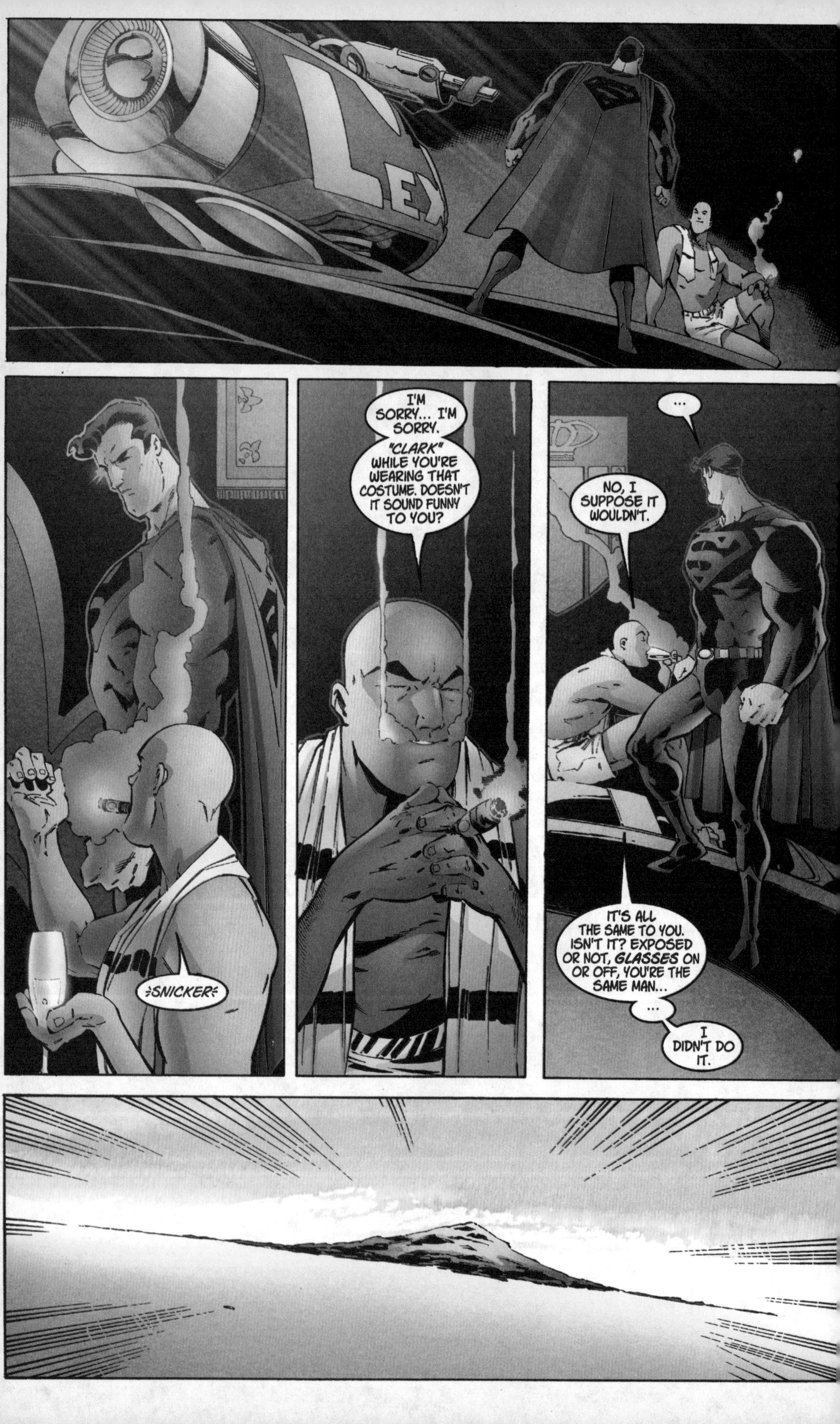
SNICKER
I'M SORRY... I'M SORRY. "CLARK" WHILE YOU'RE WEARING THAT COSTUME. DOESN'T IT SOUND FUNNY TO YOU?
...
NO, I SUPPOSE IT WOULDN'T.
IT'S ALL THE SAME TO YOU. ISN'T IT? EXPOSED OR NOT, GLASSES ON OR OFF, YOU'RE THE SAME MAN...
...
I DIDN'T DO IT.
LEX

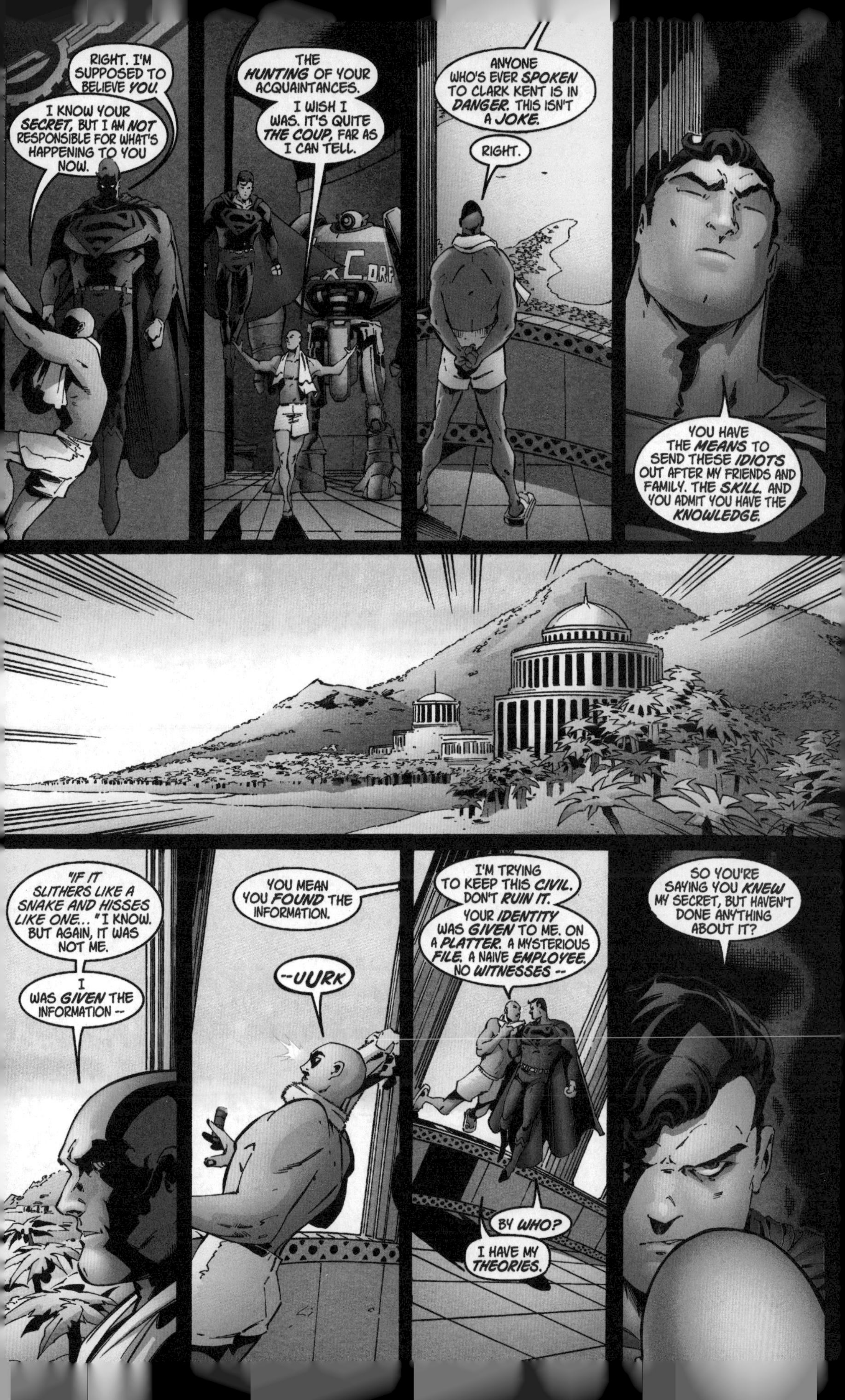
RIGHT. I'M SUPPOSED TO BELIEVE YOU.
I KNOW YOUR SECRET, BUT I AM NOT RESPONSIBLE FOR WHAT'S HAPPENING TO YOU NOW.
THE HUNTING OF YOUR ACQUAINTANCES.
I WISH I WAS. IT'S QUITE THE COUP, FAR AS I CAN TELL.
ANYONE WHO'S EVER SPOKEN TO CLARK KENT IS IN DANGER. THIS ISN'T A JOKE.
RIGHT.
YOU HAVE THE MEANS TO SEND THESE IDIOTS OUT AFTER MY FRIENDS AND FAMILY. THE SKILL. AND YOU ADMIT YOU HAVE THE KNOWLEDGE.
"IF IT SLITHERS LIKE A SNAKE AND HISSES LIKE ONE..." I KNOW. BUT AGAIN, IT WAS NOT ME.
I WAS GIVEN THE INFORMATION --
YOU MEAN YOU FOUND THE INFORMATION.
--UURK
I'M TRYING TO KEEP THIS CIVIL. DON'T RUIN IT.
YOUR IDENTITY WAS GIVEN TO ME. ON A PLATTER. A MYSTERIOUS FILE. A NAIVE EMPLOYEE. NO WITNESSES --
BY WHO?
I HAVE MY THEORIES.
SO YOU'RE SAYING YOU KNEW MY SECRET, BUT HAVEN'T DONE ANYTHING ABOUT IT?

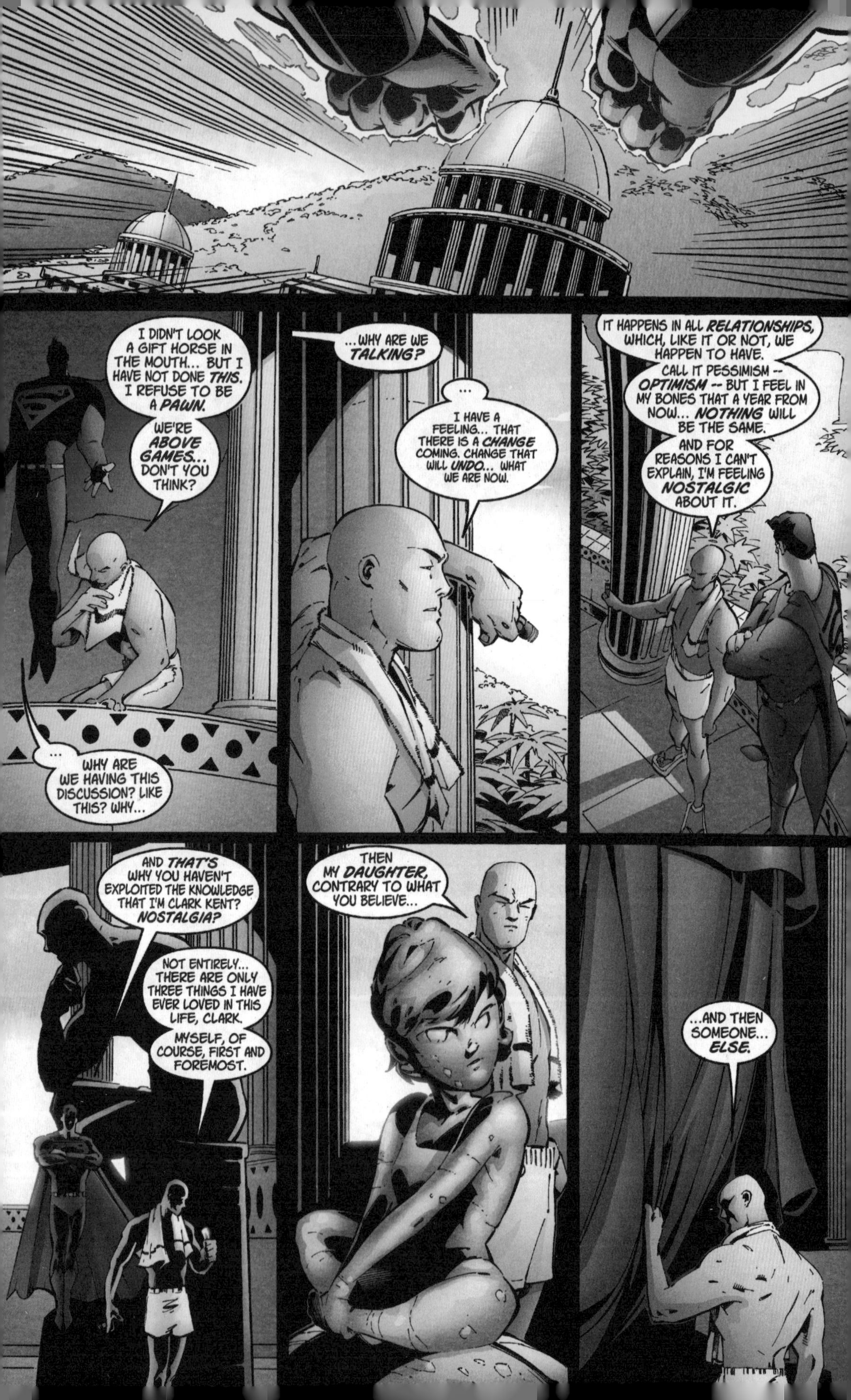
I DIDN'T LOOK A GIFT HORSE IN THE MOUTH... BUT I HAVE NOT DONE THIS. I REFUSE TO BE A PAWN.
WE'RE ABOVE GAMES... DON'T YOU THINK?
... WHY ARE WE HAVING THIS DISCUSSION? LIKE THIS? WHY...
...WHY ARE WE TALKING?
...
I HAVE A FEELING... THAT THERE IS A CHANGE COMING. CHANGE THAT WILL UNDO... WHAT WE ARE NOW.
IT HAPPENS IN ALL RELATIONSHIPS, WHICH, LIKE IT OR NOT, WE HAPPEN TO HAVE.
CALL IT PESSIMISM -- OPTIMISM -- BUT I FEEL IN MY BONES THAT A YEAR FROM NOW... NOTHING WILL BE THE SAME.
AND FOR REASONS I CAN'T EXPLAIN, I'M FEELING NOSTALGIC ABOUT IT.
AND THAT'S WHY YOU HAVEN'T EXPLOITED THE KNOWLEDGE THAT I'M CLARK KENT? NOSTALGIA?
NOT ENTIRELY... THERE ARE ONLY THREE THINGS I HAVE EVER LOVED IN THIS LIFE, CLARK.
MYSELF, OF COURSE, FIRST AND FOREMOST.
THEN MY DAUGHTER, CONTRARY TO WHAT YOU BELIEVE...
...AND THEN SOMEONE... ELSE.

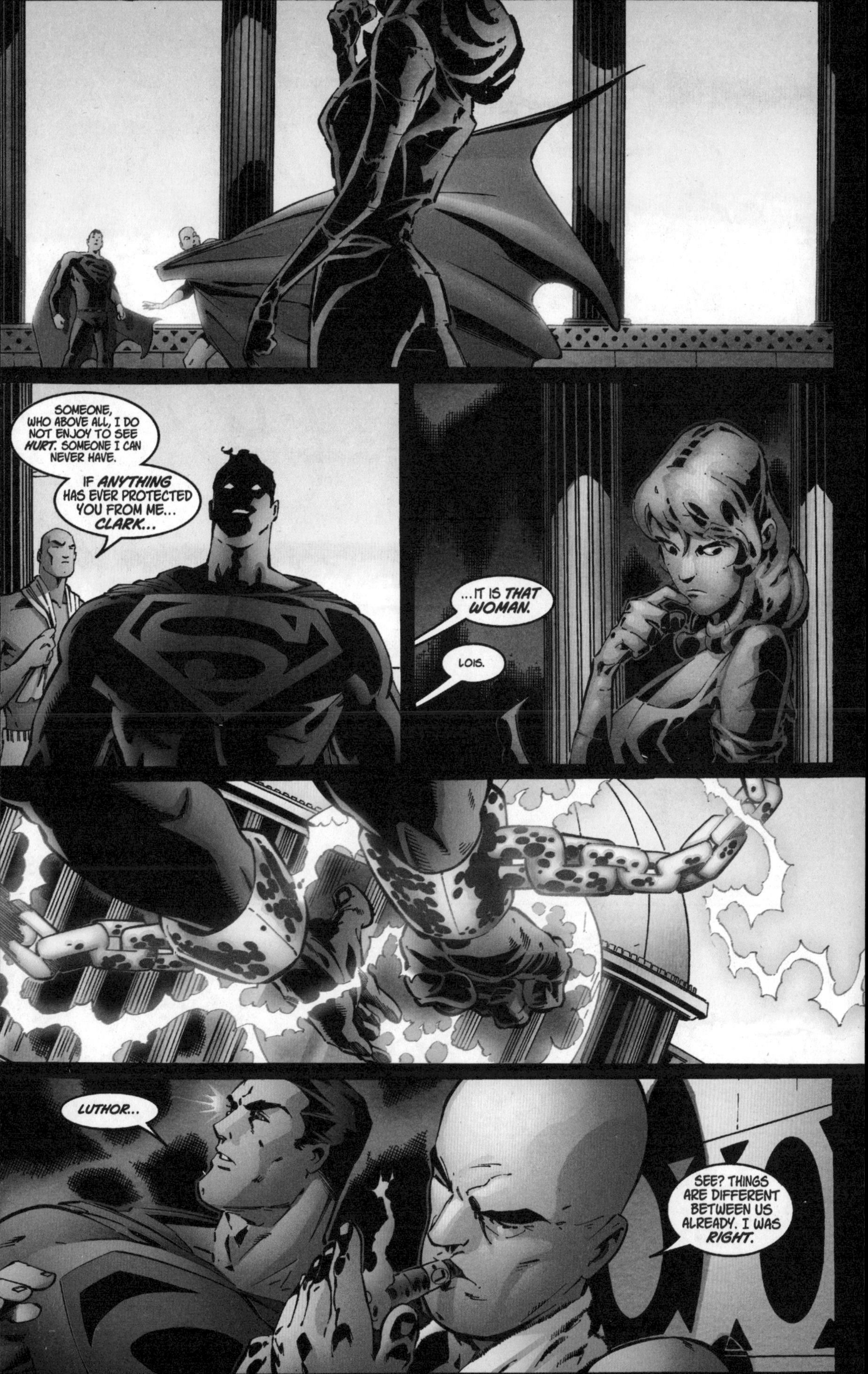
SOMEONE, WHO ABOVE ALL, I DO NOT ENJOY TO SEE HURT. SOMEONE I CAN NEVER HAVE.
IF ANYTHING HAS EVER PROTECTED YOU FROM ME... CLARK...
...IT IS THAT WOMAN.
LOIS.
LUTHOR...
SEE? THINGS ARE DIFFERENT BETWEEN US ALREADY. I WAS RIGHT.

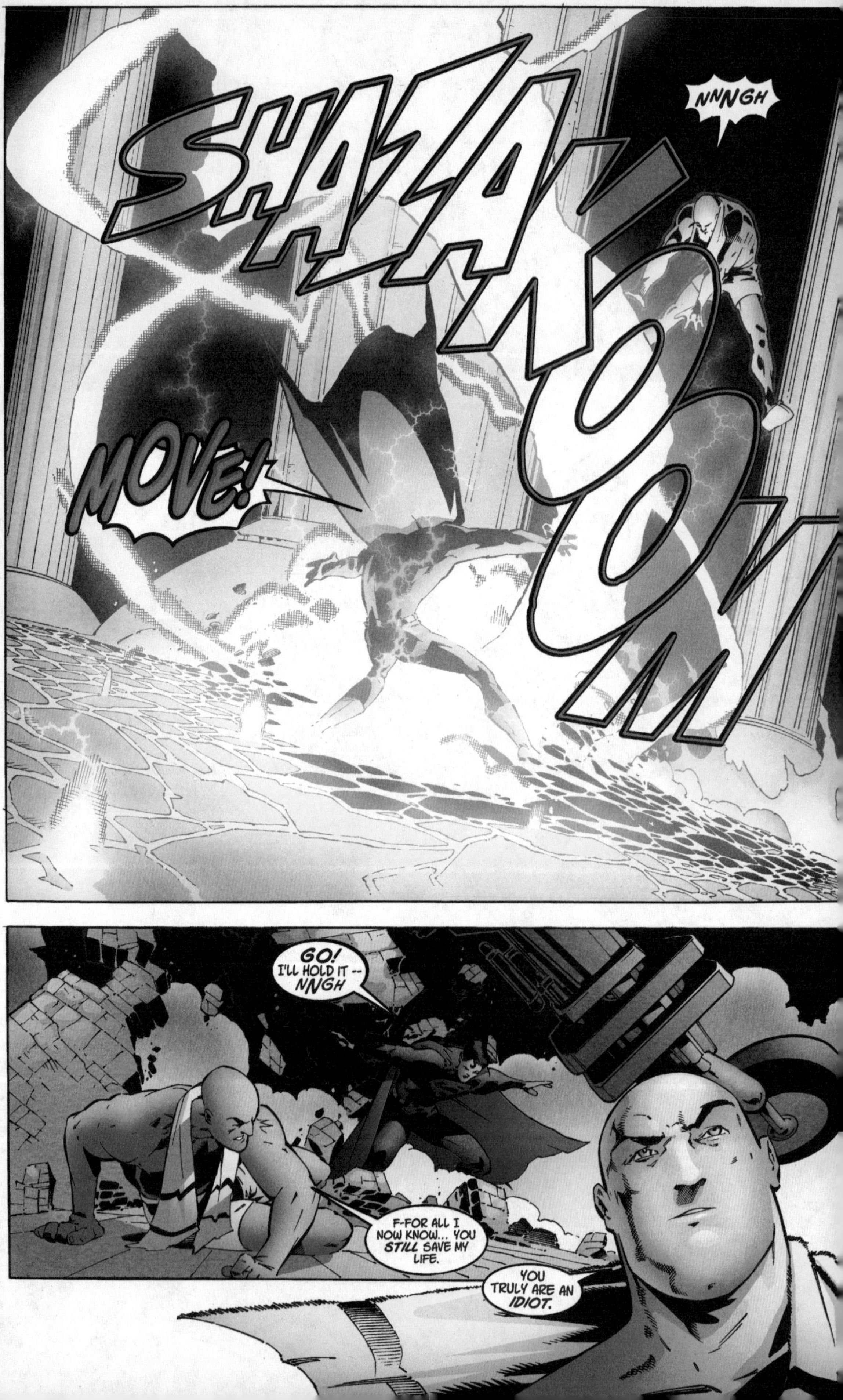
SHAZAM!
NNNGH
MOVE!
BOOOM
GO! I'LL HOLD IT -- NNGH
F-FOR ALL I NOW KNOW... YOU STILL SAVE MY LIFE.
YOU TRULY ARE AN IDIOT.

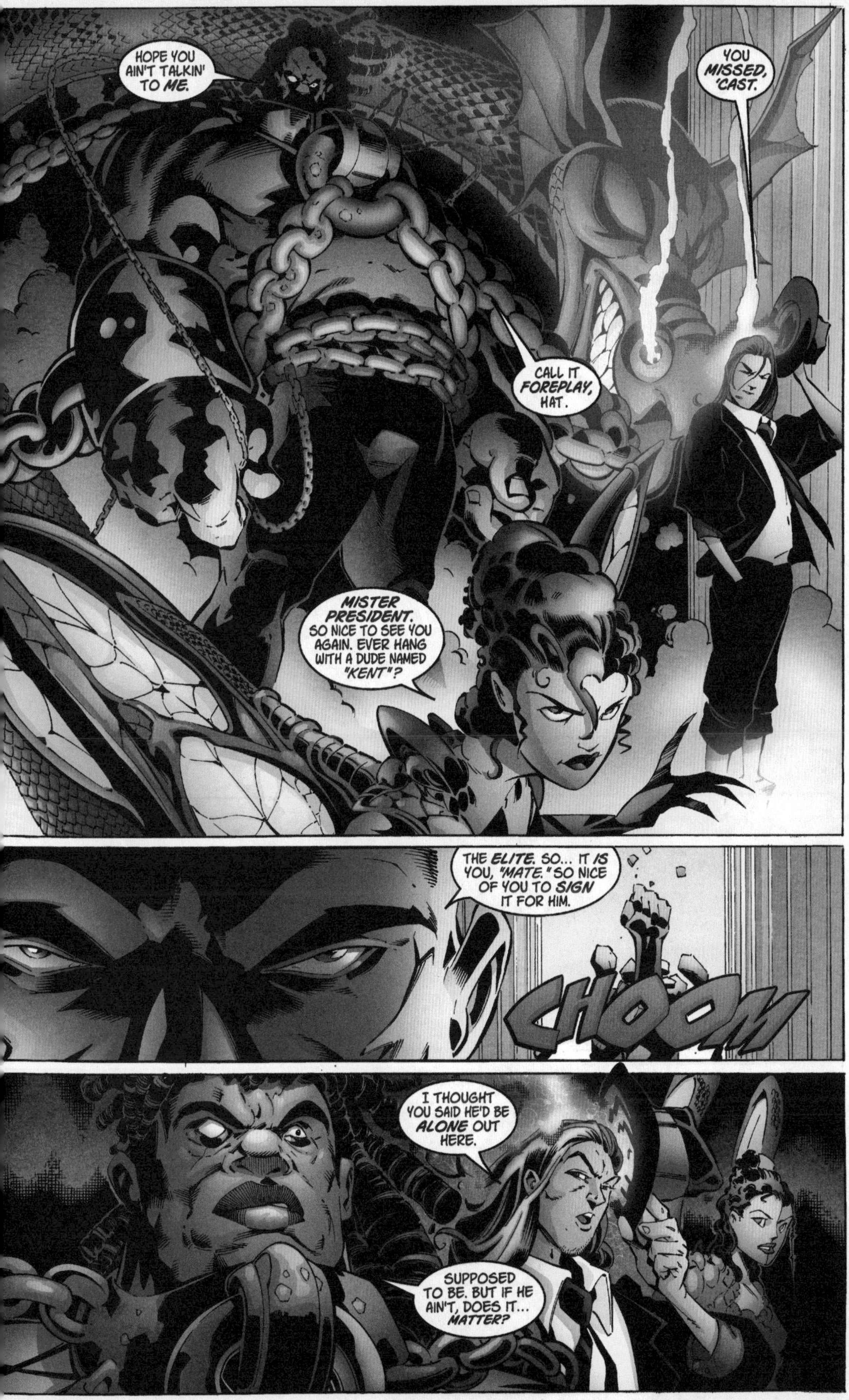
HOPE YOU AIN'T TALKIN' TO ME.
YOU MISSED, 'CAST.
CALL IT FOREPLAY, HAT.
MISTER PRESIDENT. SO NICE TO SEE YOU AGAIN. EVER HANG WITH A DUDE NAMED "KENT"?
THE ELITE. SO... IT IS YOU, "MATE." SO NICE OF YOU TO SIGN IT FOR HIM.
CHOOM
I THOUGHT YOU SAID HE'D BE ALONE OUT HERE.
SUPPOSED TO BE. BUT IF HE AIN'T, DOES IT... MATTER?

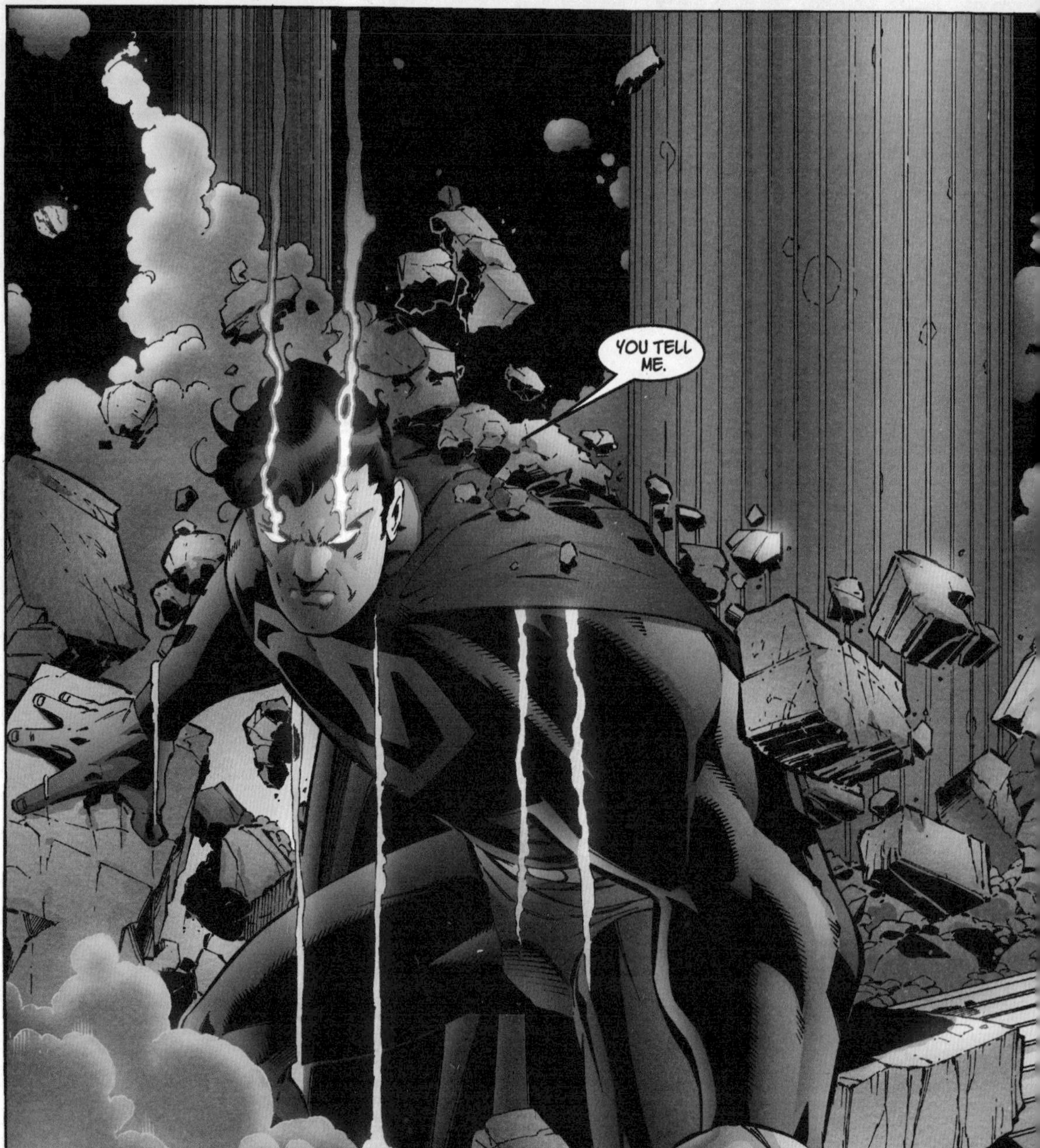
YOU TELL ME.

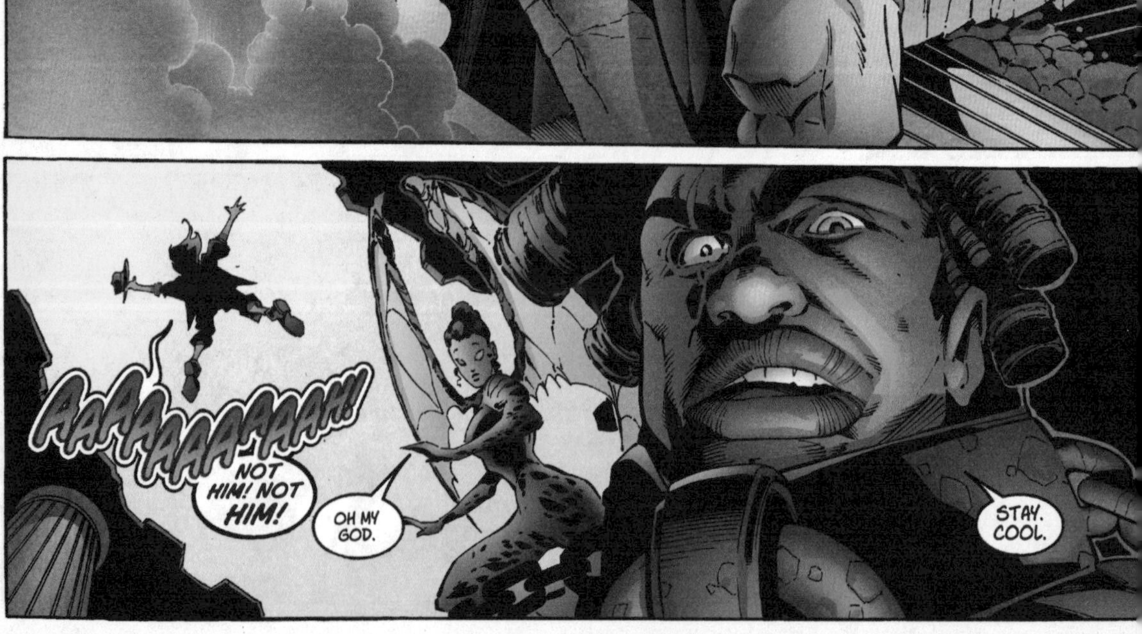
AAAAAAAAAAAH!!
NOT HIM! NOT HIM!
OH MY GOD.
STAY. COOL.

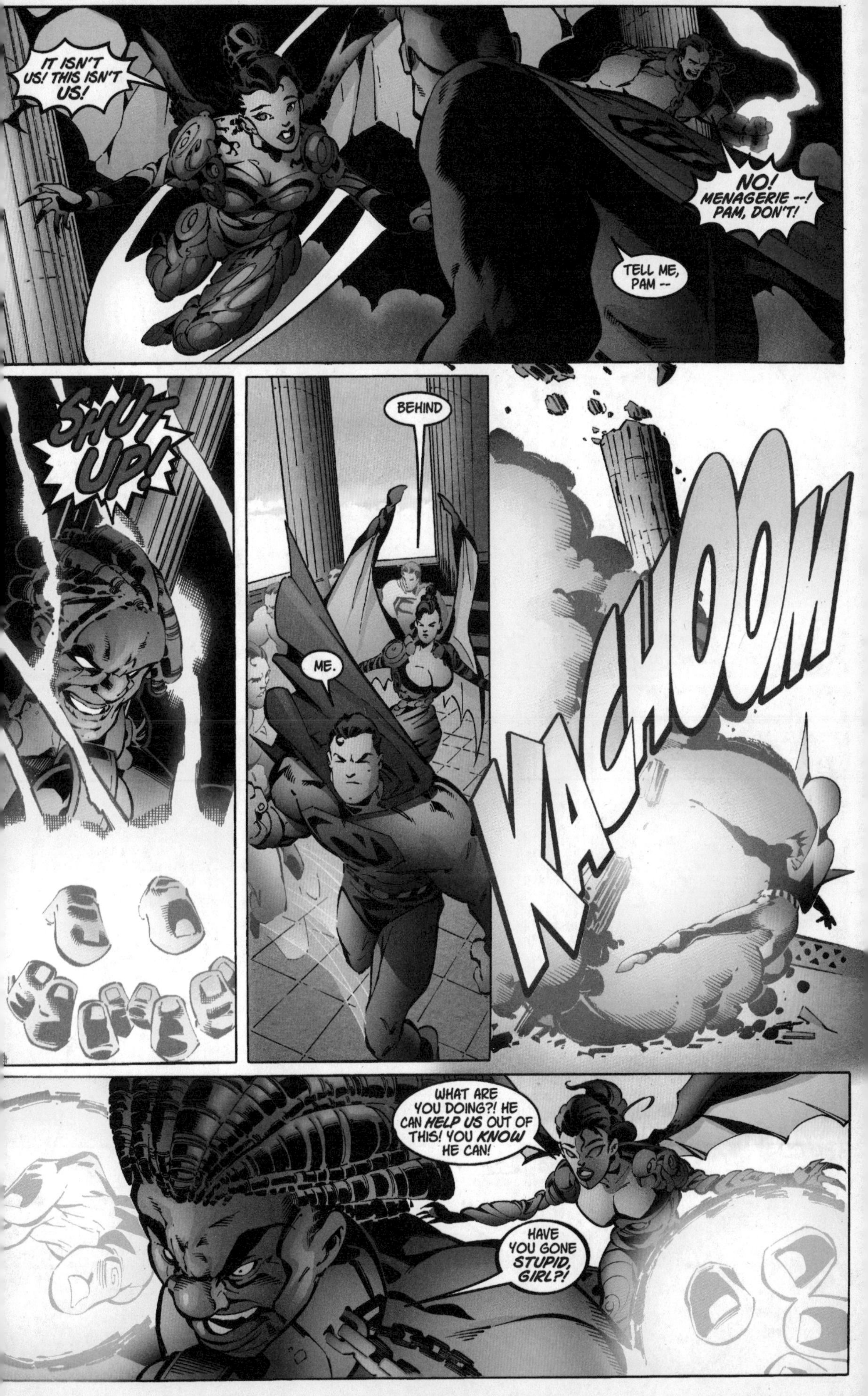
IT ISN'T US! THIS ISN'T US!
NO! MENAGERIE --! PAM, DON'T!
TELL ME, PAM --
SHUT UP!
BEHIND
ME.
KACHOOM
WHAT ARE YOU DOING?! HE CAN HELP US OUT OF THIS! YOU KNOW HE CAN!
HAVE YOU GONE STUPID, GIRL?!

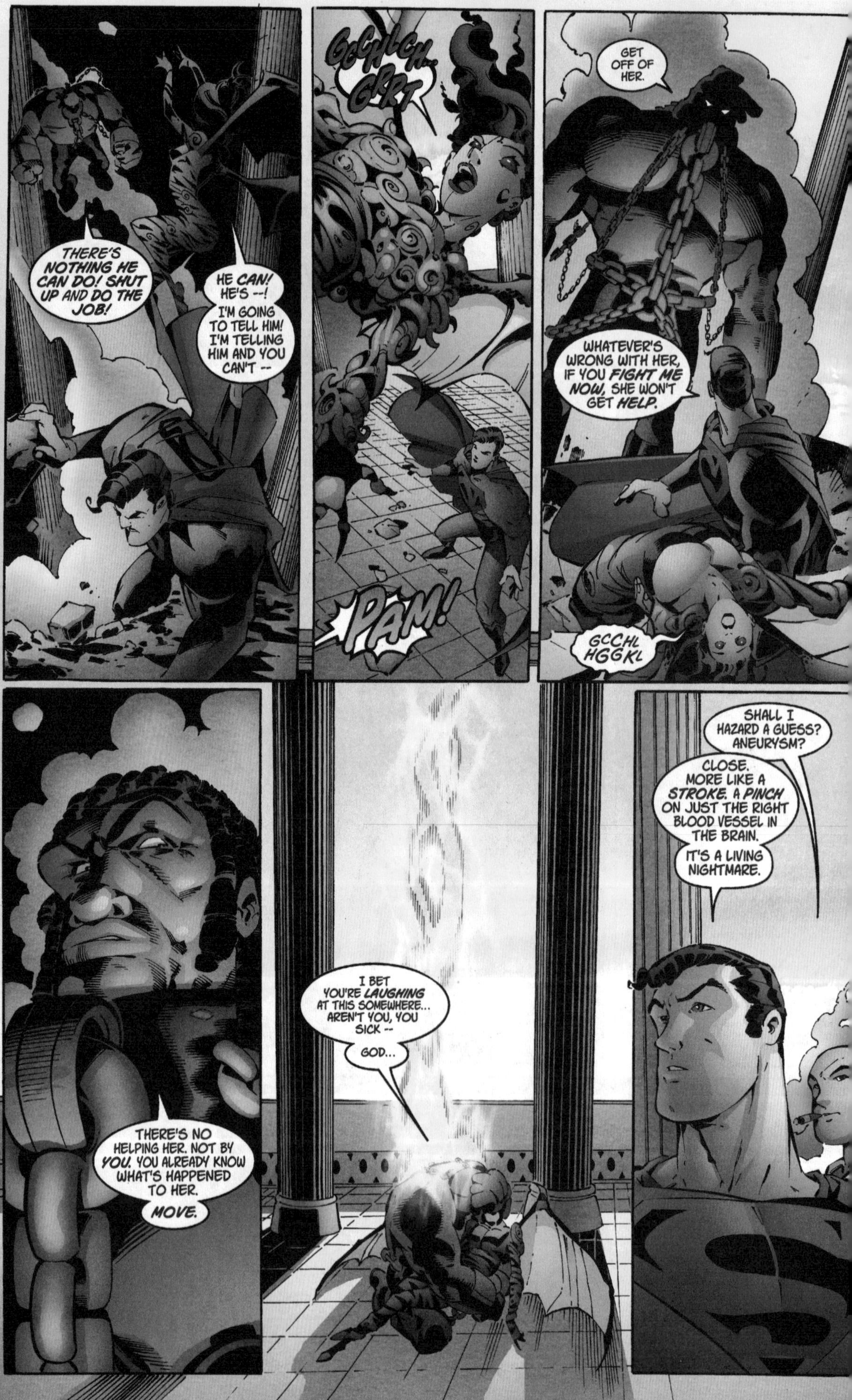

THERE'S NOTHING HE CAN DO! SHUT UP AND DO THE JOB!
HE CAN! HE'S --!
I'M GOING TO TELL HIM! I'M TELLING HIM AND YOU CAN'T --
GCGHLCH... GRRT
PAM!
GET OFF OF HER.
WHATEVER'S WRONG WITH HER, IF YOU FIGHT ME NOW, SHE WON'T GET HELP.
GCCHL HGGKL
THERE'S NO HELPING HER. NOT BY YOU. YOU ALREADY KNOW WHAT'S HAPPENED TO HER.
MOVE.
I BET YOU'RE LAUGHING AT THIS SOMEWHERE... AREN'T YOU, YOU SICK --
GOD...
SHALL I HAZARD A GUESS? ANEURYSM?
CLOSE. MORE LIKE A STROKE. A PINCH ON JUST THE RIGHT BLOOD VESSEL IN THE BRAIN.
IT'S A LIVING NIGHTMARE.

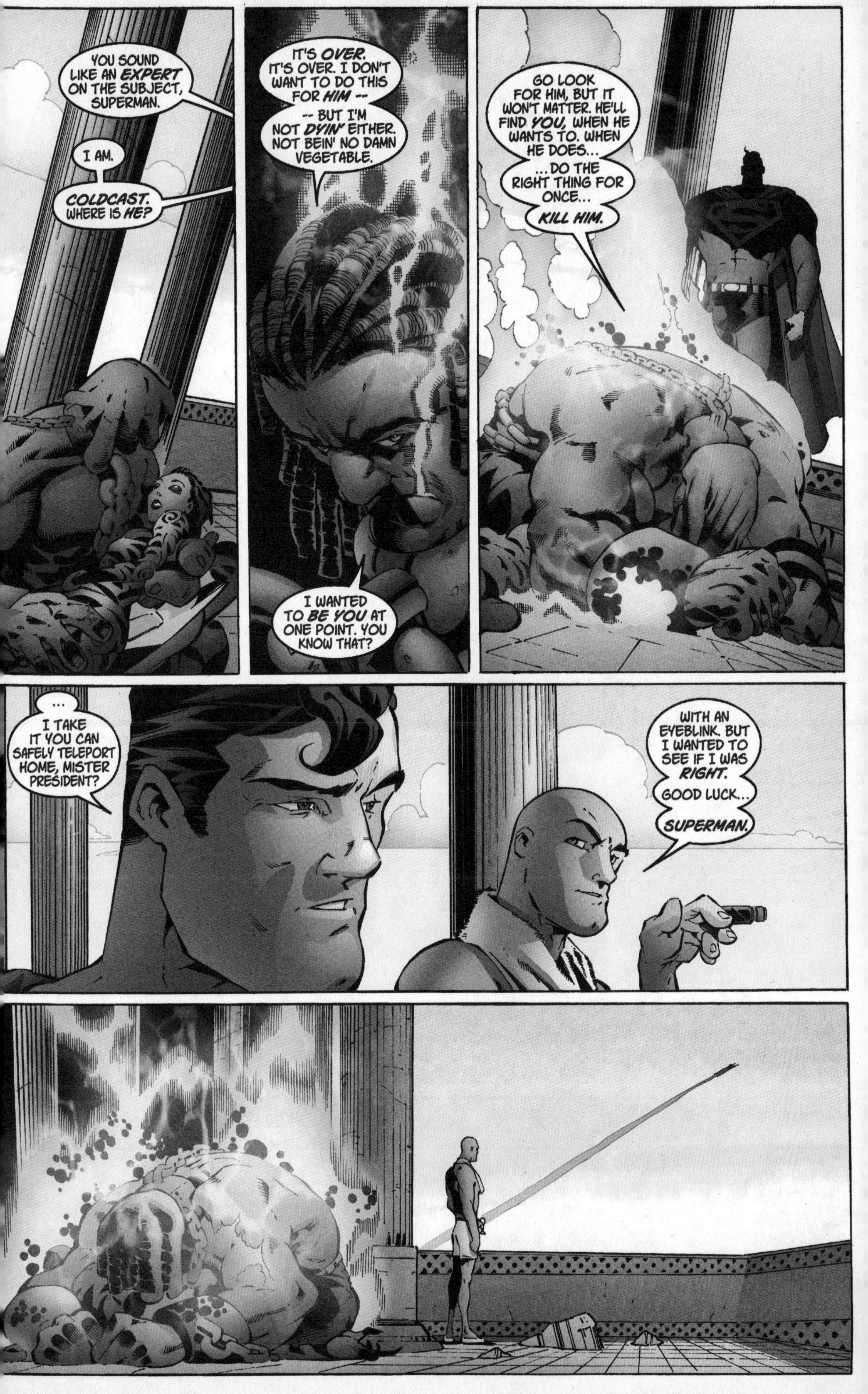
YOU SOUND LIKE AN EXPERT ON THE SUBJECT, SUPERMAN.
I AM.
COLDCAST. WHERE IS HE?
IT'S OVER. IT'S OVER. I DON'T WANT TO DO THIS FOR HIM --
-- BUT I'M NOT DYIN' EITHER. NOT BEIN' NO DAMN VEGETABLE.
I WANTED TO BE YOU AT ONE POINT. YOU KNOW THAT?
GO LOOK FOR HIM, BUT IT WON'T MATTER. HE'LL FIND YOU, WHEN HE WANTS TO. WHEN HE DOES...
...DO THE RIGHT THING FOR ONCE...
KILL HIM.
...
I TAKE IT YOU CAN SAFELY TELEPORT HOME, MISTER PRESIDENT?
WITH AN EYEBLINK. BUT I WANTED TO SEE IF I WAS RIGHT.
GOOD LUCK...
SUPERMAN.

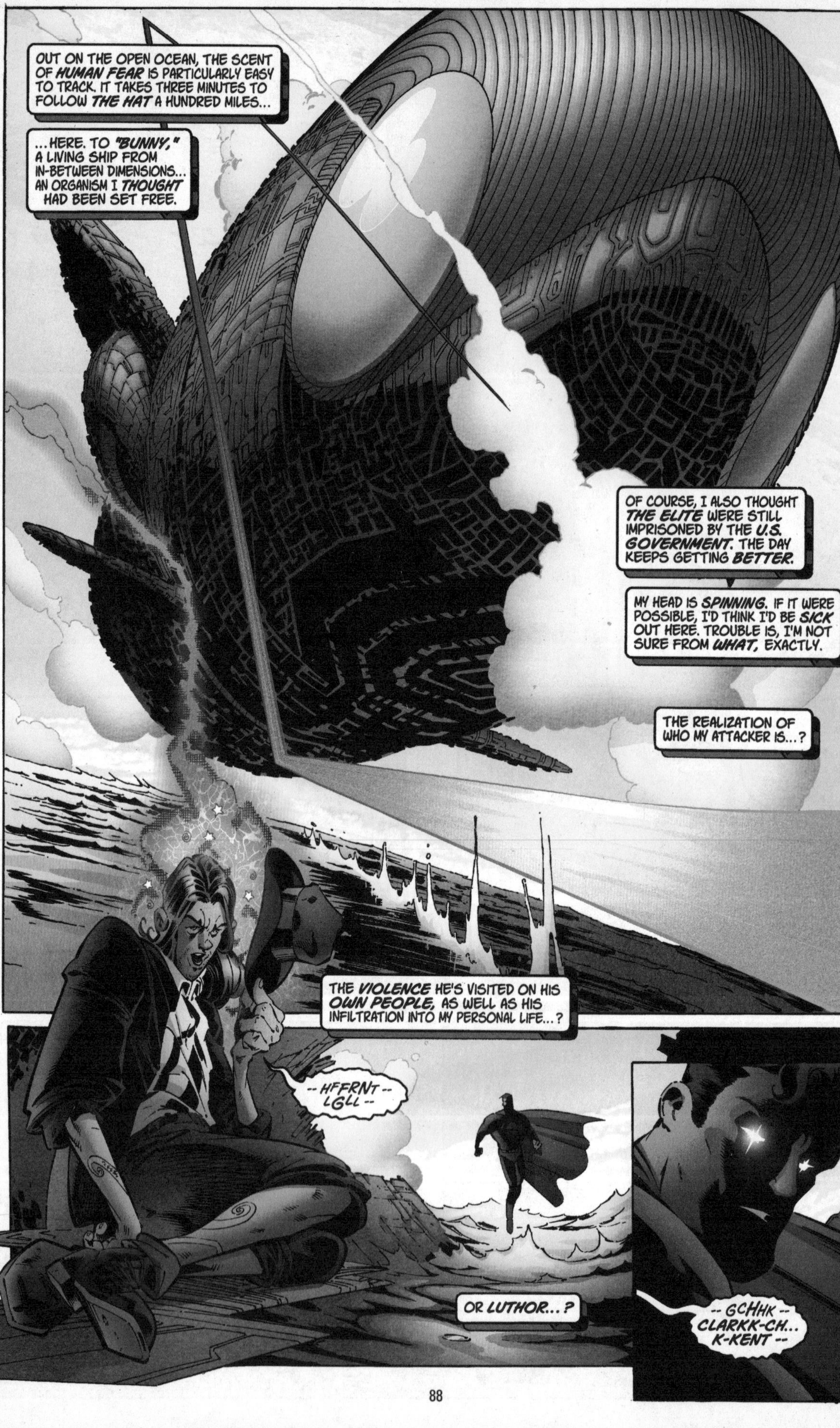

OUT ON THE OPEN OCEAN, THE SCENT OF HUMAN FEAR IS PARTICULARLY EASY TO TRACK. IT TAKES THREE MINUTES TO FOLLOW THE HAT A HUNDRED MILES...
...HERE. TO "BUNNY," A LIVING SHIP FROM IN-BETWEEN DIMENSIONS... AN ORGANISM I THOUGHT HAD BEEN SET FREE.
OF COURSE, I ALSO THOUGHT THE ELITE WERE STILL IMPRISONED BY THE U.S. GOVERNMENT. THE DAY KEEPS GETTING BETTER.
MY HEAD IS SPINNING. IF IT WERE POSSIBLE, I'D THINK I'D BE SICK OUT HERE. TROUBLE IS, I'M NOT SURE FROM WHAT, EXACTLY.
THE REALIZATION OF WHO MY ATTACKER IS...?
THE VIOLENCE HE'S VISITED ON HIS OWN PEOPLE, AS WELL AS HIS INFILTRATION INTO MY PERSONAL LIFE...?
-- HFFRNT -- LGLL --
OR LUTHOR...?
-- GCHHK -- CLARKK-CH... K-KENT --

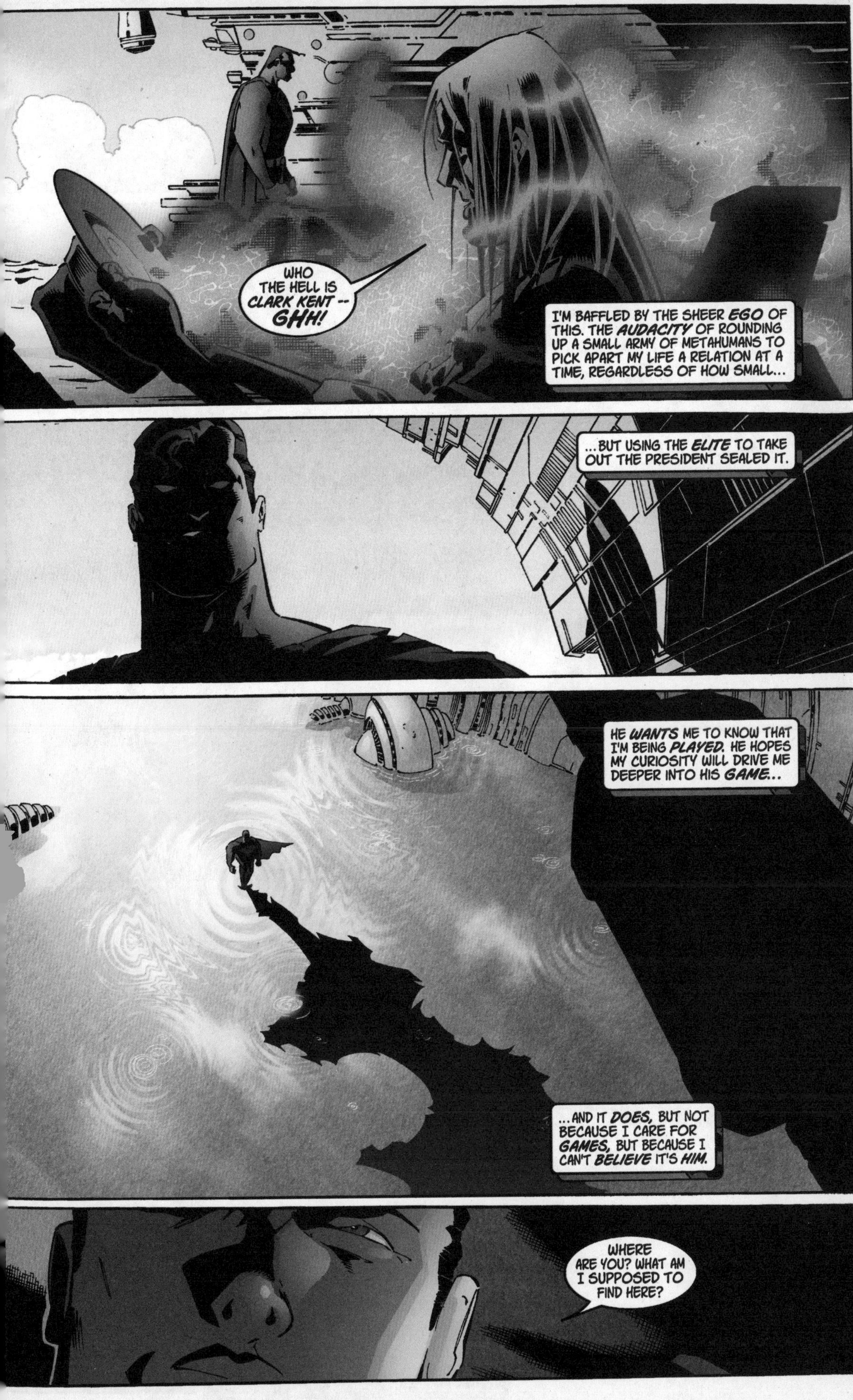
WHO THE HELL IS CLARK KENT -- GHH!
I'M BAFFLED BY THE SHEER EGO OF THIS. THE AUDACITY OF ROUNDING UP A SMALL ARMY OF METAHUMANS TO PICK APART MY LIFE A RELATION AT A TIME, REGARDLESS OF HOW SMALL...
...BUT USING THE ELITE TO TAKE OUT THE PRESIDENT SEALED IT.
HE WANTS ME TO KNOW THAT I'M BEING PLAYED. HE HOPES MY CURIOSITY WILL DRIVE ME DEEPER INTO HIS GAME...
...AND IT DOES, BUT NOT BECAUSE I CARE FOR GAMES, BUT BECAUSE I CAN'T BELIEVE IT'S HIM.
WHERE ARE YOU? WHAT AM I SUPPOSED TO FIND HERE?

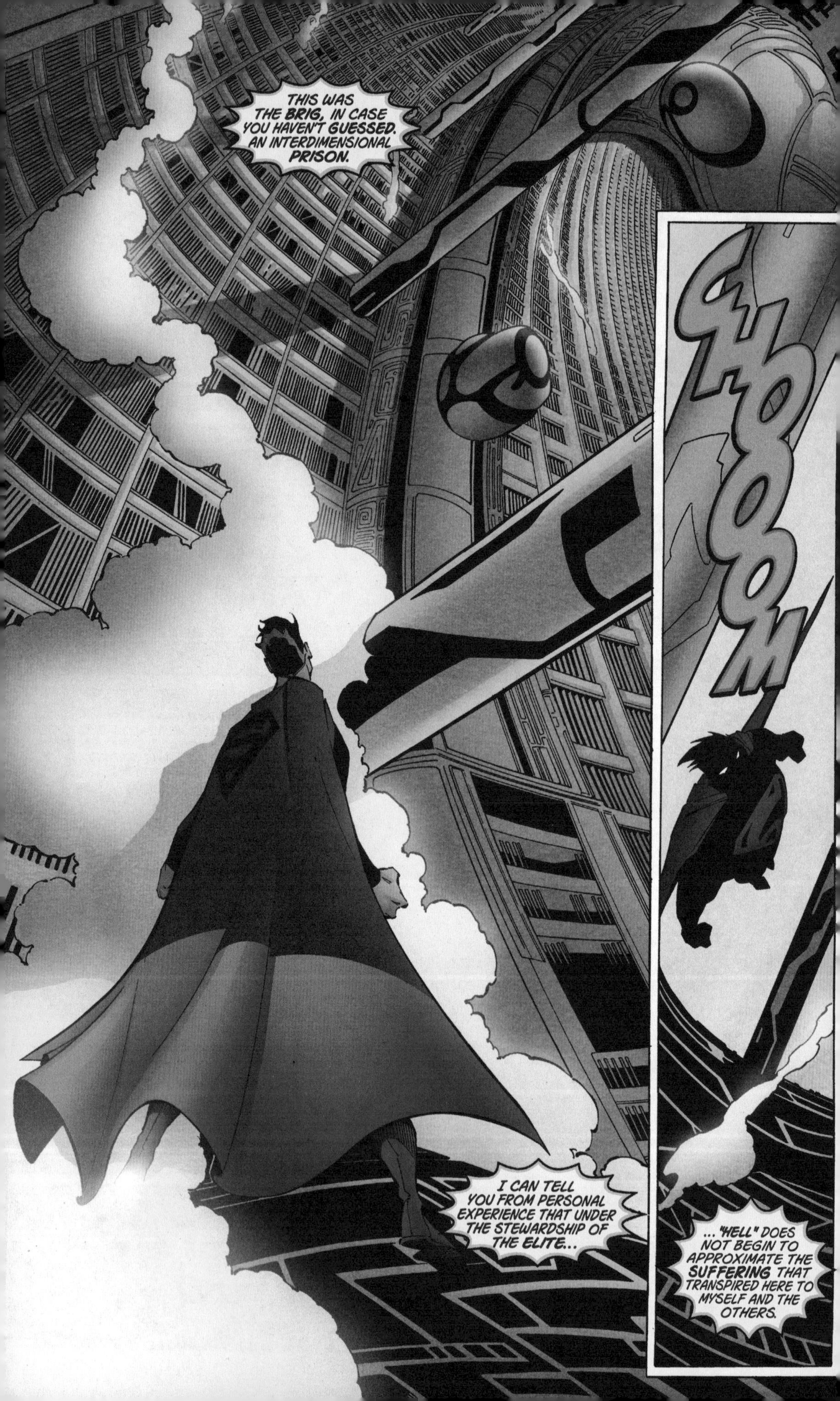
THIS WAS THE BRIG, IN CASE YOU HAVEN'T GUESSED. AN INTERDIMENSIONAL PRISON.
CHOOOOOM
I CAN TELL YOU FROM PERSONAL EXPERIENCE THAT UNDER THE STEWARDSHIP OF THE ELITE...
... "HELL" DOES NOT BEGIN TO APPROXIMATE THE SUFFERING THAT TRANSPIRED HERE TO MYSELF AND THE OTHERS.

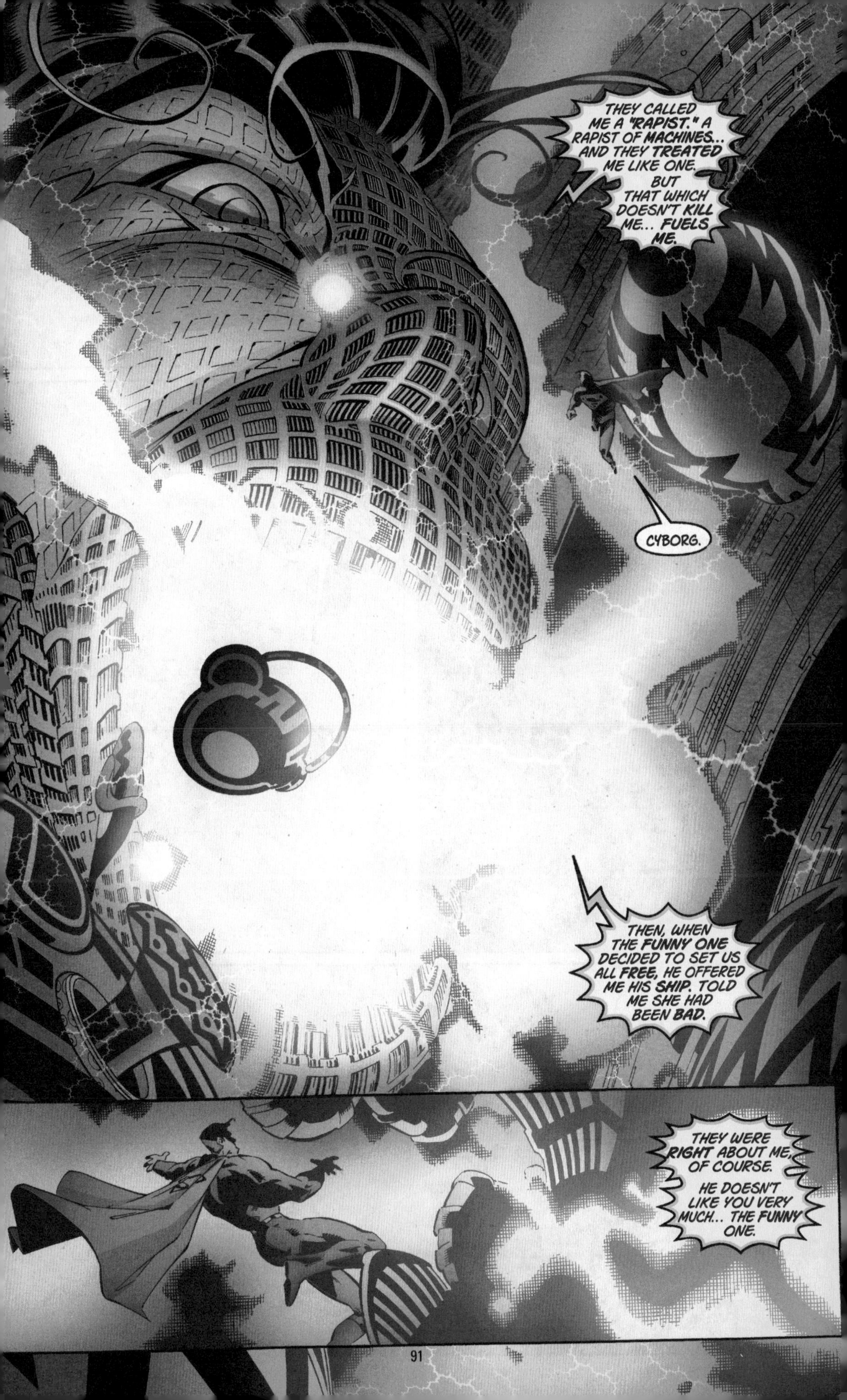
THEY CALLED ME A "RAPIST." A RAPIST OF MACHINES... AND THEY TREATED ME LIKE ONE.
BUT THAT WHICH DOESN'T KILL ME... FUELS ME.
CYBORG.
THEN, WHEN THE FUNNY ONE DECIDED TO SET US ALL FREE, HE OFFERED ME HIS SHIP. TOLD ME SHE HAD BEEN BAD.
THEY WERE RIGHT ABOUT ME, OF COURSE.
HE DOESN'T LIKE YOU VERY MUCH... THE FUNNY ONE.

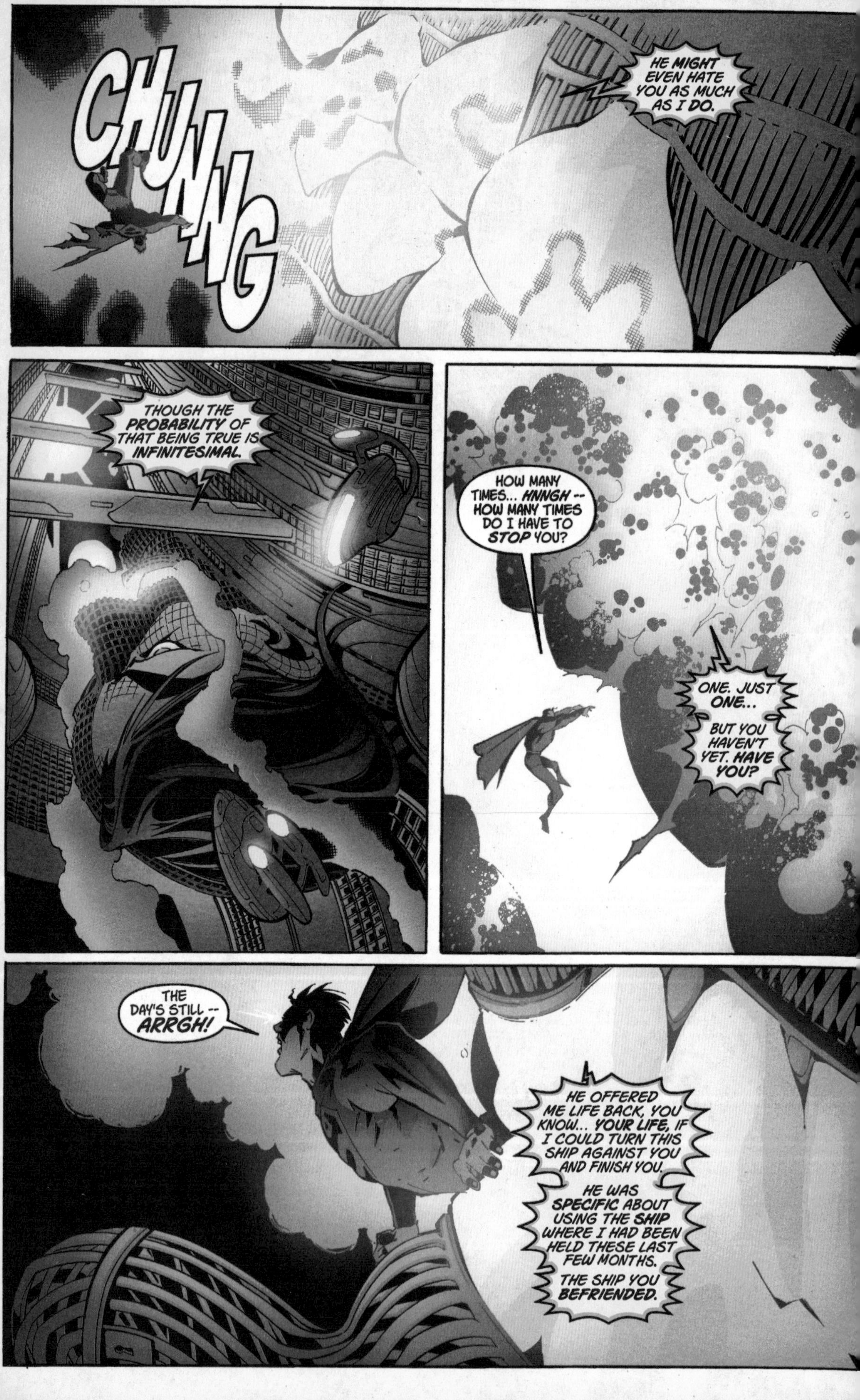
CHUNNG
HE MIGHT EVEN HATE YOU AS MUCH AS I DO.
THOUGH THE PROBABILITY OF THAT BEING TRUE IS INFINITESIMAL.
HOW MANY TIMES... HNNGH -- HOW MANY TIMES DO I HAVE TO STOP YOU?
ONE. JUST ONE...
BUT YOU HAVEN'T YET. HAVE YOU?
THE DAY'S STILL -- ARRGH!
HE OFFERED ME LIFE BACK, YOU KNOW... YOUR LIFE, IF I COULD TURN THIS SHIP AGAINST YOU AND FINISH YOU.
HE WAS SPECIFIC ABOUT USING THE SHIP WHERE I HAD BEEN HELD THESE LAST FEW MONTHS.
THE SHIP YOU BEFRIENDED.

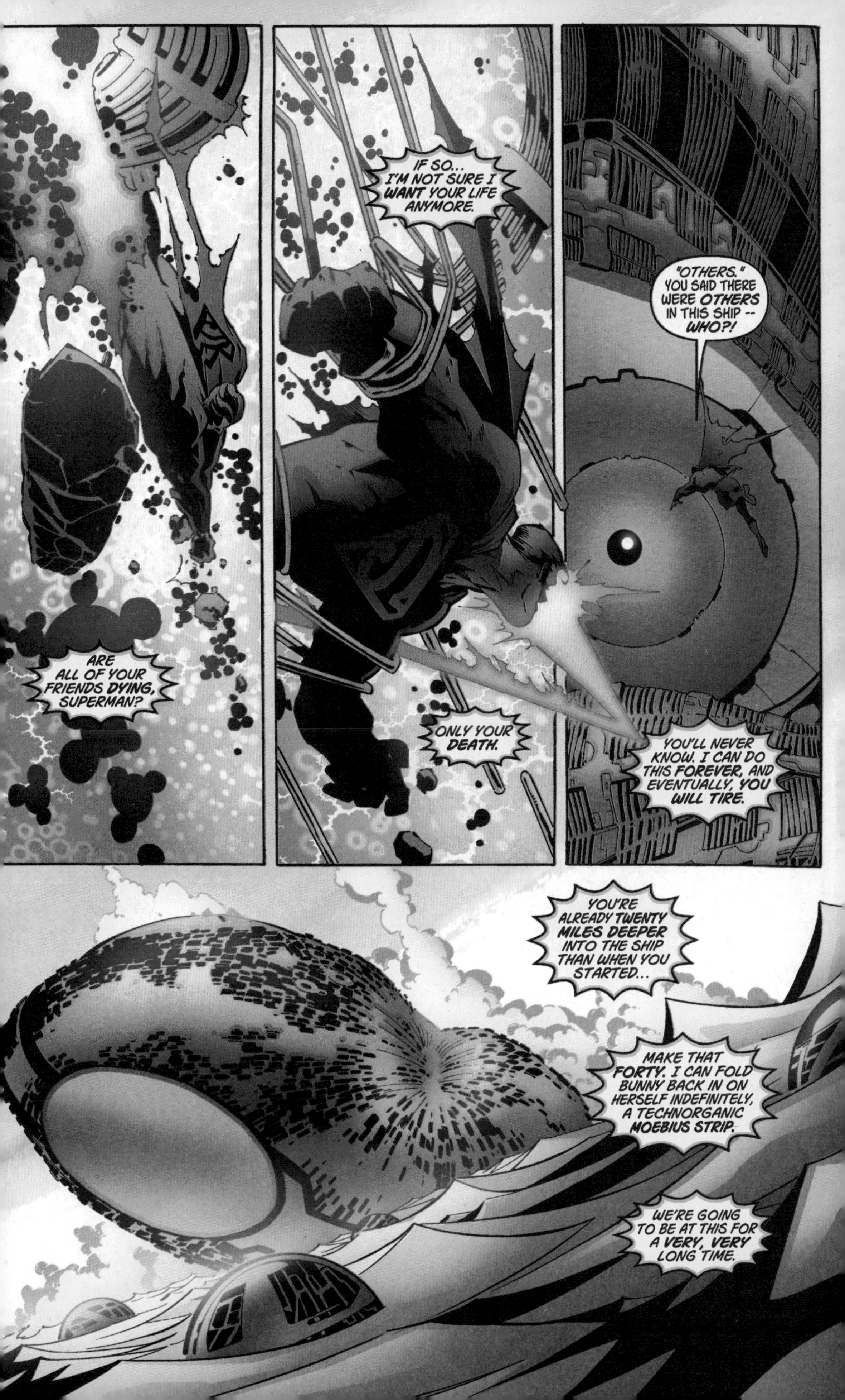
ARE ALL OF YOUR FRIENDS DYING, SUPERMAN?
IF SO... I'M NOT SURE I WANT YOUR LIFE ANYMORE.
ONLY YOUR DEATH.
"OTHERS." YOU SAID THERE WERE OTHERS IN THIS SHIP -- WHO?!
YOU'LL NEVER KNOW. I CAN DO THIS FOREVER, AND EVENTUALLY, YOU WILL TIRE.
YOU'RE ALREADY TWENTY MILES DEEPER INTO THE SHIP THAN WHEN YOU STARTED...
MAKE THAT FORTY. I CAN FOLD BUNNY BACK IN ON HERSELF INDEFINITELY, A TECHNORGANIC MOEBIUS STRIP.
WE'RE GOING TO BE AT THIS FOR A VERY, VERY LONG TIME.

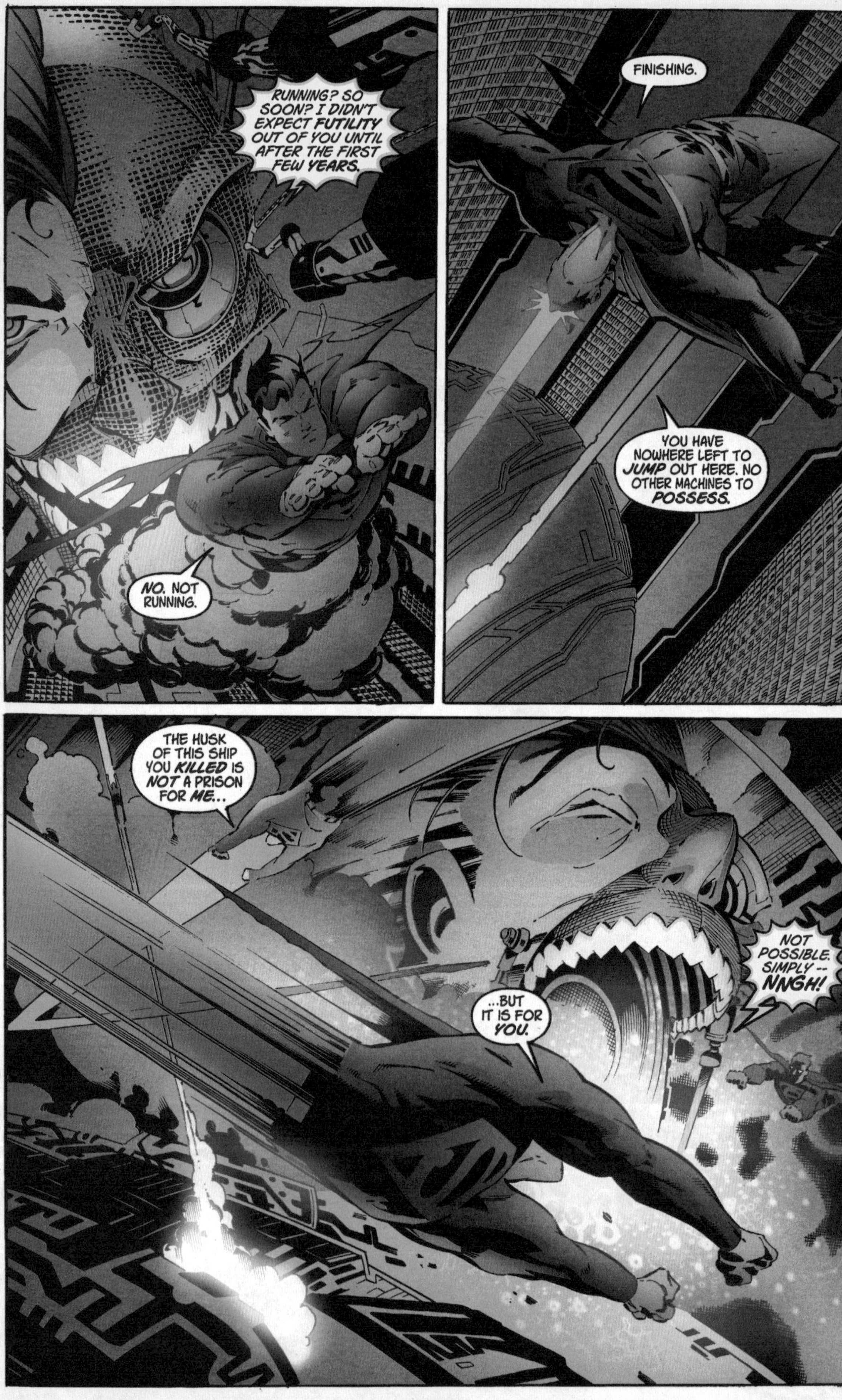
RUNNING? SO SOON? I DIDN'T EXPECT *FUTILITY* OUT OF YOU UNTIL AFTER THE FIRST FEW *YEARS.*
NO. NOT RUNNING.
FINISHING.
YOU HAVE NOWHERE LEFT TO *JUMP* OUT HERE. NO OTHER MACHINES TO *POSSESS.*
THE HUSK OF THIS SHIP YOU *KILLED* IS *NOT* A PRISON FOR *ME...*
...BUT IT IS FOR *YOU.*
NOT POSSIBLE. SIMPLY -- *NNGH!*

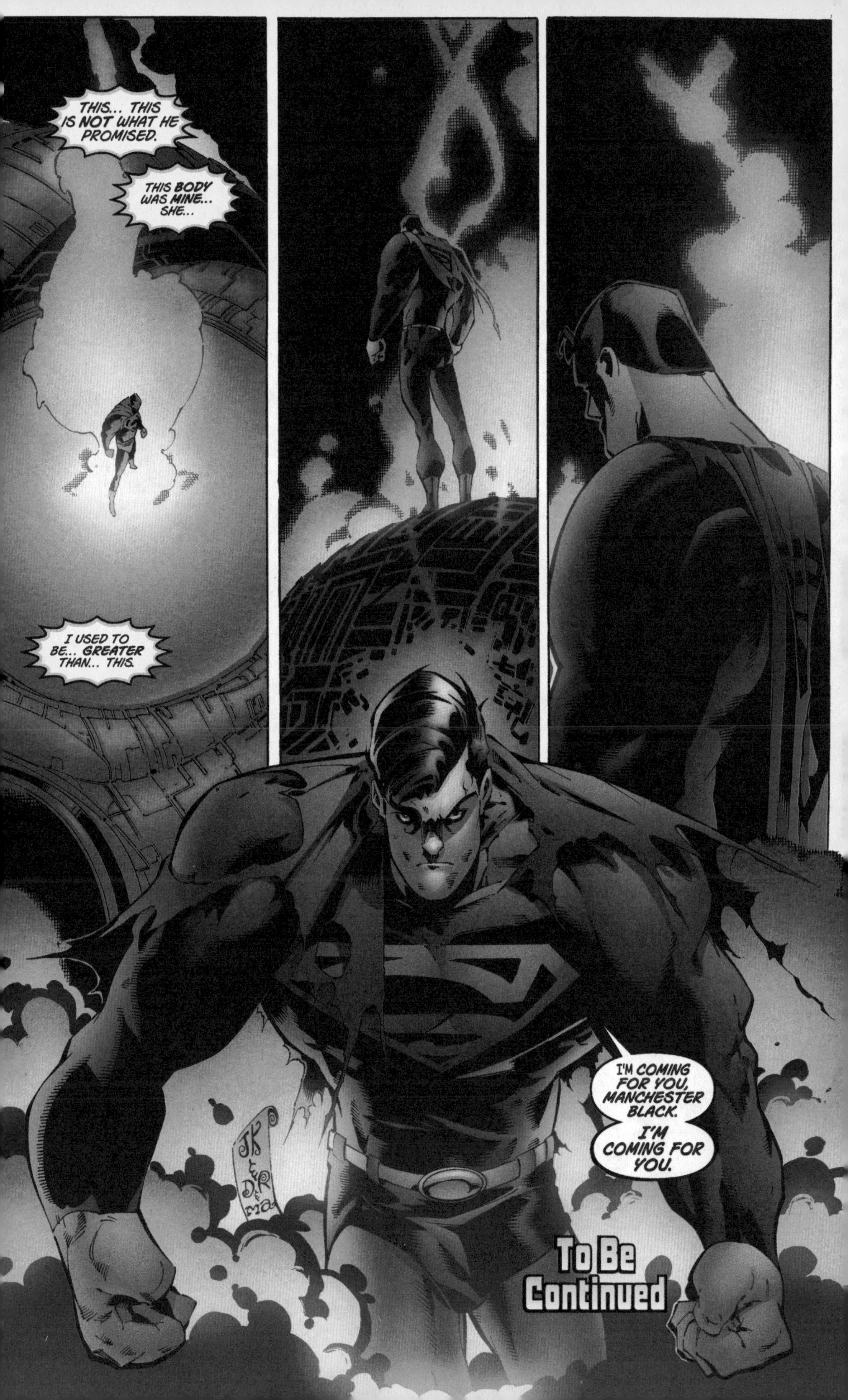
THIS... THIS IS NOT WHAT HE PROMISED.
THIS BODY WAS MINE... SHE...
I USED TO BE... GREATER THAN... THIS.
I'M COMING FOR YOU, MANCHESTER BLACK.
I'M COMING FOR YOU.
To Be Continued

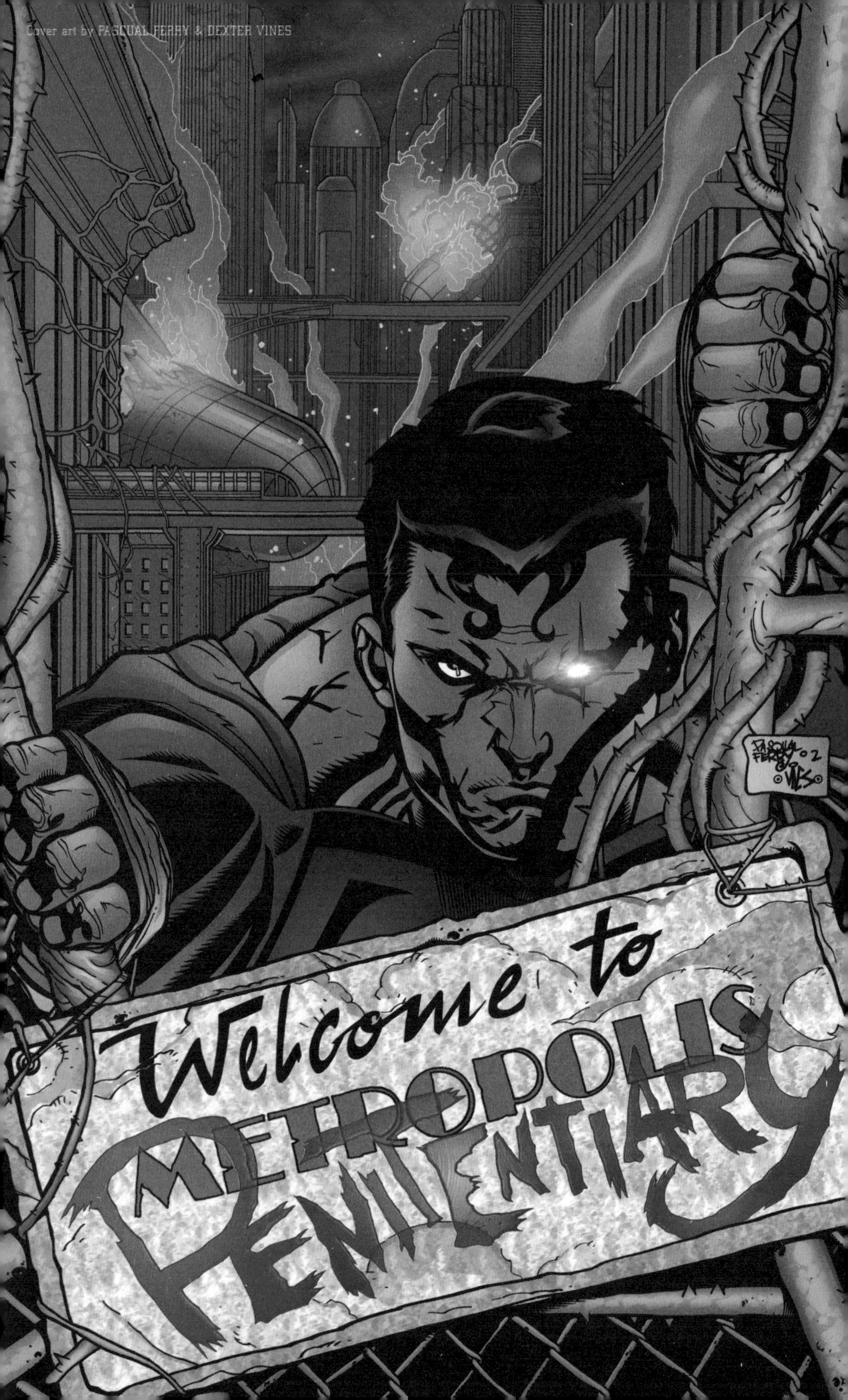
Welcome to
METROPOLIS
PENITENTIARY
Cover art by PASCUAL FERRY & DEXTER VINES

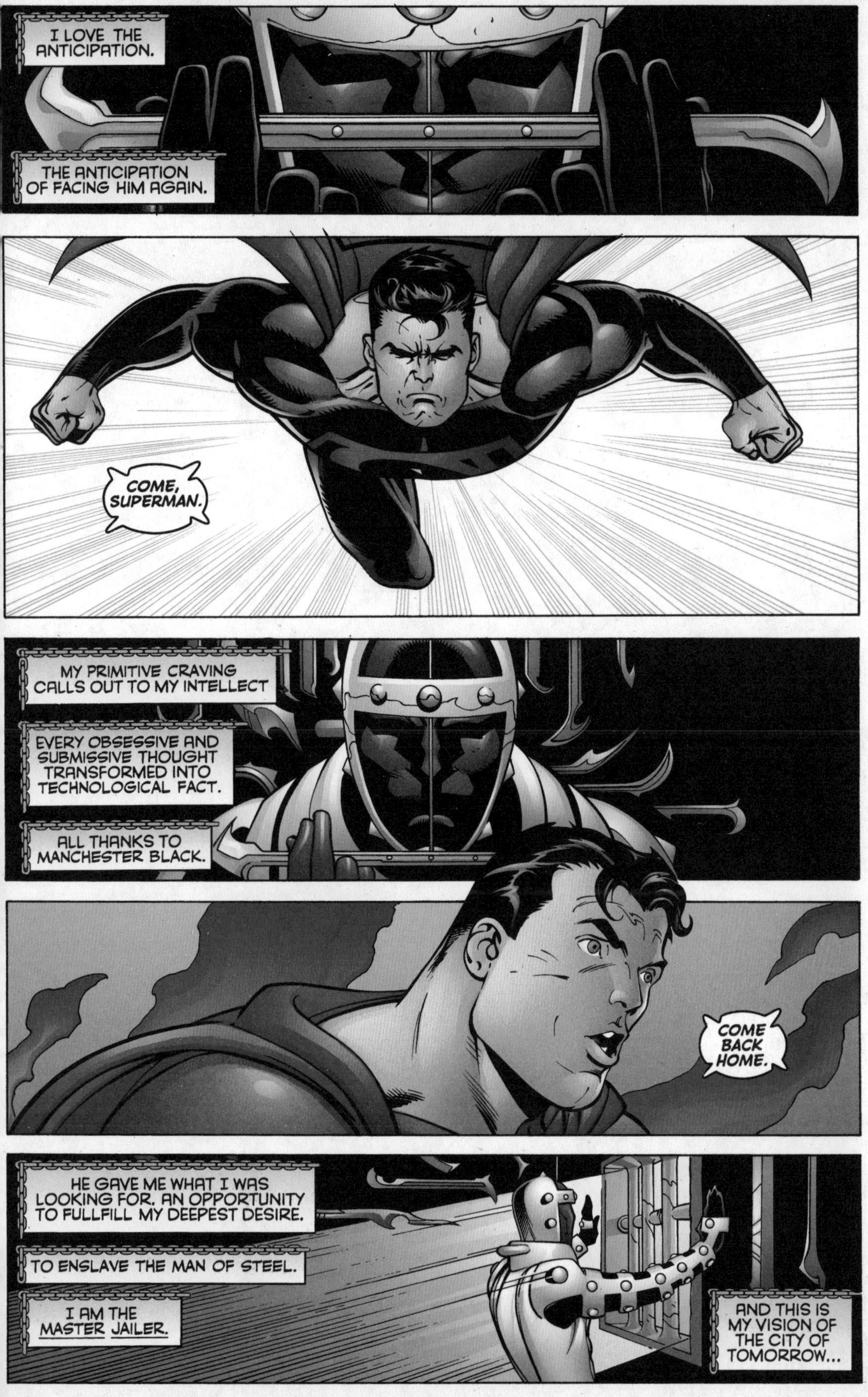
I LOVE THE ANTICIPATION.
THE ANTICIPATION OF FACING HIM AGAIN.
COME, SUPERMAN.
MY PRIMITIVE CRAVING CALLS OUT TO MY INTELLECT
EVERY OBSESSIVE AND SUBMISSIVE THOUGHT TRANSFORMED INTO TECHNOLOGICAL FACT.
ALL THANKS TO MANCHESTER BLACK.
COME BACK HOME.
HE GAVE ME WHAT I WAS LOOKING FOR. AN OPPORTUNITY TO FULLFILL MY DEEPEST DESIRE.
TO ENSLAVE THE MAN OF STEEL.
I AM THE MASTER JAILER.
AND THIS IS MY VISION OF THE CITY OF TOMORROW...

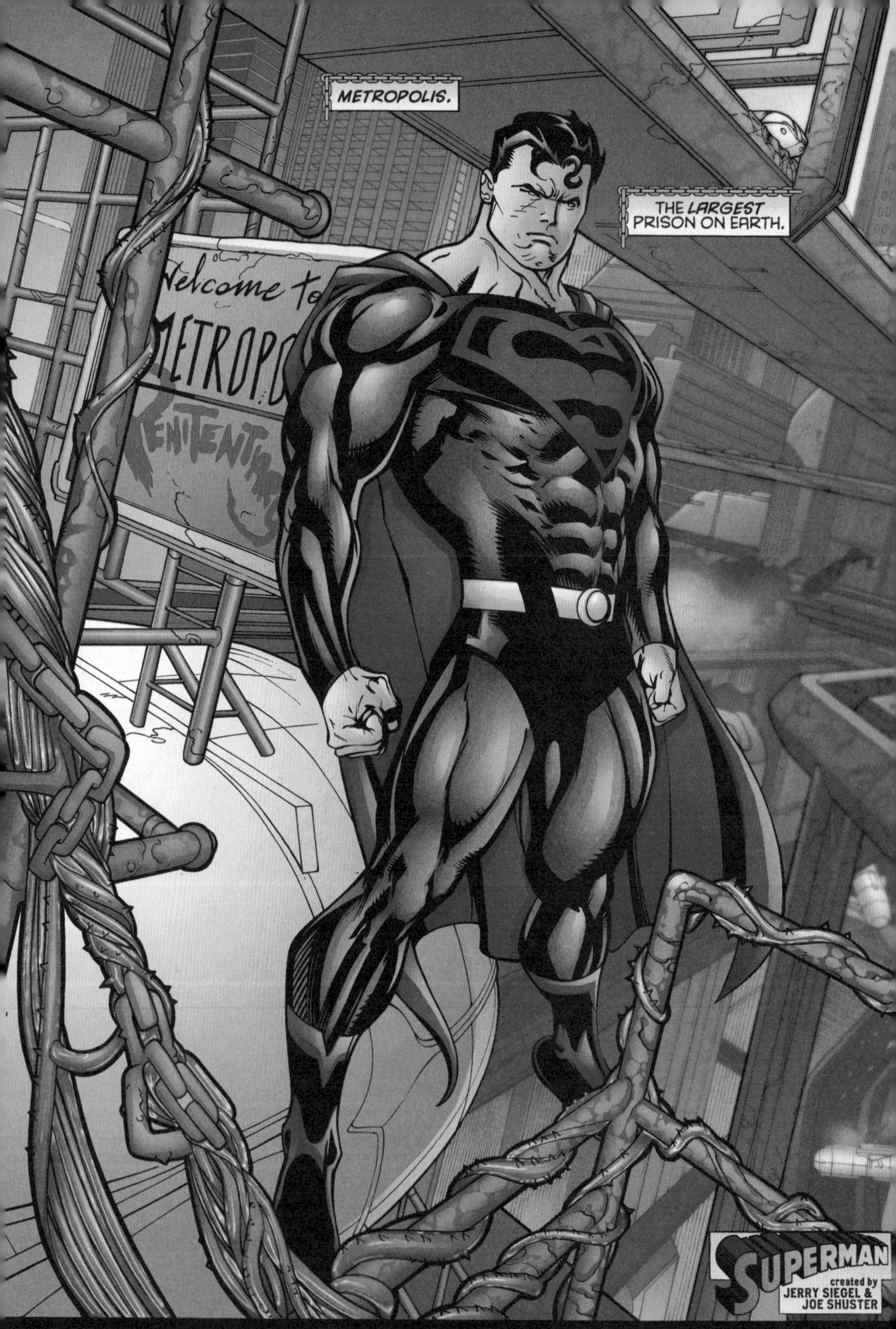
METROPOLIS.
THE *LARGEST* PRISON ON EARTH.
SUPERMAN
created by JERRY SIEGEL & JOE SHUSTER

GEOFF JOHNS story • PASCUAL FE Y pencils • MARK FARMER inks • TANYA & RICH HORIE colors

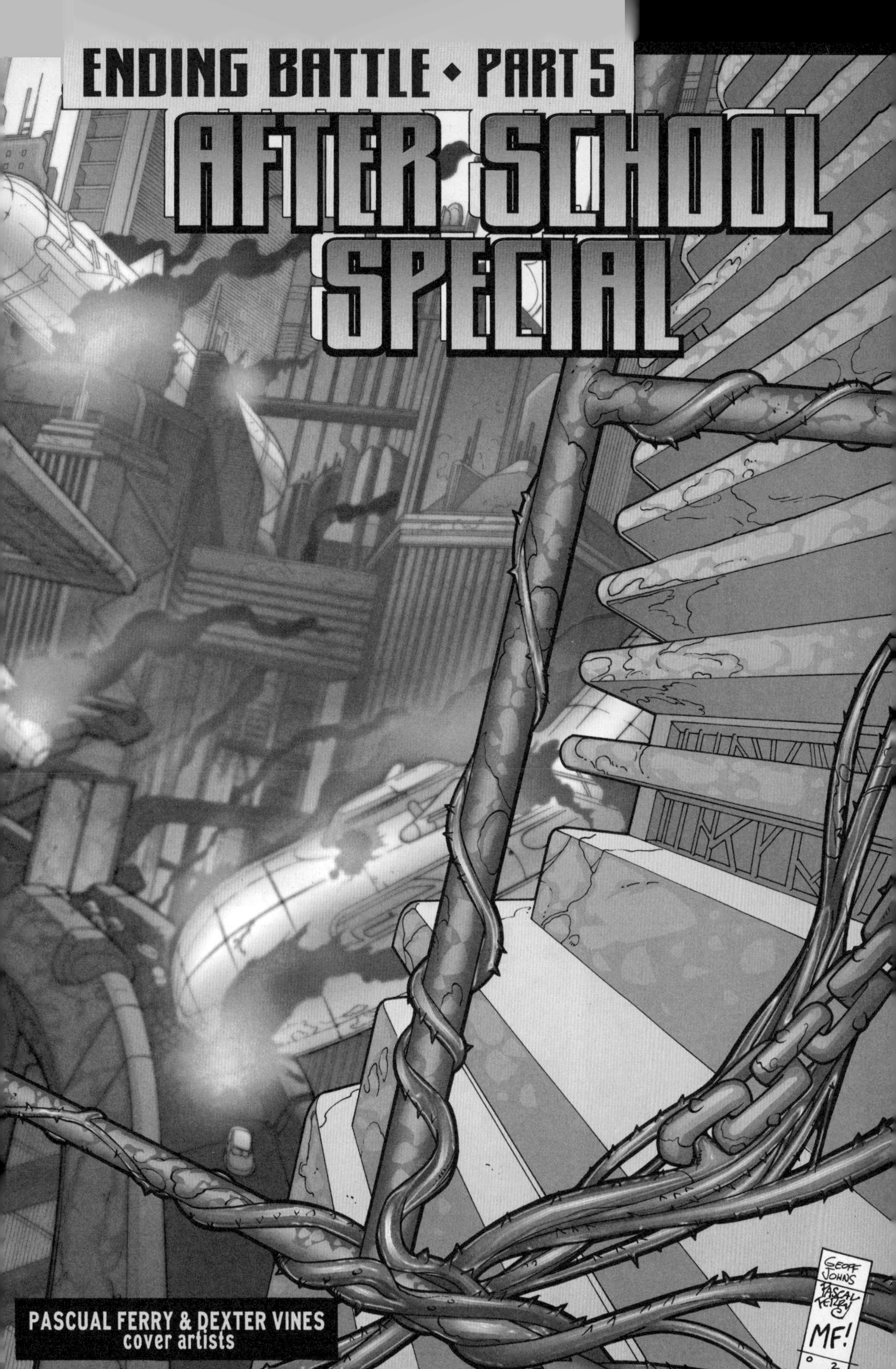
ENDING BATTLE • PART 5
AFTER SCHOOL SPECIAL
PASCUAL FERRY & DEXTER VINES
cover artists
GEOFF JOHNS
PASCAL FERRY
MF!
02

RICHARD STARKINGS letters • TOM PALMER jr. associate editor • EDDIE BERGANZA editor

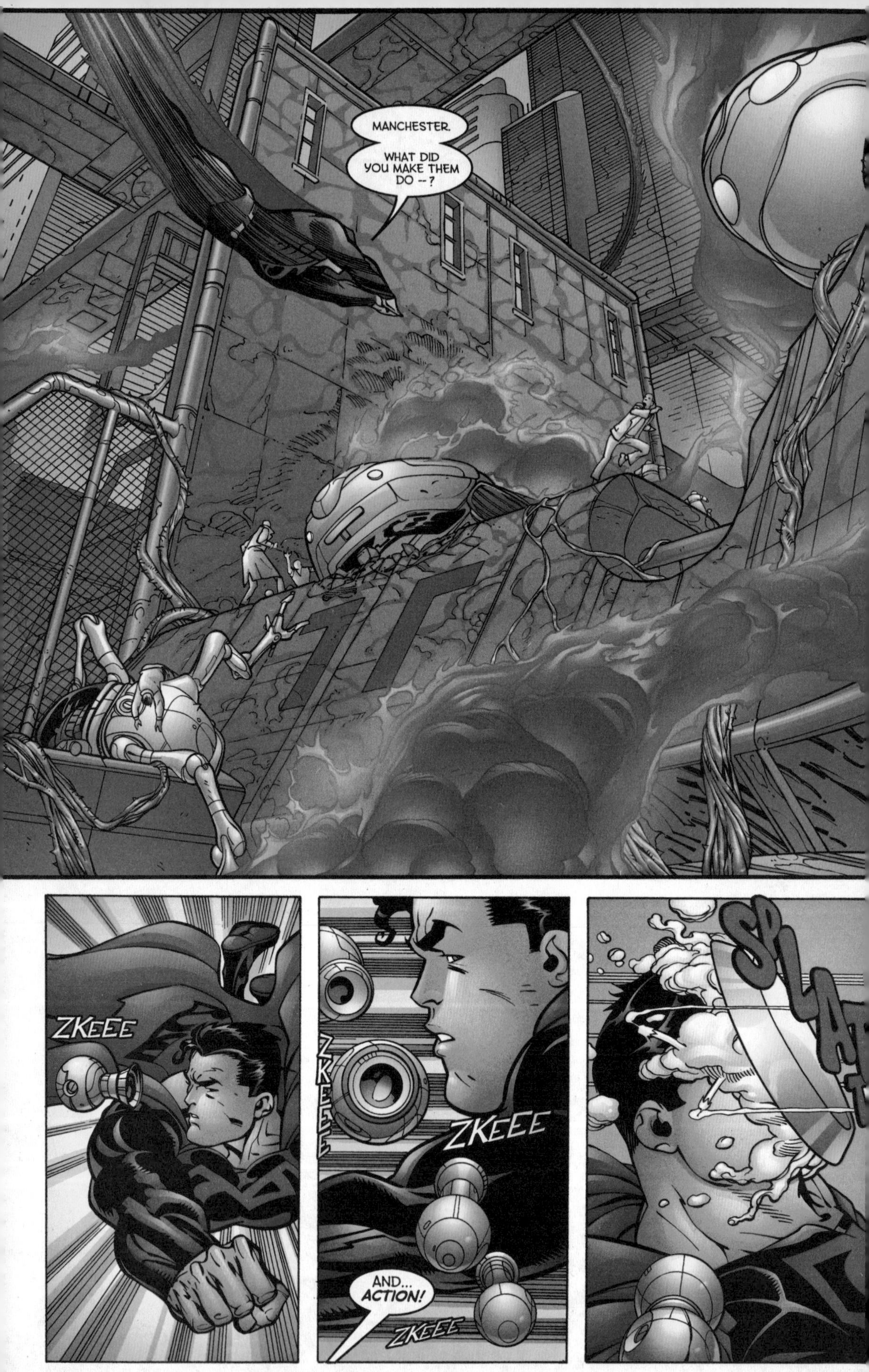
MANCHESTER.
WHAT DID YOU MAKE THEM DO --?
ZKEEE
ZKEEE
ZKEEE
AND... ACTION!
ZKEEE

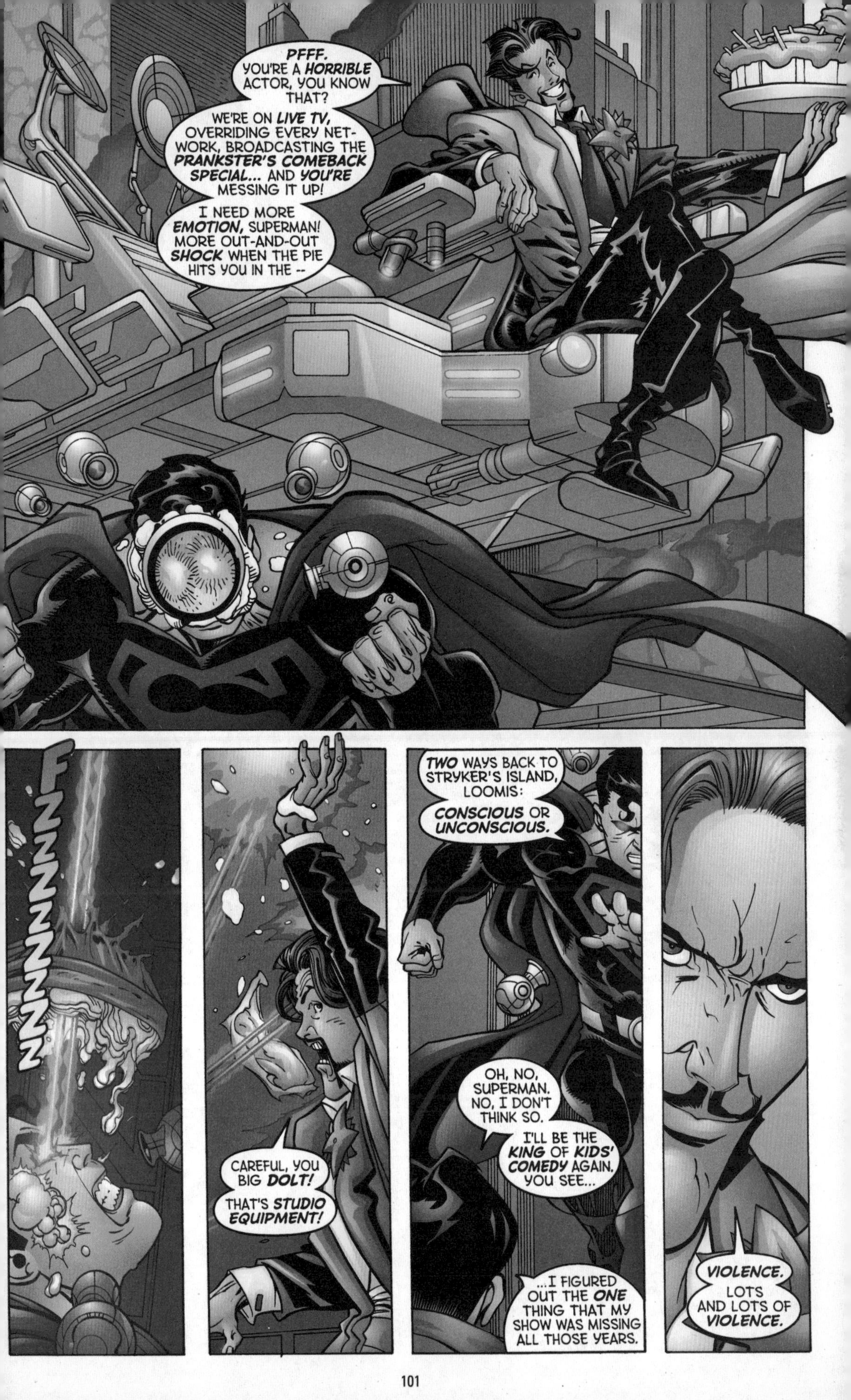
PFFF. YOU'RE A HORRIBLE ACTOR, YOU KNOW THAT?
WE'RE ON LIVE TV, OVERRIDING EVERY NET-WORK, BROADCASTING THE PRANKSTER'S COMEBACK SPECIAL... AND YOU'RE MESSING IT UP!
I NEED MORE EMOTION, SUPERMAN! MORE OUT-AND-OUT SHOCK WHEN THE PIE HITS YOU IN THE --
FZZZZZZZZZZ
CAREFUL, YOU BIG DOLT!
THAT'S STUDIO EQUIPMENT!
TWO WAYS BACK TO STRYKER'S ISLAND, LOOMIS:
CONSCIOUS OR UNCONSCIOUS.
OH, NO, SUPERMAN. NO, I DON'T THINK SO.
I'LL BE THE KING OF KIDS' COMEDY AGAIN, YOU SEE...
...I FIGURED OUT THE ONE THING THAT MY SHOW WAS MISSING ALL THOSE YEARS.
VIOLENCE.
LOTS AND LOTS OF VIOLENCE.

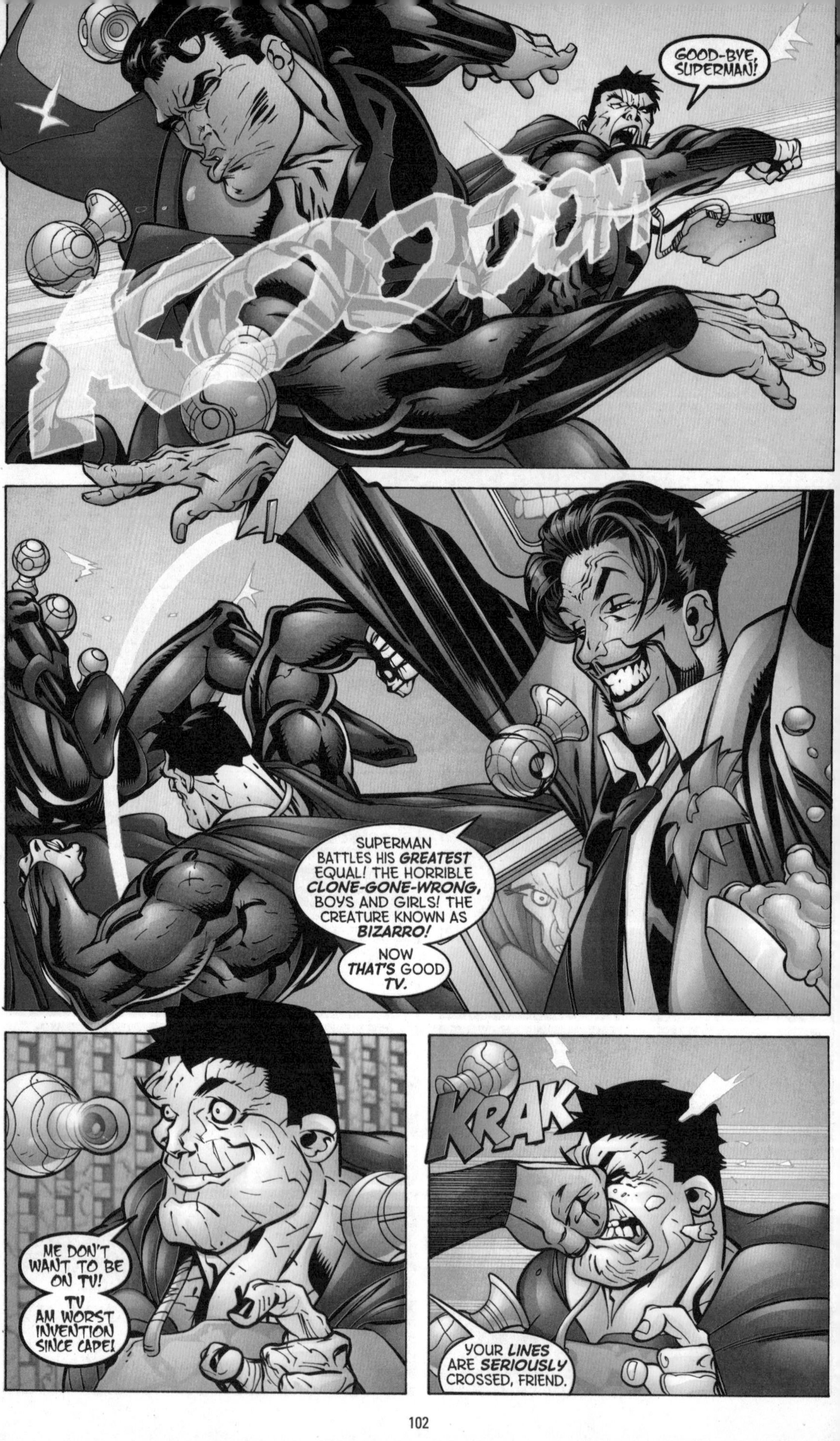
GOOD-BYE, SUPERMAN!
KOOOOOM
SUPERMAN BATTLES HIS GREATEST EQUAL! THE HORRIBLE CLONE-GONE-WRONG, BOYS AND GIRLS! THE CREATURE KNOWN AS BIZARRO!
NOW THAT'S GOOD TV.
ME DON'T WANT TO BE ON TV!
TV AM WORST INVENTION SINCE CAPE!
KRAK
YOUR LINES ARE SERIOUSLY CROSSED, FRIEND.

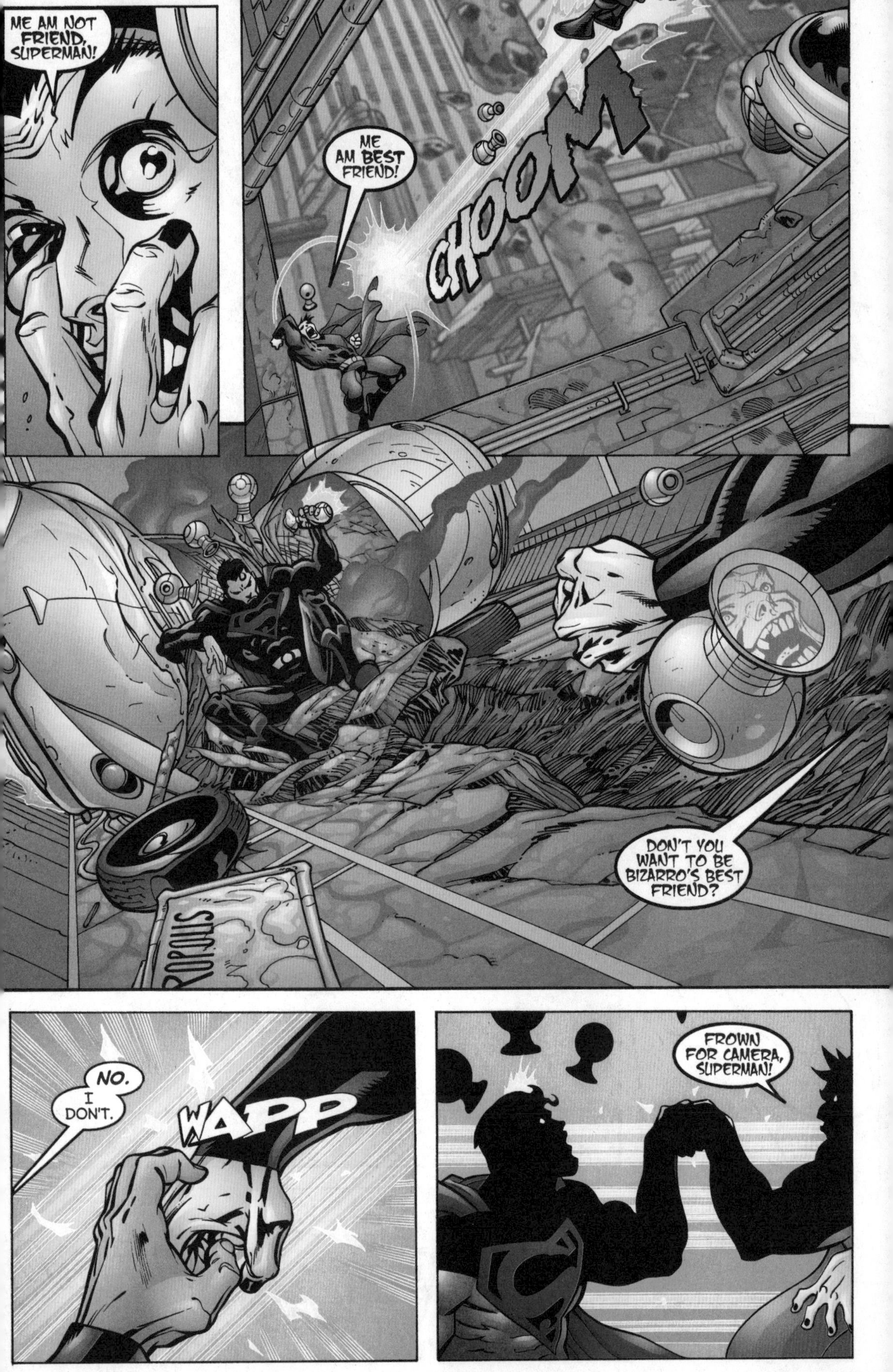
ME AM NOT FRIEND, SUPERMAN!
ME AM BEST FRIEND!
CHOOM
DON'T YOU WANT TO BE BIZARRO'S BEST FRIEND?
ROPOLIS
NO. I DON'T.
WAPP
FROWN FOR CAMERA, SUPERMAN!

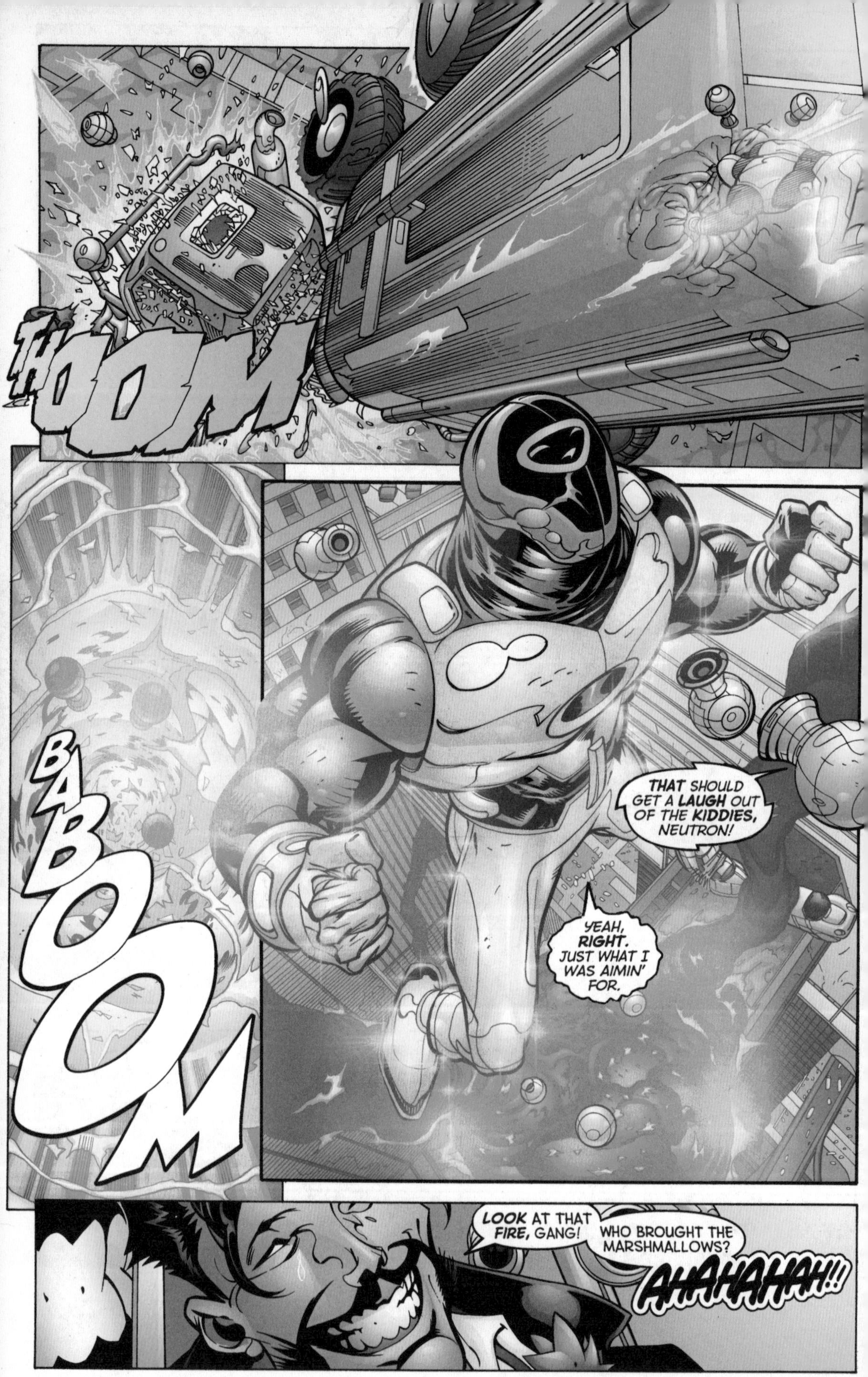
THOOM
BABOOOM
THAT SHOULD GET A LAUGH OUT OF THE KIDDIES, NEUTRON!
YEAH, RIGHT. JUST WHAT I WAS AIMIN' FOR.
LOOK AT THAT FIRE, GANG!
WHO BROUGHT THE MARSHMALLOWS?
AHAHAHAH!!

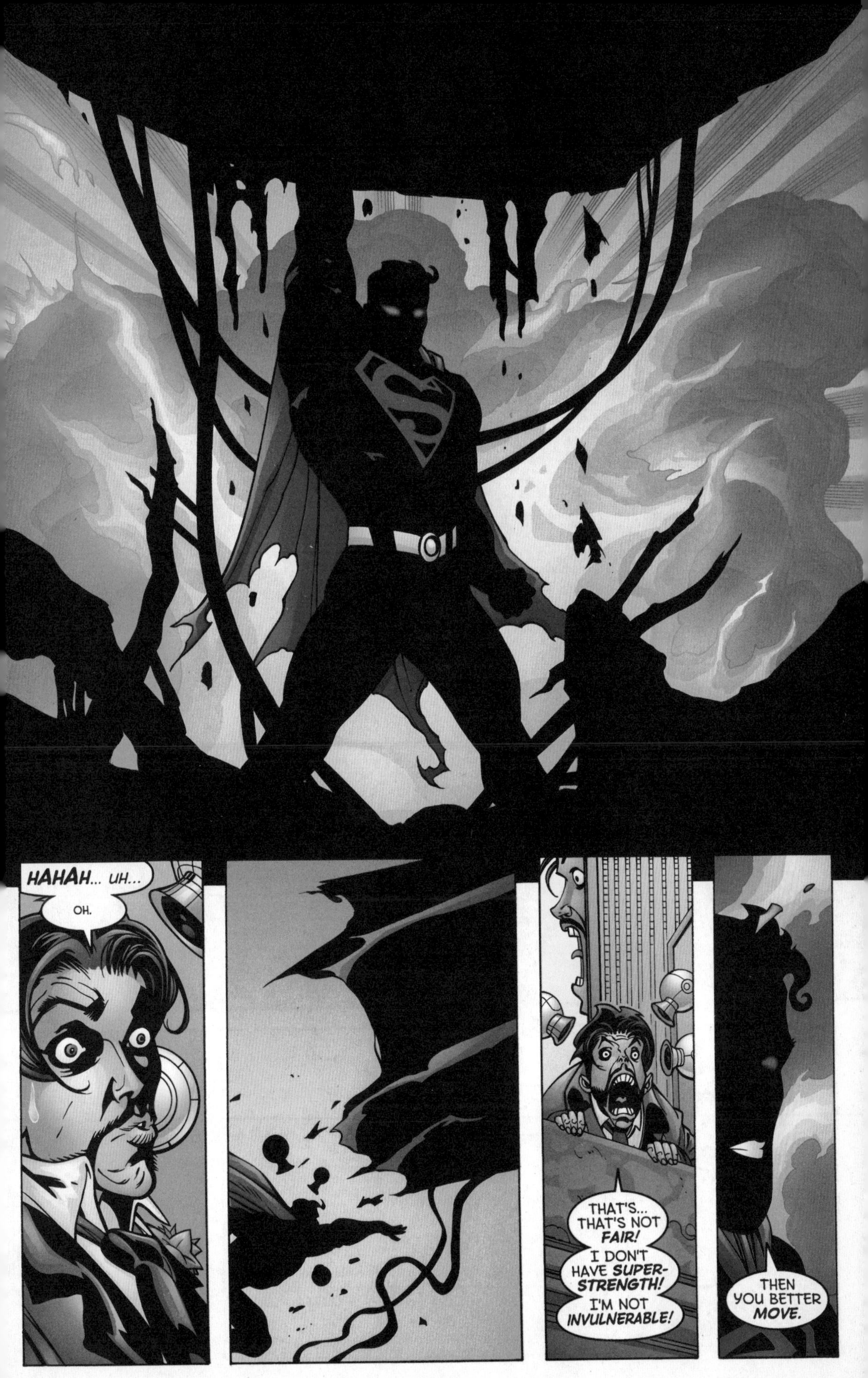
HAHAH... UH...
OH.
THAT'S... THAT'S NOT FAIR! I DON'T HAVE SUPER-STRENGTH! I'M NOT INVULNERABLE!
THEN YOU BETTER MOVE.

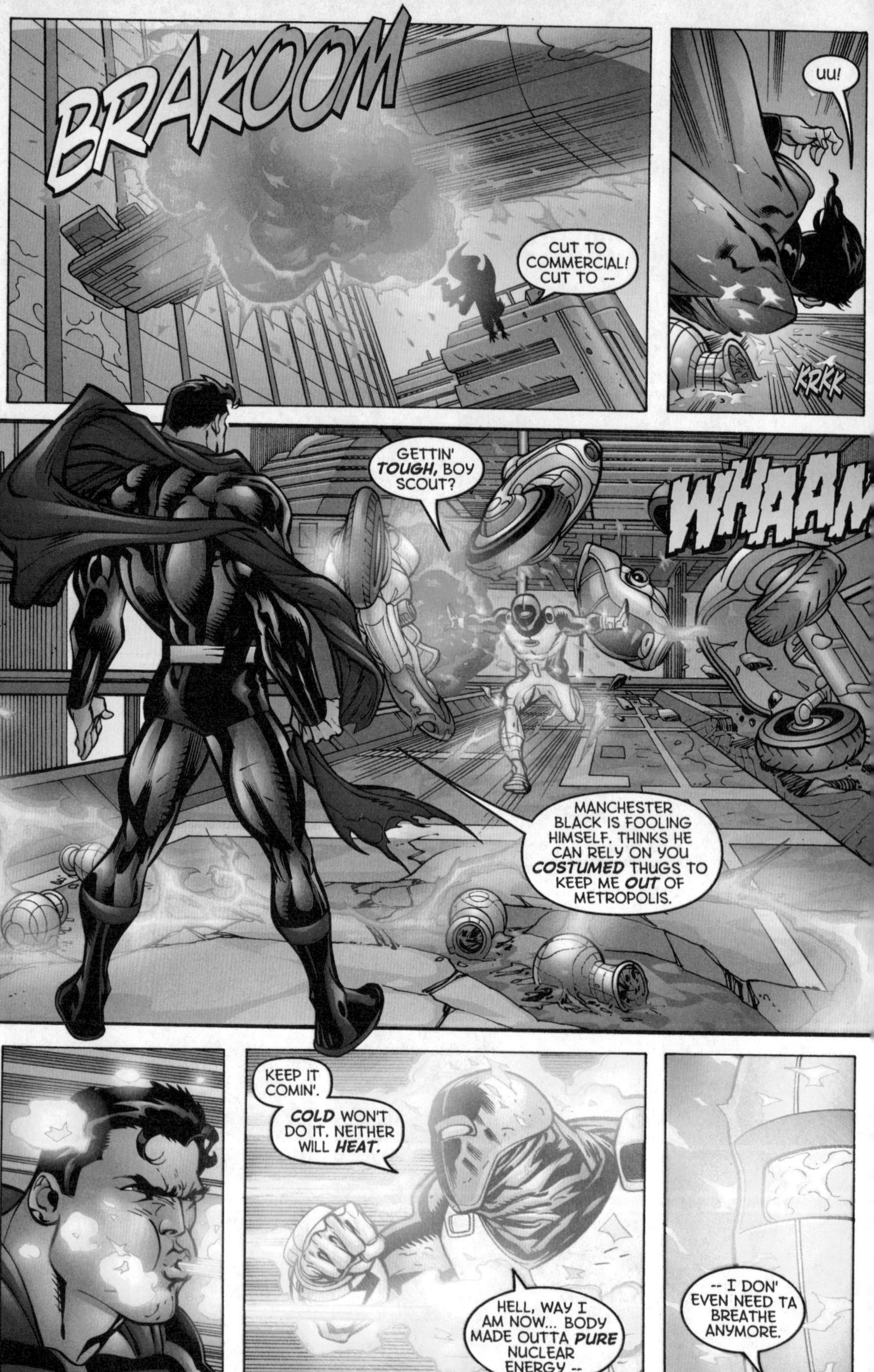
BRAKOOM
CUT TO COMMERCIAL! CUT TO --
UU!
KRKK
GETTIN' TOUGH, BOY SCOUT?
WHAAM
MANCHESTER BLACK IS FOOLING HIMSELF. THINKS HE CAN RELY ON YOU COSTUMED THUGS TO KEEP ME OUT OF METROPOLIS.
KEEP IT COMIN'.
COLD WON'T DO IT. NEITHER WILL HEAT.
HELL, WAY I AM NOW... BODY MADE OUTTA PURE NUCLEAR ENERGY --
-- I DON' EVEN NEED TA BREATHE ANYMORE.

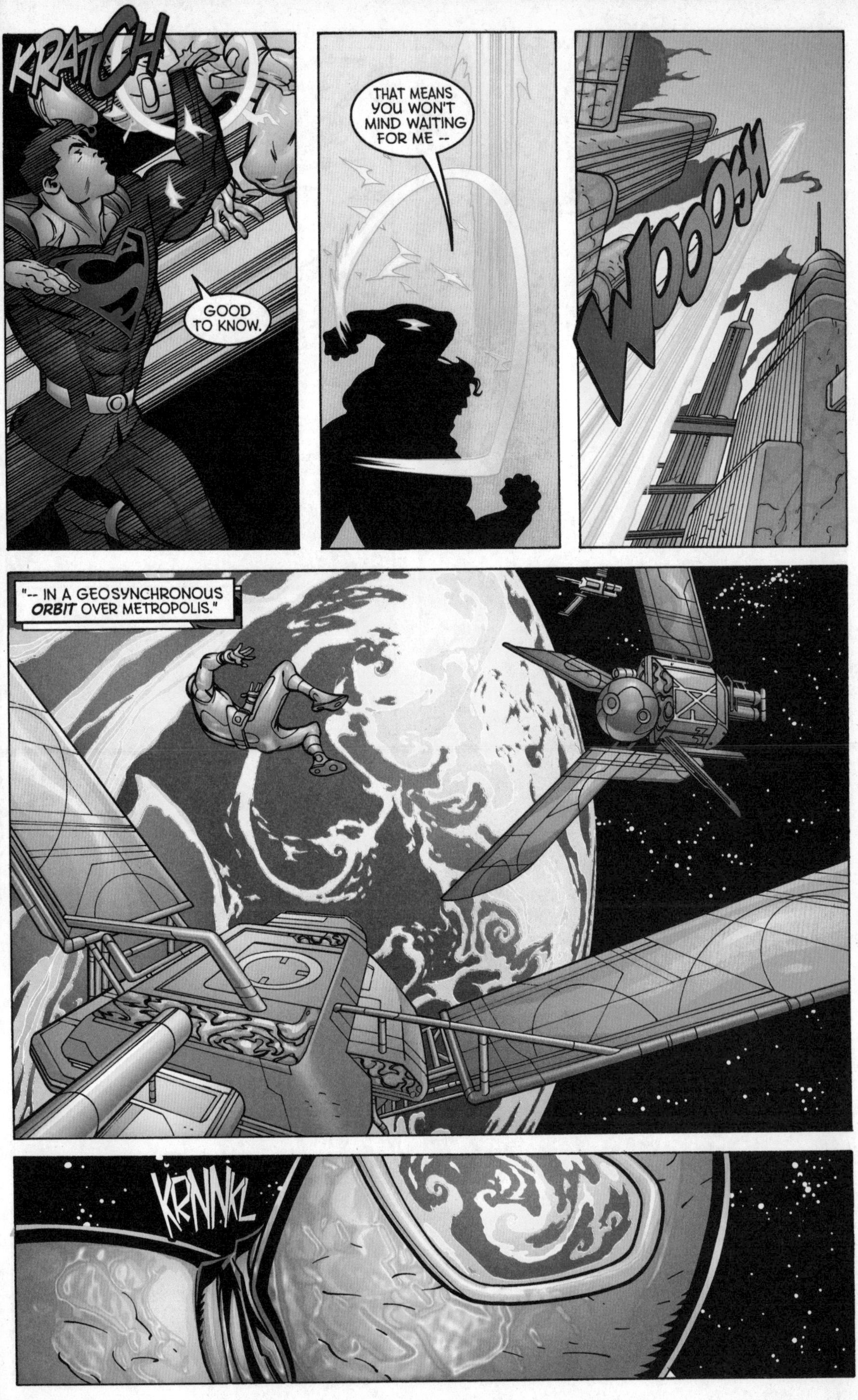
KRATCH
GOOD TO KNOW.
THAT MEANS YOU WON'T MIND WAITING FOR ME --
WOOOSH
"-- IN A GEOSYNCHRONOUS ORBIT OVER METROPOLIS."
KRNNKL

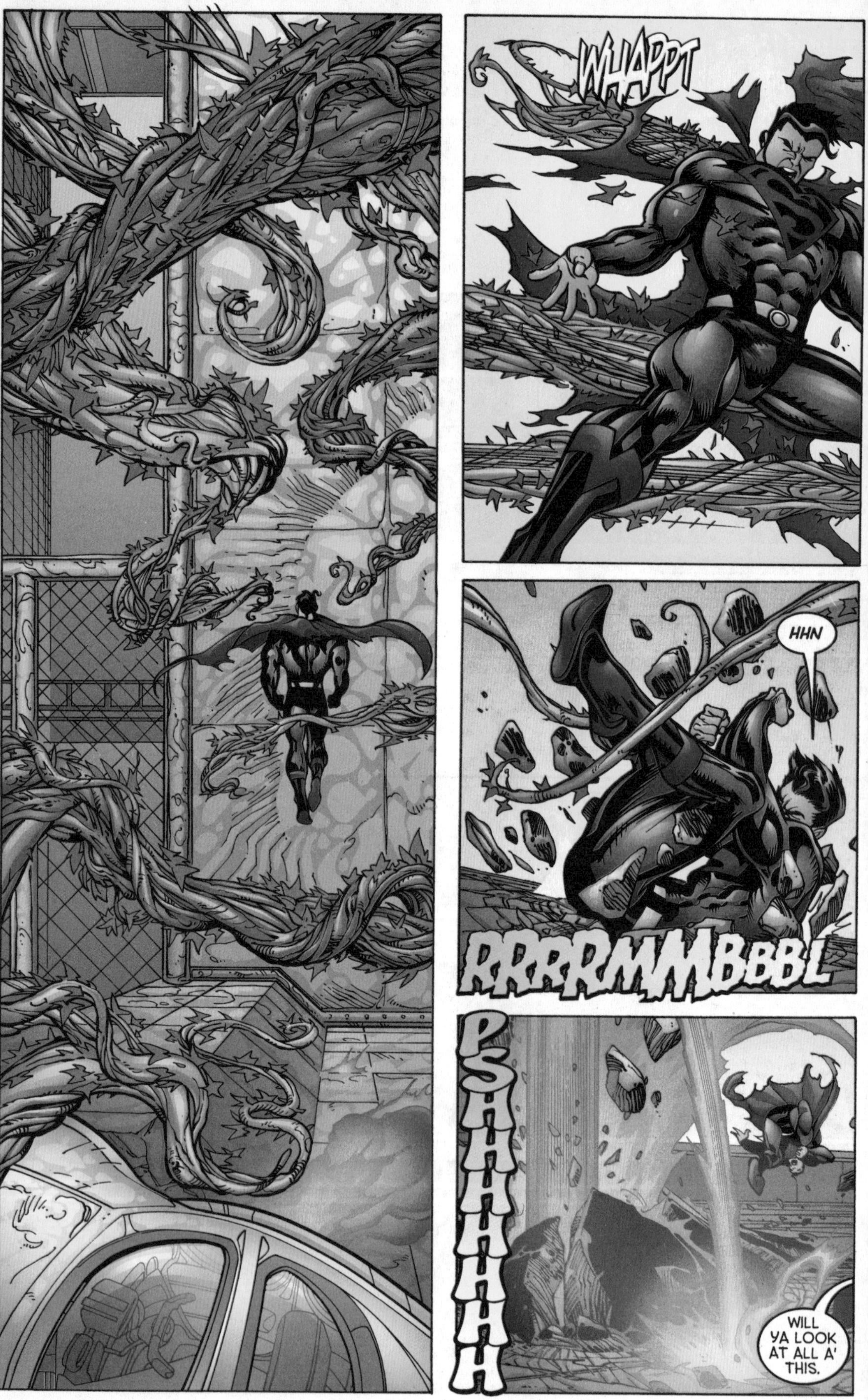
WHAPPT
HHN
RRRRMMBBBL
PSHHHHHHHH
WILL YA LOOK AT ALL A' THIS.

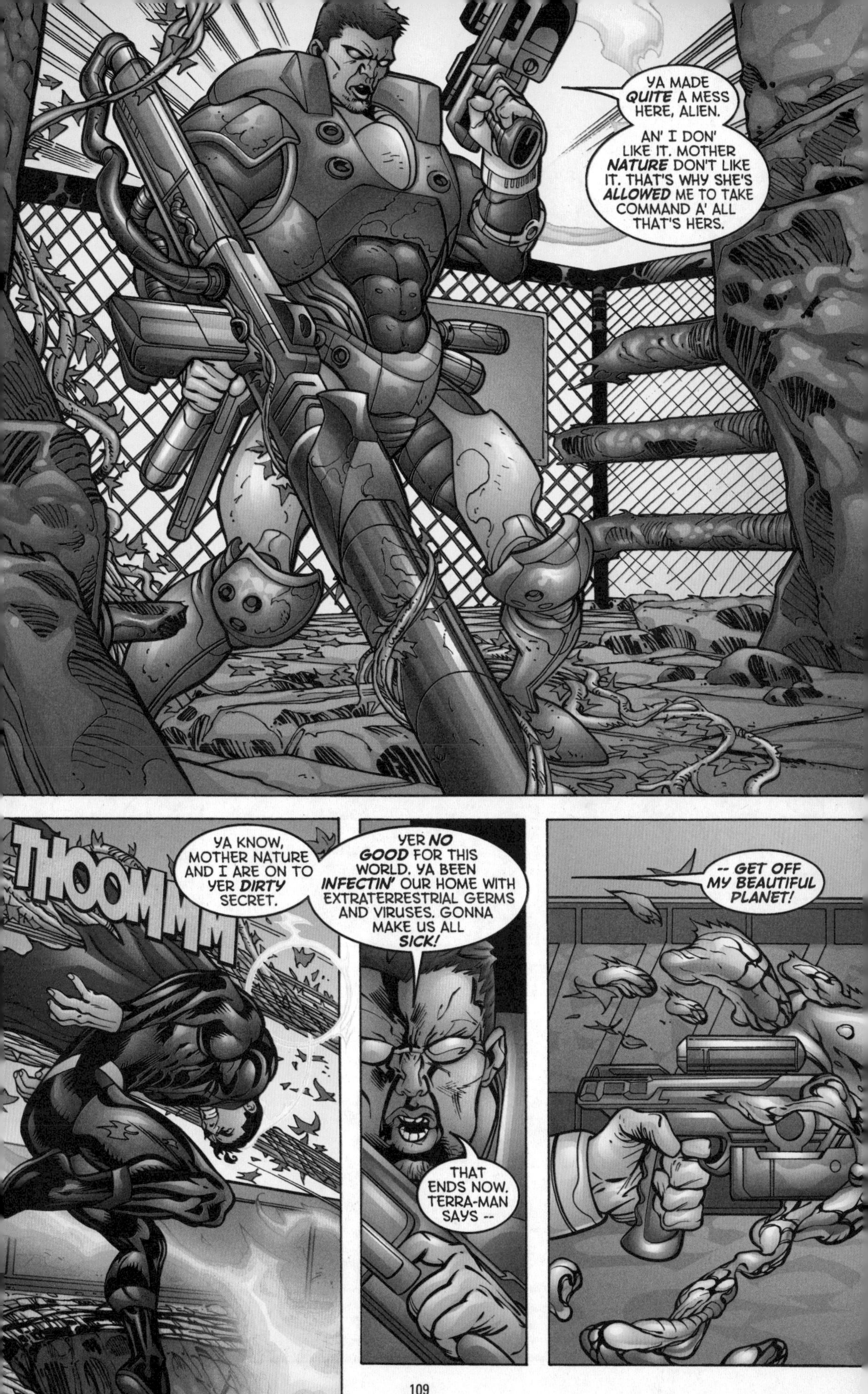
YA MADE QUITE A MESS HERE, ALIEN.
AN' I DON' LIKE IT. MOTHER NATURE DON'T LIKE IT. THAT'S WHY SHE'S ALLOWED ME TO TAKE COMMAND A' ALL THAT'S HERS.
THOOMMM
YA KNOW, MOTHER NATURE AND I ARE ON TO YER DIRTY SECRET.
YER NO GOOD FOR THIS WORLD. YA BEEN INFECTIN' OUR HOME WITH EXTRATERRESTRIAL GERMS AND VIRUSES. GONNA MAKE US ALL SICK!
THAT ENDS NOW. TERRA-MAN SAYS --
-- GET OFF MY BEAUTIFUL PLANET!

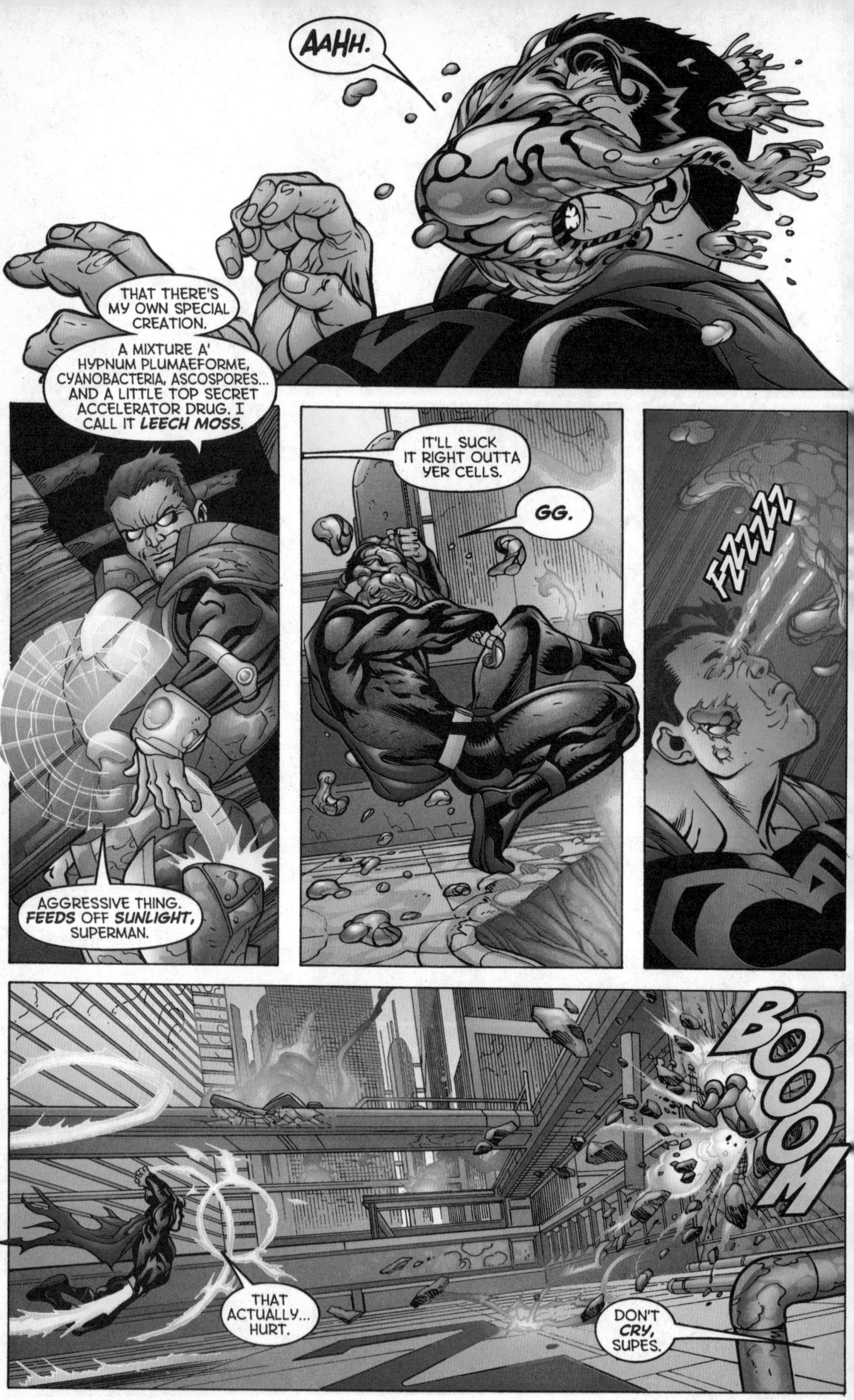
AAHH.
THAT THERE'S MY OWN SPECIAL CREATION.
A MIXTURE A' HYPNUM PLUMAEFORME, CYANOBACTERIA, ASCOSPORES... AND A LITTLE TOP SECRET ACCELERATOR DRUG. I CALL IT LEECH MOSS.
AGGRESSIVE THING. FEEDS OFF SUNLIGHT, SUPERMAN.
IT'LL SUCK IT RIGHT OUTTA YER CELLS.
GG.
FZZZZZZ
BOOOOM
THAT ACTUALLY... HURT.
DON'T CRY, SUPES.

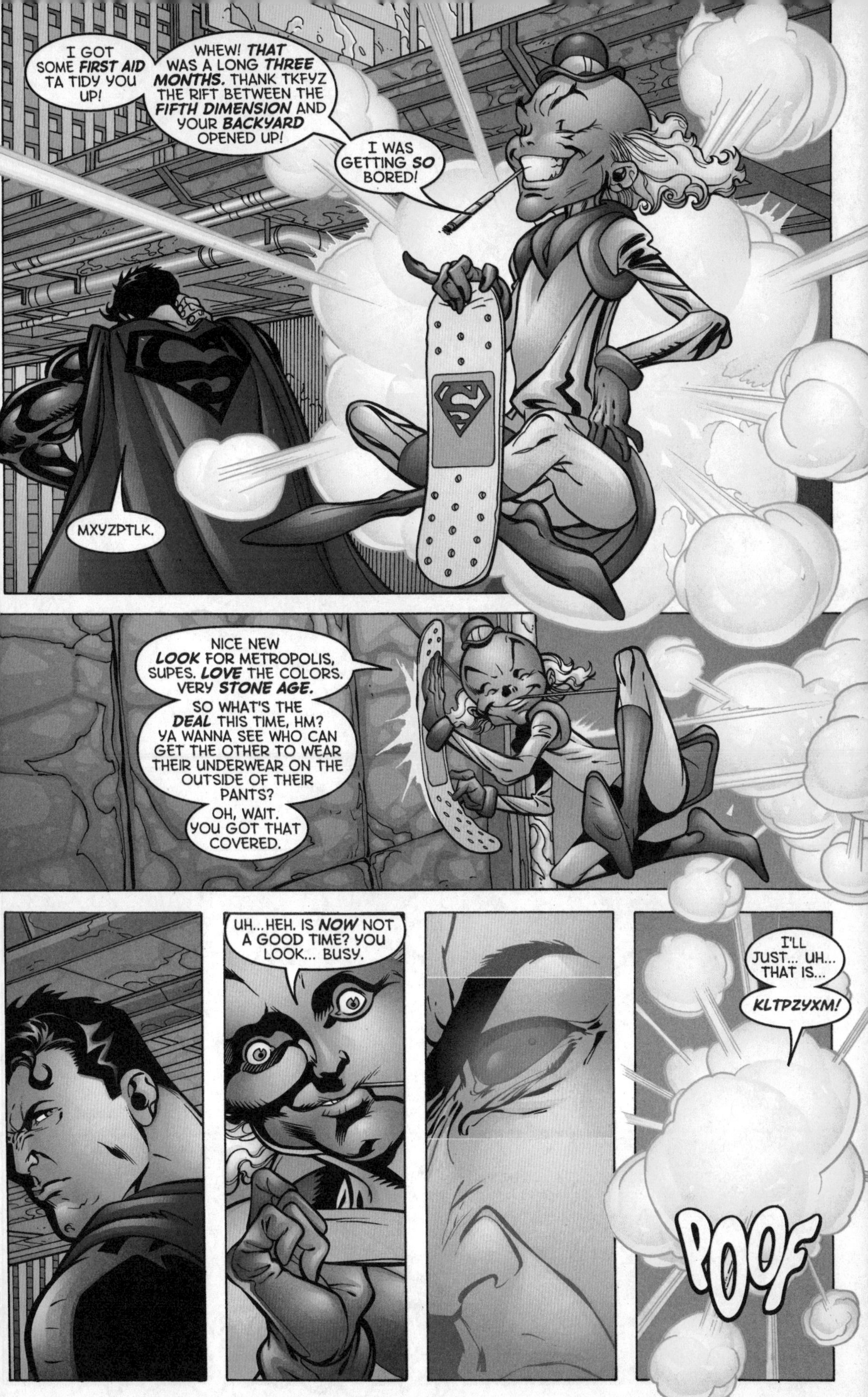
I GOT SOME FIRST AID TA TIDY YOU UP!
WHEW! THAT WAS A LONG THREE MONTHS. THANK TKFYZ THE RIFT BETWEEN THE FIFTH DIMENSION AND YOUR BACKYARD OPENED UP!
I WAS GETTING SO BORED!
MXYZPTLK.
NICE NEW LOOK FOR METROPOLIS, SUPES. LOVE THE COLORS. VERY STONE AGE.
SO WHAT'S THE DEAL THIS TIME, HM? YA WANNA SEE WHO CAN GET THE OTHER TO WEAR THEIR UNDERWEAR ON THE OUTSIDE OF THEIR PANTS?
OH, WAIT. YOU GOT THAT COVERED.
UH...HEH. IS NOW NOT A GOOD TIME? YOU LOOK... BUSY.
I'LL JUST... UH... THAT IS...
KLTPZYXM!
POOF

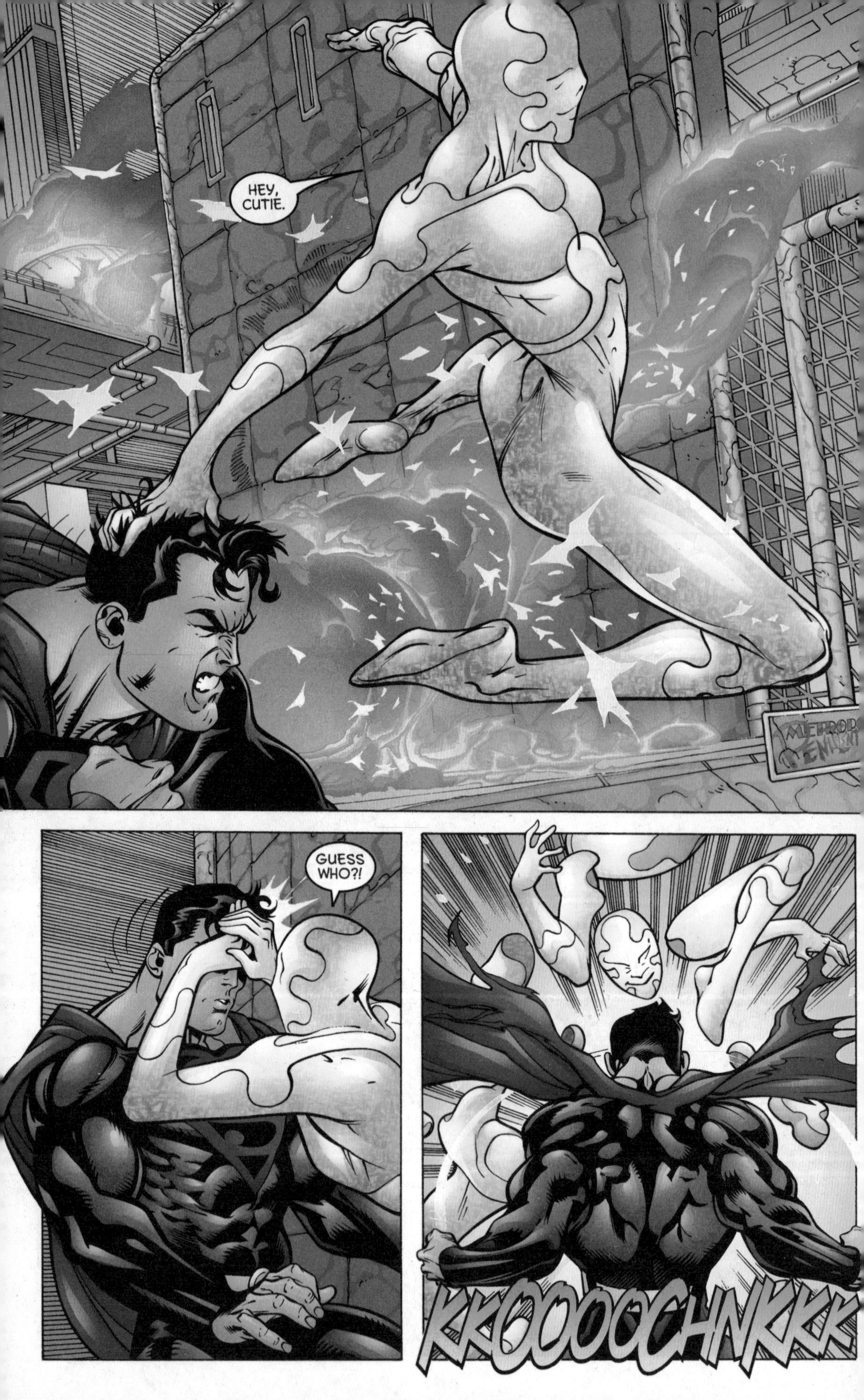
HEY, CUTIE.
GUESS WHO?!
KKOOOOCHNKKK

FWMMPP
FWMMPP

CHAK
CHAK
CHAK

OKAY, OKAY. I'LL *TELL* YOU SPOIL-SPORT.

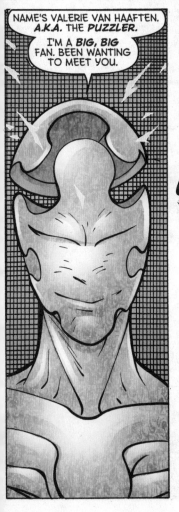

NAME'S VALERIE VAN HAAFTEN, *A.K.A.* THE *PUZZLER*.

I'M A *BIG, BIG* FAN. BEEN WANTING TO MEET YOU.

'COURSE I COULD *NEVER* JOIN THE JUSTICE LEAGUE. HECK, EVEN THE *OUTSIDERS* WOULDN'T RETURN MY *E-MAILS*.

SO I THOUGHT GETTING YOUR ATTENTION WOULD BE EASIER THIS WAY.

I'M GONNA BE ONE OF YOUR *ARCHVILLAINS*... WELL, AT THE LEAST I'LL BE A *REALLY* GOOD *THIEF*, YA KNOW, LEAVIN' CLUES FOR YOU TO FOLLOW...

I *LOVE* YOUR SHOULDERS.

YOU *SINGLE?*

THAT'S NONE OF YOUR BUSINESS.

HEY! I'M MAKIN' IT MY BUSINESS.

LIKE IT OR NOT, YOU AND I ARE GONNA FIT TOGETHER LIKE PIECES IN A PUZZ --

BWOOSSHHH

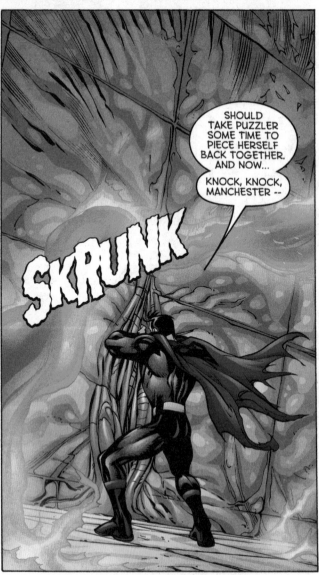

SHOULD TAKE PUZZLER SOME TIME TO PIECE HERSELF BACK TOGETHER. AND NOW...

KNOCK, KNOCK, MANCHESTER --

SKRUNK

-- BLACK?

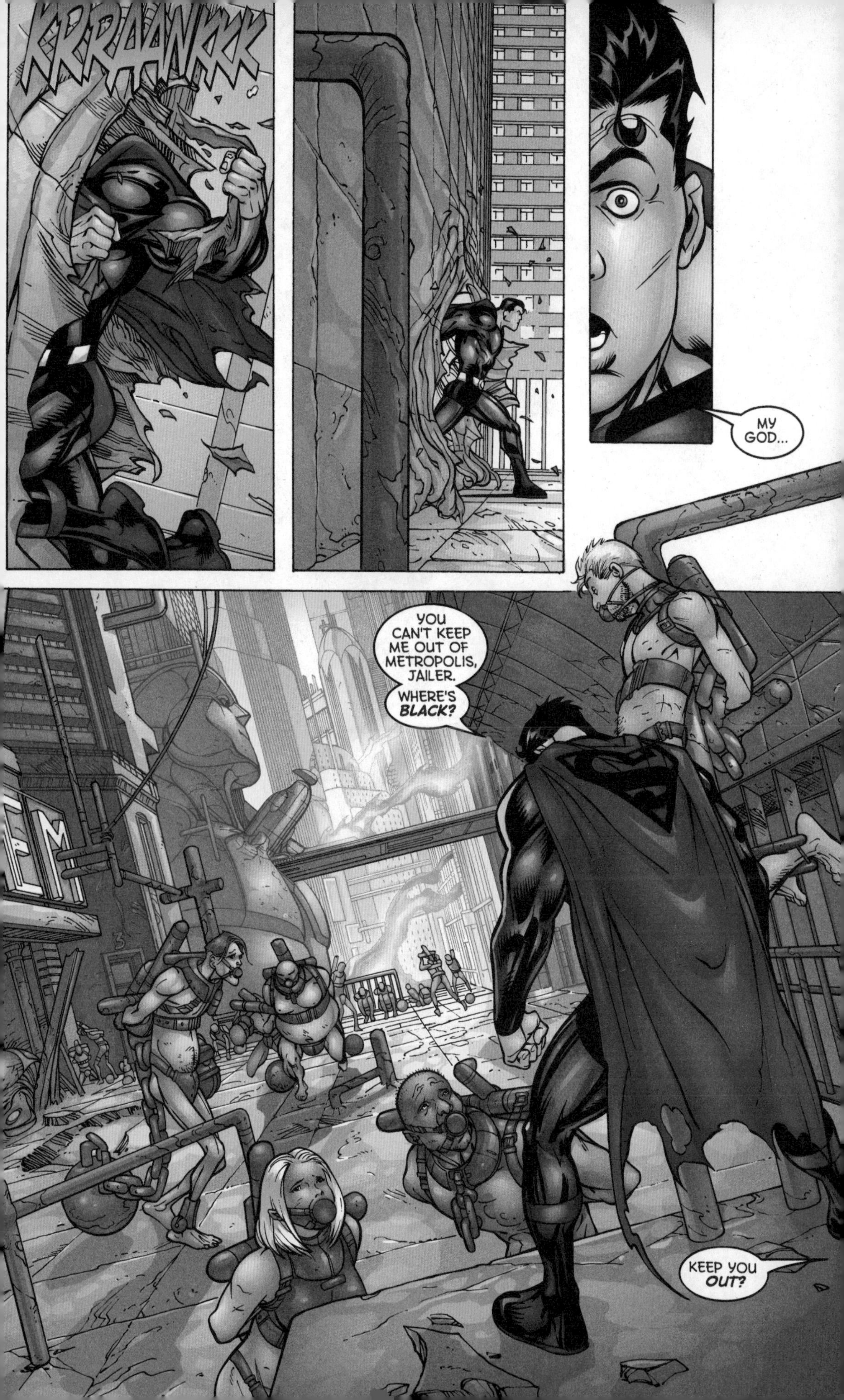
KRRAANKK
MY GOD...
YOU CAN'T KEEP ME OUT OF METROPOLIS, JAILER.
WHERE'S *BLACK?*
KEEP YOU *OUT?*

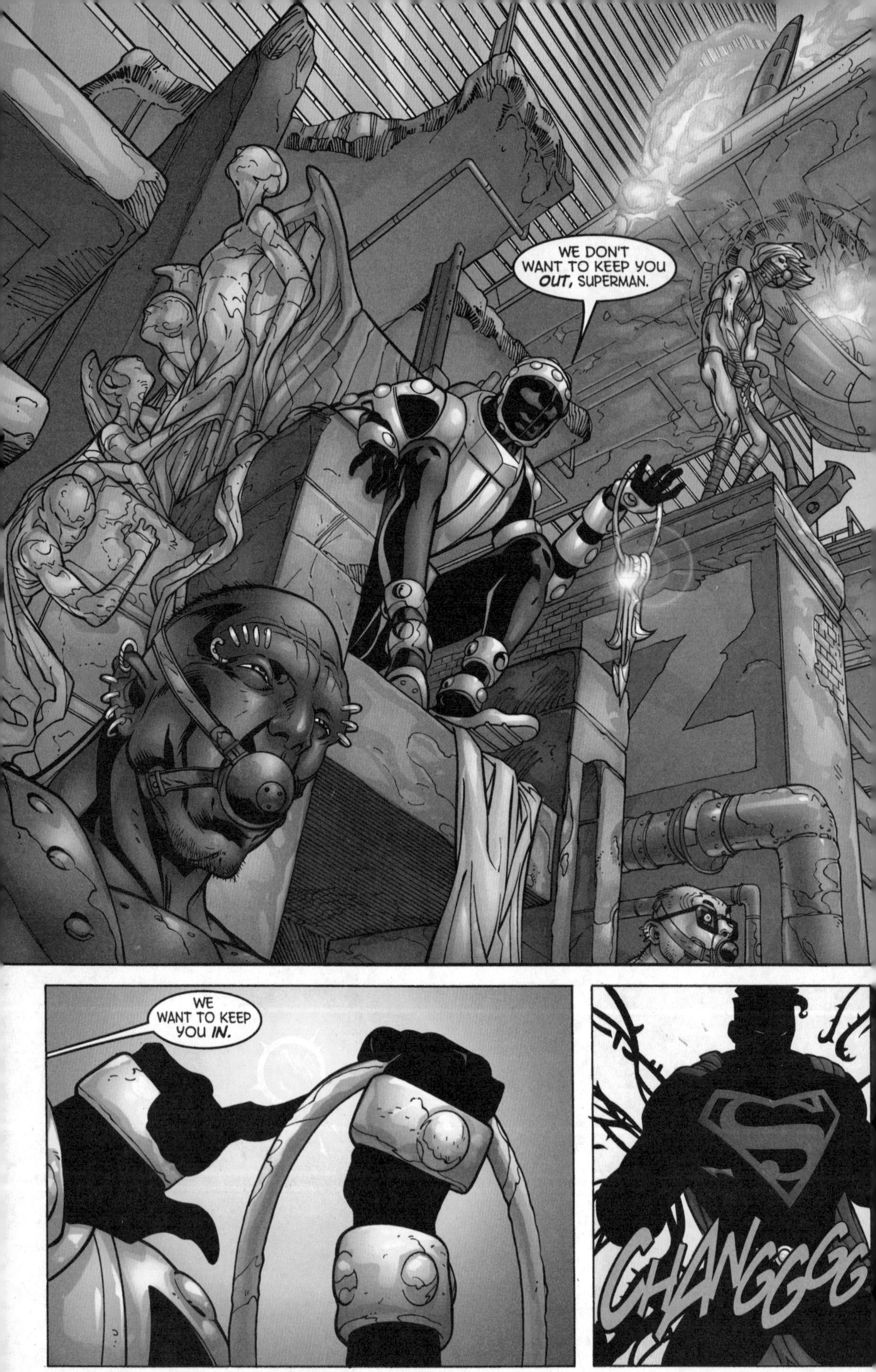
WE DON'T WANT TO KEEP YOU *OUT,* SUPERMAN.
WE WANT TO KEEP YOU *IN.*
CHANGGGG

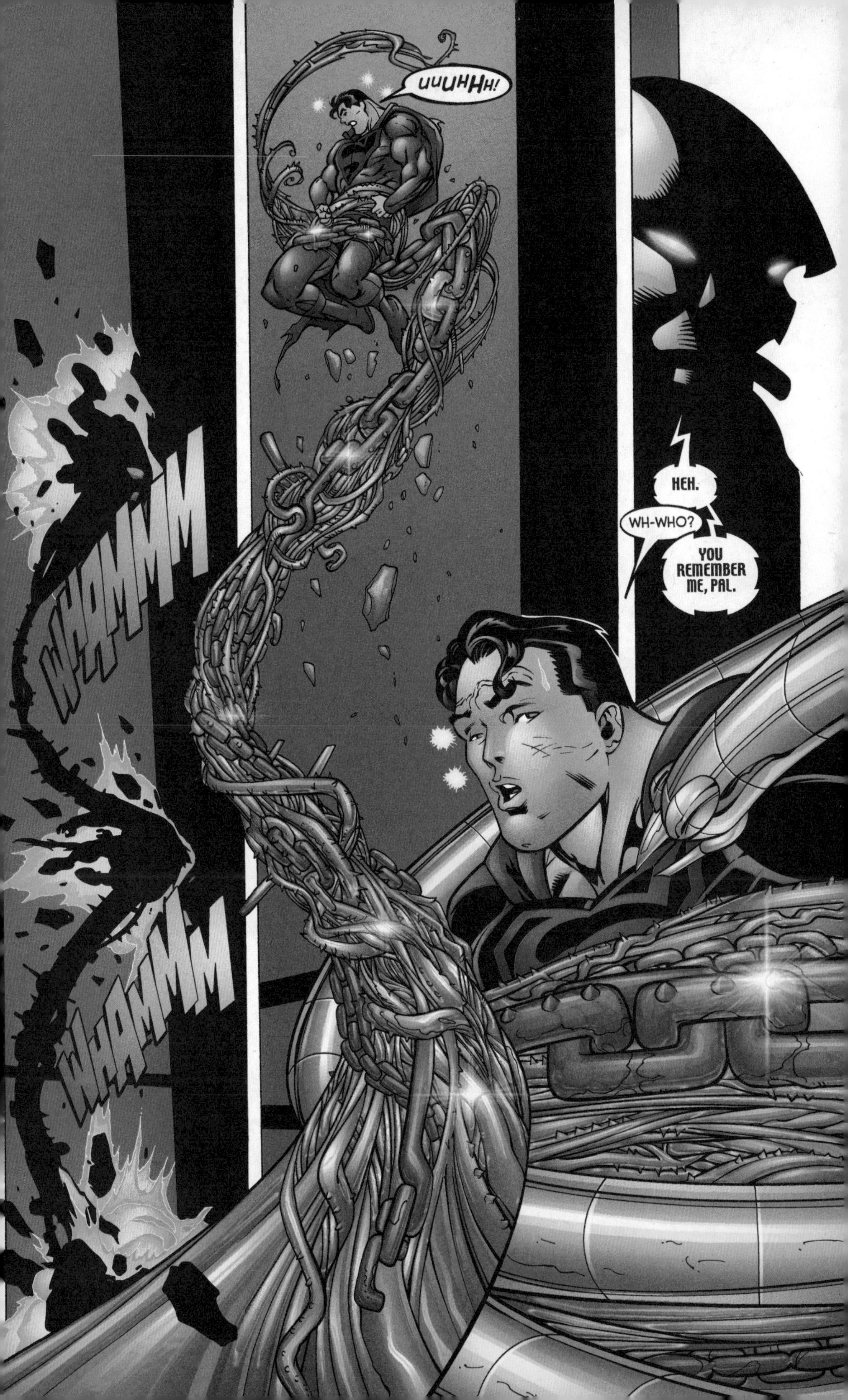
WHAMMM
WHAMMM
UUUHHH!
HEH.
WH-WHO?
YOU REMEMBER ME, PAL.

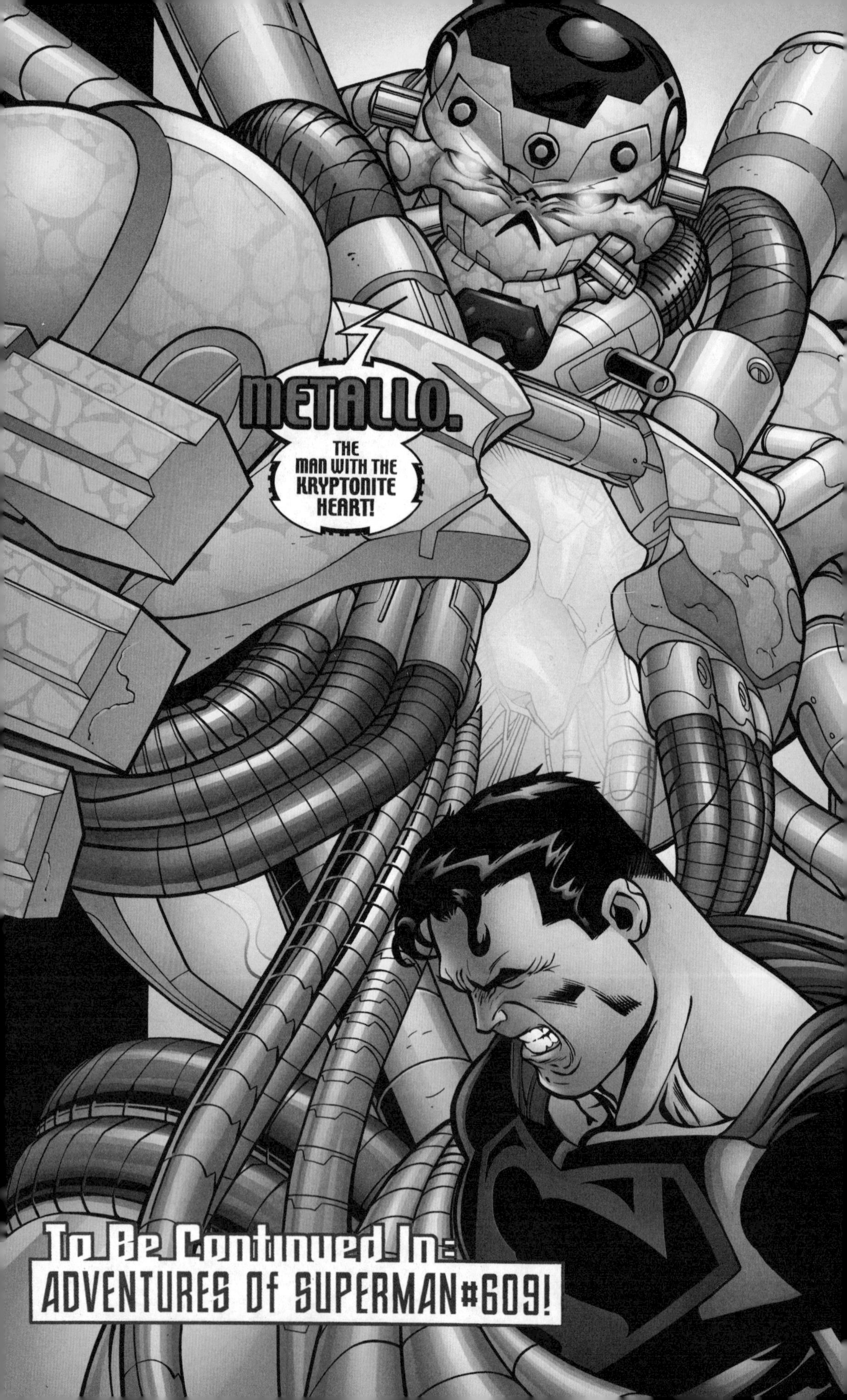
METALLO.
THE MAN WITH THE KRYPTONITE HEART!
To Be Continued In:
ADVENTURES Of SUPERMAN#609!

Cover art by KEVIN NOWLAN

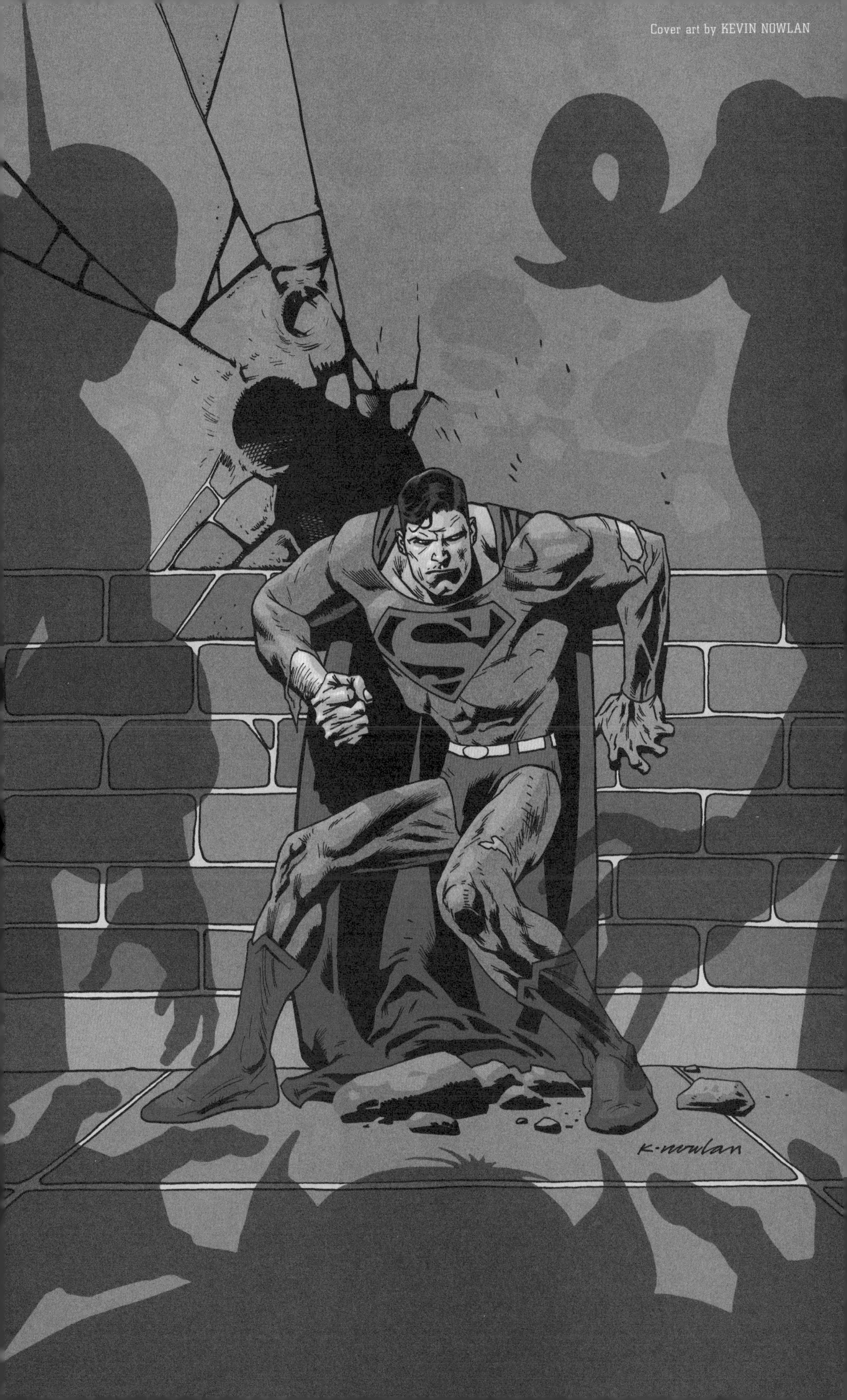
K-nowlan

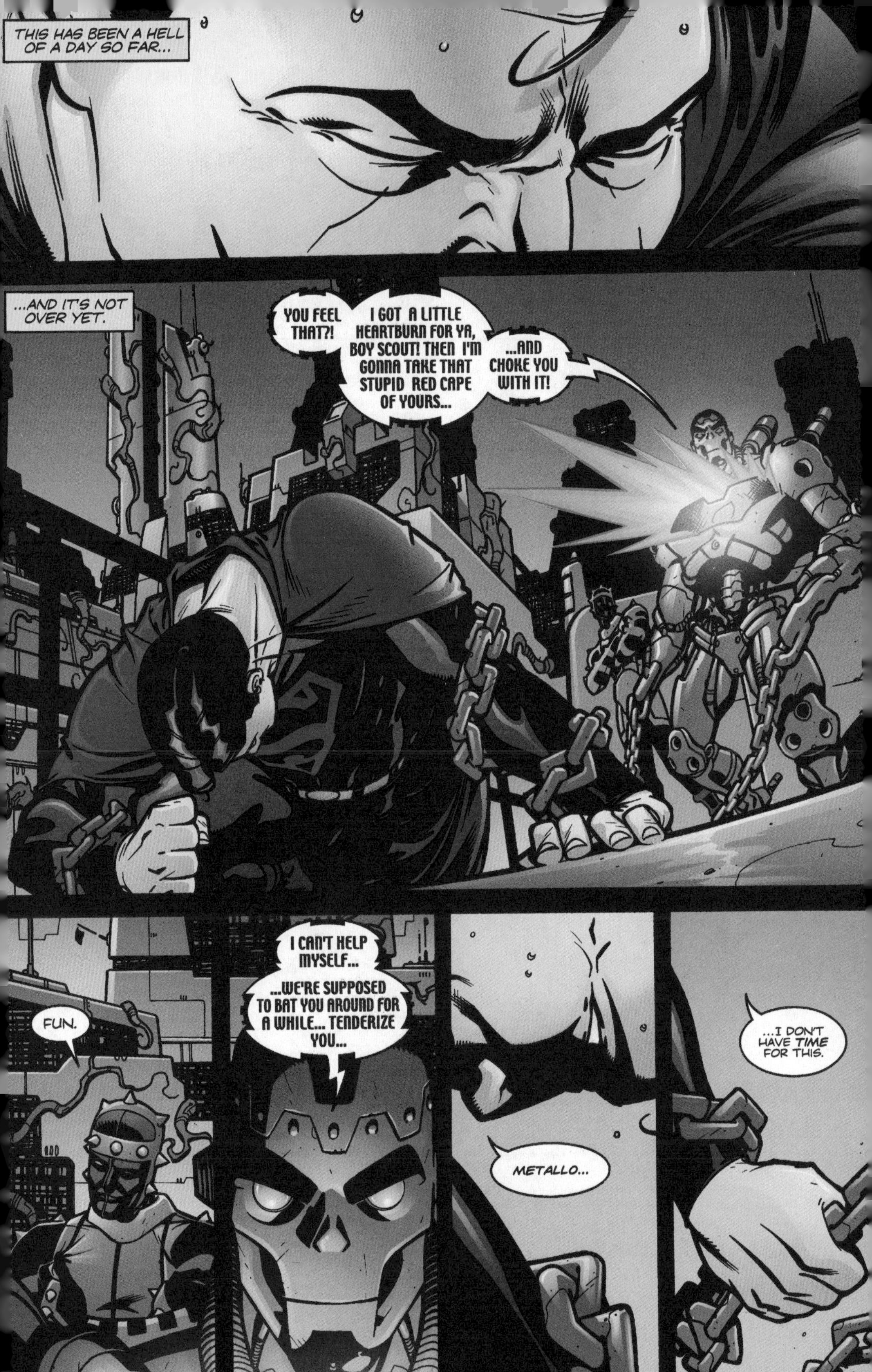
THIS HAS BEEN A HELL OF A DAY SO FAR...
...AND IT'S NOT OVER YET.
YOU FEEL THAT?!
I GOT A LITTLE HEARTBURN FOR YA, BOY SCOUT! THEN I'M GONNA TAKE THAT STUPID RED CAPE OF YOURS...
...AND CHOKE YOU WITH IT!
FUN.
I CAN'T HELP MYSELF...
...WE'RE SUPPOSED TO BAT YOU AROUND FOR A WHILE... TENDERIZE YOU...
METALLO...
...I DON'T HAVE TIME FOR THIS.

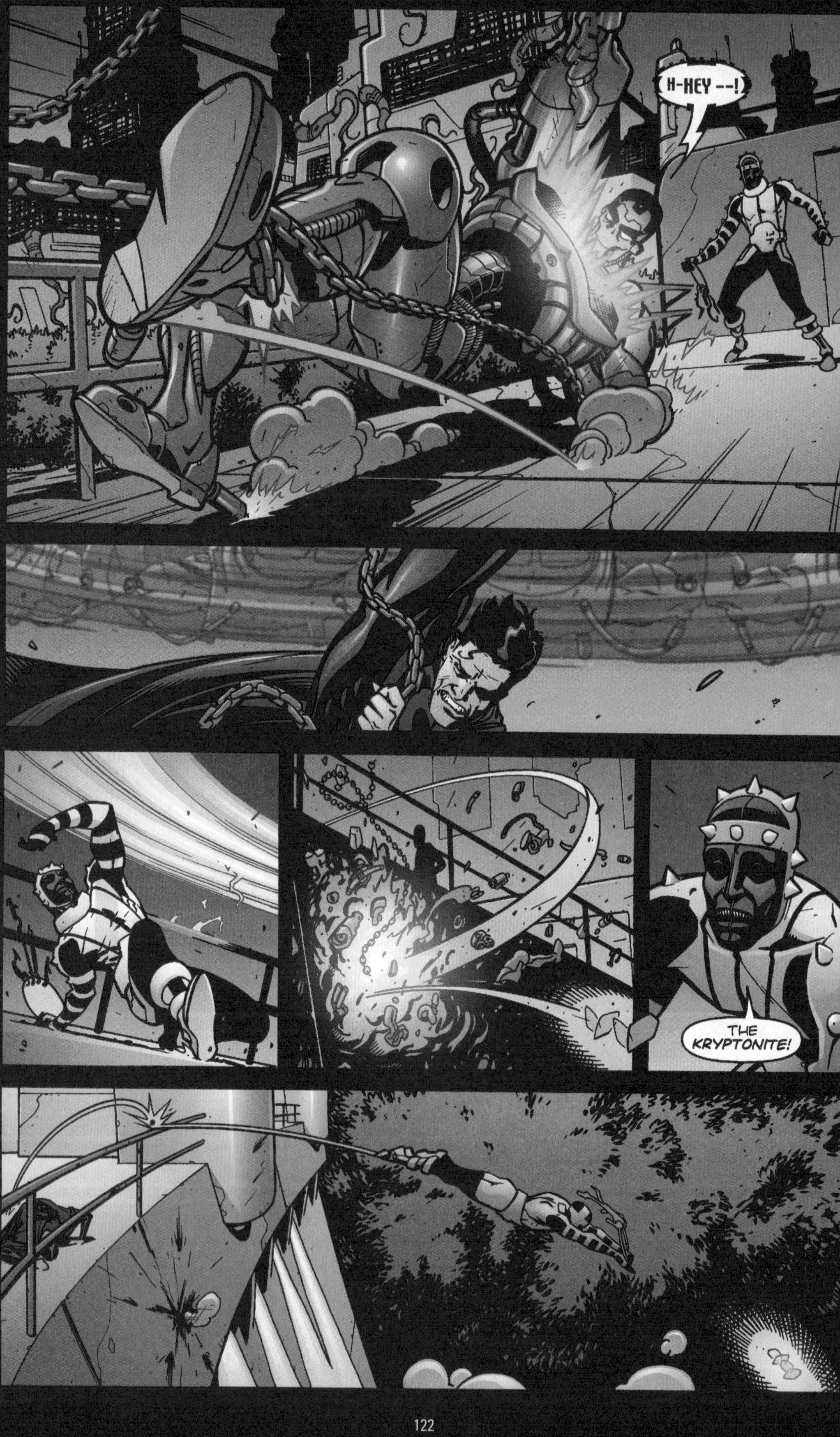
H-HEY --!
THE KRYPTONITE!

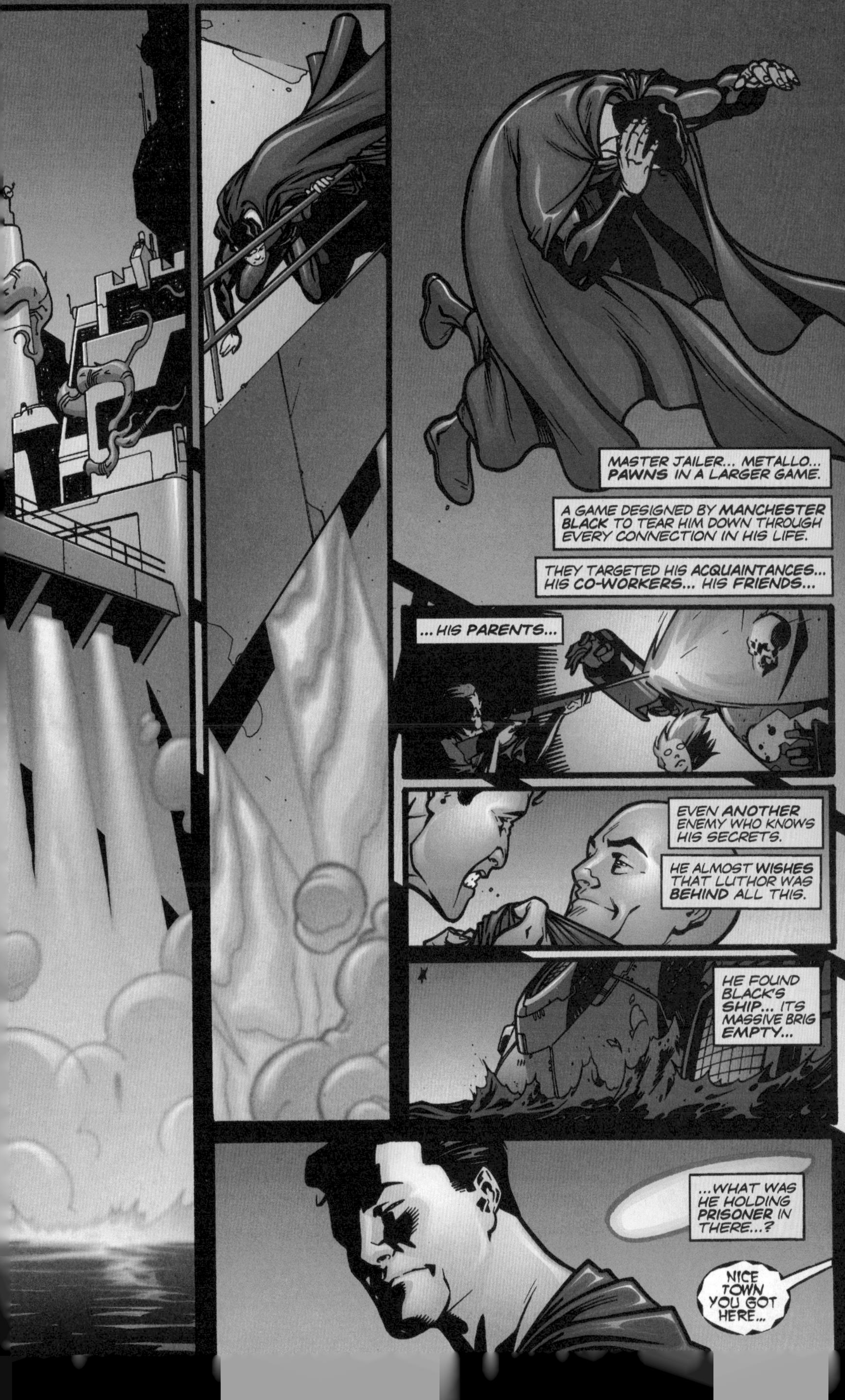
MASTER JAILER... METALLO... PAWNS IN A LARGER GAME.
A GAME DESIGNED BY MANCHESTER BLACK TO TEAR HIM DOWN THROUGH EVERY CONNECTION IN HIS LIFE.
THEY TARGETED HIS ACQUAINTANCES... HIS CO-WORKERS... HIS FRIENDS...
...HIS PARENTS...
EVEN ANOTHER ENEMY WHO KNOWS HIS SECRETS.
HE ALMOST WISHES THAT LUTHOR WAS BEHIND ALL THIS.
HE FOUND BLACK'S SHIP... ITS MASSIVE BRIG EMPTY...
...WHAT WAS HE HOLDING PRISONER IN THERE...?
NICE TOWN YOU GOT HERE...

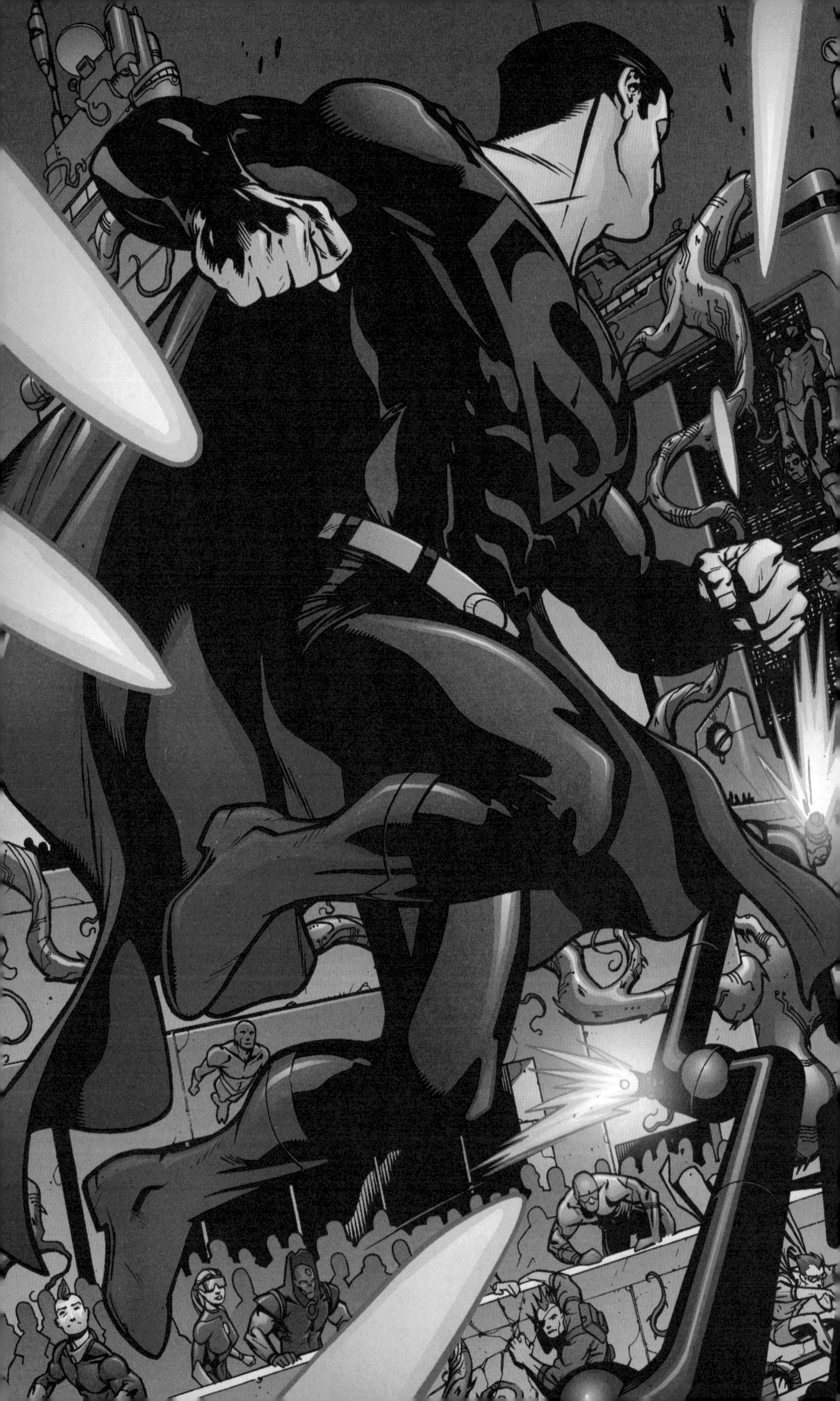

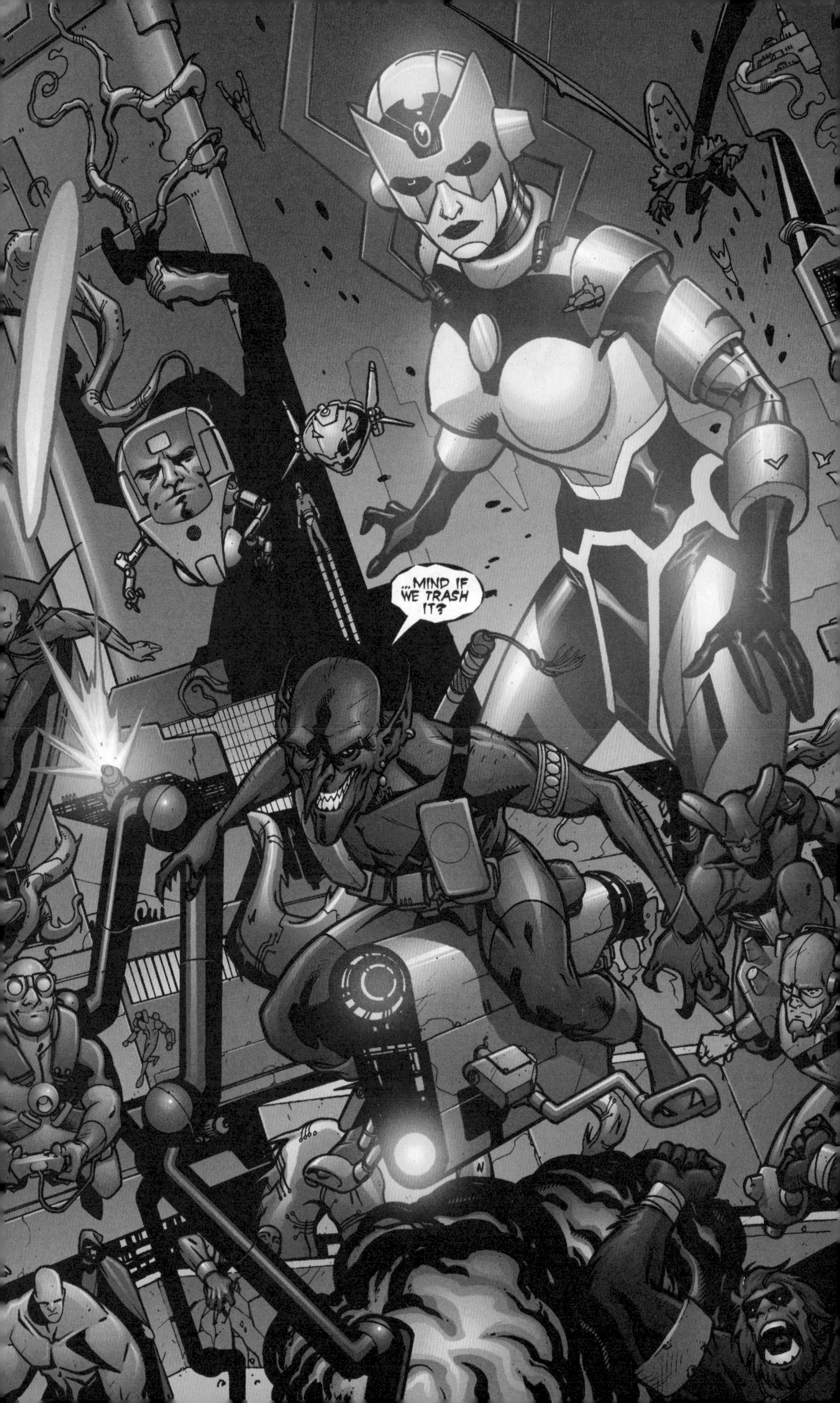
...MIND IF WE TRASH IT?

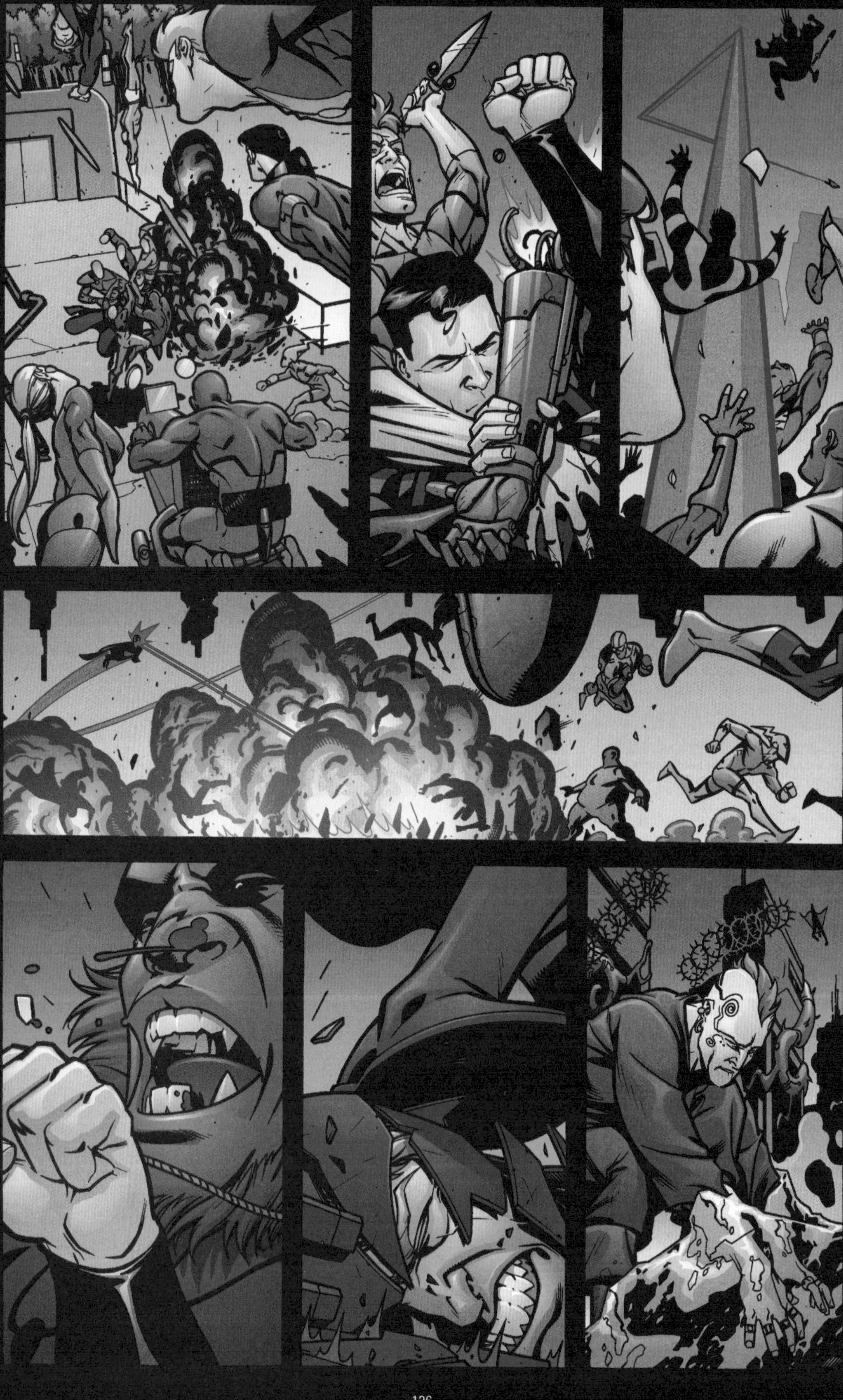

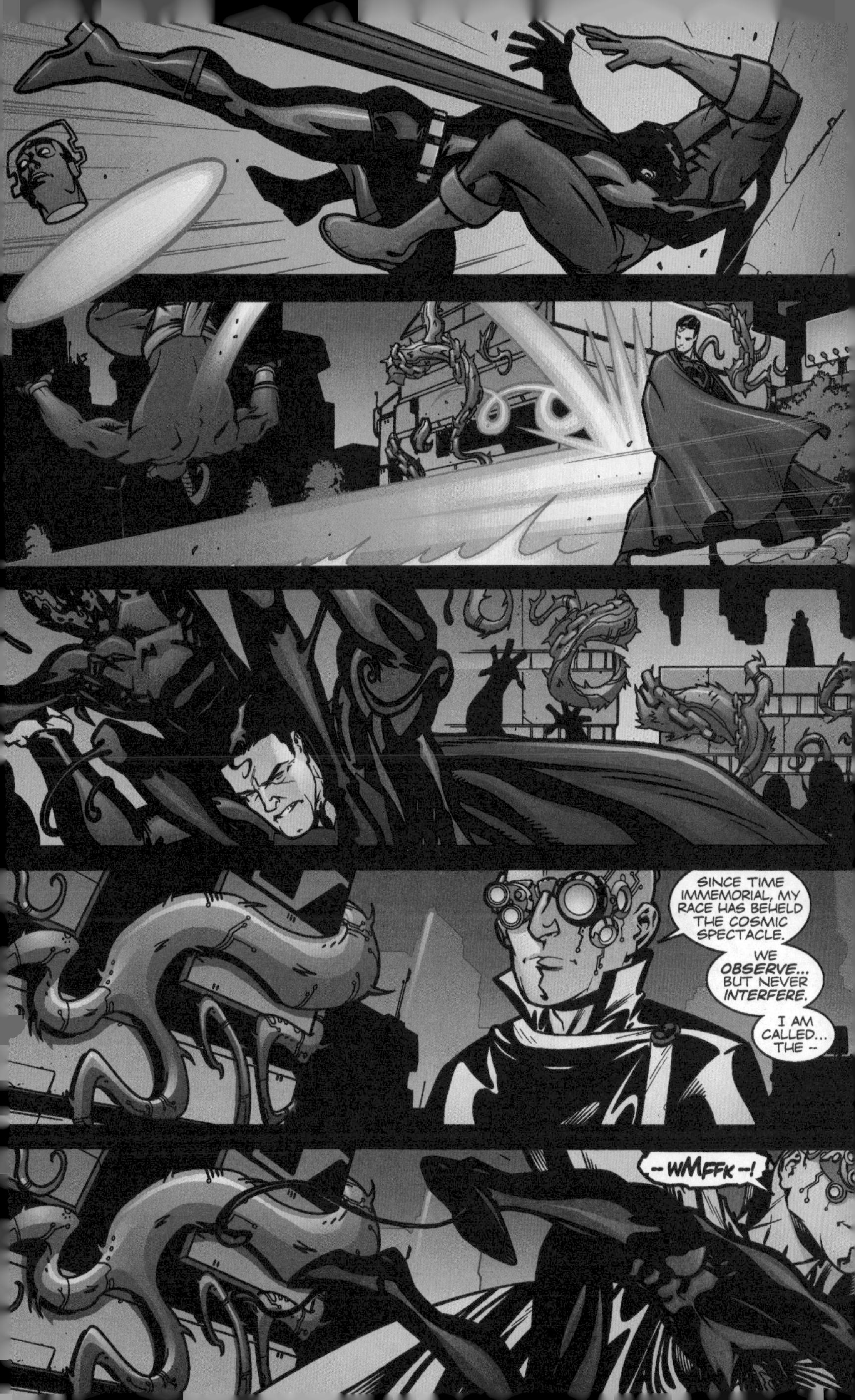
SINCE TIME IMMEMORIAL, MY RACE HAS BEHELD THE COSMIC SPECTACLE.
WE OBSERVE... BUT NEVER INTERFERE.
I AM CALLED... THE --
-- WMFFK --!

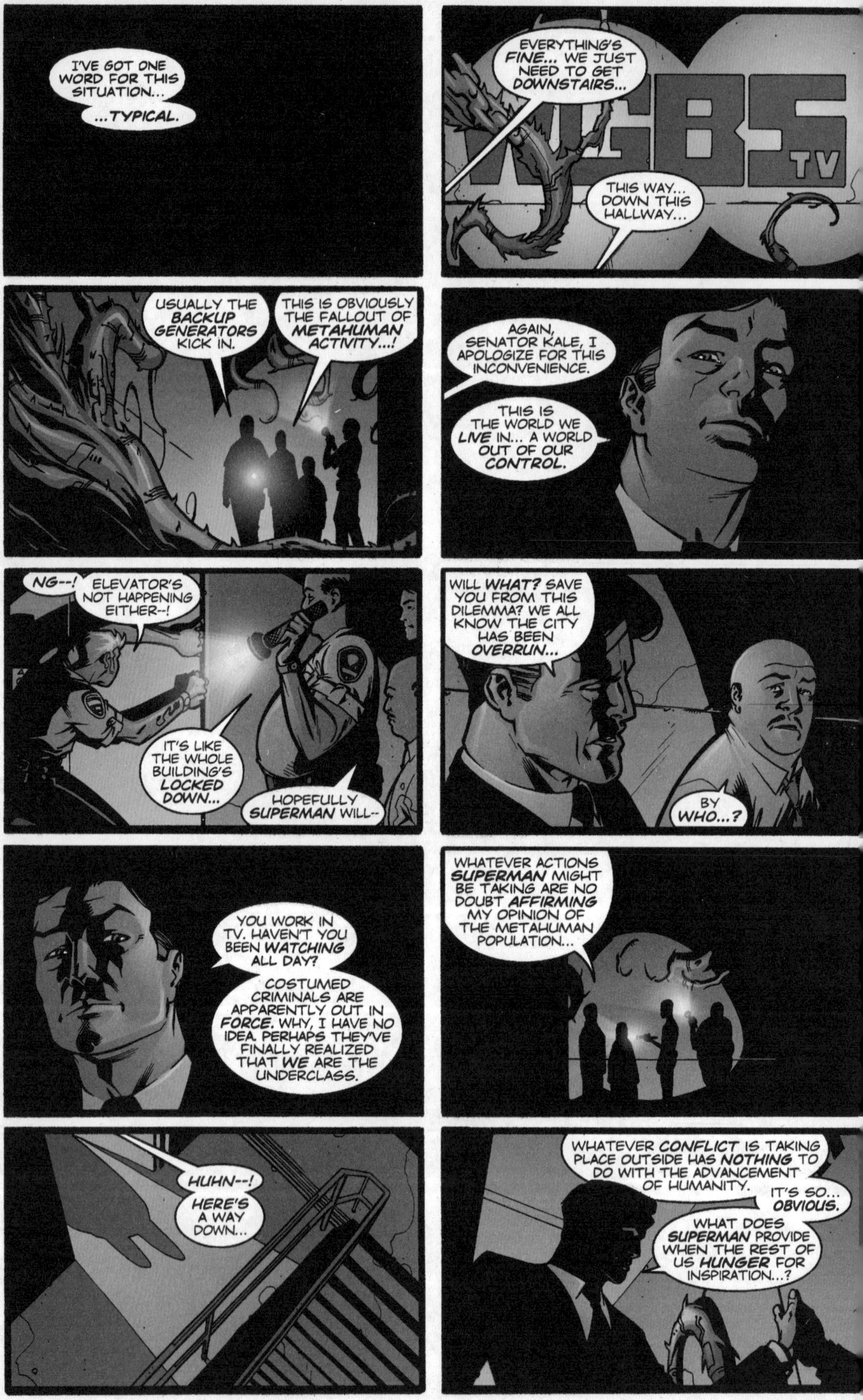
I'VE GOT ONE WORD FOR THIS SITUATION...
...TYPICAL.
EVERYTHING'S FINE... WE JUST NEED TO GET DOWNSTAIRS...
WGBS TV
THIS WAY... DOWN THIS HALLWAY...
USUALLY THE BACKUP GENERATORS KICK IN.
THIS IS OBVIOUSLY THE FALLOUT OF METAHUMAN ACTIVITY...!
AGAIN, SENATOR KALE, I APOLOGIZE FOR THIS INCONVENIENCE.
THIS IS THE WORLD WE LIVE IN... A WORLD OUT OF OUR CONTROL.
NG--!
ELEVATOR'S NOT HAPPENING EITHER--!
IT'S LIKE THE WHOLE BUILDING'S LOCKED DOWN...
HOPEFULLY SUPERMAN WILL--
WILL WHAT? SAVE YOU FROM THIS DILEMMA? WE ALL KNOW THE CITY HAS BEEN OVERRUN...
BY WHO...?
YOU WORK IN TV. HAVEN'T YOU BEEN WATCHING ALL DAY?
COSTUMED CRIMINALS ARE APPARENTLY OUT IN FORCE. WHY, I HAVE NO IDEA. PERHAPS THEY'VE FINALLY REALIZED THAT WE ARE THE UNDERCLASS.
WHATEVER ACTIONS SUPERMAN MIGHT BE TAKING ARE NO DOUBT AFFIRMING MY OPINION OF THE METAHUMAN POPULATION...
HUHN--!
HERE'S A WAY DOWN...
WHATEVER CONFLICT IS TAKING PLACE OUTSIDE HAS NOTHING TO DO WITH THE ADVANCEMENT OF HUMANITY.
IT'S SO... OBVIOUS.
WHAT DOES SUPERMAN PROVIDE WHEN THE REST OF US HUNGER FOR INSPIRATION...?

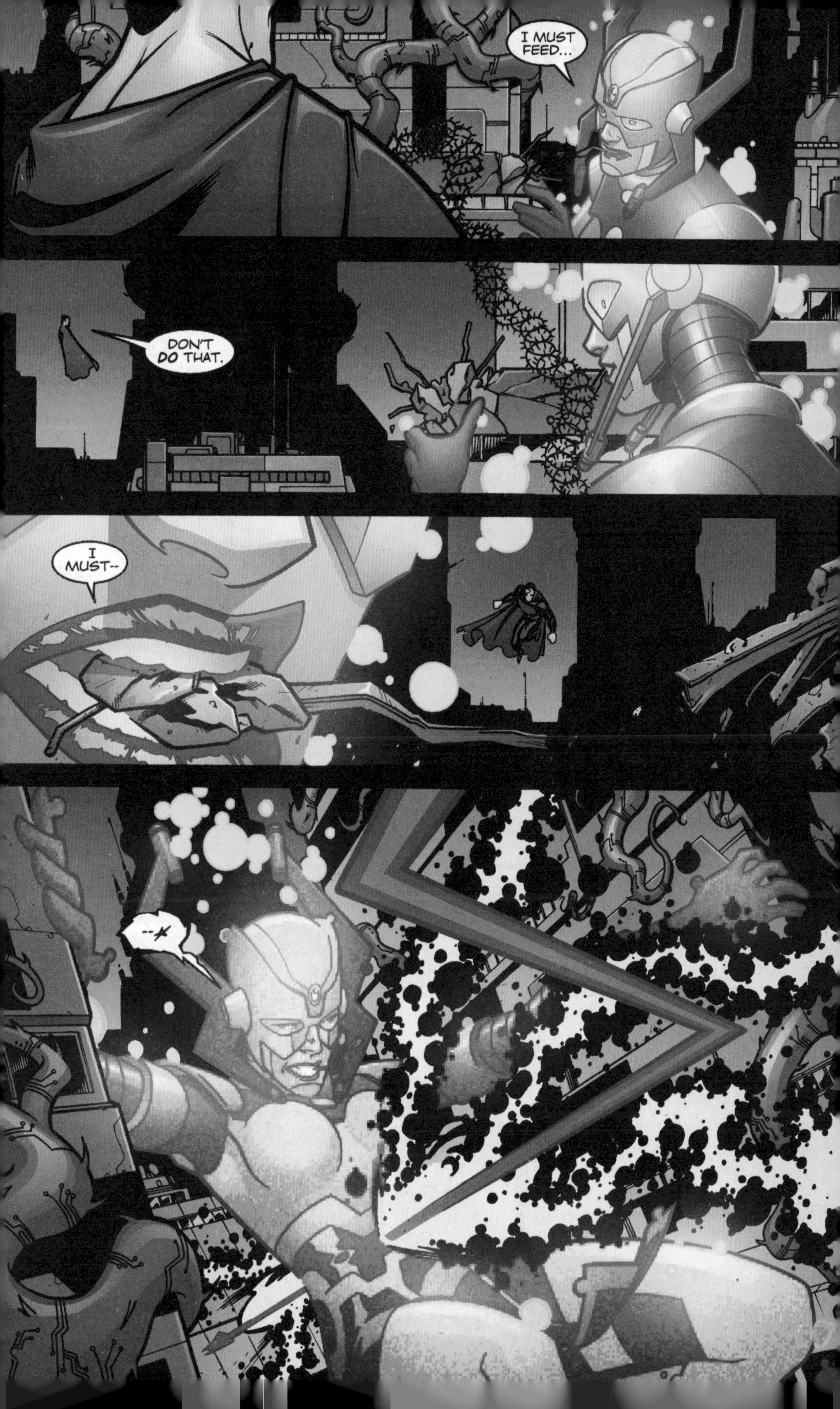
I MUST FEED...
DON'T DO THAT.
I MUST--
--*

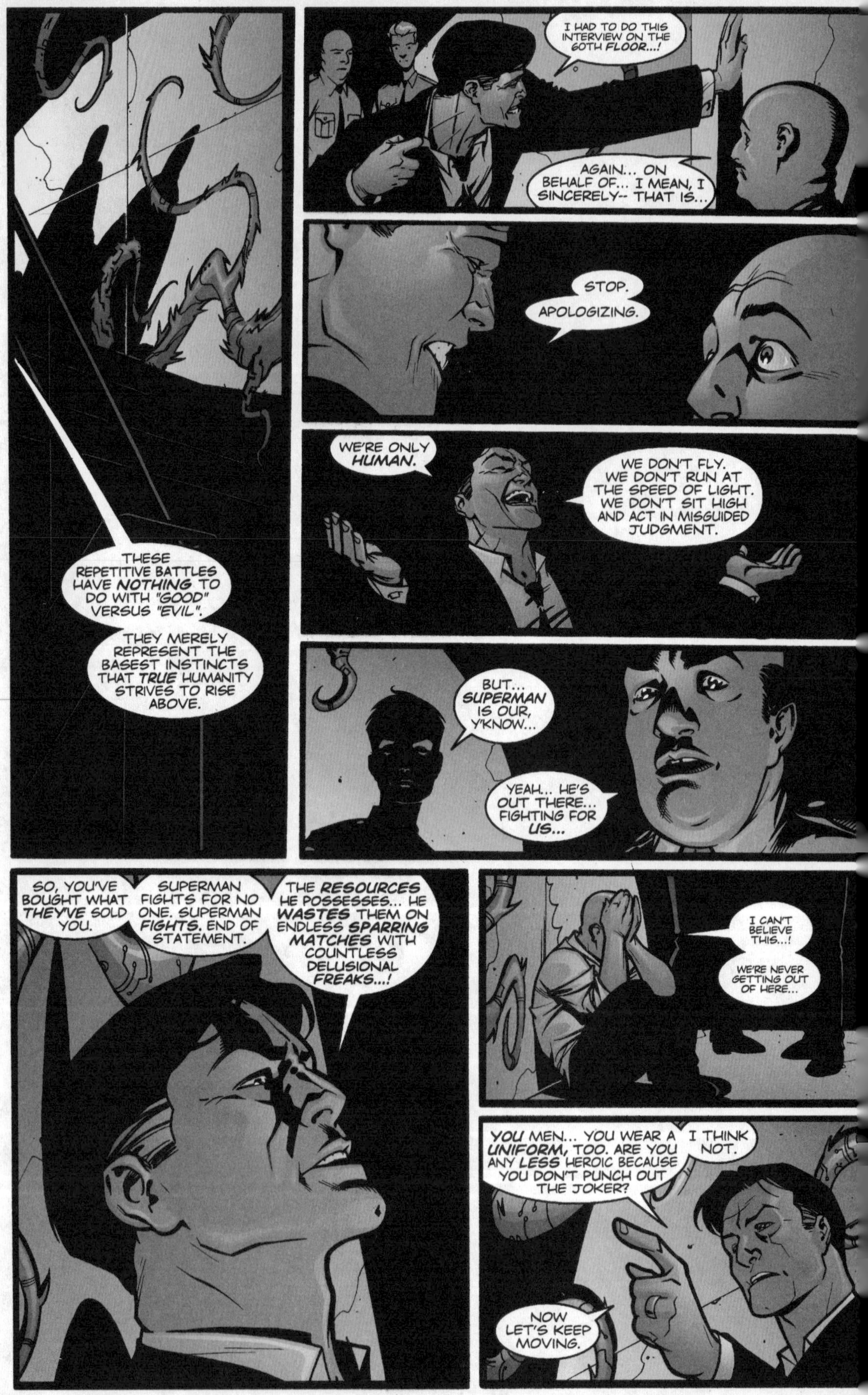
I HAD TO DO THIS INTERVIEW ON THE 60TH FLOOR...!
AGAIN... ON BEHALF OF... I MEAN, I SINCERELY-- THAT IS...
STOP.
APOLOGIZING.
WE'RE ONLY HUMAN.
WE DON'T FLY. WE DON'T RUN AT THE SPEED OF LIGHT. WE DON'T SIT HIGH AND ACT IN MISGUIDED JUDGMENT.
THESE REPETITIVE BATTLES HAVE NOTHING TO DO WITH "GOOD" VERSUS "EVIL".
THEY MERELY REPRESENT THE BASEST INSTINCTS THAT TRUE HUMANITY STRIVES TO RISE ABOVE.
BUT... SUPERMAN IS OUR, Y'KNOW...
YEAH... HE'S OUT THERE... FIGHTING FOR US...
SO, YOU'VE BOUGHT WHAT THEY'VE SOLD YOU.
SUPERMAN FIGHTS FOR NO ONE. SUPERMAN FIGHTS. END OF STATEMENT.
THE RESOURCES HE POSSESSES... HE WASTES THEM ON ENDLESS SPARRING MATCHES WITH COUNTLESS DELUSIONAL FREAKS...!
I CAN'T BELIEVE THIS...!
WE'RE NEVER GETTING OUT OF HERE...
YOU MEN... YOU WEAR A UNIFORM, TOO. ARE YOU ANY LESS HEROIC BECAUSE YOU DON'T PUNCH OUT THE JOKER?
I THINK NOT.
NOW LET'S KEEP MOVING.

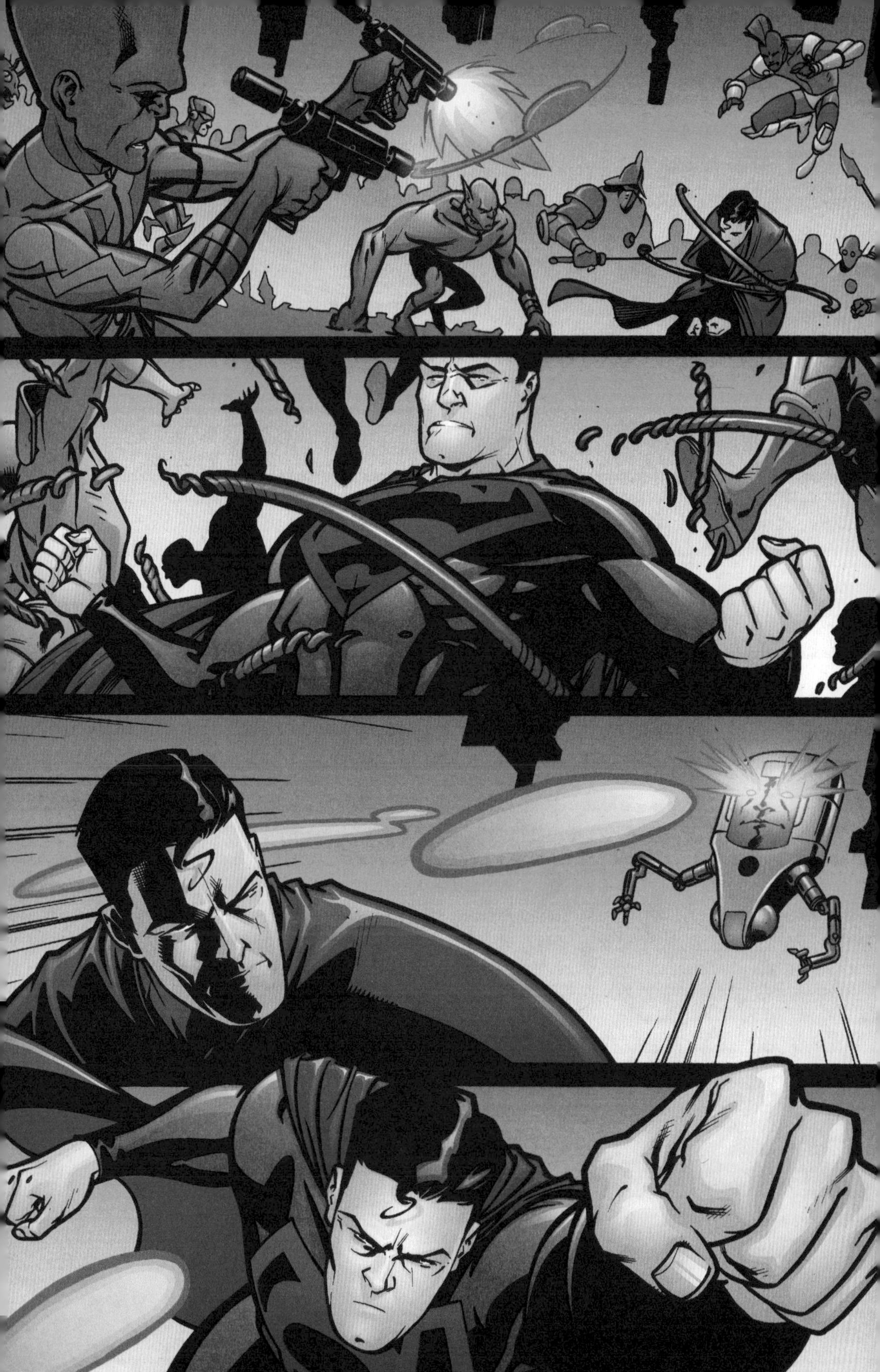

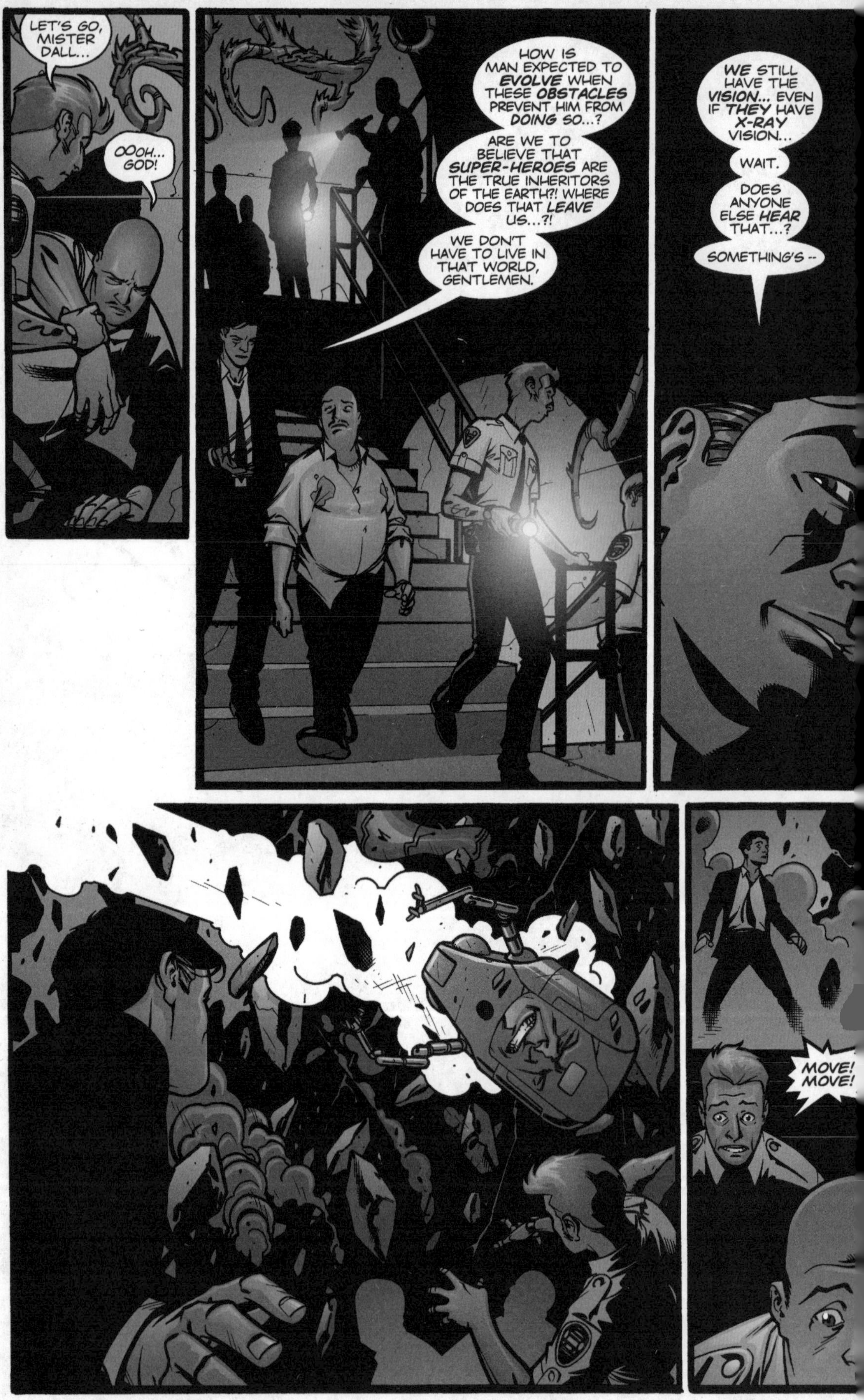
LET'S GO, MISTER DALL...
OOOH... GOD!
HOW IS MAN EXPECTED TO EVOLVE WHEN THESE OBSTACLES PREVENT HIM FROM DOING SO...?
ARE WE TO BELIEVE THAT SUPER-HEROES ARE THE TRUE INHERITORS OF THE EARTH?! WHERE DOES THAT LEAVE US...?!
WE DON'T HAVE TO LIVE IN THAT WORLD, GENTLEMEN.
WE STILL HAVE THE VISION... EVEN IF THEY HAVE X-RAY VISION...
WAIT.
DOES ANYONE ELSE HEAR THAT...?
SOMETHING'S --
MOVE! MOVE!

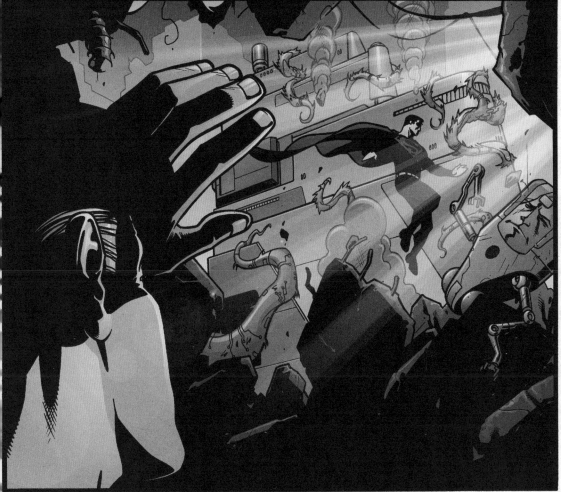

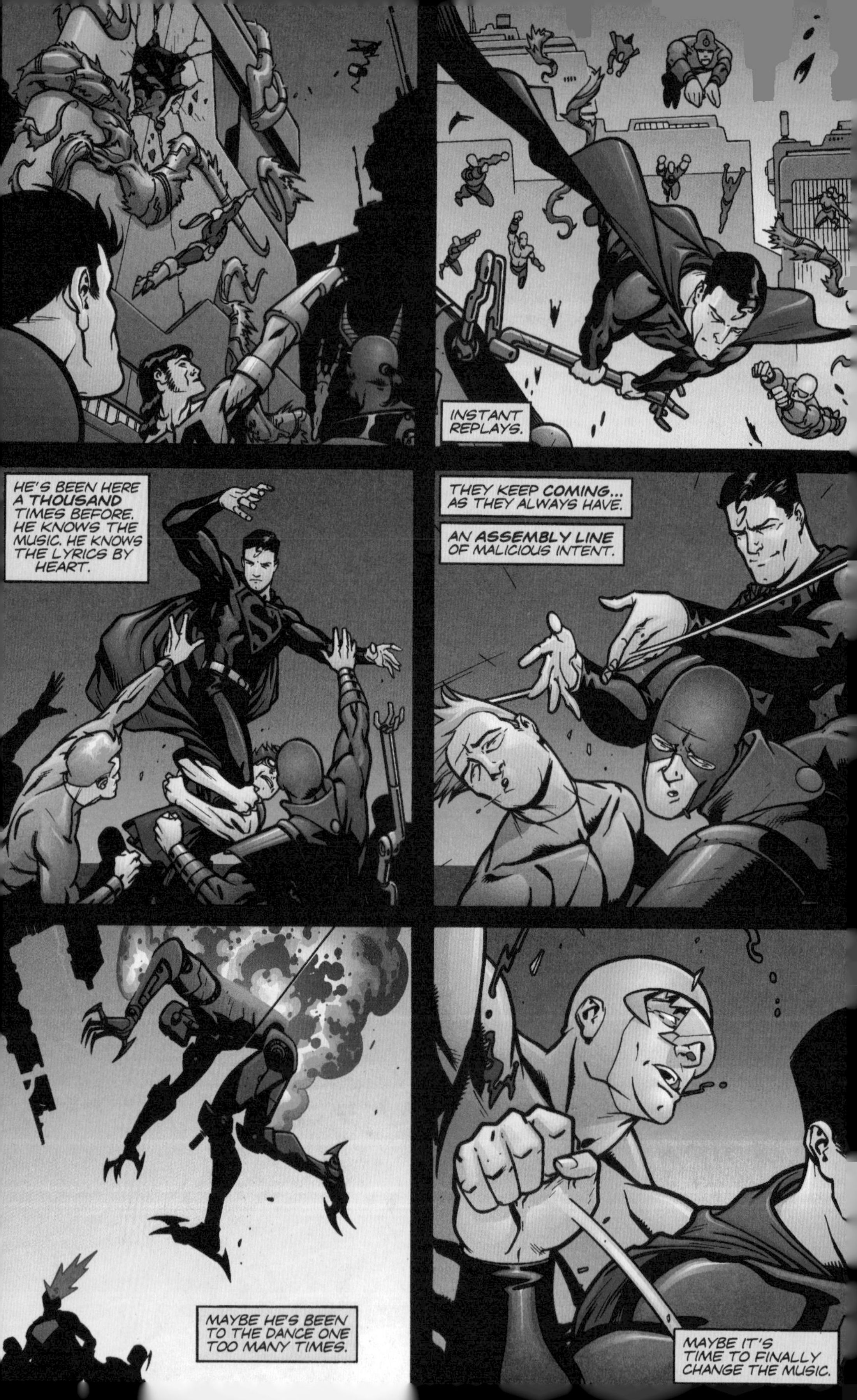
INSTANT REPLAYS.
HE'S BEEN HERE A THOUSAND TIMES BEFORE. HE KNOWS THE MUSIC. HE KNOWS THE LYRICS BY HEART.
THEY KEEP COMING... AS THEY ALWAYS HAVE.
AN ASSEMBLY LINE OF MALICIOUS INTENT.
MAYBE HE'S BEEN TO THE DANCE ONE TOO MANY TIMES.
MAYBE IT'S TIME TO FINALLY CHANGE THE MUSIC.

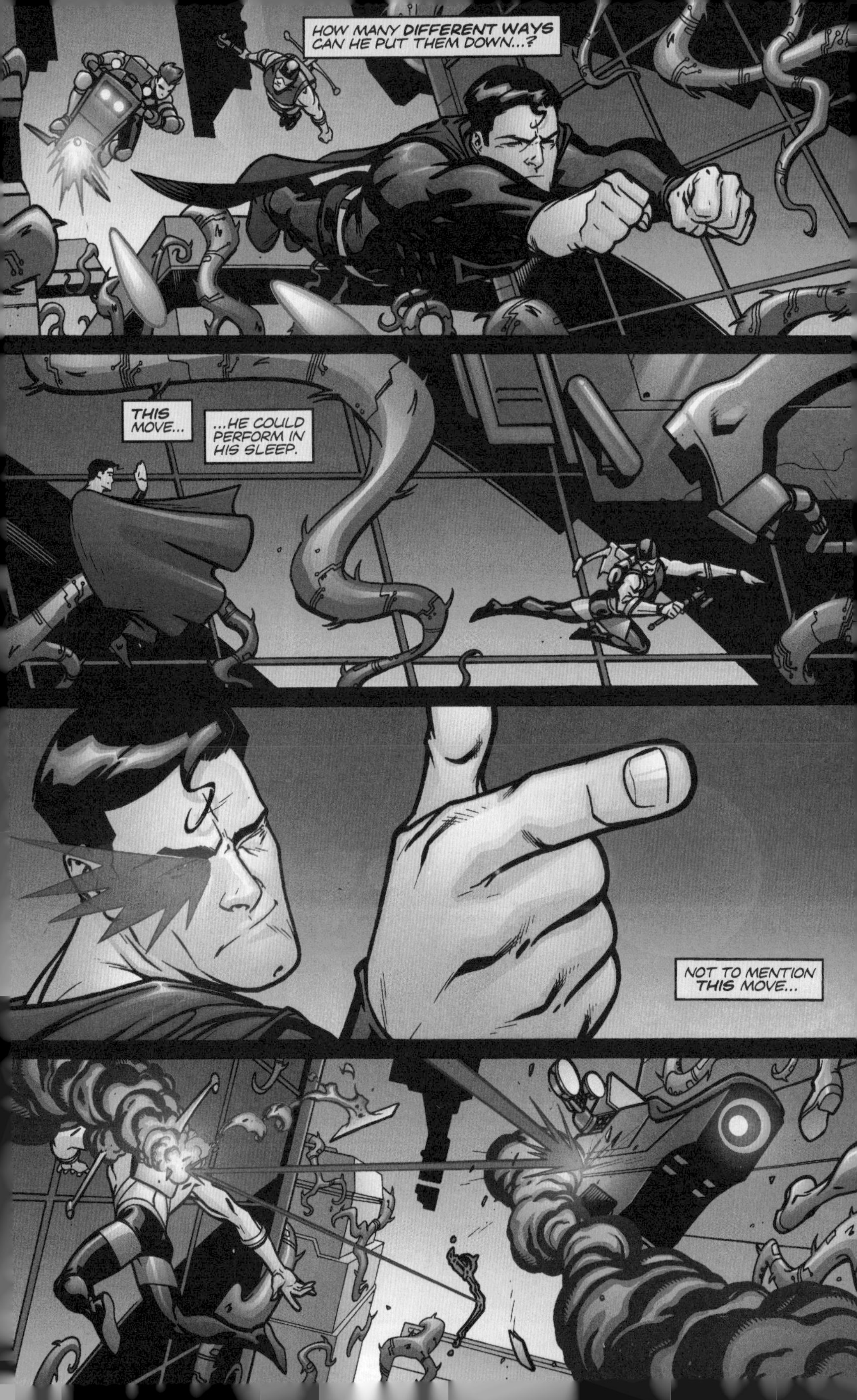
HOW MANY DIFFERENT WAYS CAN HE PUT THEM DOWN...?
THIS MOVE...
...HE COULD PERFORM IN HIS SLEEP.
NOT TO MENTION THIS MOVE...

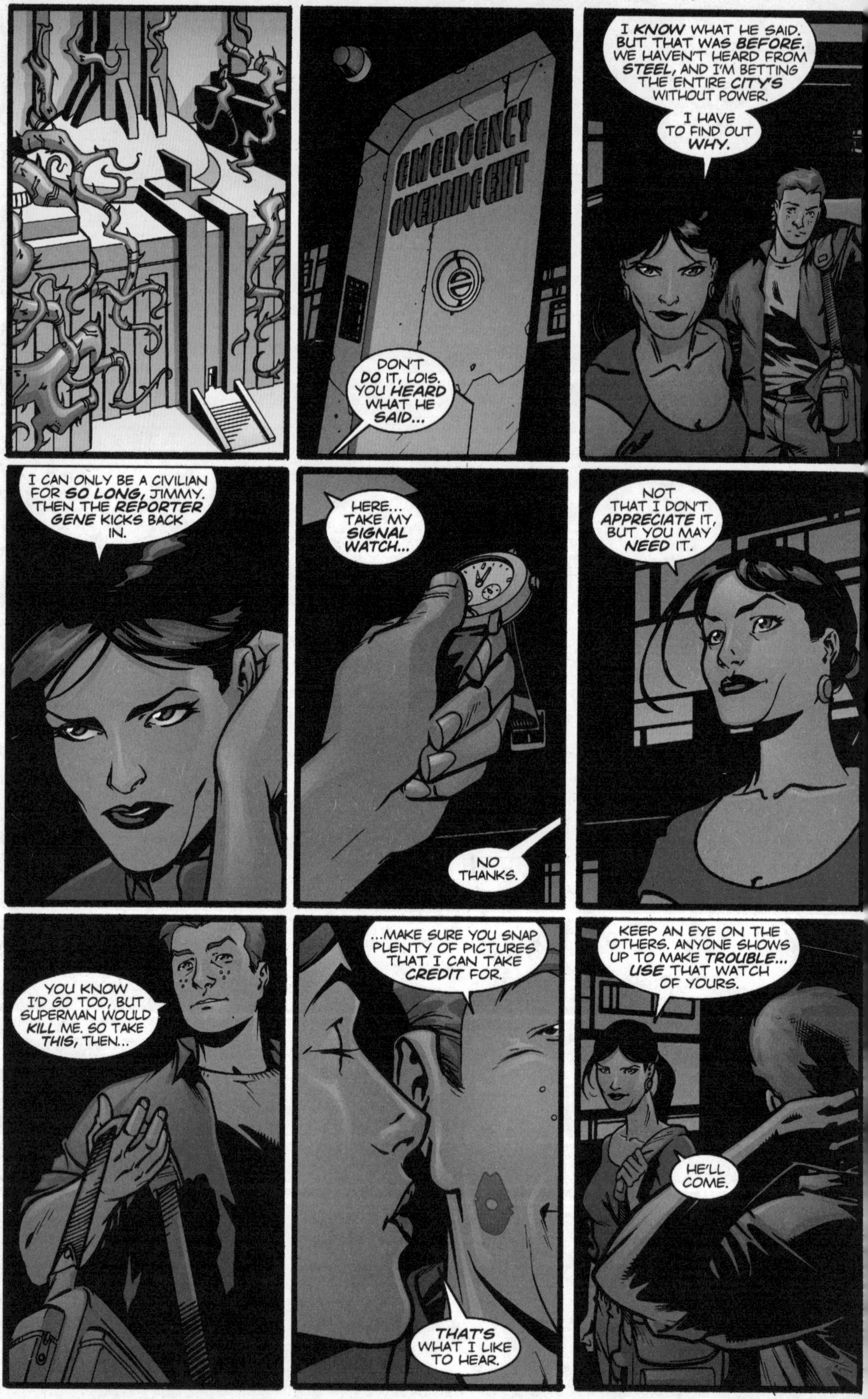
EMERGENCY OVERRIDE EXIT
DON'T DO IT, LOIS. YOU HEARD WHAT HE SAID...
I KNOW WHAT HE SAID. BUT THAT WAS BEFORE. WE HAVEN'T HEARD FROM STEEL, AND I'M BETTING THE ENTIRE CITY'S WITHOUT POWER.
I HAVE TO FIND OUT WHY.
I CAN ONLY BE A CIVILIAN FOR SO LONG, JIMMY. THEN THE REPORTER GENE KICKS BACK IN.
HERE... TAKE MY SIGNAL WATCH...
NO THANKS.
NOT THAT I DON'T APPRECIATE IT, BUT YOU MAY NEED IT.
YOU KNOW I'D GO TOO, BUT SUPERMAN WOULD KILL ME. SO TAKE THIS, THEN...
...MAKE SURE YOU SNAP PLENTY OF PICTURES THAT I CAN TAKE CREDIT FOR.
THAT'S WHAT I LIKE TO HEAR.
KEEP AN EYE ON THE OTHERS. ANYONE SHOWS UP TO MAKE TROUBLE... USE THAT WATCH OF YOURS.
HE'LL COME.

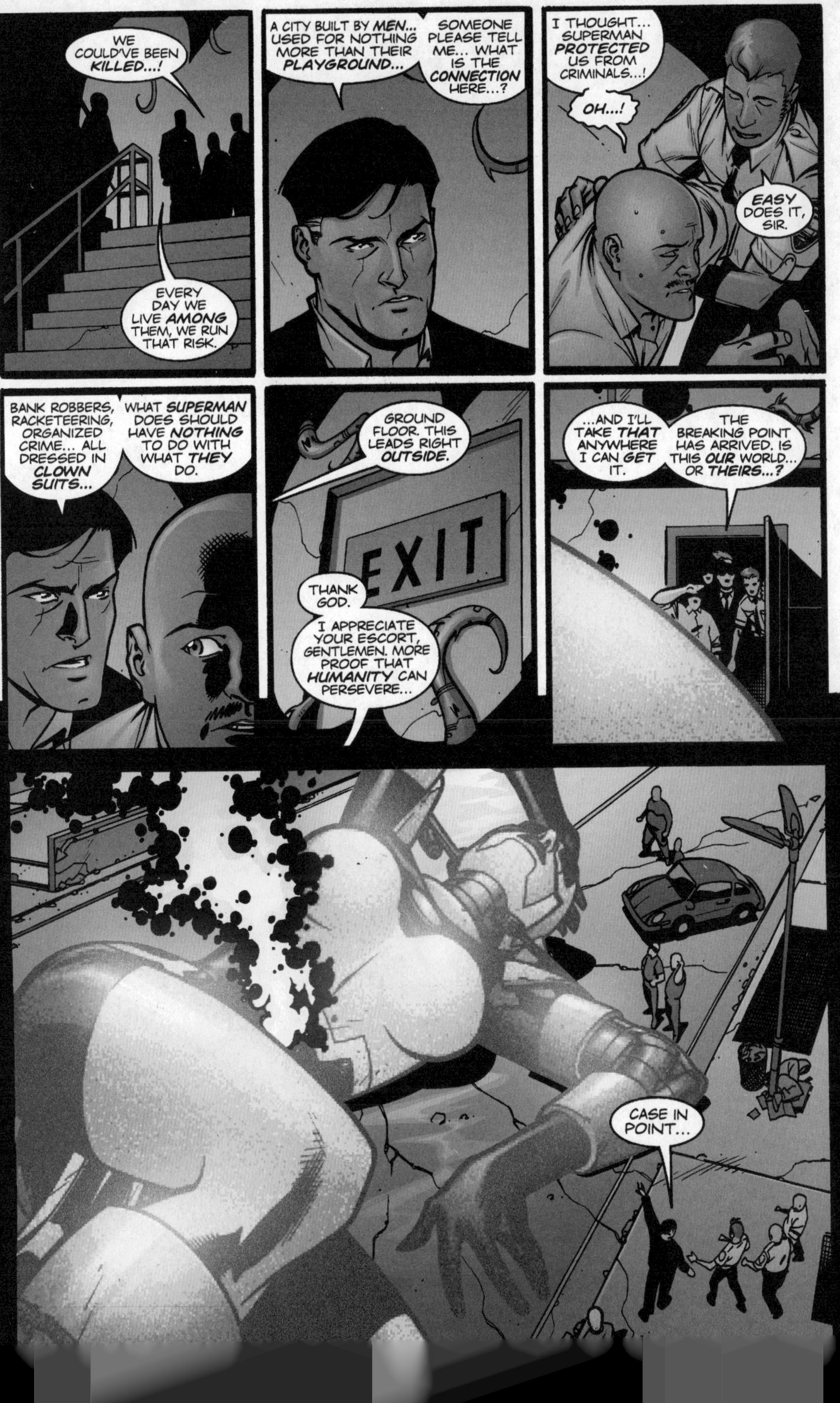

WE COULD'VE BEEN KILLED...!
EVERY DAY WE LIVE AMONG THEM, WE RUN THAT RISK.
A CITY BUILT BY MEN... USED FOR NOTHING MORE THAN THEIR PLAYGROUND...
SOMEONE PLEASE TELL ME... WHAT IS THE CONNECTION HERE...?
I THOUGHT... SUPERMAN PROTECTED US FROM CRIMINALS...!
OH...!
EASY DOES IT, SIR.
BANK ROBBERS, RACKETEERING, ORGANIZED CRIME... ALL DRESSED IN CLOWN SUITS...
WHAT SUPERMAN DOES SHOULD HAVE NOTHING TO DO WITH WHAT THEY DO.
GROUND FLOOR. THIS LEADS RIGHT OUTSIDE.
EXIT
THANK GOD.
I APPRECIATE YOUR ESCORT, GENTLEMEN. MORE PROOF THAT HUMANITY CAN PERSEVERE...
...AND I'LL TAKE THAT ANYWHERE I CAN GET IT.
THE BREAKING POINT HAS ARRIVED. IS THIS OUR WORLD... OR THEIRS...?
CASE IN POINT...

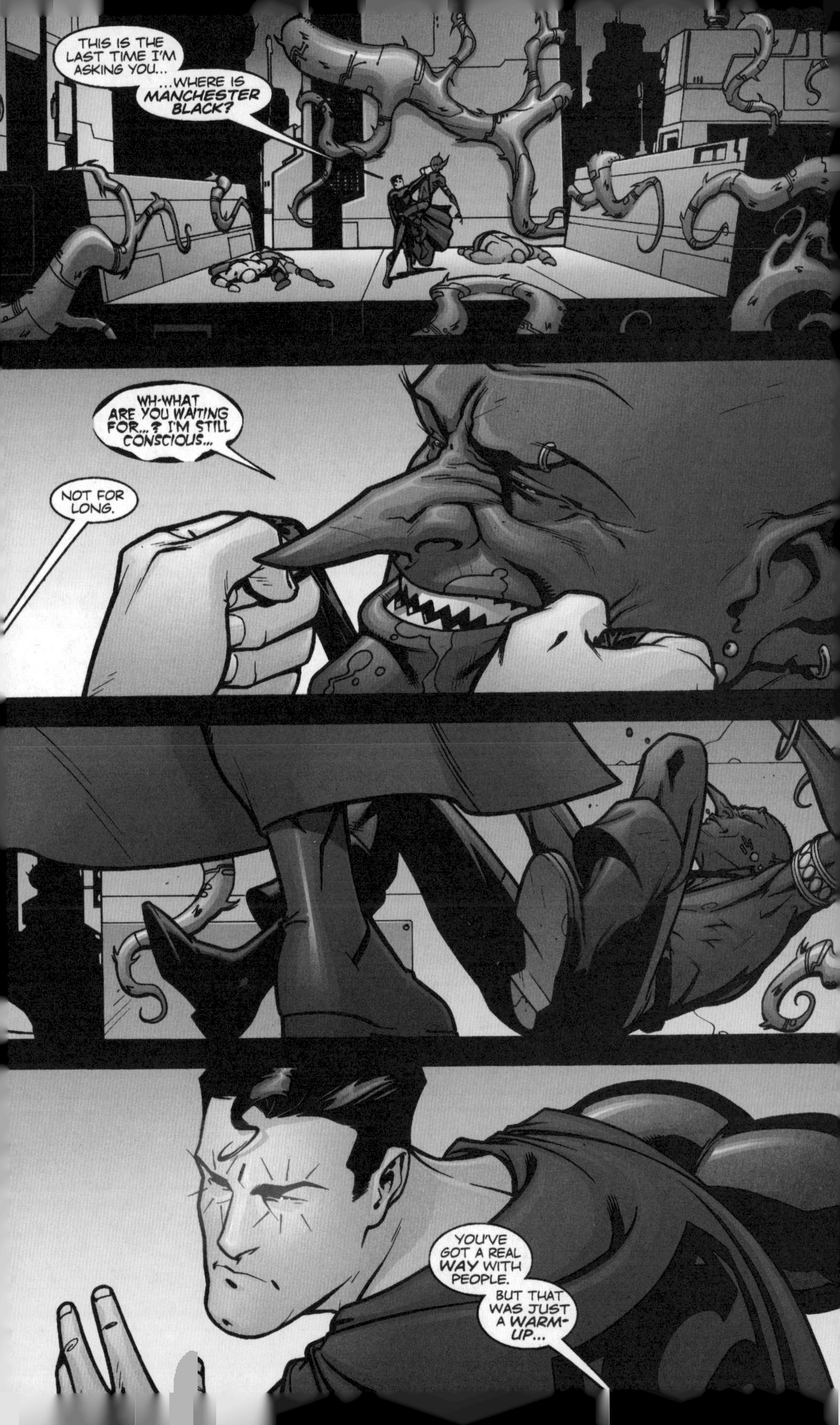
THIS IS THE LAST TIME I'M ASKING YOU...
...WHERE IS MANCHESTER BLACK?
WH-WHAT ARE YOU WAITING FOR...? I'M STILL CONSCIOUS...
NOT FOR LONG.
YOU'VE GOT A REAL WAY WITH PEOPLE.
BUT THAT WAS JUST A WARM-UP...

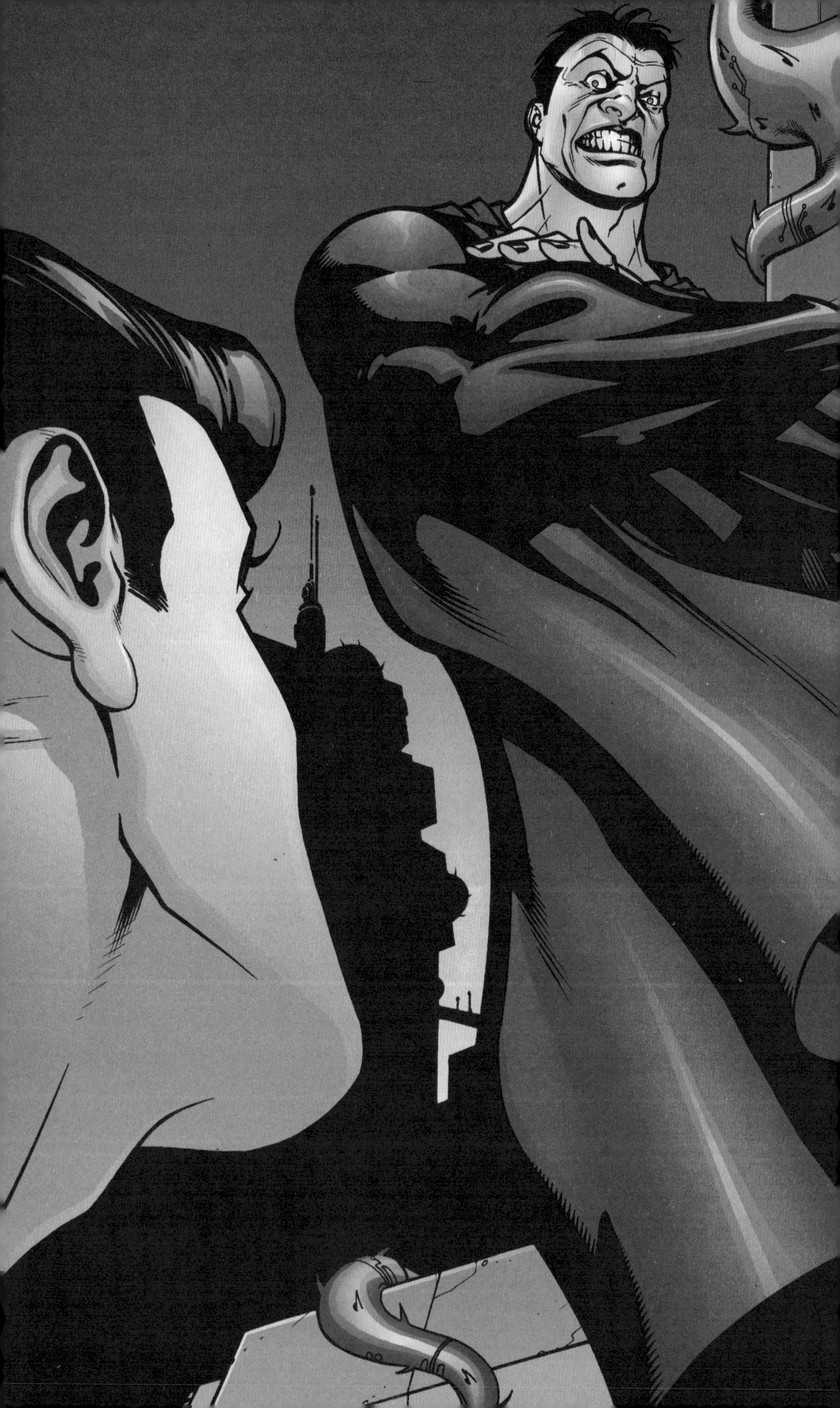

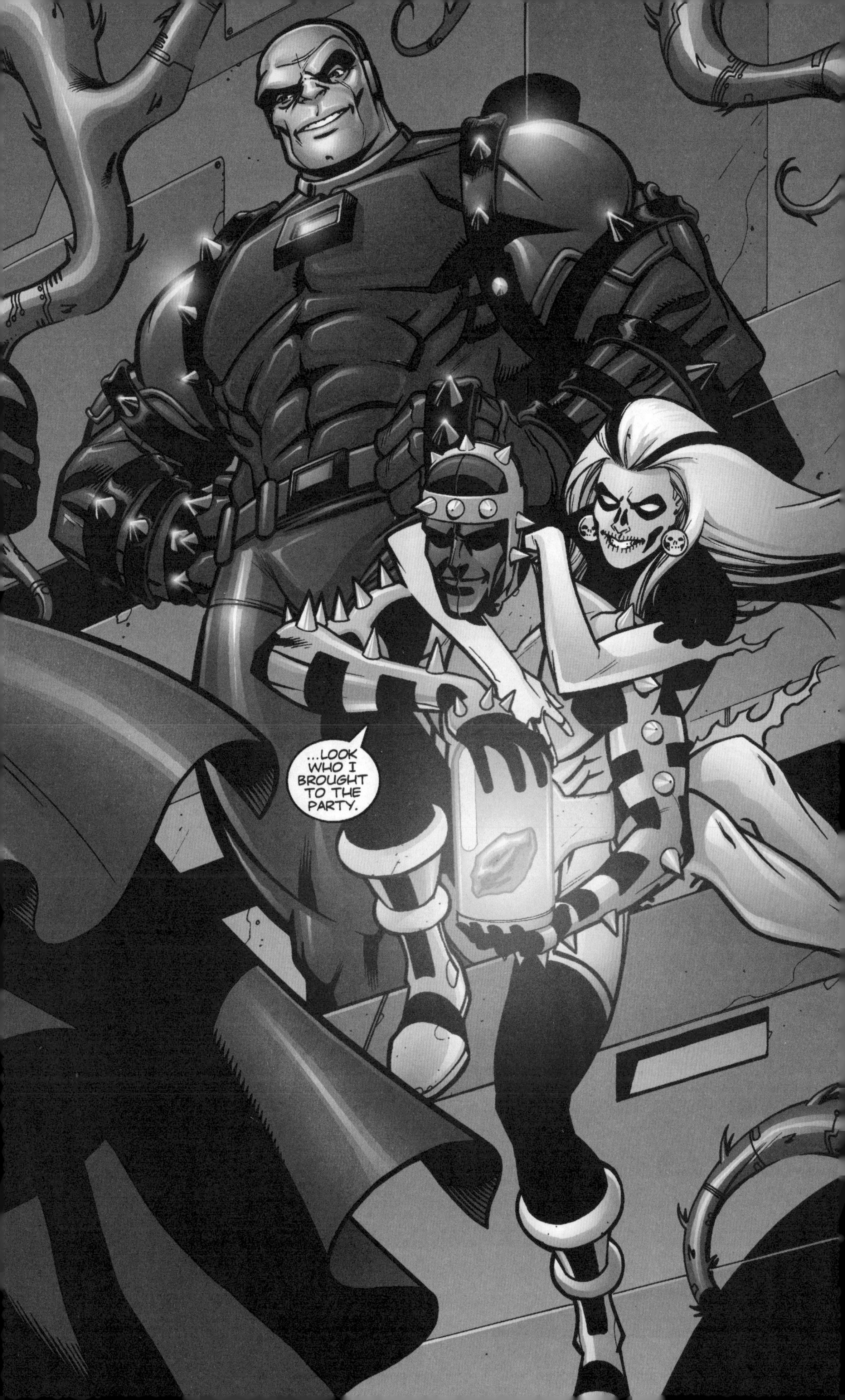
...LOOK WHO I BROUGHT TO THE PARTY.

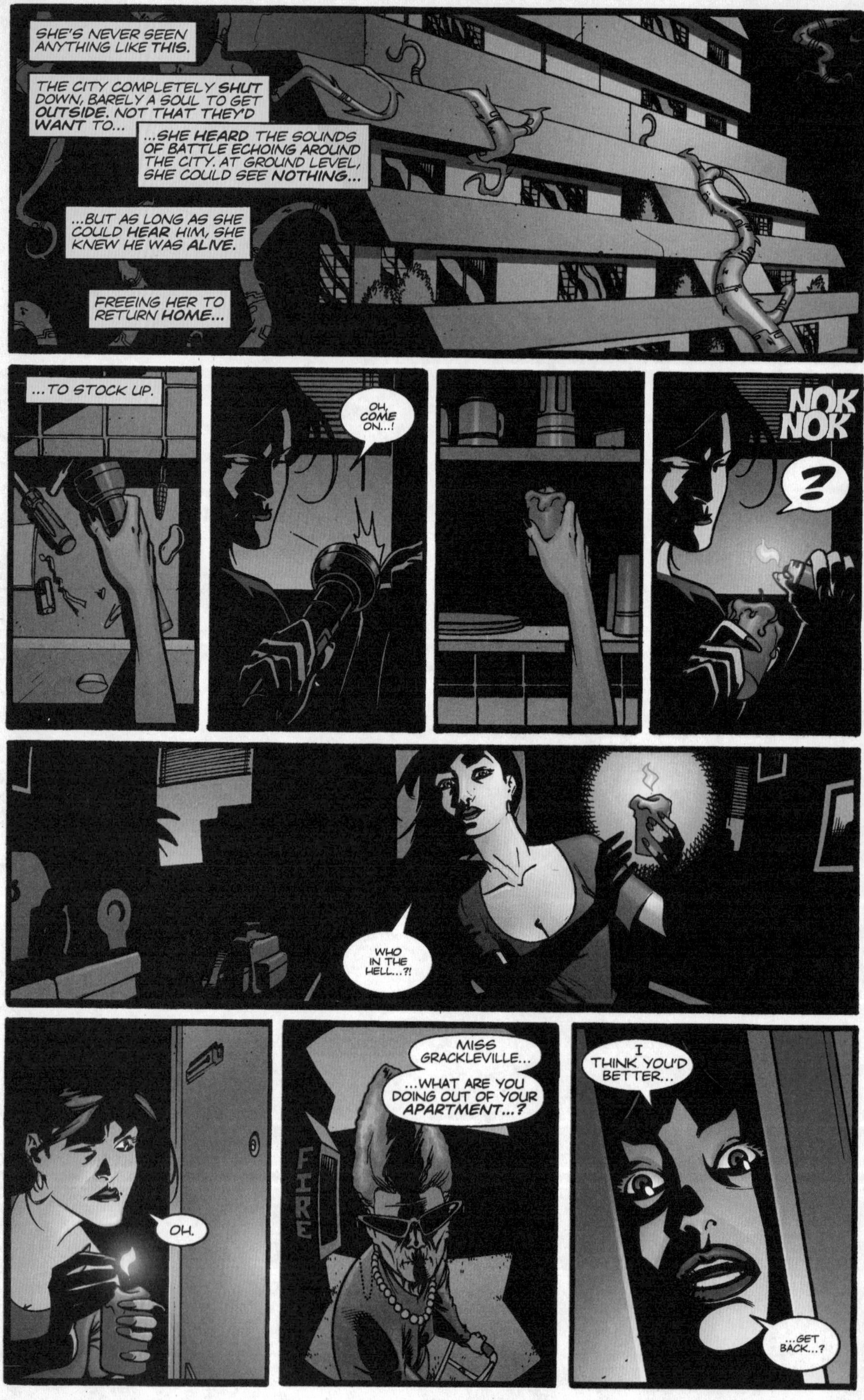
SHE'S NEVER SEEN ANYTHING LIKE THIS.
THE CITY COMPLETELY SHUT DOWN, BARELY A SOUL TO GET OUTSIDE. NOT THAT THEY'D WANT TO...
...SHE HEARD THE SOUNDS OF BATTLE ECHOING AROUND THE CITY. AT GROUND LEVEL, SHE COULD SEE NOTHING...
...BUT AS LONG AS SHE COULD HEAR HIM, SHE KNEW HE WAS ALIVE.
FREEING HER TO RETURN HOME...
...TO STOCK UP.
OH, COME ON...!
NOK NOK
?
WHO IN THE HELL...?!
OH.
MISS GRACKLEVILLE...
...WHAT ARE YOU DOING OUT OF YOUR APARTMENT...?
FIRE
I THINK YOU'D BETTER...
...GET BACK...?

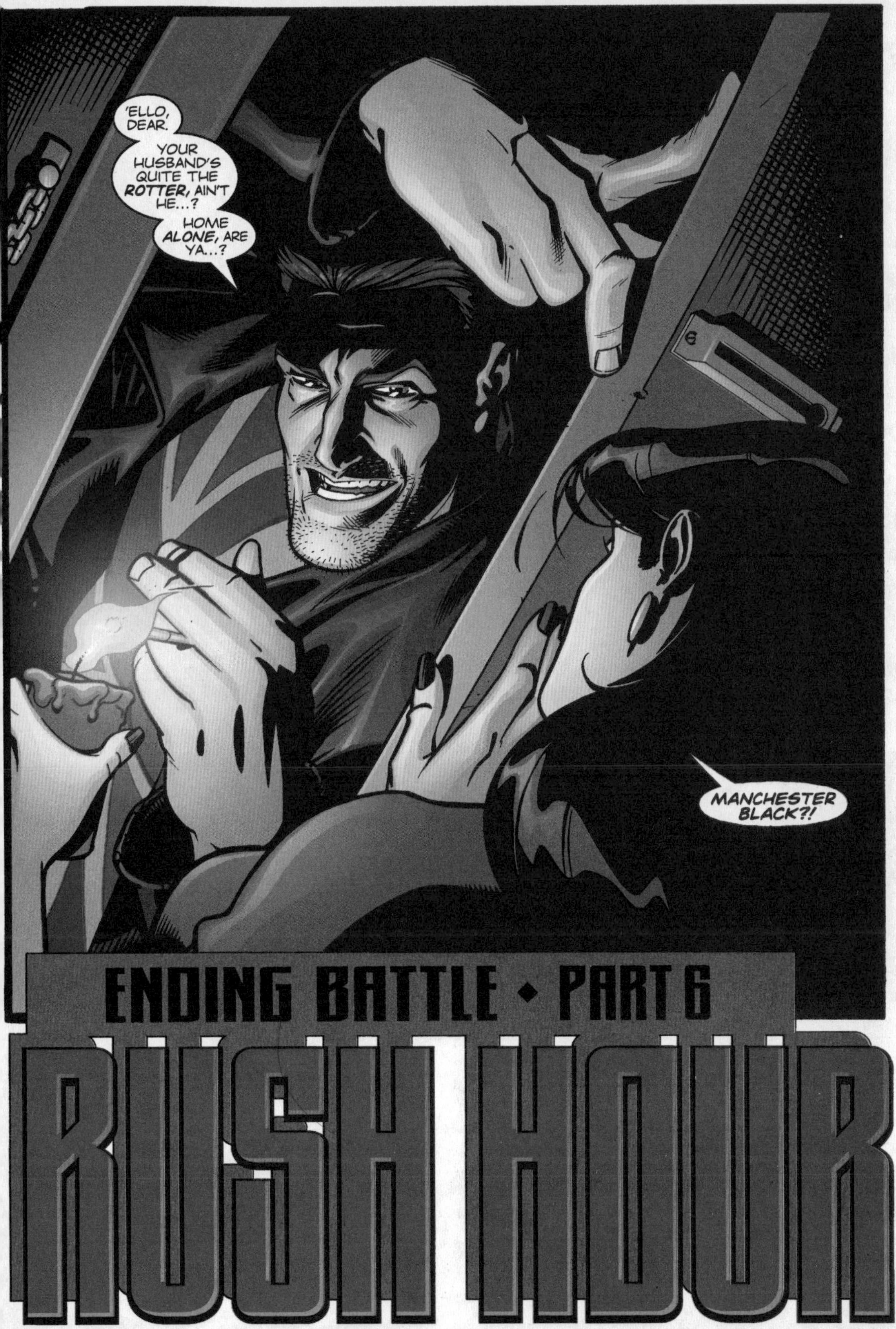
'ELLO, DEAR.
YOUR HUSBAND'S QUITE THE *ROTTER,* AIN'T HE...?
HOME *ALONE,* ARE YA...?
MANCHESTER BLACK?!

ENDING BATTLE • PART 6

RUSH HOUR

JOE CASEY story • **DEREC AUCOIN** art • **ROB RO & ALEX BLEYAERT** colors
COMICRAFT letters • **TOM PALMER JR.** associate editor • **EDDIE BERGANZA** editor
SUPERMAN created by **JERRY SIEGEL & JOE SHUSTER**

Cover art by CARLOS PACHECO & JESUS MERINO

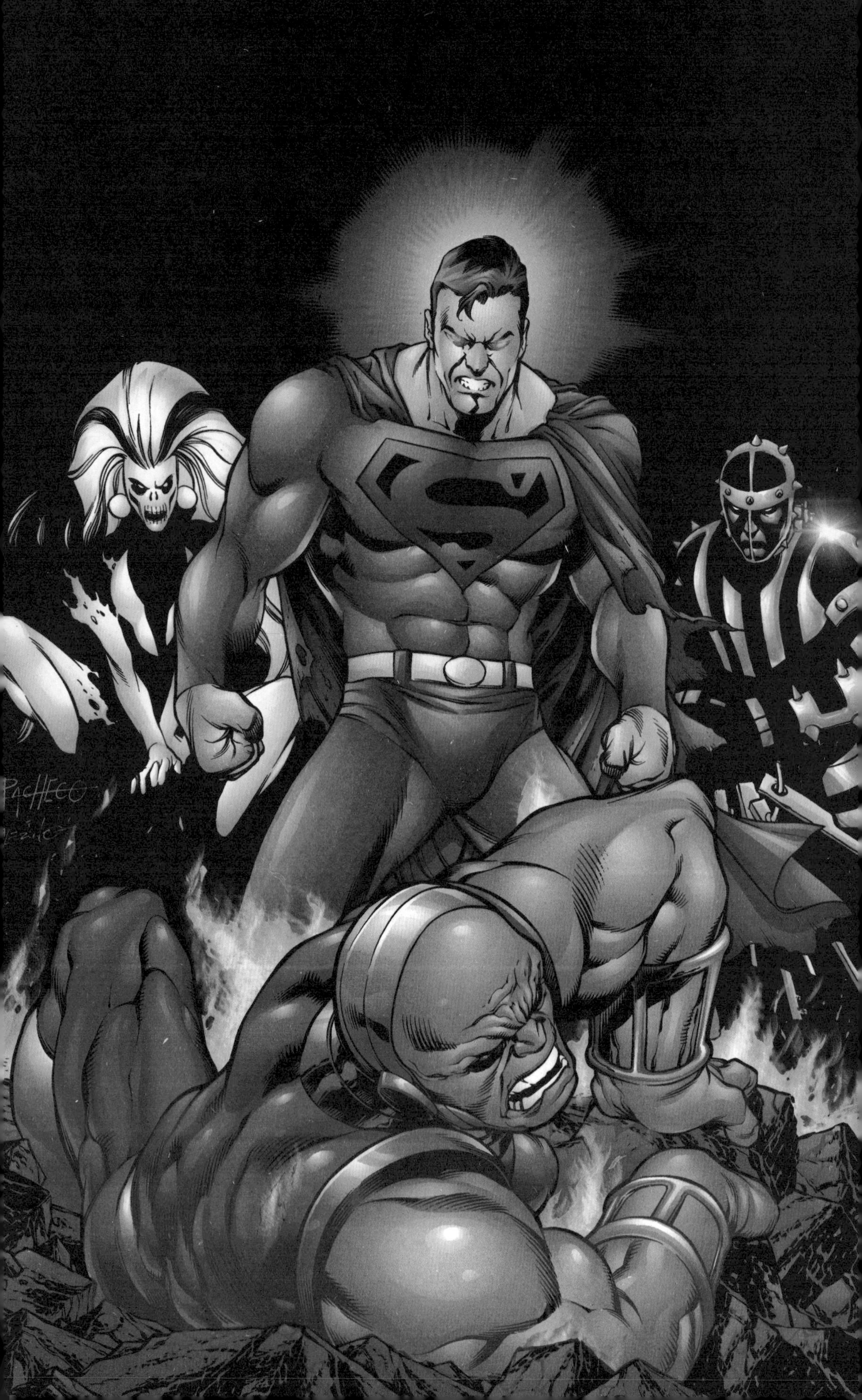
PACHECO

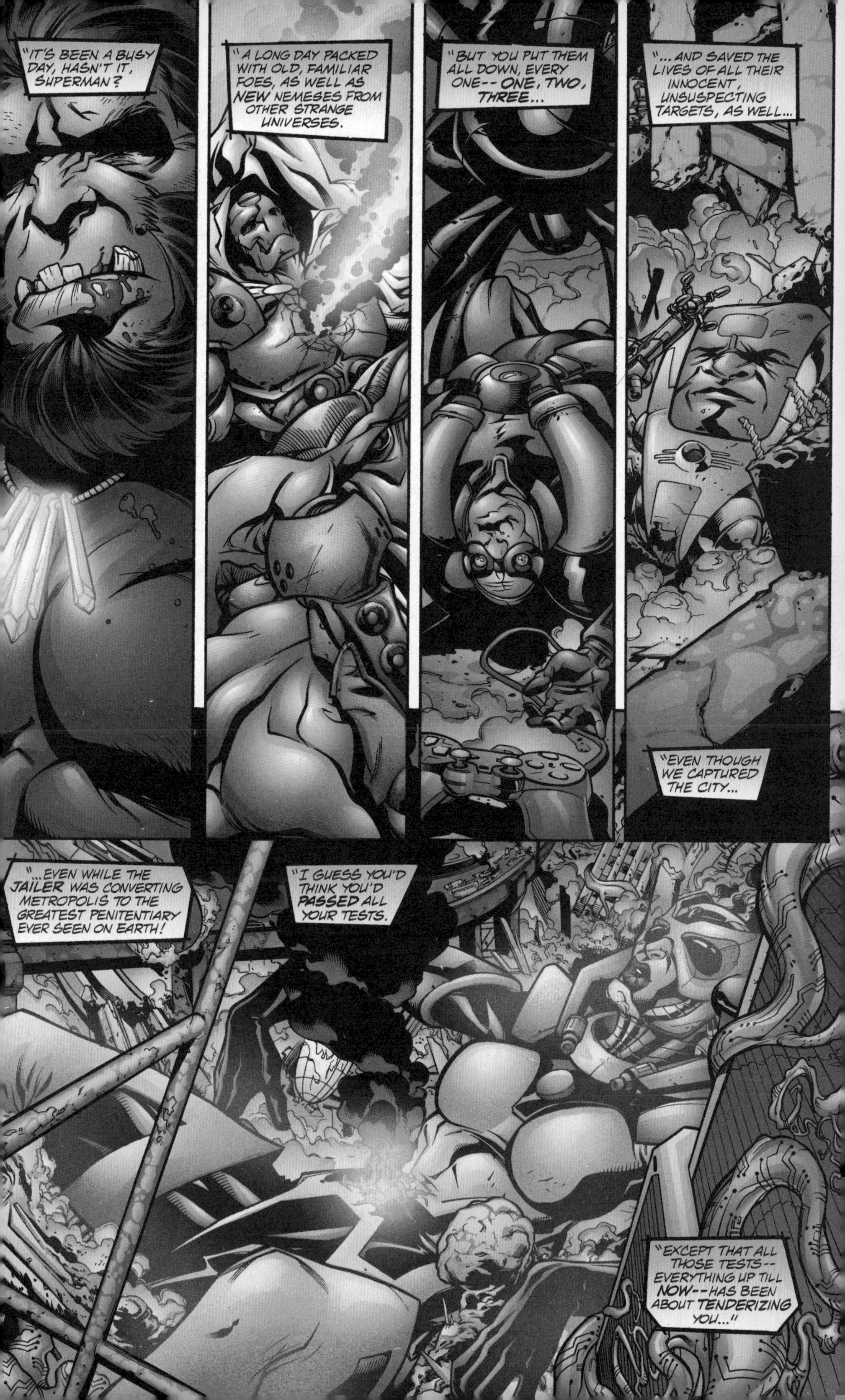
"IT'S BEEN A BUSY DAY, HASN'T IT, SUPERMAN?
"A LONG DAY PACKED WITH OLD, FAMILIAR FOES, AS WELL AS NEW NEMESES FROM OTHER STRANGE UNIVERSES.
"BUT YOU PUT THEM ALL DOWN, EVERY ONE-- ONE, TWO, THREE...
"...AND SAVED THE LIVES OF ALL THEIR INNOCENT, UNSUSPECTING TARGETS, AS WELL...
"EVEN THOUGH WE CAPTURED THE CITY...
"...EVEN WHILE THE JAILER WAS CONVERTING METROPOLIS TO THE GREATEST PENITENTIARY EVER SEEN ON EARTH!
"I GUESS YOU'D THINK YOU'D PASSED ALL YOUR TESTS.
"EXCEPT THAT ALL THOSE TESTS-- EVERYTHING UP TILL NOW--HAS BEEN ABOUT TENDERIZING YOU..."

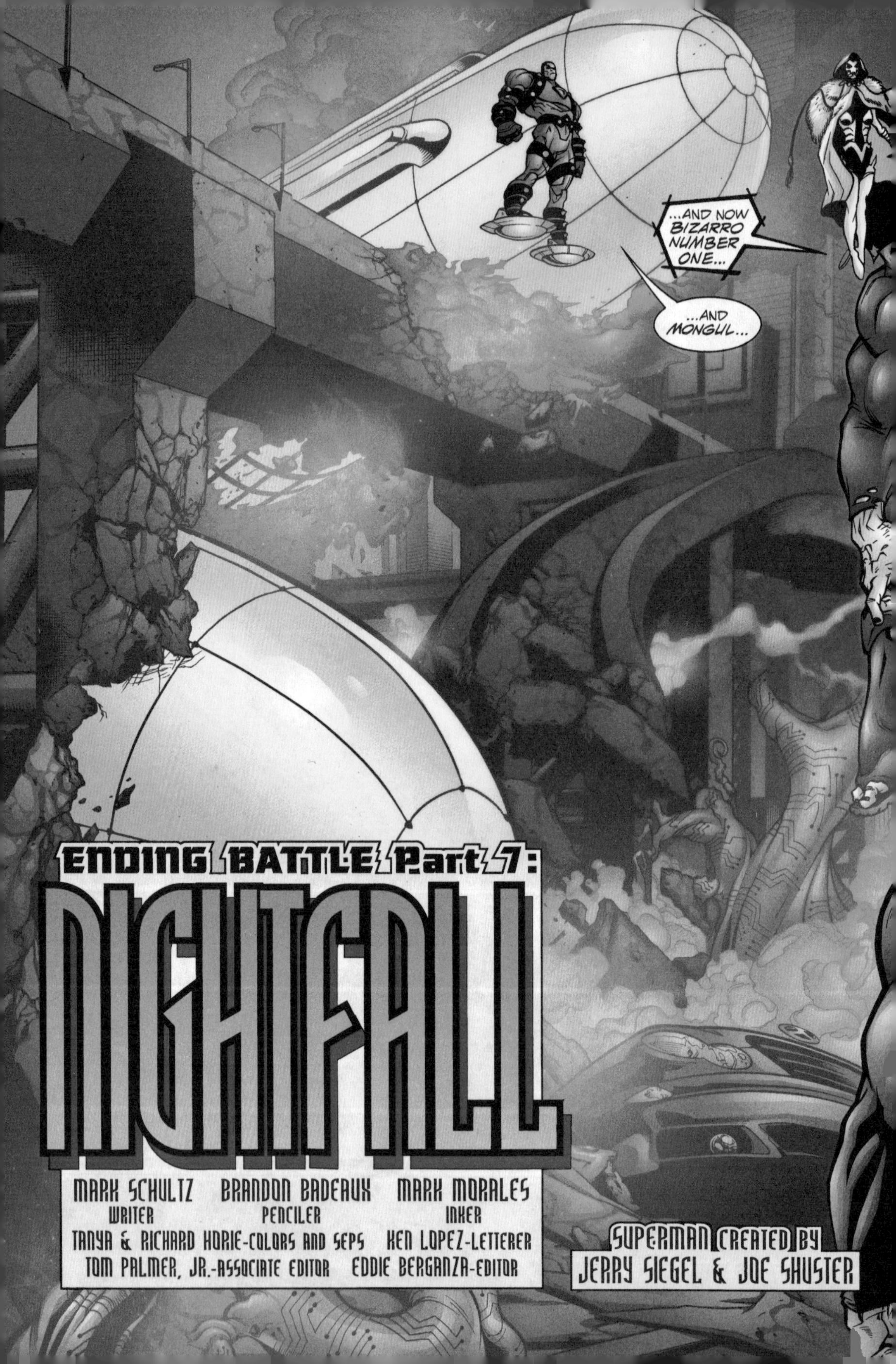
...AND NOW BIZARRO NUMBER ONE...
...AND MONGUL...
ENDING BATTLE Part 7:
NIGHTFALL
MARK SCHULTZ WRITER
BRANDON BADEAUX PENCILER
MARK MORALES INKER
TANYA & RICHARD HORIE-COLORS AND SEPS
KEN LOPEZ-LETTERER
TOM PALMER, JR.-ASSOCIATE EDITOR
EDDIE BERGANZA-EDITOR
SUPERMAN CREATED BY JERRY SIEGEL & JOE SHUSTER

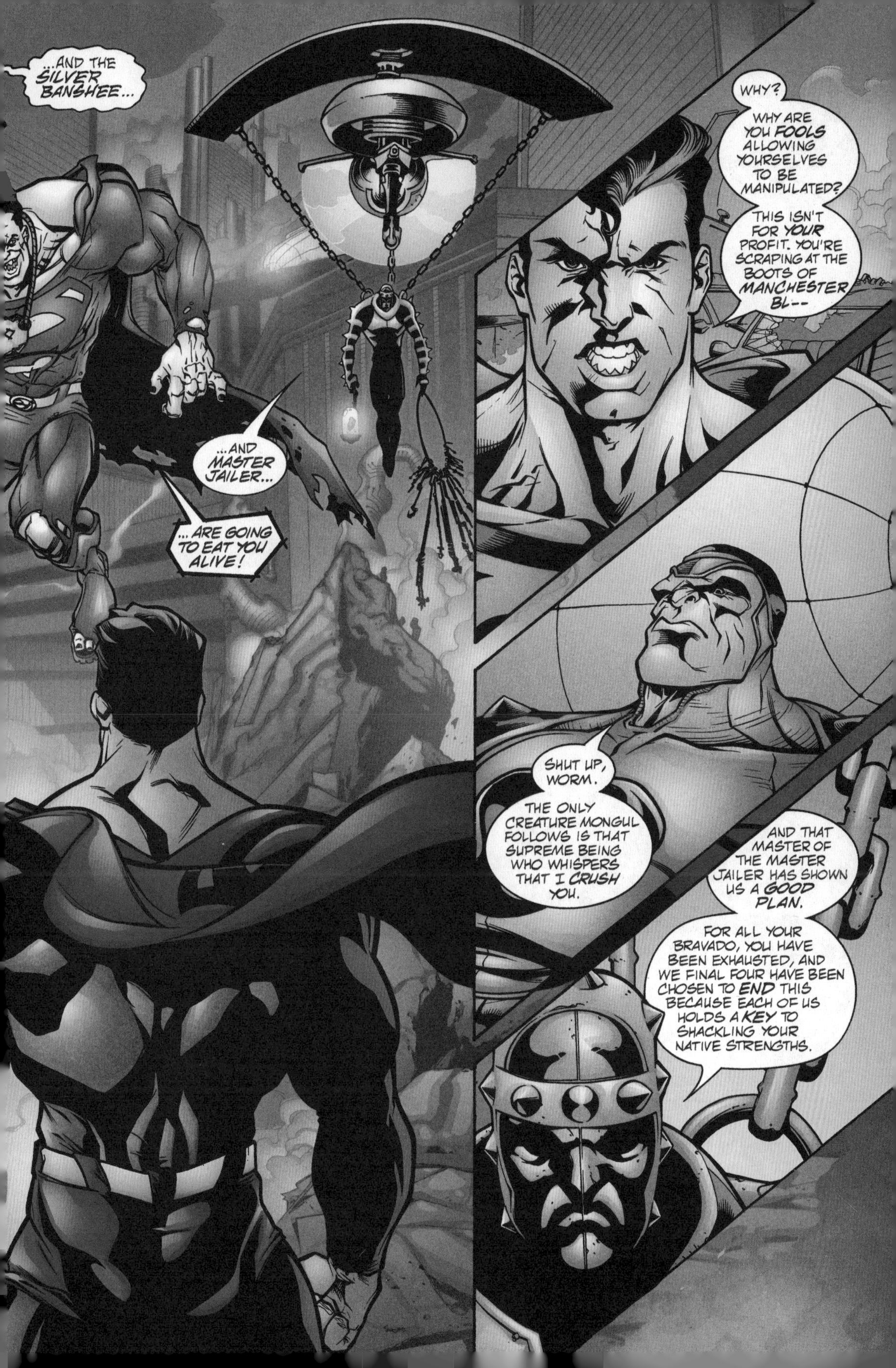
...AND THE SILVER BANSHEE...
...AND MASTER JAILER...
...ARE GOING TO EAT YOU ALIVE!
WHY?
WHY ARE YOU FOOLS ALLOWING YOURSELVES TO BE MANIPULATED?
THIS ISN'T FOR YOUR PROFIT. YOU'RE SCRAPING AT THE BOOTS OF MANCHESTER BL--
SHUT UP, WORM.
THE ONLY CREATURE MONGUL FOLLOWS IS THAT SUPREME BEING WHO WHISPERS THAT I CRUSH YOU.
AND THAT MASTER OF THE MASTER JAILER HAS SHOWN US A GOOD PLAN.
FOR ALL YOUR BRAVADO, YOU HAVE BEEN EXHAUSTED, AND WE FINAL FOUR HAVE BEEN CHOSEN TO END THIS BECAUSE EACH OF US HOLDS A KEY TO SHACKLING YOUR NATIVE STRENGTHS.

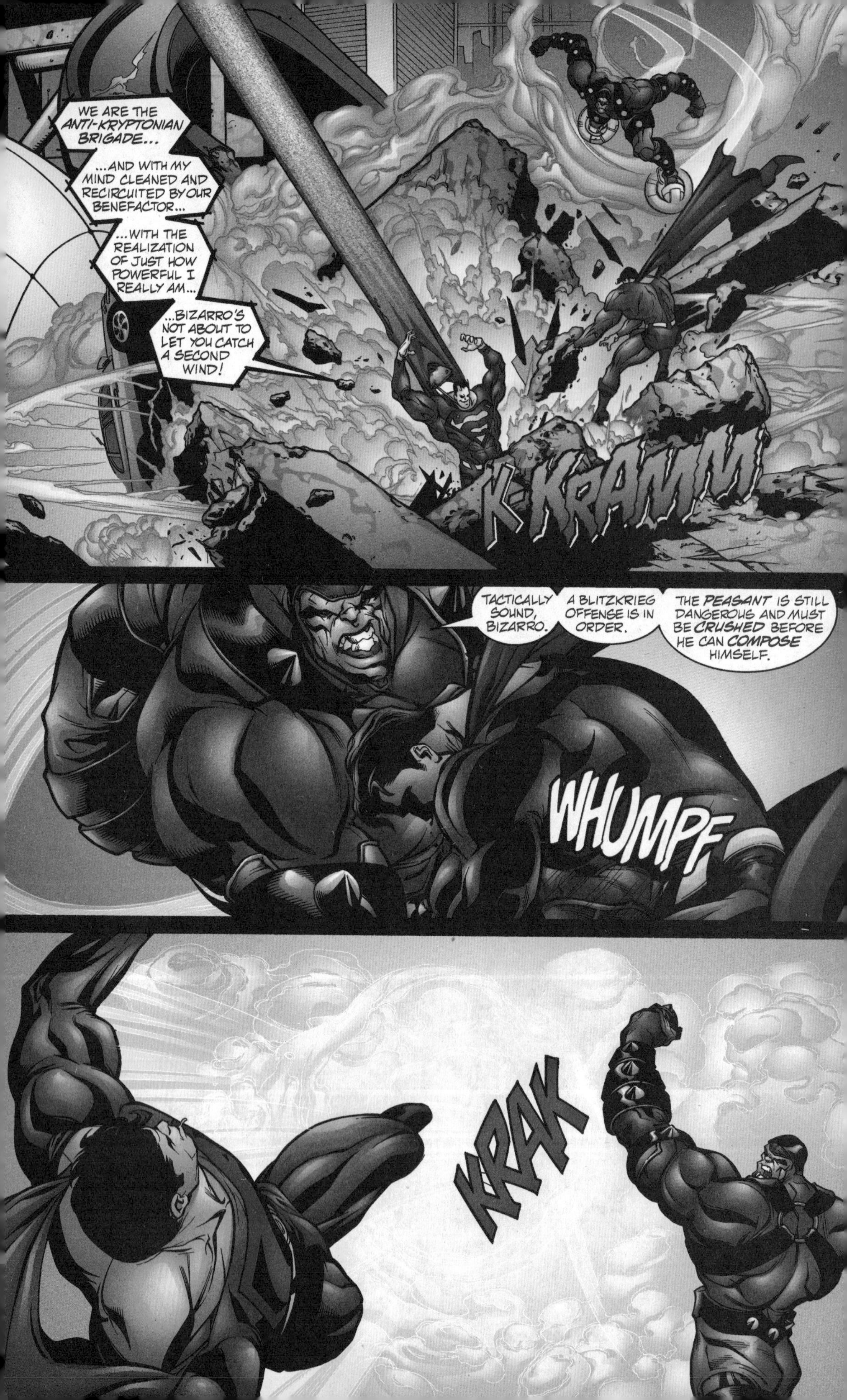
WE ARE THE ANTI-KRYPTONIAN BRIGADE...
...AND WITH MY MIND CLEANED AND RECIRCUITED BY OUR BENEFACTOR...
...WITH THE REALIZATION OF JUST HOW POWERFUL I REALLY AM...
...BIZARRO'S NOT ABOUT TO LET YOU CATCH A SECOND WIND!
K-KRAMM
TACTICALLY SOUND, BIZARRO.
A BLITZKRIEG OFFENSE IS IN ORDER.
THE PEASANT IS STILL DANGEROUS AND MUST BE CRUSHED BEFORE HE CAN COMPOSE HIMSELF.
WHUMPF
KRAK

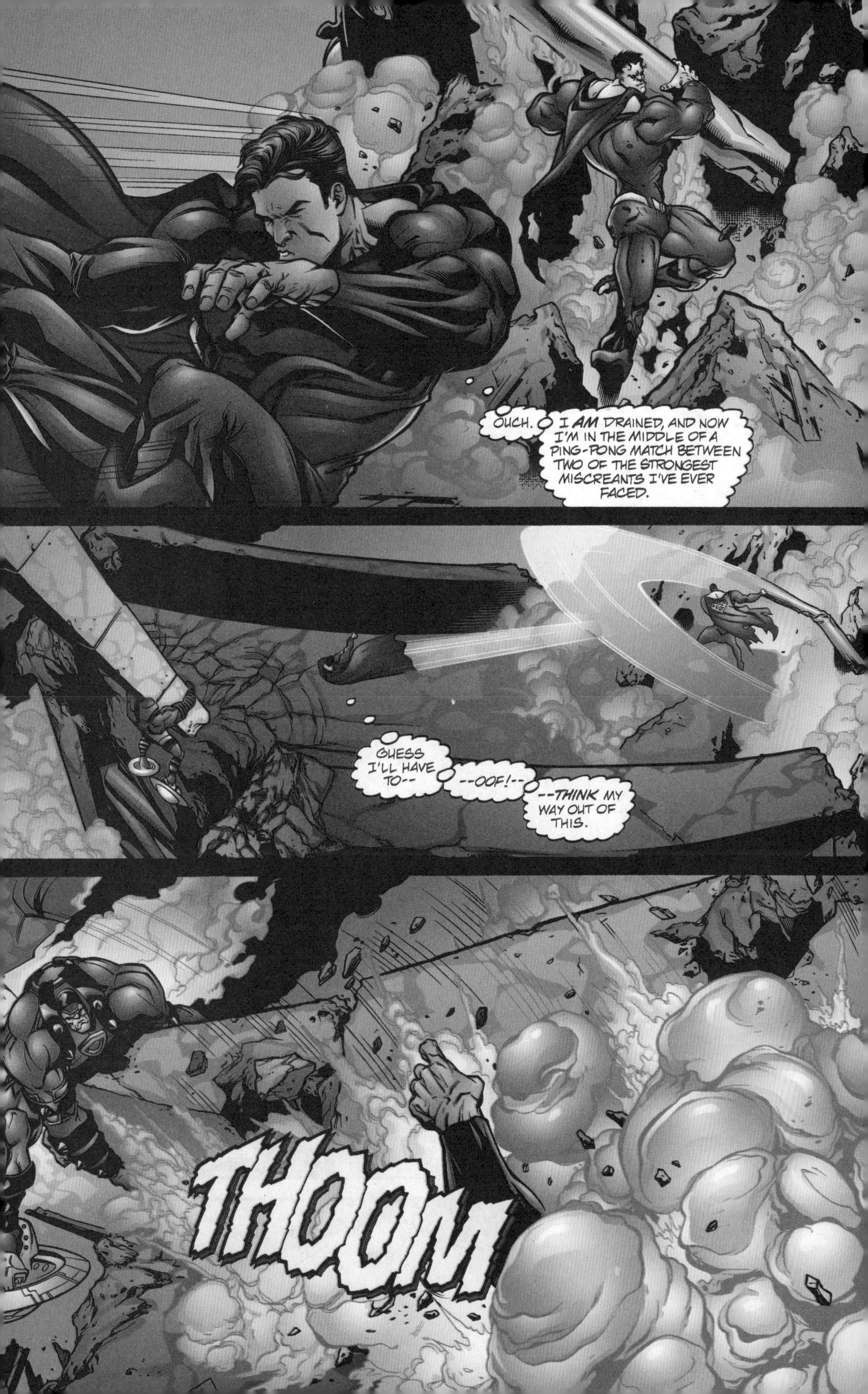
OUCH.
I AM DRAINED, AND NOW I'M IN THE MIDDLE OF A PING-PONG MATCH BETWEEN TWO OF THE STRONGEST MISCREANTS I'VE EVER FACED.
GUESS I'LL HAVE TO--
--OOF!--
--THINK MY WAY OUT OF THIS.
THOOM

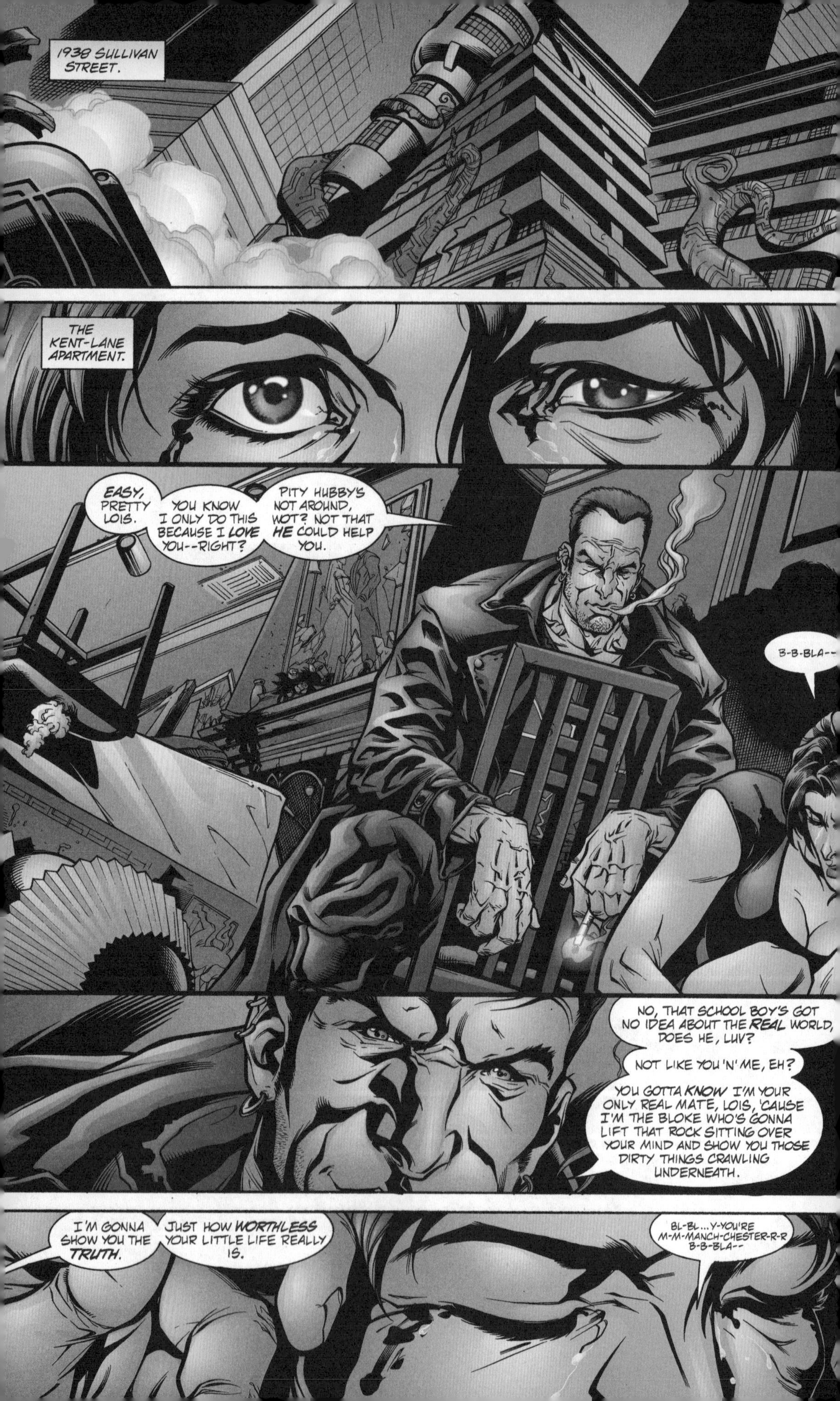

1938 SULLIVAN STREET.
THE KENT-LANE APARTMENT.
EASY, PRETTY LOIS.
YOU KNOW I ONLY DO THIS BECAUSE I LOVE YOU--RIGHT?
PITY HUBBY'S NOT AROUND, WOT? NOT THAT HE COULD HELP YOU.
B-B-BLA--
NO, THAT SCHOOL BOY'S GOT NO IDEA ABOUT THE REAL WORLD, DOES HE, LUV?
NOT LIKE YOU'N' ME, EH?
YOU GOTTA KNOW I'M YOUR ONLY REAL MATE, LOIS, 'CAUSE I'M THE BLOKE WHO'S GONNA LIFT THAT ROCK SITTING OVER YOUR MIND AND SHOW YOU THOSE DIRTY THINGS CRAWLING UNDERNEATH.
I'M GONNA SHOW YOU THE TRUTH.
JUST HOW WORTHLESS YOUR LITTLE LIFE REALLY IS.
BL-BL...Y-YOU'RE M-M-MANCH-CHESTER-R-R B-B-BLA--

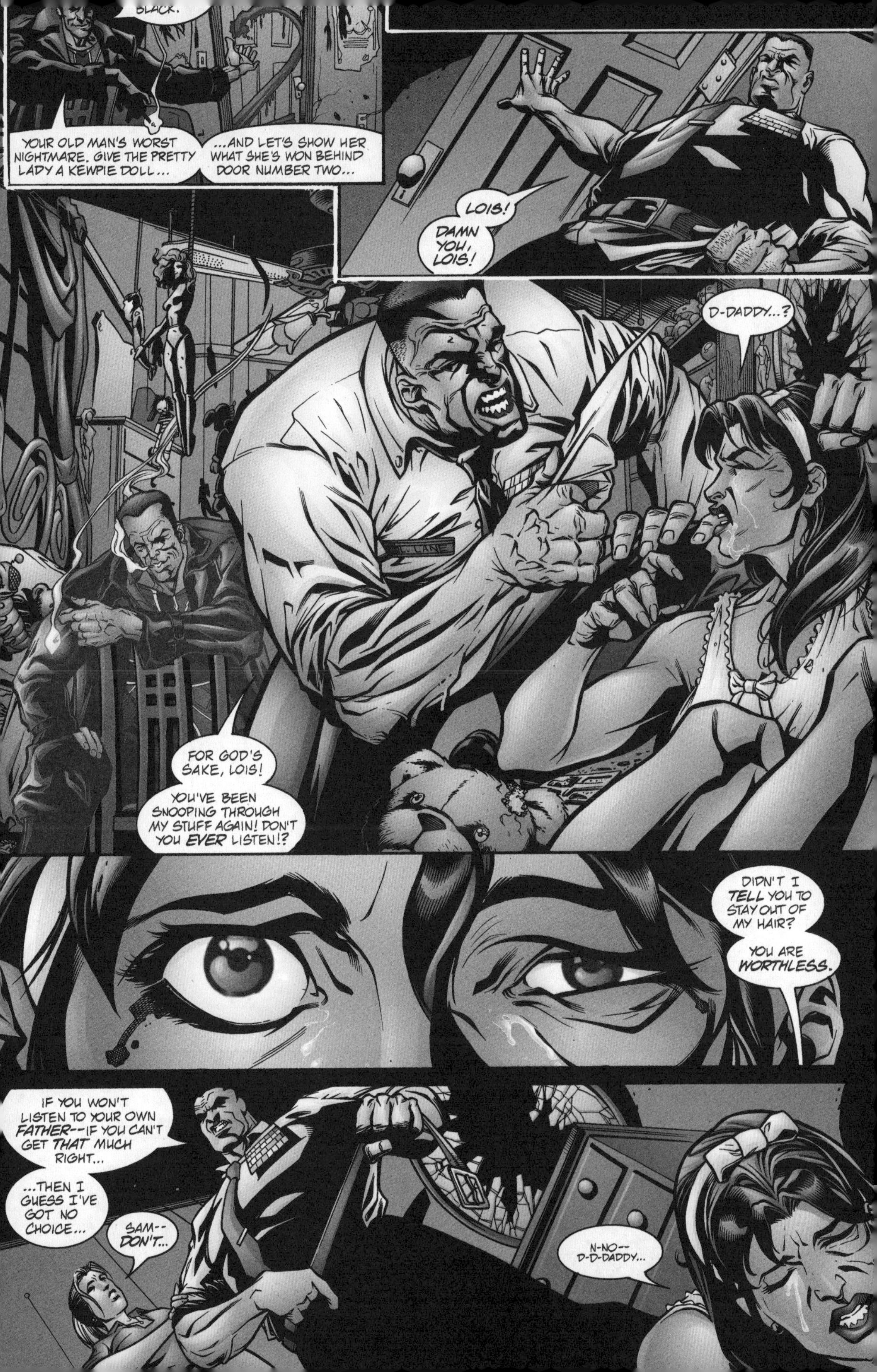
BLACK.
YOUR OLD MAN'S WORST NIGHTMARE. GIVE THE PRETTY LADY A KEWPIE DOLL...
...AND LET'S SHOW HER WHAT SHE'S WON BEHIND DOOR NUMBER TWO...
LOIS! DAMN YOU, LOIS!
D-DADDY...?
FOR GOD'S SAKE, LOIS!
YOU'VE BEEN SNOOPING THROUGH MY STUFF AGAIN! DON'T YOU EVER LISTEN!?
DIDN'T I TELL YOU TO STAY OUT OF MY HAIR?
YOU ARE WORTHLESS.
IF YOU WON'T LISTEN TO YOUR OWN FATHER--IF YOU CAN'T GET THAT MUCH RIGHT...
...THEN I GUESS I'VE GOT NO CHOICE...
SAM--DON'T...
N-NO-- D-D-DADDY...

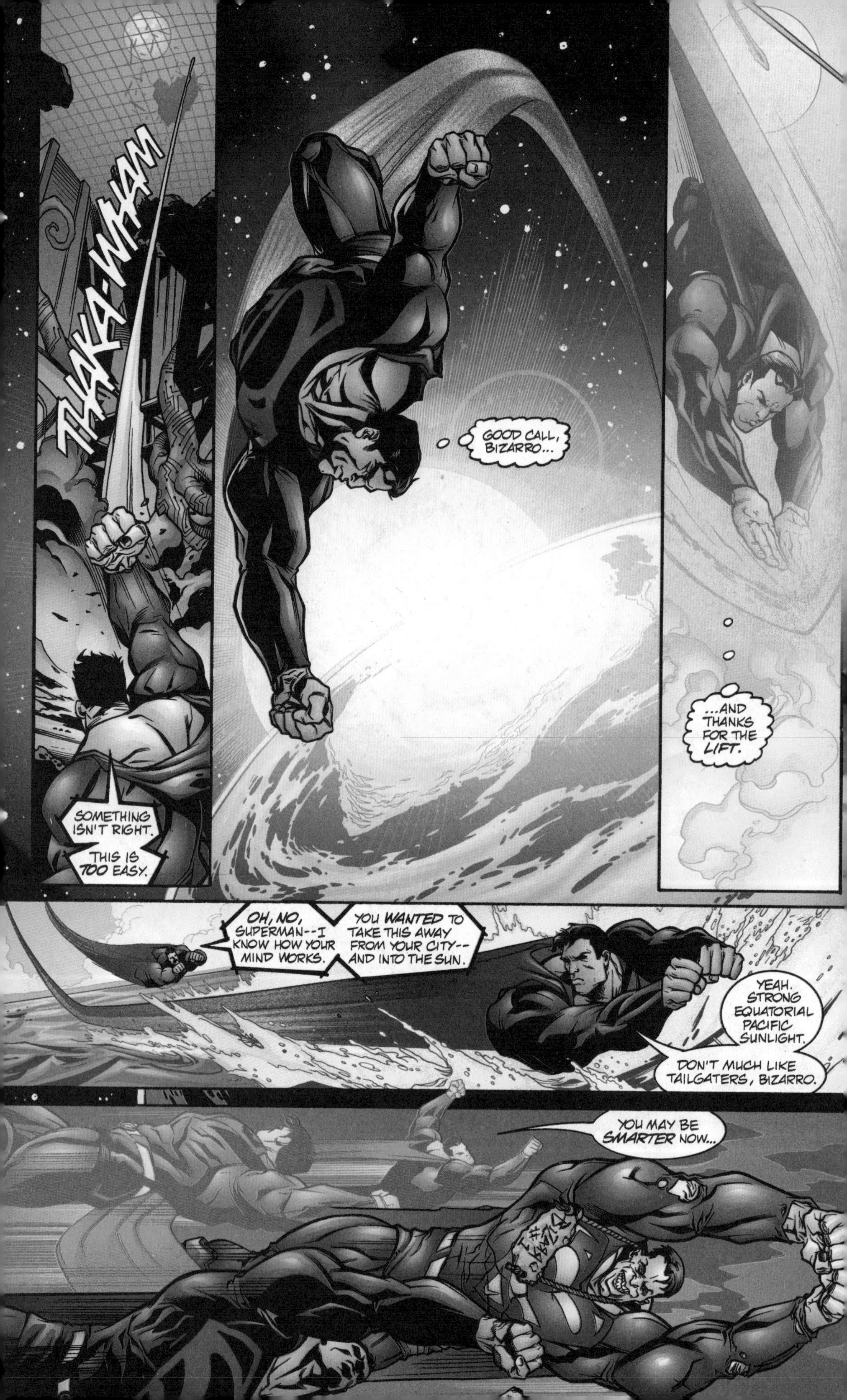
THAKA-WHAM
SOMETHING ISN'T RIGHT.
THIS IS TOO EASY.
GOOD CALL, BIZARRO...
...AND THANKS FOR THE LIFT.
OH, NO, SUPERMAN--I KNOW HOW YOUR MIND WORKS.
YOU WANTED TO TAKE THIS AWAY FROM YOUR CITY--AND INTO THE SUN.
YEAH. STRONG EQUATORIAL PACIFIC SUNLIGHT.
DON'T MUCH LIKE TAILGATERS, BIZARRO.
YOU MAY BE SMARTER NOW...

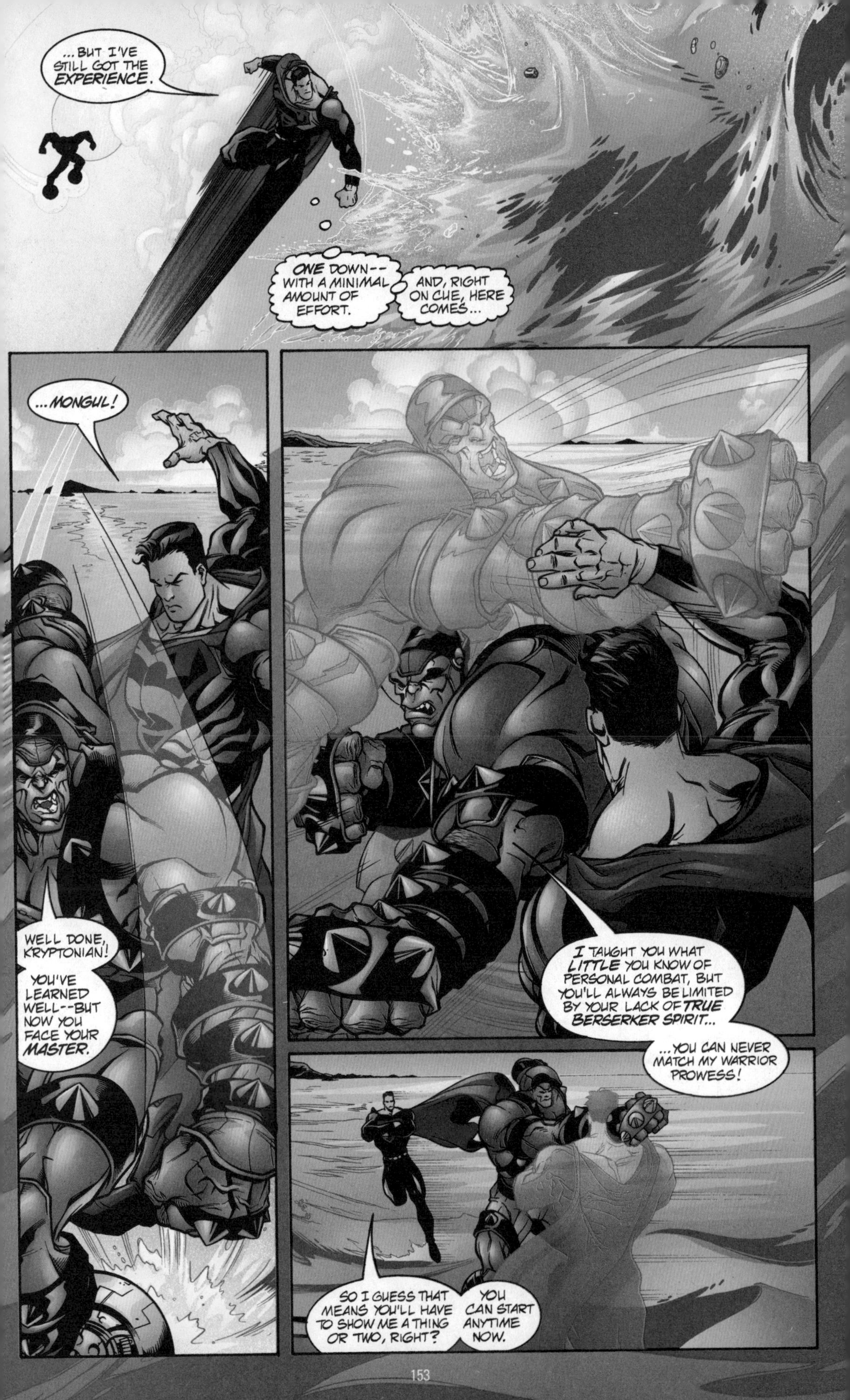

...BUT I'VE STILL GOT THE EXPERIENCE.
ONE DOWN-- WITH A MINIMAL AMOUNT OF EFFORT.
AND, RIGHT ON CUE, HERE COMES...
...MONGUL!
WELL DONE, KRYPTONIAN!
YOU'VE LEARNED WELL--BUT NOW YOU FACE YOUR MASTER.
I TAUGHT YOU WHAT LITTLE YOU KNOW OF PERSONAL COMBAT, BUT YOU'LL ALWAYS BE LIMITED BY YOUR LACK OF TRUE BERSERKER SPIRIT...
...YOU CAN NEVER MATCH MY WARRIOR PROWESS!
SO I GUESS THAT MEANS YOU'LL HAVE TO SHOW ME A THING OR TWO, RIGHT?
YOU CAN START ANYTIME NOW.

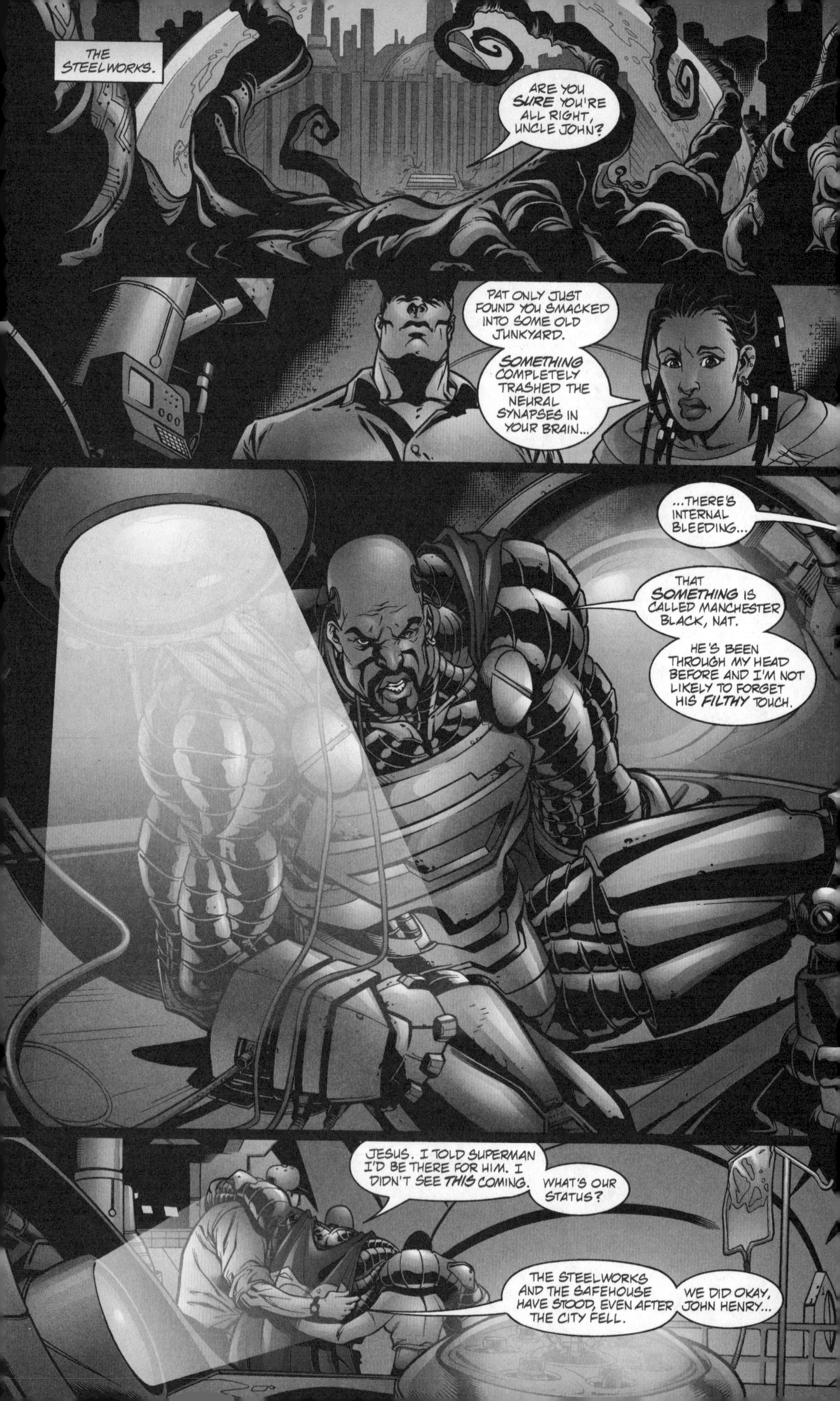
THE STEELWORKS.
ARE YOU SURE YOU'RE ALL RIGHT, UNCLE JOHN?
PAT ONLY JUST FOUND YOU SMACKED INTO SOME OLD JUNKYARD.
SOMETHING COMPLETELY TRASHED THE NEURAL SYNAPSES IN YOUR BRAIN...
...THERE'S INTERNAL BLEEDING...
THAT SOMETHING IS CALLED MANCHESTER BLACK, NAT.
HE'S BEEN THROUGH MY HEAD BEFORE AND I'M NOT LIKELY TO FORGET HIS FILTHY TOUCH.
JESUS. I TOLD SUPERMAN I'D BE THERE FOR HIM. I DIDN'T SEE THIS COMING.
WHAT'S OUR STATUS?
THE STEELWORKS AND THE SAFEHOUSE HAVE STOOD, EVEN AFTER THE CITY FELL.
WE DID OKAY, JOHN HENRY...

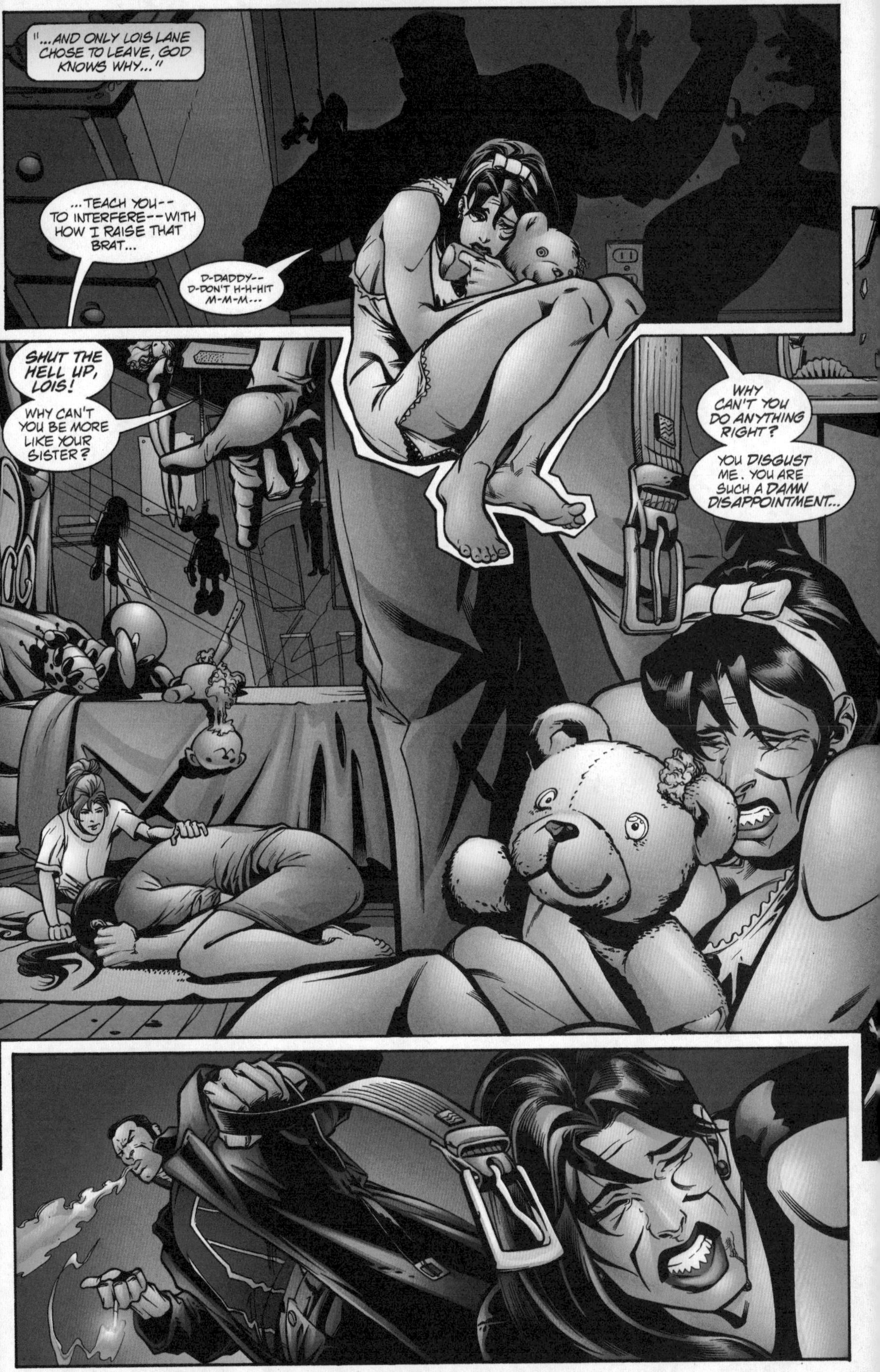
"...AND ONLY LOIS LANE CHOSE TO LEAVE, GOD KNOWS WHY..."
...TEACH YOU-- TO INTERFERE--WITH HOW I RAISE THAT BRAT...
D-DADDY-- D-DON'T H-H-HIT M-M-M...
SHUT THE HELL UP, LOIS!
WHY CAN'T YOU BE MORE LIKE YOUR SISTER?
WHY CAN'T YOU DO ANYTHING RIGHT?
YOU DISGUST ME. YOU ARE SUCH A DAMN DISAPPOINTMENT...

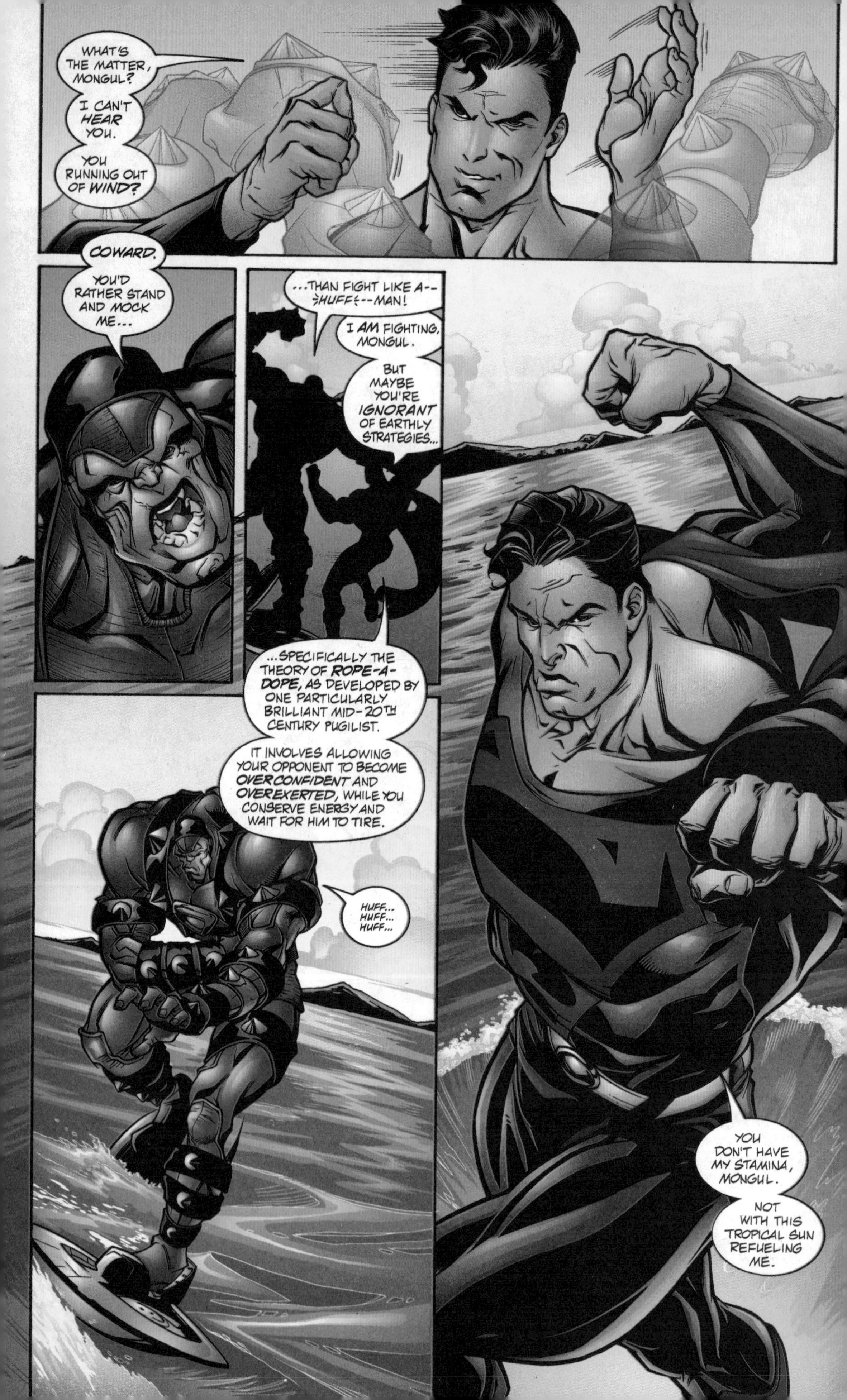
WHAT'S THE MATTER, MONGUL?
I CAN'T HEAR YOU.
YOU RUNNING OUT OF WIND?
COWARD.
YOU'D RATHER STAND AND MOCK ME...
...THAN FIGHT LIKE A-- *HUFF*--MAN!
I AM FIGHTING, MONGUL.
BUT MAYBE YOU'RE IGNORANT OF EARTHLY STRATEGIES...
...SPECIFICALLY THE THEORY OF ROPE-A-DOPE, AS DEVELOPED BY ONE PARTICULARLY BRILLIANT MID-20TH CENTURY PUGILIST.
IT INVOLVES ALLOWING YOUR OPPONENT TO BECOME OVERCONFIDENT AND OVEREXERTED, WHILE YOU CONSERVE ENERGY AND WAIT FOR HIM TO TIRE.
HUFF... HUFF... HUFF...
YOU DON'T HAVE MY STAMINA, MONGUL.
NOT WITH THIS TROPICAL SUN REFUELING ME.

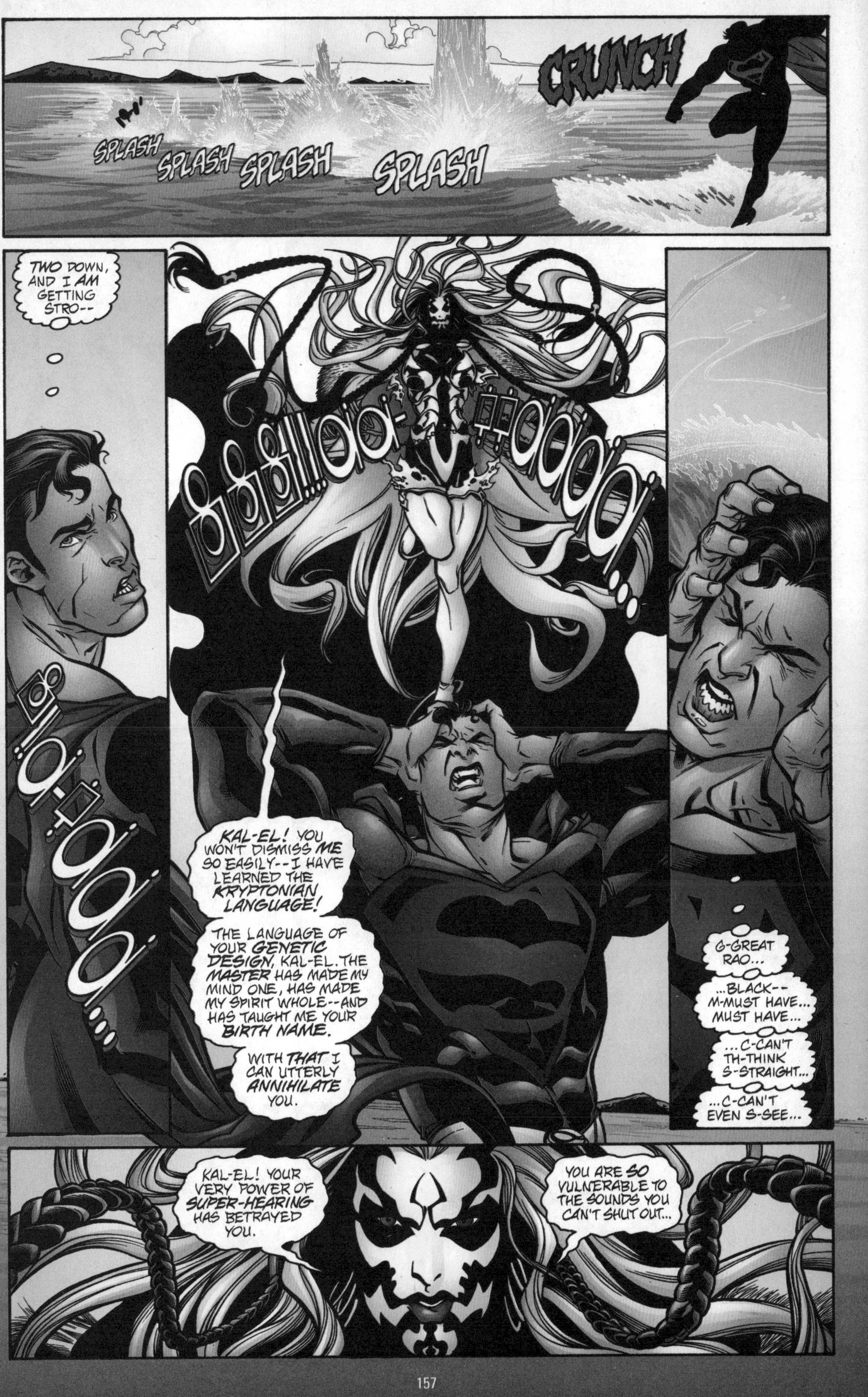
SPLASH
SPLASH
SPLASH
SPLASH
CRUNCH
TWO DOWN, AND I AM GETTING STRO--
KAL-EL! YOU WON'T DISMISS ME SO EASILY--I HAVE LEARNED THE KRYPTONIAN LANGUAGE!
THE LANGUAGE OF YOUR GENETIC DESIGN, KAL-EL. THE MASTER HAS MADE MY MIND ONE, HAS MADE MY SPIRIT WHOLE--AND HAS TAUGHT ME YOUR BIRTH NAME.
WITH THAT I CAN UTTERLY ANNIHILATE YOU.
G-GREAT RAO...
...BLACK-- M-MUST HAVE... MUST HAVE...
...C-CAN'T TH-THINK S-STRAIGHT...
...C-CAN'T EVEN S-SEE...
KAL-EL! YOUR VERY POWER OF SUPER-HEARING HAS BETRAYED YOU.
YOU ARE SO VULNERABLE TO THE SOUNDS YOU CAN'T SHUT OUT...

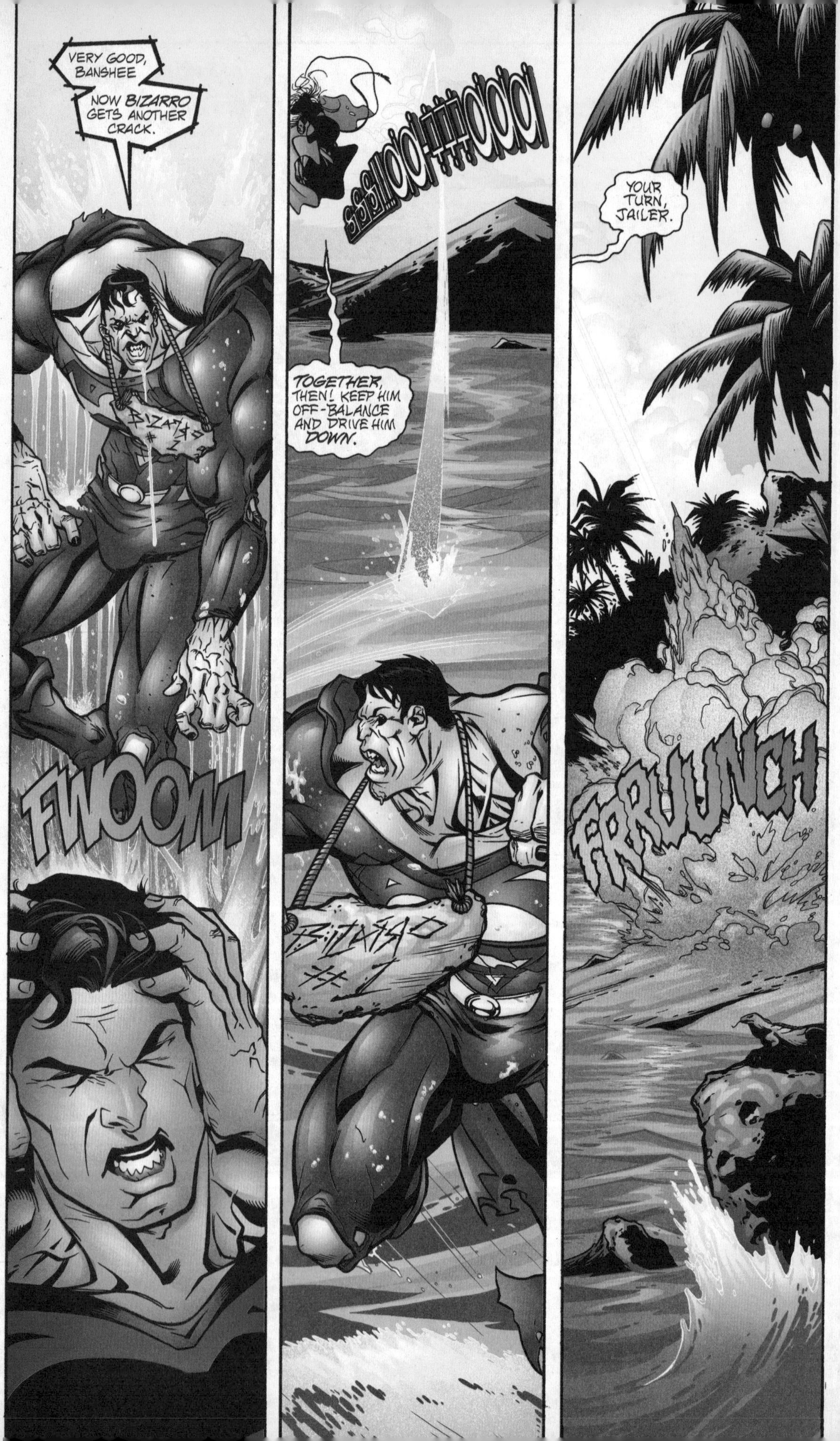
VERY GOOD, BANSHEE
NOW BIZARRO GETS ANOTHER CRACK.
FWOOM
TOGETHER, THEN! KEEP HIM OFF-BALANCE AND DRIVE HIM DOWN.
YOUR TURN, JAILER.
FRRUUNCH

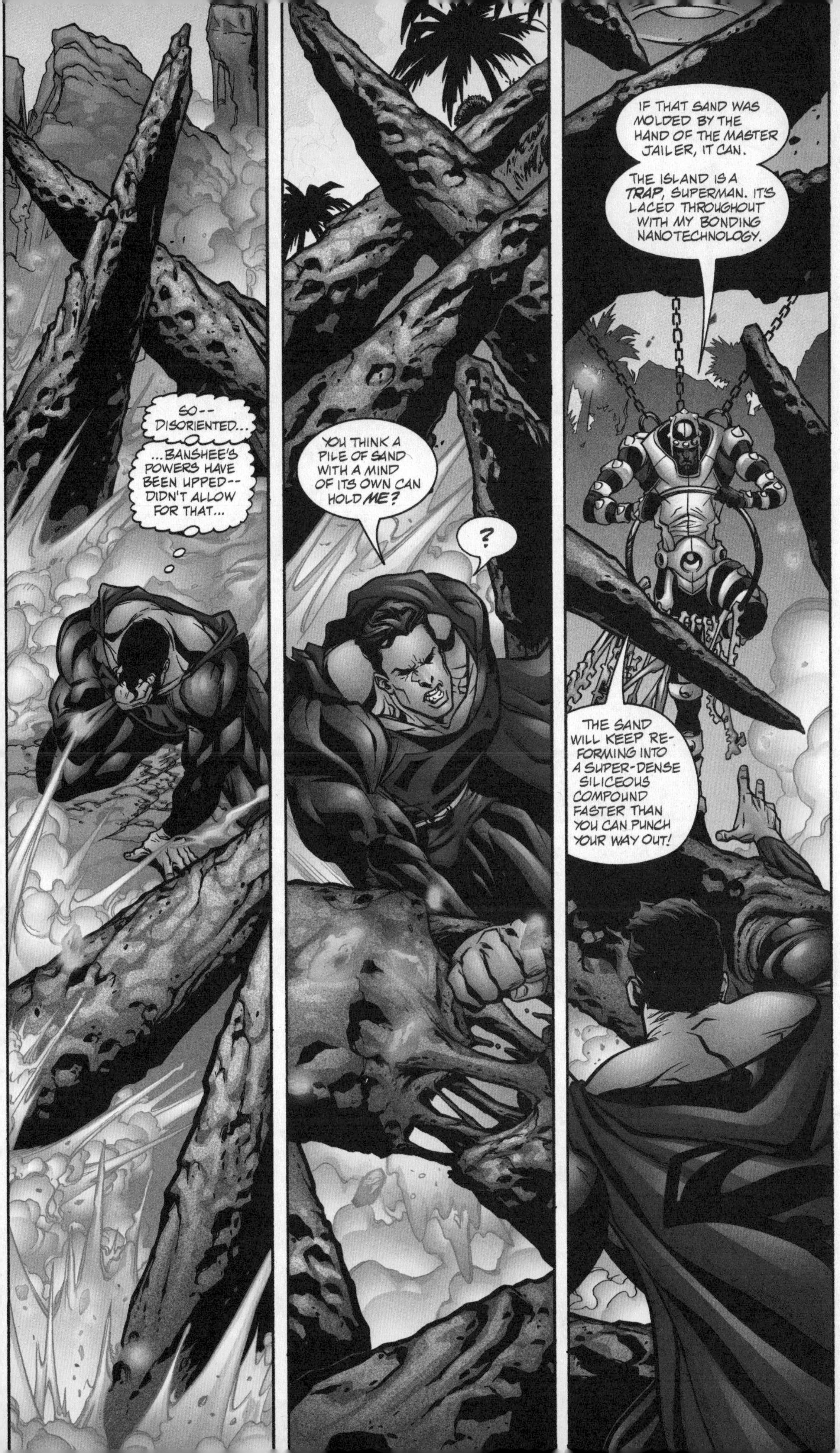
SO-- DISORIENTED...
...BANSHEE'S POWERS HAVE BEEN UPPED-- DIDN'T ALLOW FOR THAT...
YOU THINK A PILE OF SAND WITH A MIND OF ITS OWN CAN HOLD *ME*?
?
IF THAT SAND WAS MOLDED BY THE HAND OF THE MASTER JAILER, IT CAN.
THE ISLAND IS A *TRAP*, SUPERMAN. IT'S LACED THROUGHOUT WITH MY BONDING NANOTECHNOLOGY.
THE SAND WILL KEEP RE-FORMING INTO A SUPER-DENSE SILICEOUS COMPOUND FASTER THAN YOU CAN PUNCH YOUR WAY OUT!

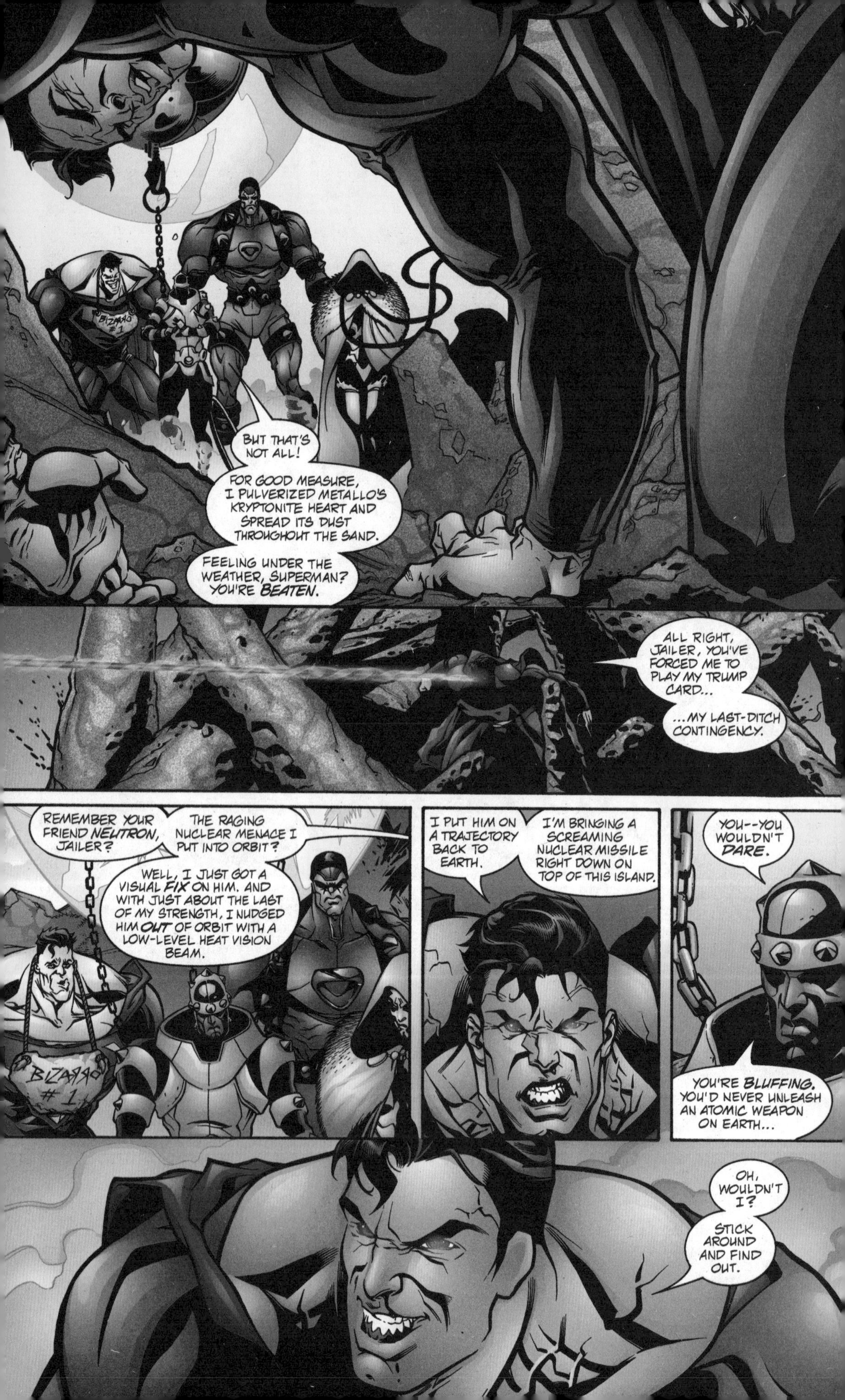

BIZARRO #1
BUT THAT'S NOT ALL!
FOR GOOD MEASURE, I PULVERIZED METALLO'S KRYPTONITE HEART AND SPREAD ITS DUST THROUGHOUT THE SAND.
FEELING UNDER THE WEATHER, SUPERMAN? YOU'RE BEATEN.
ALL RIGHT, JAILER, YOU'VE FORCED ME TO PLAY MY TRUMP CARD...
...MY LAST-DITCH CONTINGENCY.
REMEMBER YOUR FRIEND NEUTRON, JAILER?
THE RAGING NUCLEAR MENACE I PUT INTO ORBIT?
WELL, I JUST GOT A VISUAL FIX ON HIM. AND WITH JUST ABOUT THE LAST OF MY STRENGTH, I NUDGED HIM OUT OF ORBIT WITH A LOW-LEVEL HEAT VISION BEAM.
BIZARRO #1
I PUT HIM ON A TRAJECTORY BACK TO EARTH.
I'M BRINGING A SCREAMING NUCLEAR MISSILE RIGHT DOWN ON TOP OF THIS ISLAND.
YOU--YOU WOULDN'T DARE.
YOU'RE BLUFFING. YOU'D NEVER UNLEASH AN ATOMIC WEAPON ON EARTH...
OH, WOULDN'T I?
STICK AROUND AND FIND OUT.

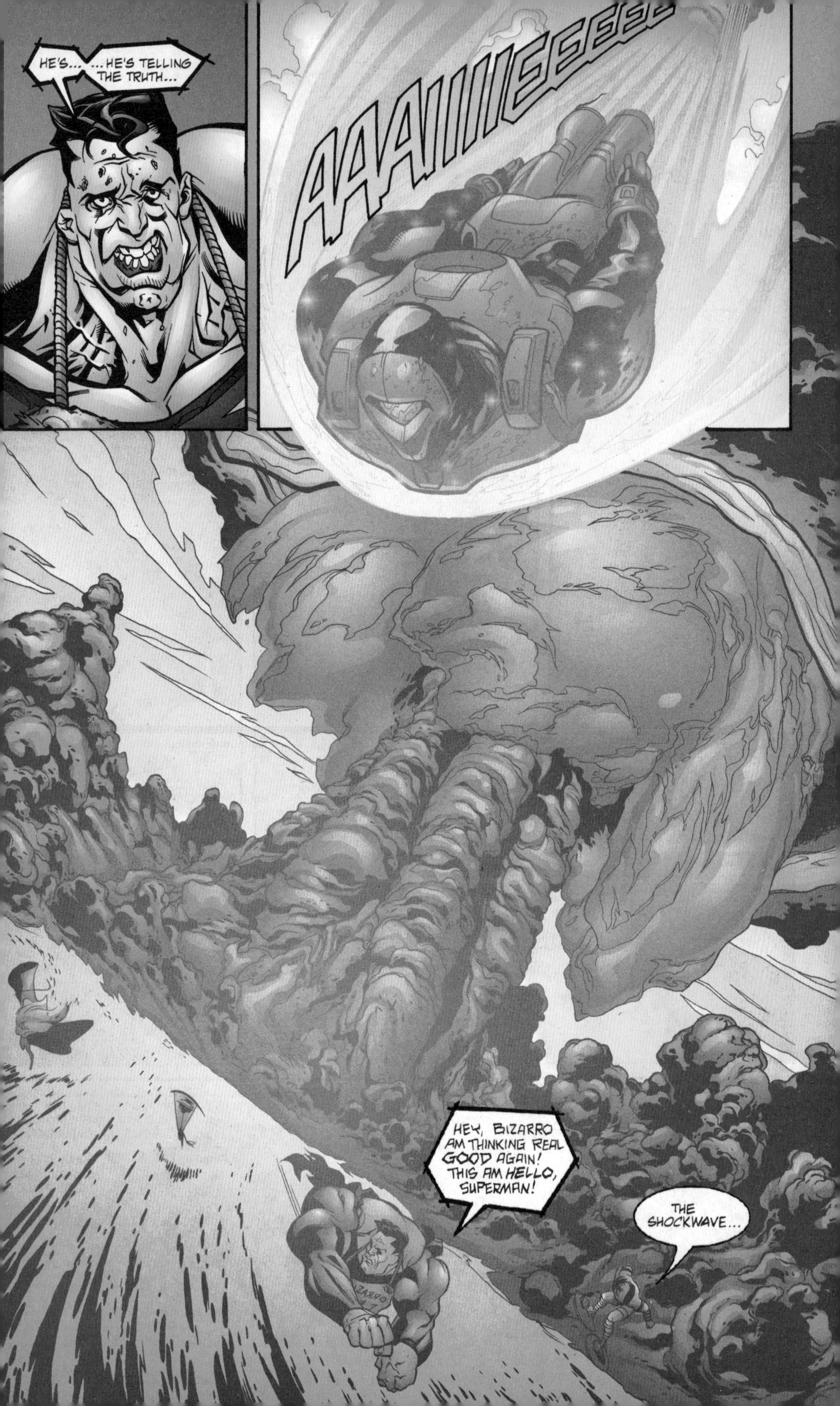

HE'S... ...HE'S TELLING THE TRUTH...
AAAIIIIEEEE!
HEY, BIZARRO AM THINKING REAL GOOD AGAIN! THIS AM HELLO, SUPERMAN!
THE SHOCKWAVE...

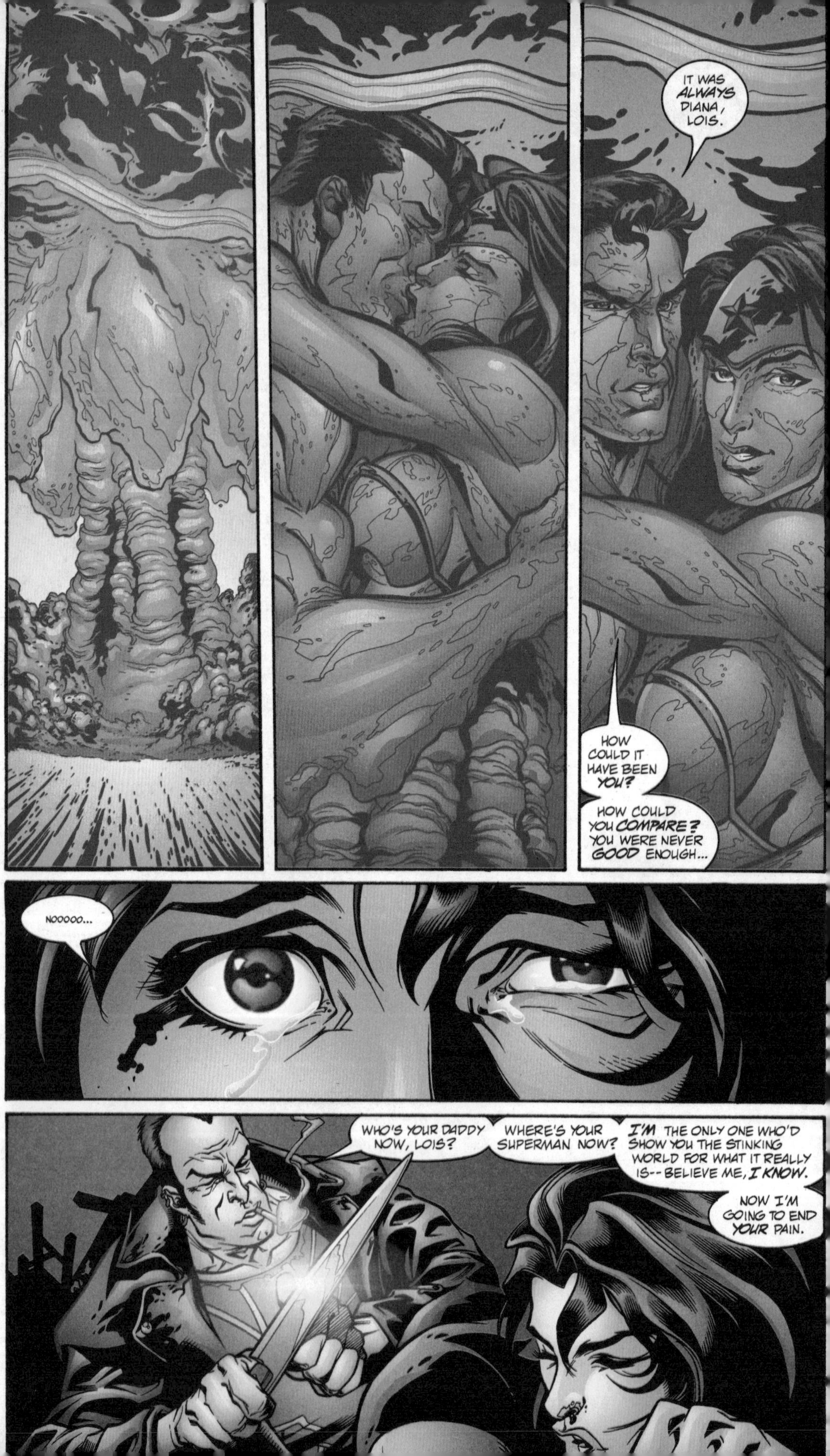
IT WAS ALWAYS DIANA, LOIS.
HOW COULD IT HAVE BEEN YOU?
HOW COULD YOU COMPARE? YOU WERE NEVER GOOD ENOUGH...
NOOOOO...
WHO'S YOUR DADDY NOW, LOIS?
WHERE'S YOUR SUPERMAN NOW?
I'M THE ONLY ONE WHO'D SHOW YOU THE STINKING WORLD FOR WHAT IT REALLY IS-- BELIEVE ME, I KNOW.
NOW I'M GOING TO END YOUR PAIN.

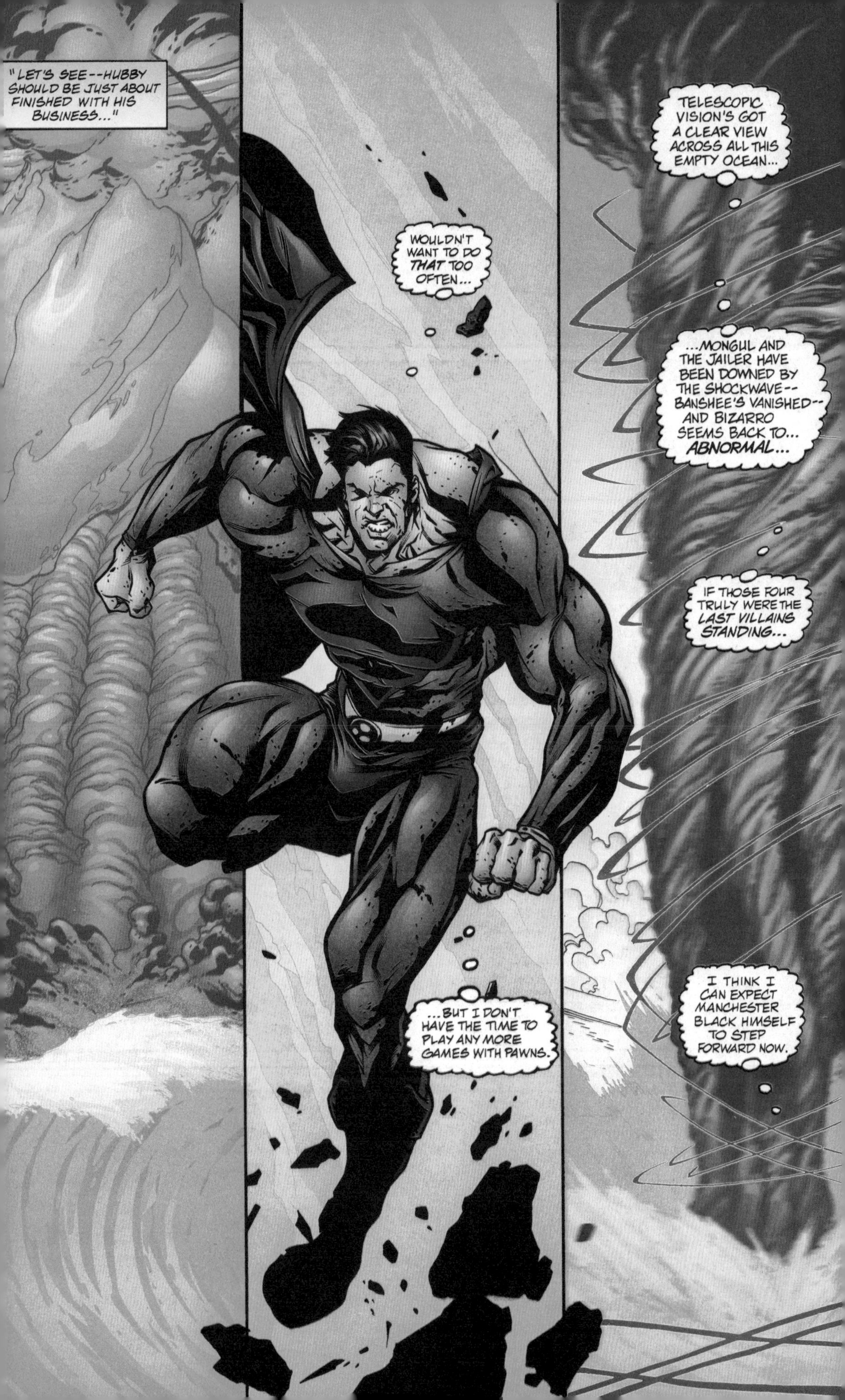
"LET'S SEE--HUBBY SHOULD BE JUST ABOUT FINISHED WITH HIS BUSINESS..."
WOULDN'T WANT TO DO THAT TOO OFTEN...
...BUT I DON'T HAVE THE TIME TO PLAY ANY MORE GAMES WITH PAWNS.
TELESCOPIC VISION'S GOT A CLEAR VIEW ACROSS ALL THIS EMPTY OCEAN...
...MONGUL AND THE JAILER HAVE BEEN DOWNED BY THE SHOCKWAVE--BANSHEE'S VANISHED--AND BIZARRO SEEMS BACK TO... ABNORMAL...
IF THOSE FOUR TRULY WERE THE LAST VILLAINS STANDING...
I THINK I CAN EXPECT MANCHESTER BLACK HIMSELF TO STEP FORWARD NOW.

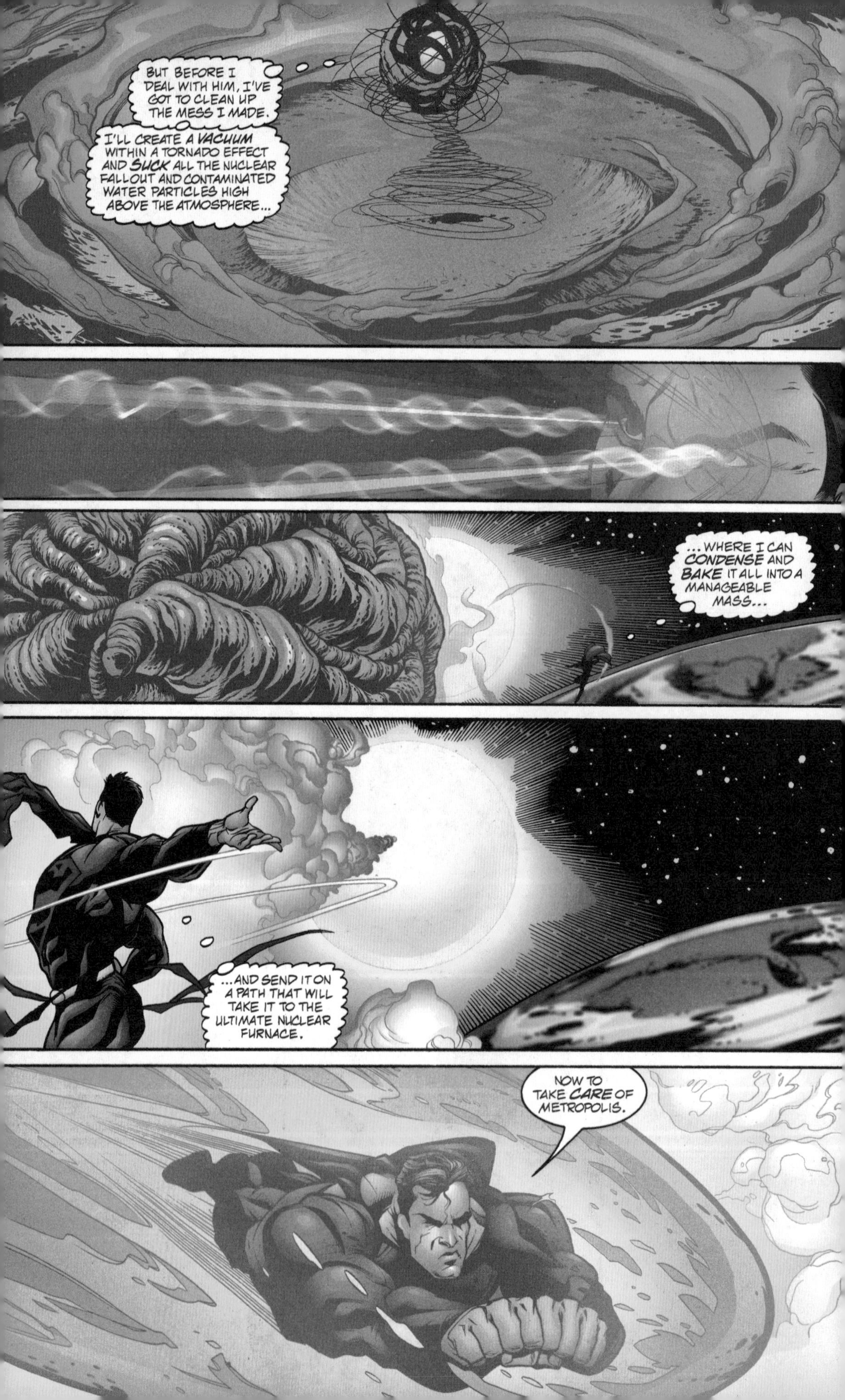
BUT BEFORE I DEAL WITH HIM, I'VE GOT TO CLEAN UP THE MESS I MADE.
I'LL CREATE A VACUUM WITHIN A TORNADO EFFECT AND SUCK ALL THE NUCLEAR FALLOUT AND CONTAMINATED WATER PARTICLES HIGH ABOVE THE ATMOSPHERE...
...WHERE I CAN CONDENSE AND BAKE IT ALL INTO A MANAGEABLE MASS...
...AND SEND IT ON A PATH THAT WILL TAKE IT TO THE ULTIMATE NUCLEAR FURNACE.
NOW TO TAKE CARE OF METROPOLIS.

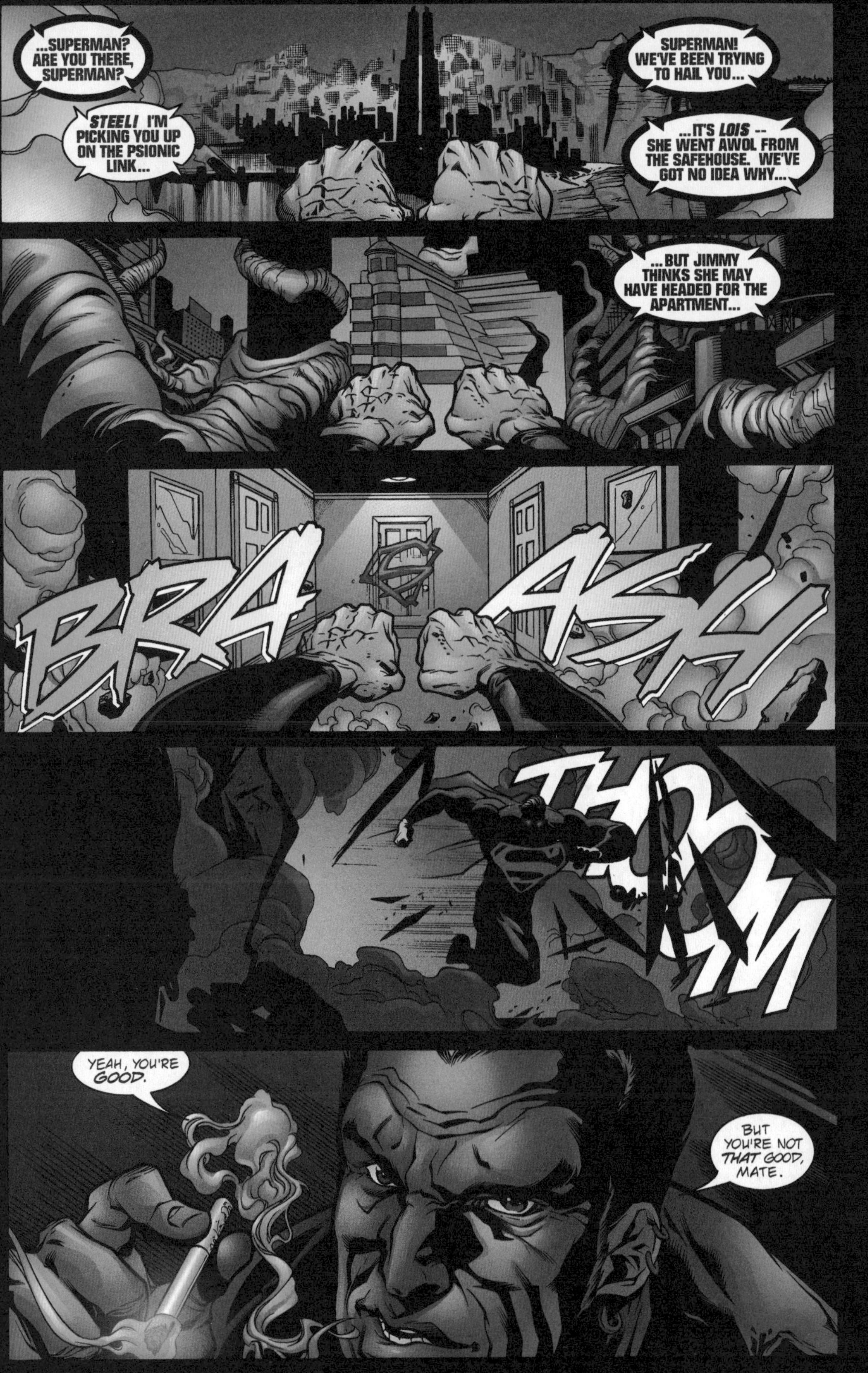
...SUPERMAN? ARE YOU THERE, SUPERMAN?
STEEL! I'M PICKING YOU UP ON THE PSIONIC LINK...
SUPERMAN! WE'VE BEEN TRYING TO HAIL YOU...
...IT'S LOIS -- SHE WENT AWOL FROM THE SAFEHOUSE. WE'VE GOT NO IDEA WHY...
...BUT JIMMY THINKS SHE MAY HAVE HEADED FOR THE APARTMENT...
BRAASH
YEAH, YOU'RE GOOD.
BUT YOU'RE NOT THAT GOOD, MATE.

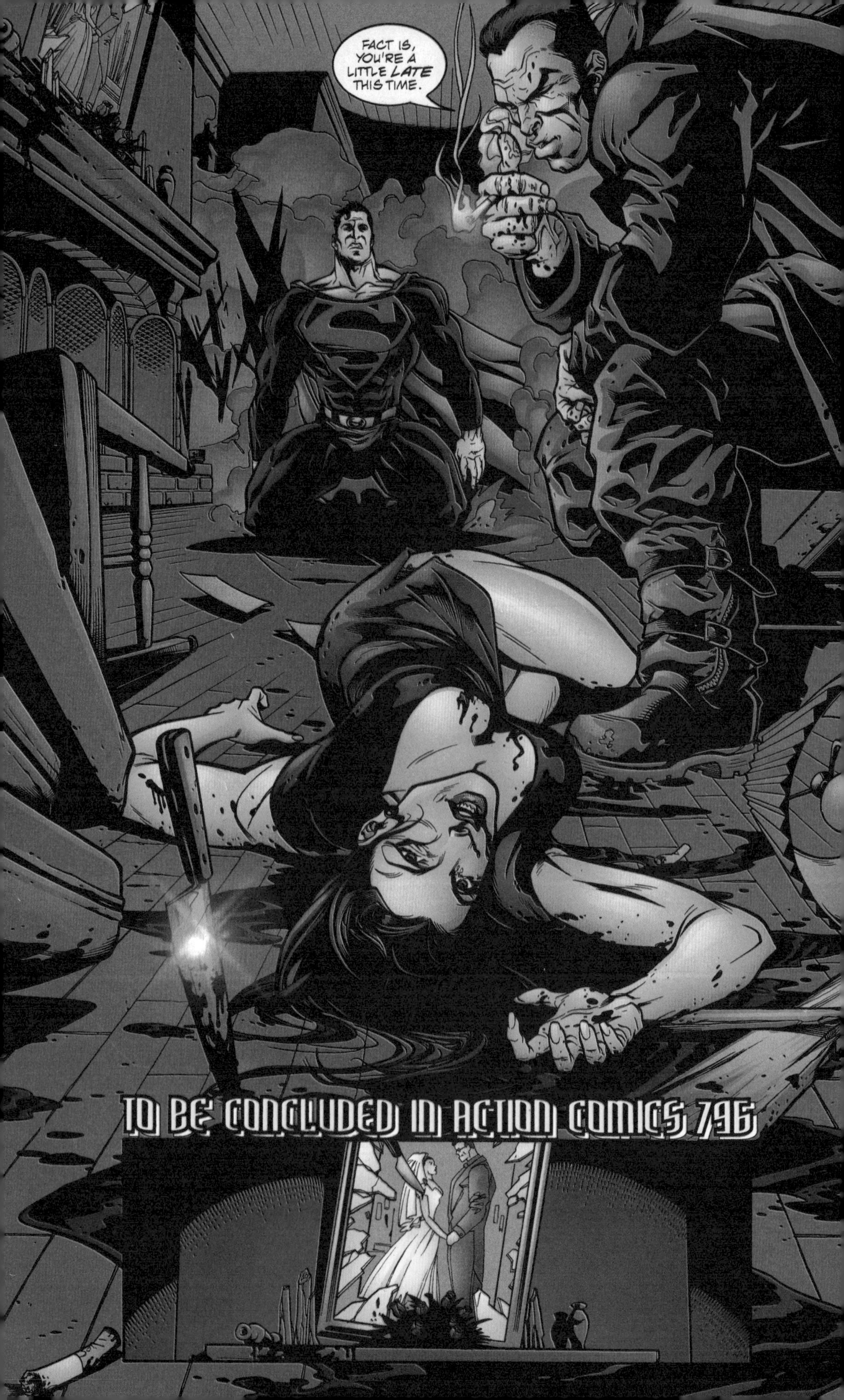
FACT IS, YOU'RE A LITTLE *LATE* THIS TIME.
TO BE CONCLUDED IN ACTION COMICS 796

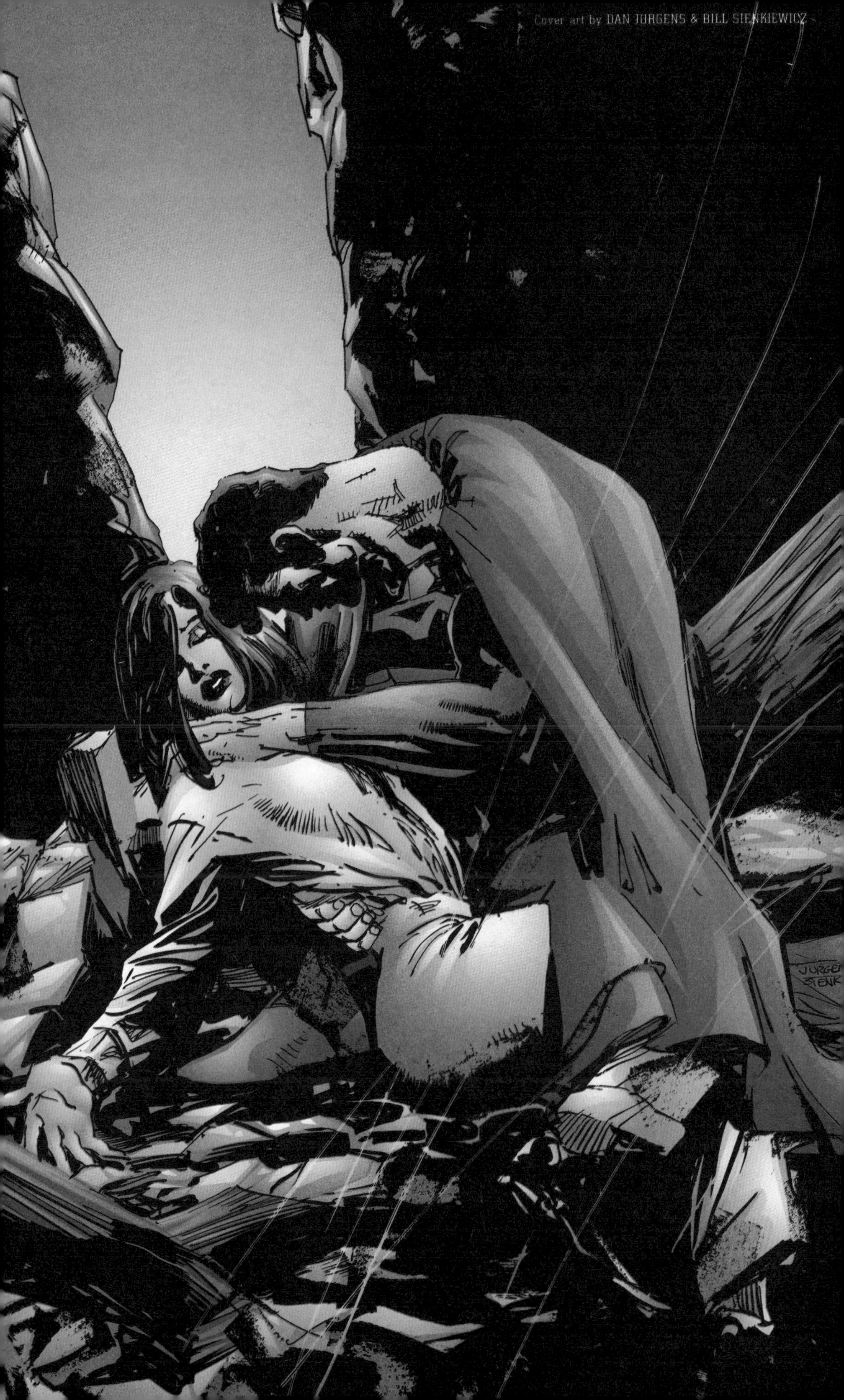

Cover art by DAN JURGENS & BILL SIENKIEWICZ

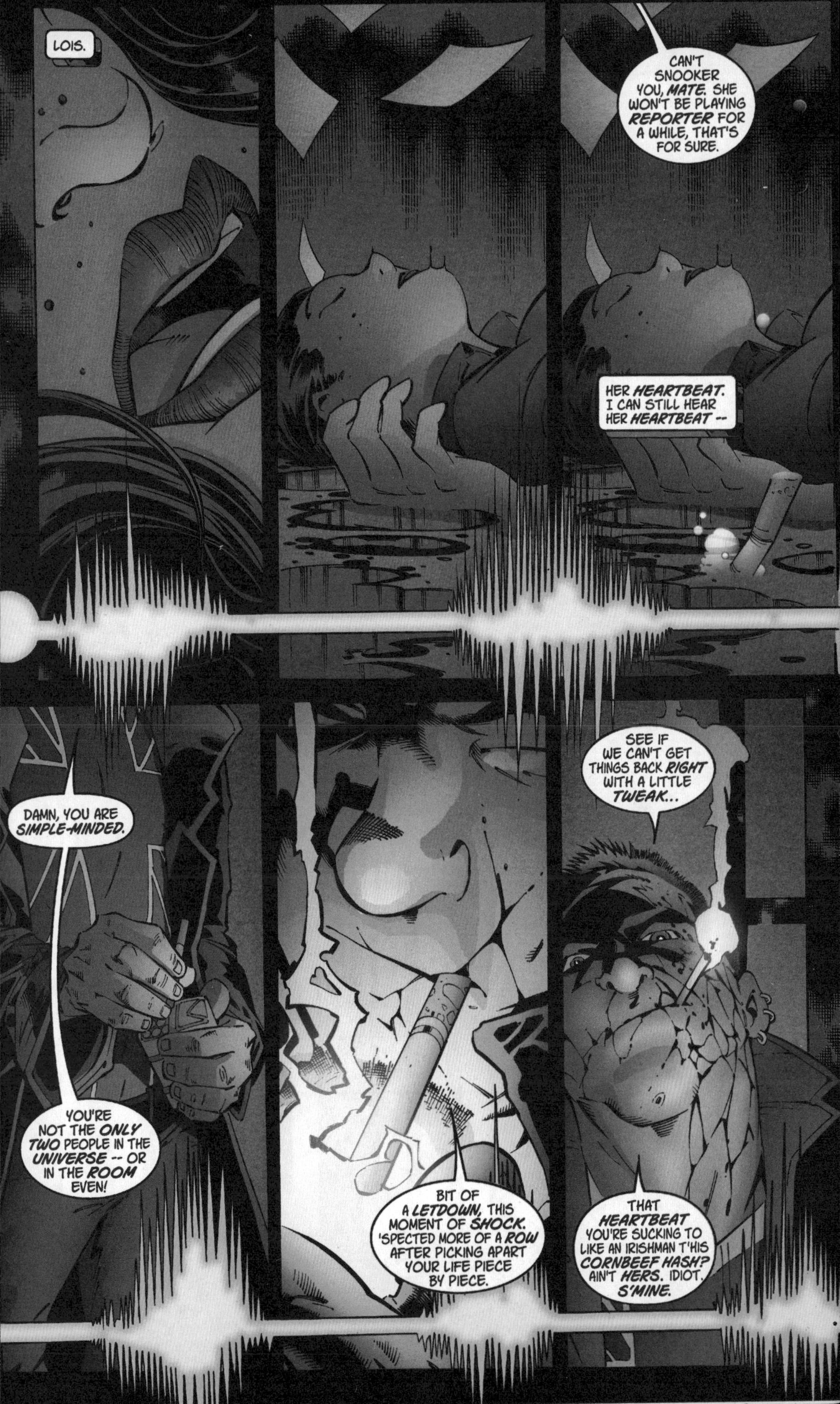
LOIS.
CAN'T SNOOKER YOU, MATE. SHE WON'T BE PLAYING REPORTER FOR A WHILE, THAT'S FOR SURE.
HER HEARTBEAT. I CAN STILL HEAR HER HEARTBEAT --
DAMN, YOU ARE SIMPLE-MINDED.
YOU'RE NOT THE ONLY TWO PEOPLE IN THE UNIVERSE -- OR IN THE ROOM EVEN!
BIT OF A LETDOWN, THIS MOMENT OF SHOCK. 'SPECTED MORE OF A ROW AFTER PICKING APART YOUR LIFE PIECE BY PIECE.
SEE IF WE CAN'T GET THINGS BACK RIGHT WITH A LITTLE TWEAK...
THAT HEARTBEAT YOU'RE SUCKING TO LIKE AN IRISHMAN T'HIS CORNBEEF HASH? AIN'T HERS. IDIOT. S'MINE.

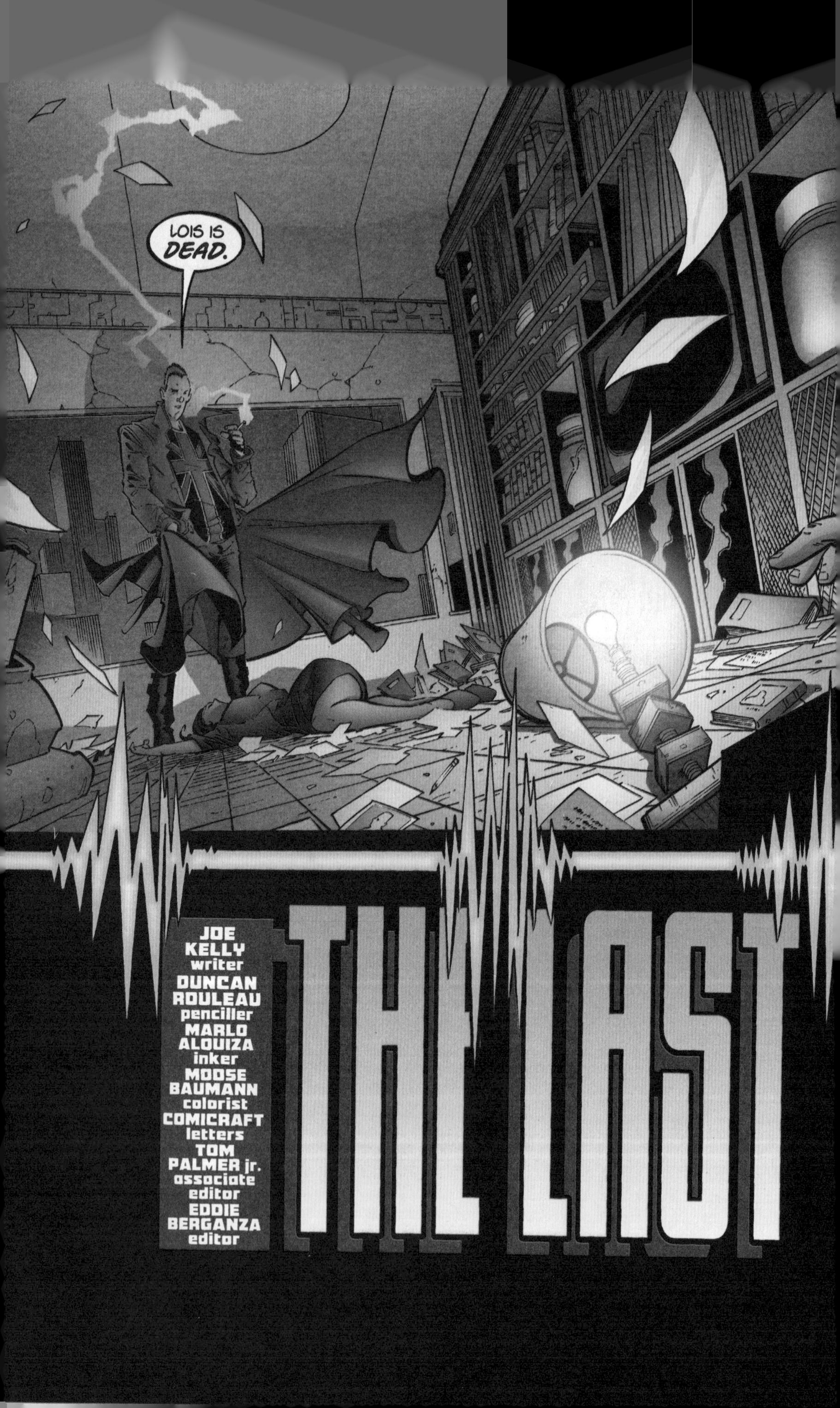

LOIS IS DEAD.
JOE KELLY writer
DUNCAN ROULEAU penciller
MARLO ALOUIZA inker
MOOSE BAUMANN colorist
COMICRAFT letters
TOM PALMER jr. associate editor
EDDIE BERGANZA editor
THE LAST

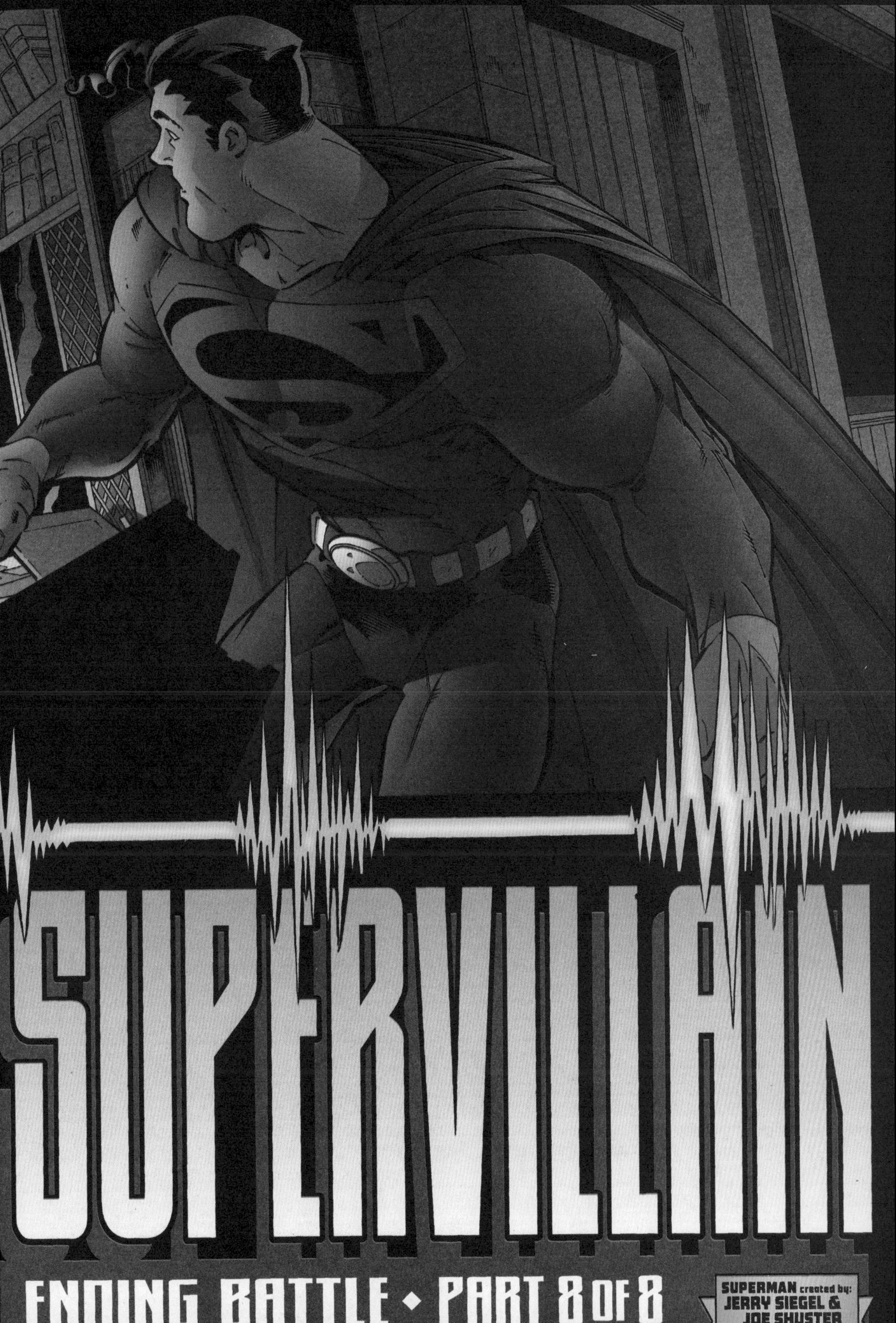
SUPERVILLAIN
ENDING BATTLE ◆ PART 8 OF 8
SUPERMAN created by:
JERRY SIEGEL &
JOE SHUSTER

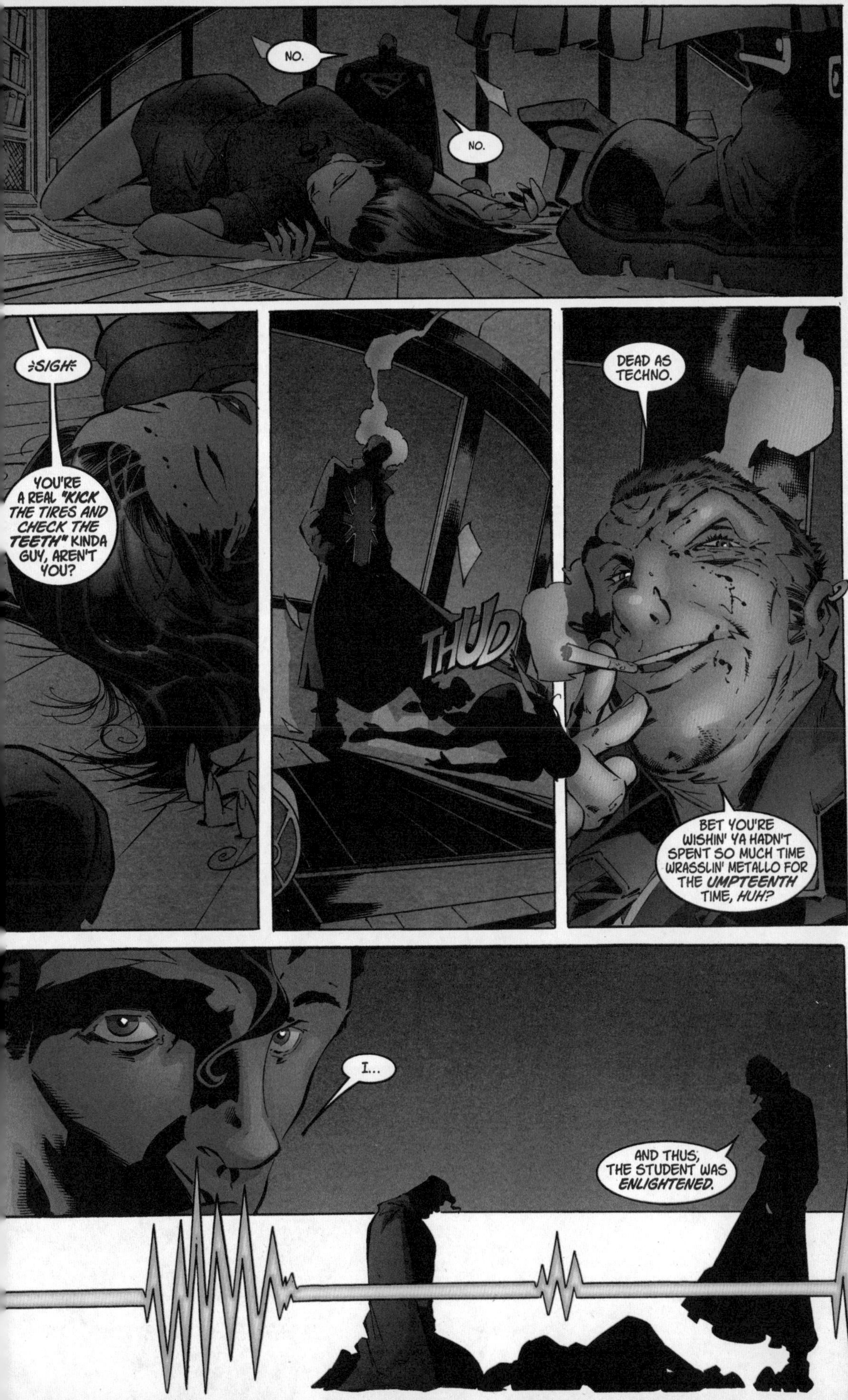

NO.
NO.
SIGH
YOU'RE A REAL "KICK THE TIRES AND CHECK THE TEETH" KINDA GUY, AREN'T YOU?
THUD
DEAD AS TECHNO.
BET YOU'RE WISHIN' YA HADN'T SPENT SO MUCH TIME WRASSLIN' METALLO FOR THE UMPTEENTH TIME, HUH?
I...
AND THUS, THE STUDENT WAS ENLIGHTENED.

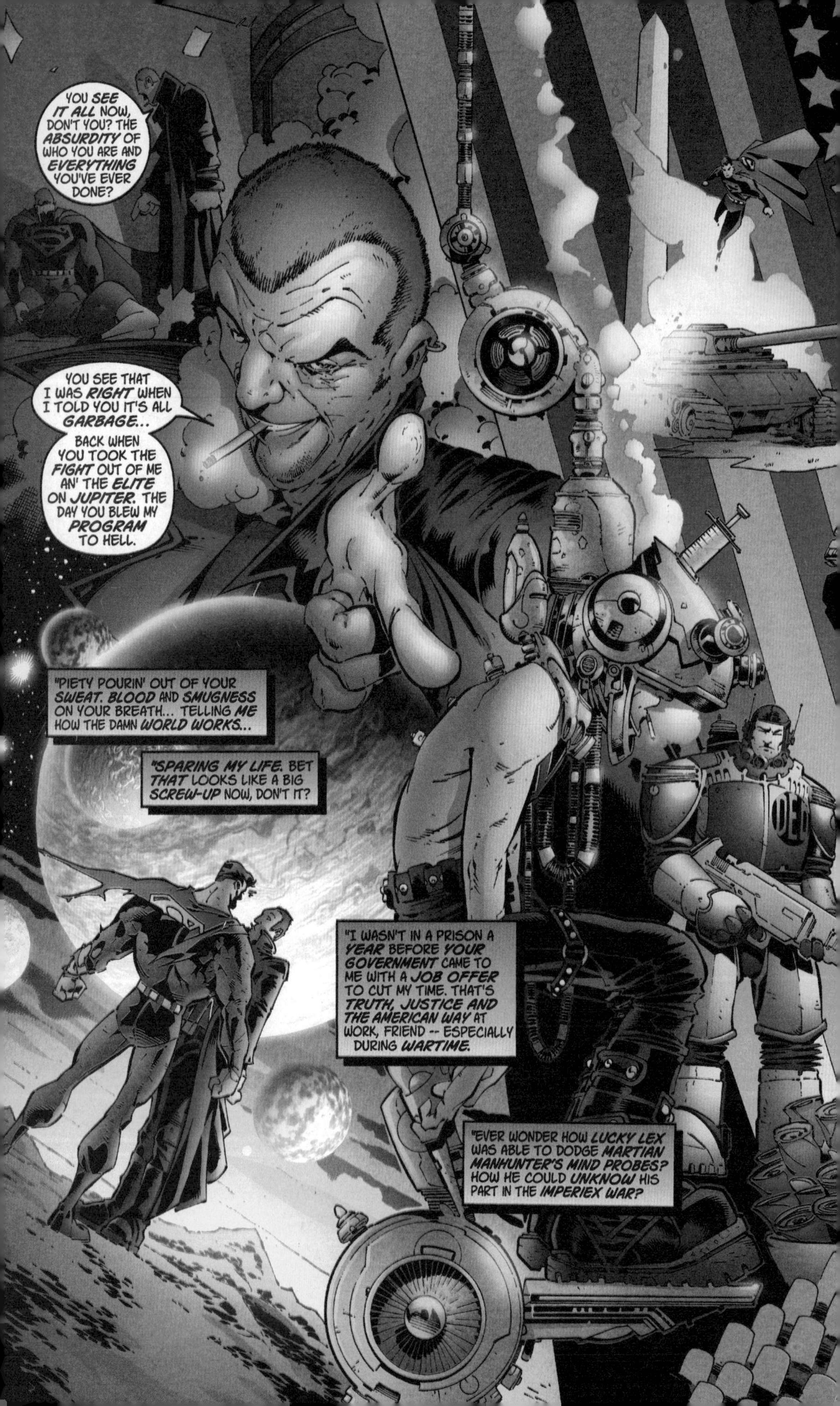
YOU SEE IT ALL NOW, DON'T YOU? THE ABSURDITY OF WHO YOU ARE AND EVERYTHING YOU'VE EVER DONE?
YOU SEE THAT I WAS RIGHT WHEN I TOLD YOU IT'S ALL GARBAGE...
BACK WHEN YOU TOOK THE FIGHT OUT OF ME AN' THE ELITE ON JUPITER. THE DAY YOU BLEW MY PROGRAM TO HELL.
"PIETY POURIN' OUT OF YOUR SWEAT. BLOOD AND SMUGNESS ON YOUR BREATH... TELLING ME HOW THE DAMN WORLD WORKS...
"SPARING MY LIFE. BET THAT LOOKS LIKE A BIG SCREW-UP NOW, DON'T IT?
"I WASN'T IN A PRISON A YEAR BEFORE YOUR GOVERNMENT CAME TO ME WITH A JOB OFFER TO CUT MY TIME. THAT'S TRUTH, JUSTICE AND THE AMERICAN WAY AT WORK, FRIEND -- ESPECIALLY DURING WARTIME.
"EVER WONDER HOW LUCKY LEX WAS ABLE TO DODGE MARTIAN MANHUNTER'S MIND PROBES? HOW HE COULD UNKNOW HIS PART IN THE IMPERIEX WAR?

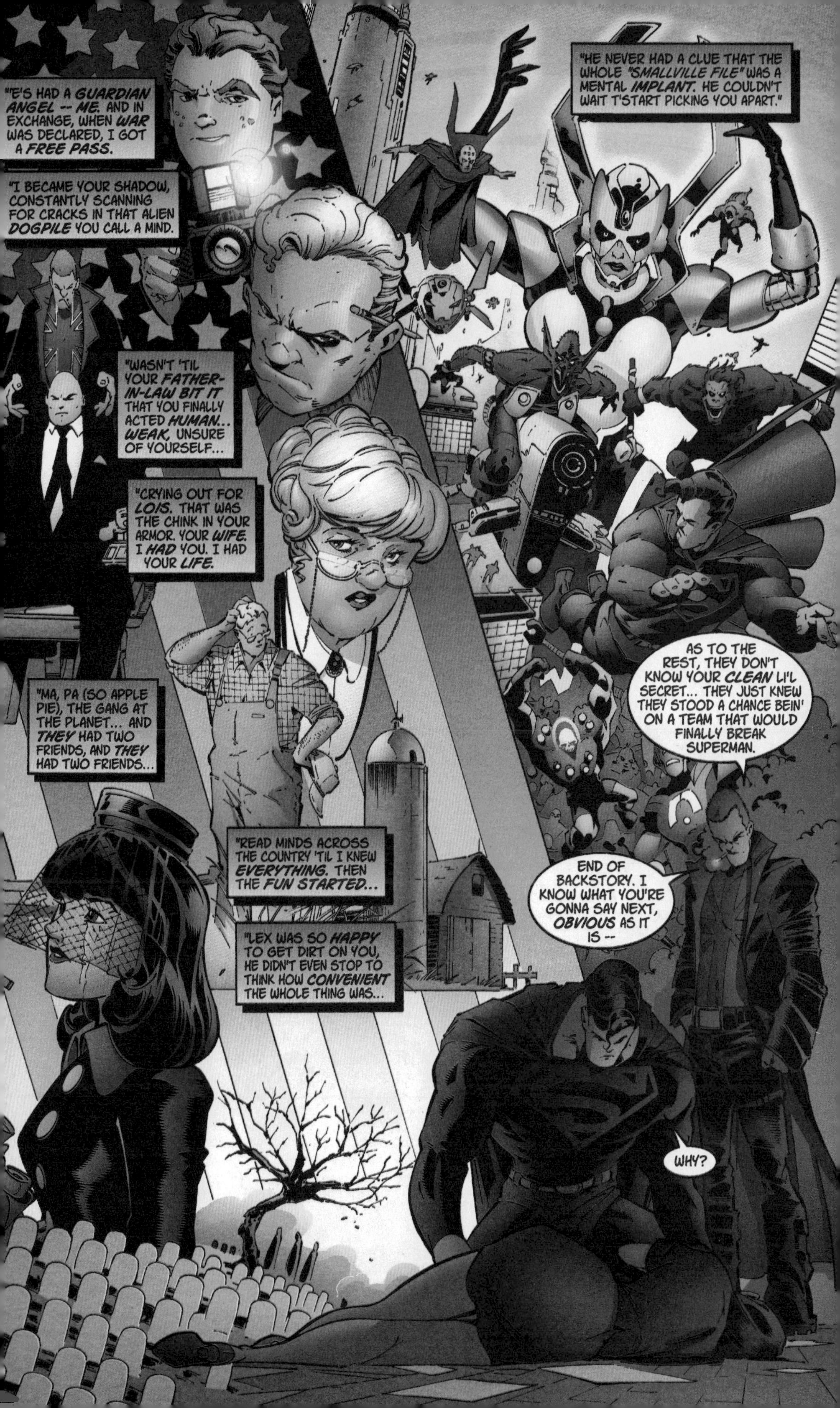
"E'S HAD A GUARDIAN ANGEL -- ME. AND IN EXCHANGE, WHEN WAR WAS DECLARED, I GOT A FREE PASS.
"I BECAME YOUR SHADOW, CONSTANTLY SCANNING FOR CRACKS IN THAT ALIEN DOGPILE YOU CALL A MIND.
"WASN'T 'TIL YOUR FATHER-IN-LAW BIT IT THAT YOU FINALLY ACTED HUMAN... WEAK, UNSURE OF YOURSELF...
"CRYING OUT FOR LOIS. THAT WAS THE CHINK IN YOUR ARMOR. YOUR WIFE. I HAD YOU. I HAD YOUR LIFE.
"MA, PA (SO APPLE PIE), THE GANG AT THE PLANET... AND THEY HAD TWO FRIENDS, AND THEY HAD TWO FRIENDS...
"READ MINDS ACROSS THE COUNTRY 'TIL I KNEW EVERYTHING. THEN THE FUN STARTED...
"LEX WAS SO HAPPY TO GET DIRT ON YOU, HE DIDN'T EVEN STOP TO THINK HOW CONVENIENT THE WHOLE THING WAS...
"HE NEVER HAD A CLUE THAT THE WHOLE "SMALLVILLE FILE" WAS A MENTAL IMPLANT. HE COULDN'T WAIT T'START PICKING YOU APART."
AS TO THE REST, THEY DON'T KNOW YOUR CLEAN LI'L SECRET... THEY JUST KNEW THEY STOOD A CHANCE BEIN' ON A TEAM THAT WOULD FINALLY BREAK SUPERMAN.
END OF BACKSTORY. I KNOW WHAT YOU'RE GONNA SAY NEXT, OBVIOUS AS IT IS --
WHY?

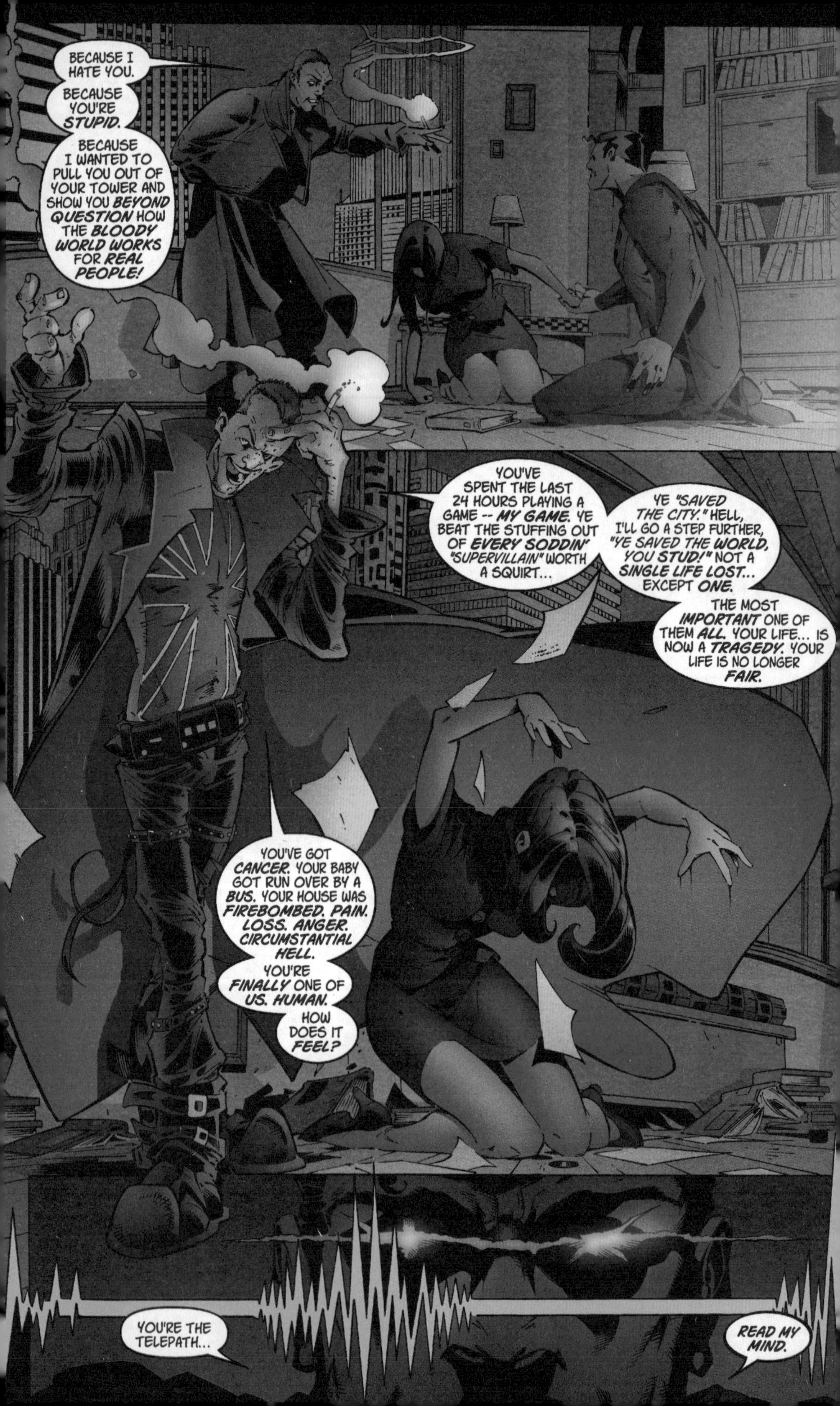

BECAUSE I HATE YOU.
BECAUSE YOU'RE *STUPID.*
BECAUSE I WANTED TO PULL YOU OUT OF YOUR TOWER AND SHOW YOU *BEYOND QUESTION* HOW THE *BLOODY WORLD WORKS* FOR *REAL PEOPLE!*
YOU'VE SPENT THE LAST 24 HOURS PLAYING A GAME -- *MY GAME.* YE BEAT THE STUFFING OUT OF *EVERY SODDIN'* "SUPERVILLAIN" WORTH A SQUIRT...
YE *"SAVED THE CITY."* HELL, I'LL GO A STEP FURTHER, *"YE SAVED THE WORLD, YOU STUD!"* NOT A *SINGLE LIFE LOST...* EXCEPT *ONE.*
THE MOST *IMPORTANT* ONE OF THEM *ALL.* YOUR LIFE... IS NOW A *TRAGEDY.* YOUR LIFE IS NO LONGER *FAIR.*
YOU'VE GOT *CANCER.* YOUR BABY GOT RUN OVER BY A *BUS.* YOUR HOUSE WAS *FIREBOMBED. PAIN. LOSS. ANGER. CIRCUMSTANTIAL HELL.*
YOU'RE *FINALLY* ONE OF *US. HUMAN.*
HOW DOES IT *FEEL?*
YOU'RE THE TELEPATH...
READ MY MIND.

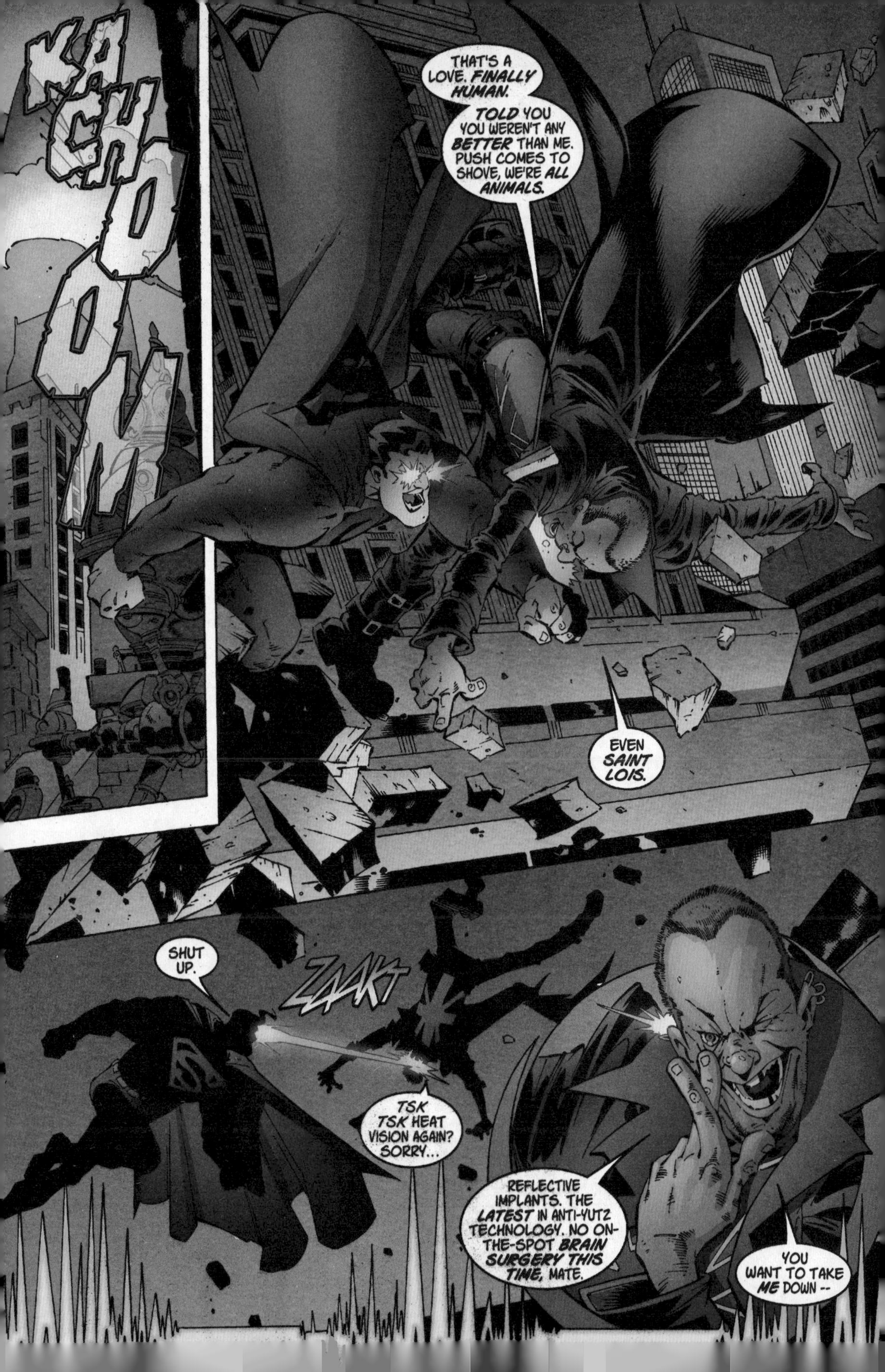

KA CHOOM
THAT'S A LOVE. FINALLY HUMAN.
TOLD YOU YOU WEREN'T ANY BETTER THAN ME. PUSH COMES TO SHOVE, WE'RE ALL ANIMALS.
EVEN SAINT LOIS.
SHUT UP.
ZZAKT
TSK TSK HEAT VISION AGAIN? SORRY...
REFLECTIVE IMPLANTS. THE LATEST IN ANTI-YUTZ TECHNOLOGY. NO ON-THE-SPOT BRAIN SURGERY THIS TIME, MATE.
YOU WANT TO TAKE ME DOWN --

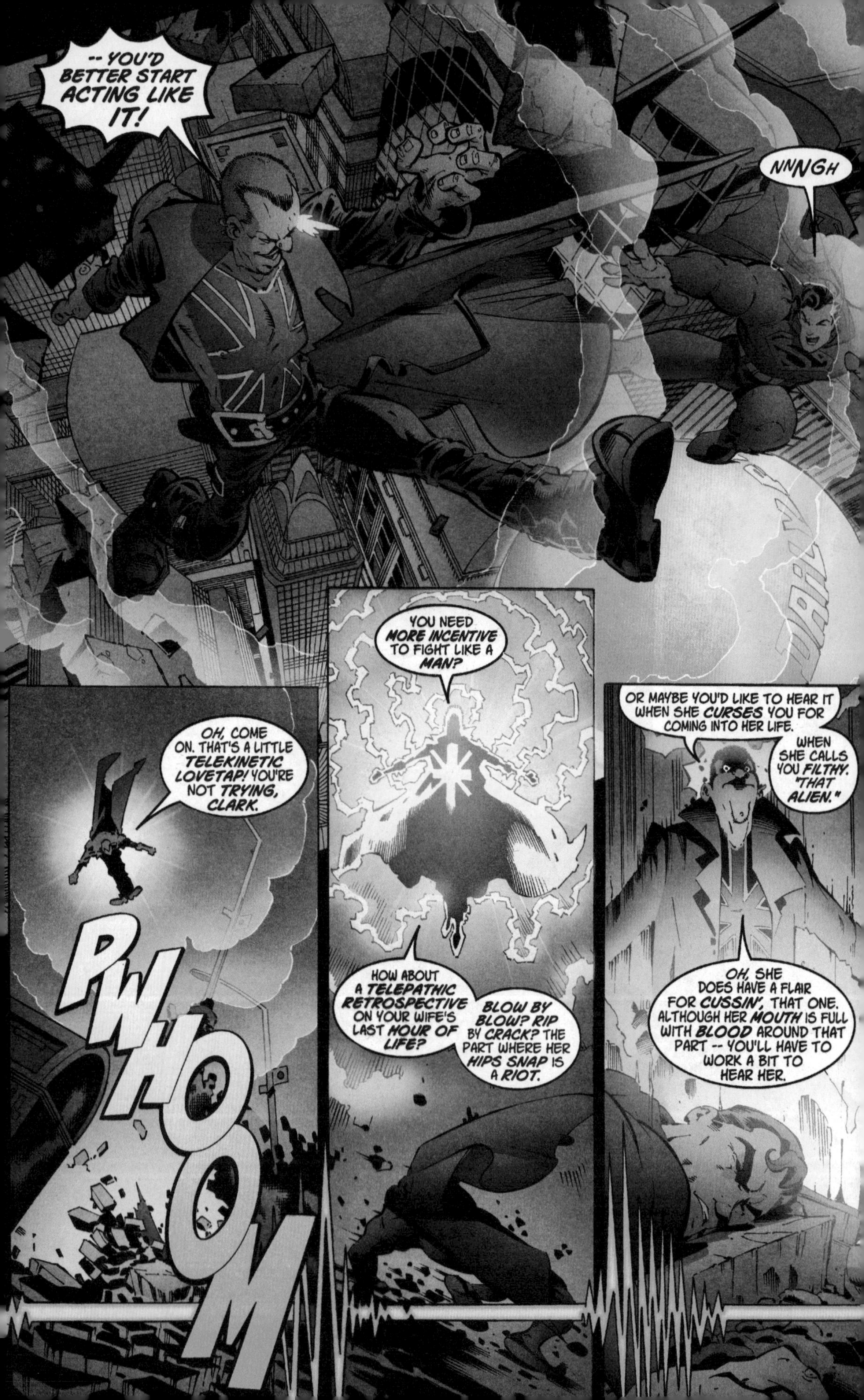
-- YOU'D BETTER START ACTING LIKE IT!
NNNGH
OH, COME ON. THAT'S A LITTLE TELEKINETIC LOVETAP! YOU'RE NOT TRYING, CLARK.
PWHOOM
YOU NEED MORE INCENTIVE TO FIGHT LIKE A MAN?
HOW ABOUT A TELEPATHIC RETROSPECTIVE ON YOUR WIFE'S LAST HOUR OF LIFE?
BLOW BY BLOW? RIP BY CRACK? THE PART WHERE HER HIPS SNAP IS A RIOT.
OR MAYBE YOU'D LIKE TO HEAR IT WHEN SHE CURSES YOU FOR COMING INTO HER LIFE.
WHEN SHE CALLS YOU FILTHY. "THAT ALIEN."
OH, SHE DOES HAVE A FLAIR FOR CUSSIN', THAT ONE. ALTHOUGH HER MOUTH IS FULL WITH BLOOD AROUND THAT PART -- YOU'LL HAVE TO WORK A BIT TO HEAR HER.

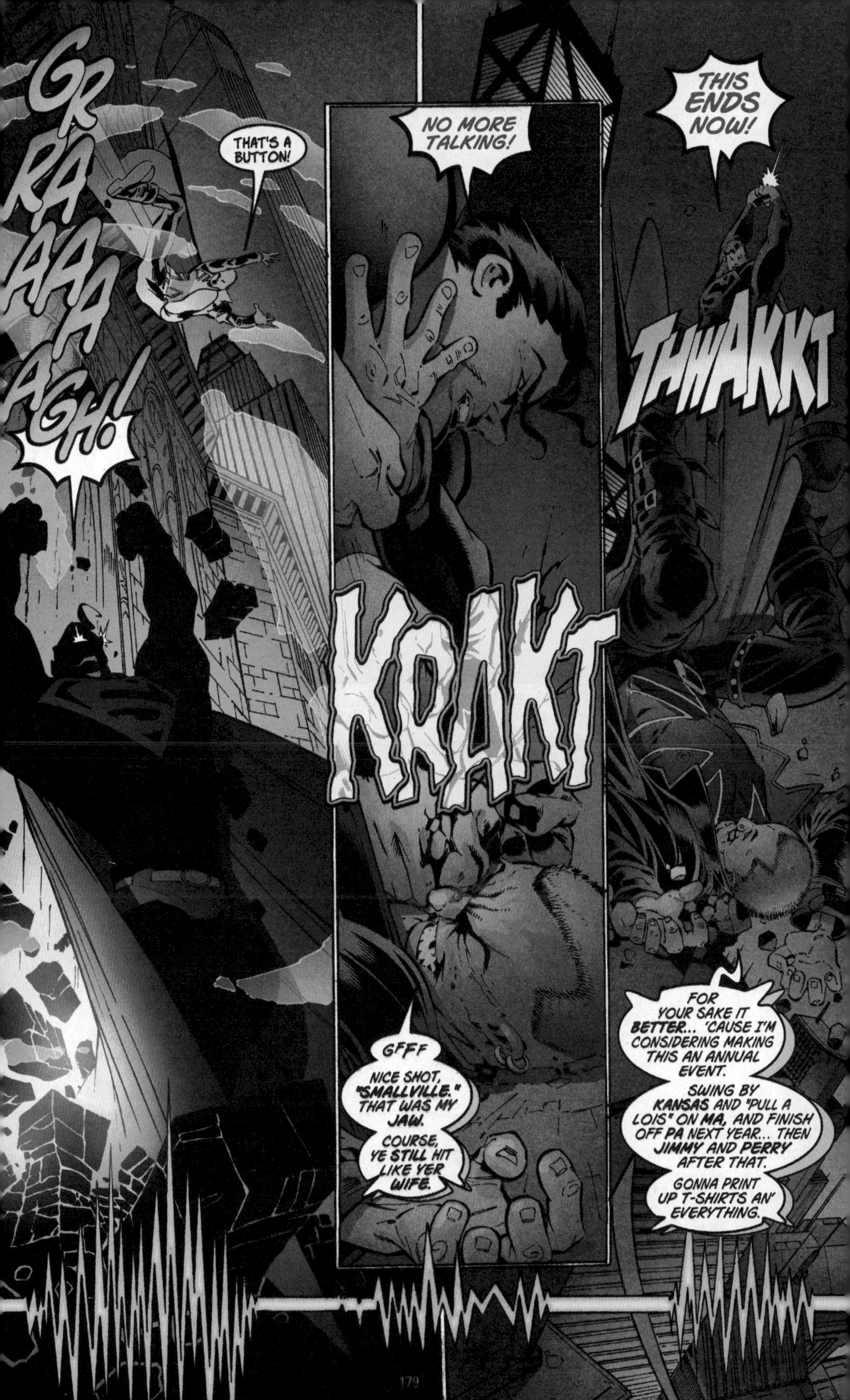

GRRAAAAAAAGH!!
THAT'S A BUTTON!
NO MORE TALKING!
KRAKT
GFFF
NICE SHOT, "SMALLVILLE." THAT WAS MY JAW.
COURSE, YE STILL HIT LIKE YER WIFE.
THIS ENDS NOW!
THWAKKT
FOR YOUR SAKE IT BETTER... 'CAUSE I'M CONSIDERING MAKING THIS AN ANNUAL EVENT.
SWING BY KANSAS AND "PULL A LOIS" ON MA, AND FINISH OFF PA NEXT YEAR... THEN JIMMY AND PERRY AFTER THAT.
GONNA PRINT UP T-SHIRTS AN' EVERYTHING.

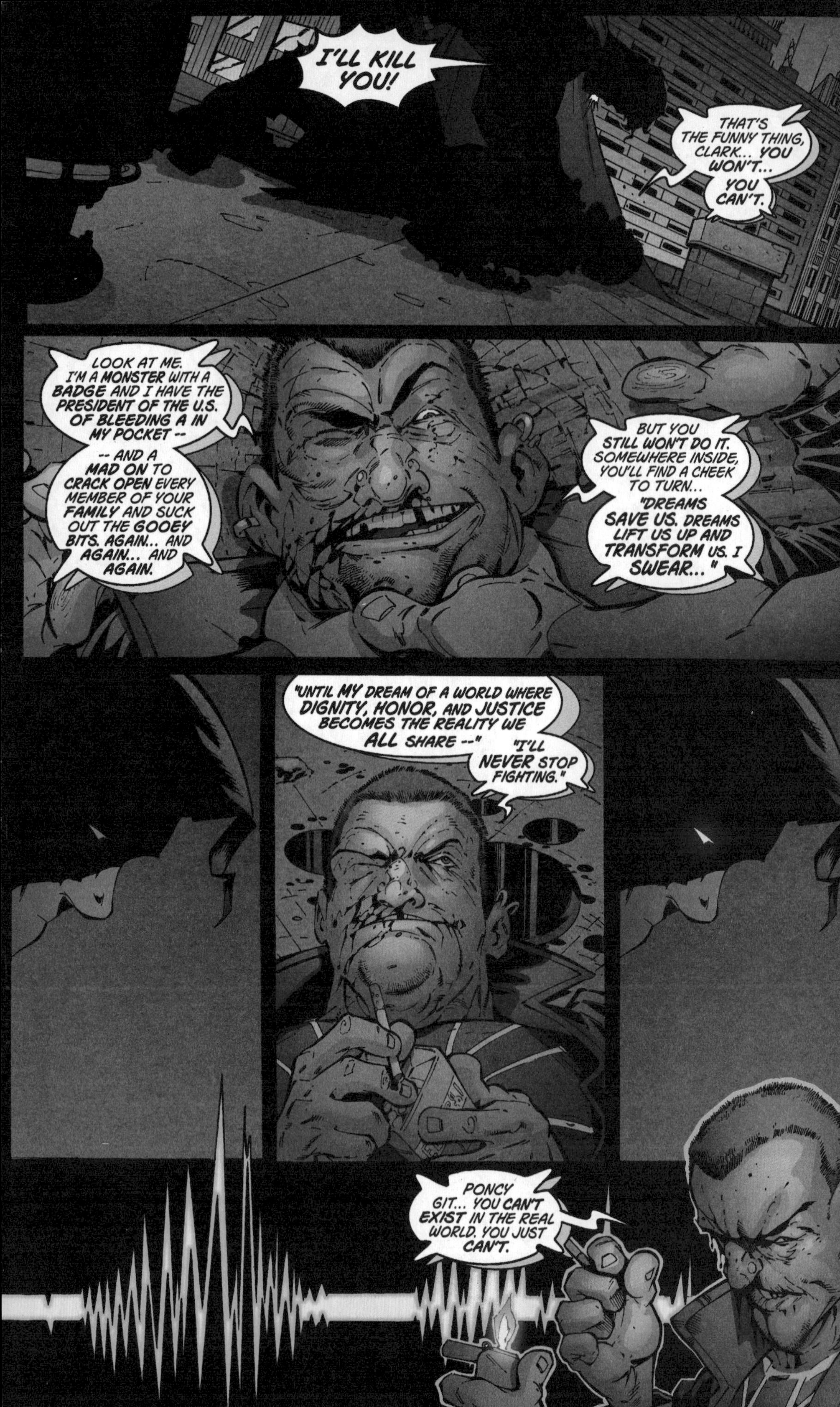
I'LL KILL YOU!
THAT'S THE FUNNY THING, CLARK... YOU WON'T... YOU CAN'T.
LOOK AT ME. I'M A MONSTER WITH A BADGE AND I HAVE THE PRESIDENT OF THE U.S. OF BLEEDING A IN MY POCKET --
-- AND A MAD ON TO CRACK OPEN EVERY MEMBER OF YOUR FAMILY AND SUCK OUT THE GOOEY BITS. AGAIN... AND AGAIN... AND AGAIN.
BUT YOU STILL WON'T DO IT. SOMEWHERE INSIDE, YOU'LL FIND A CHEEK TO TURN...
"DREAMS SAVE US. DREAMS LIFT US UP AND TRANSFORM US. I SWEAR..."
"UNTIL MY DREAM OF A WORLD WHERE DIGNITY, HONOR, AND JUSTICE BECOMES THE REALITY WE ALL SHARE --"
"I'LL NEVER STOP FIGHTING."
PONCY GIT... YOU CAN'T EXIST IN THE REAL WORLD. YOU JUST CAN'T.

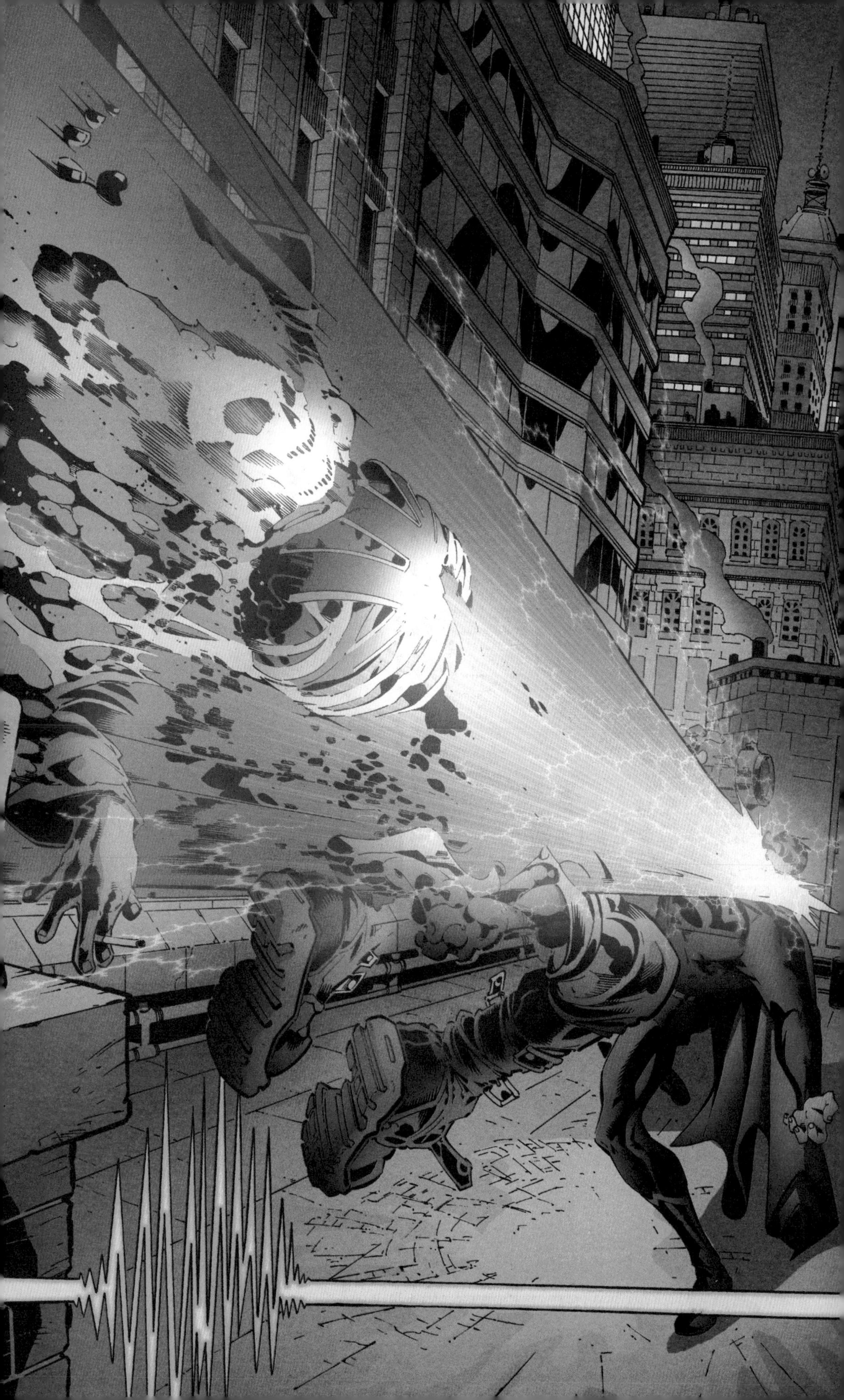

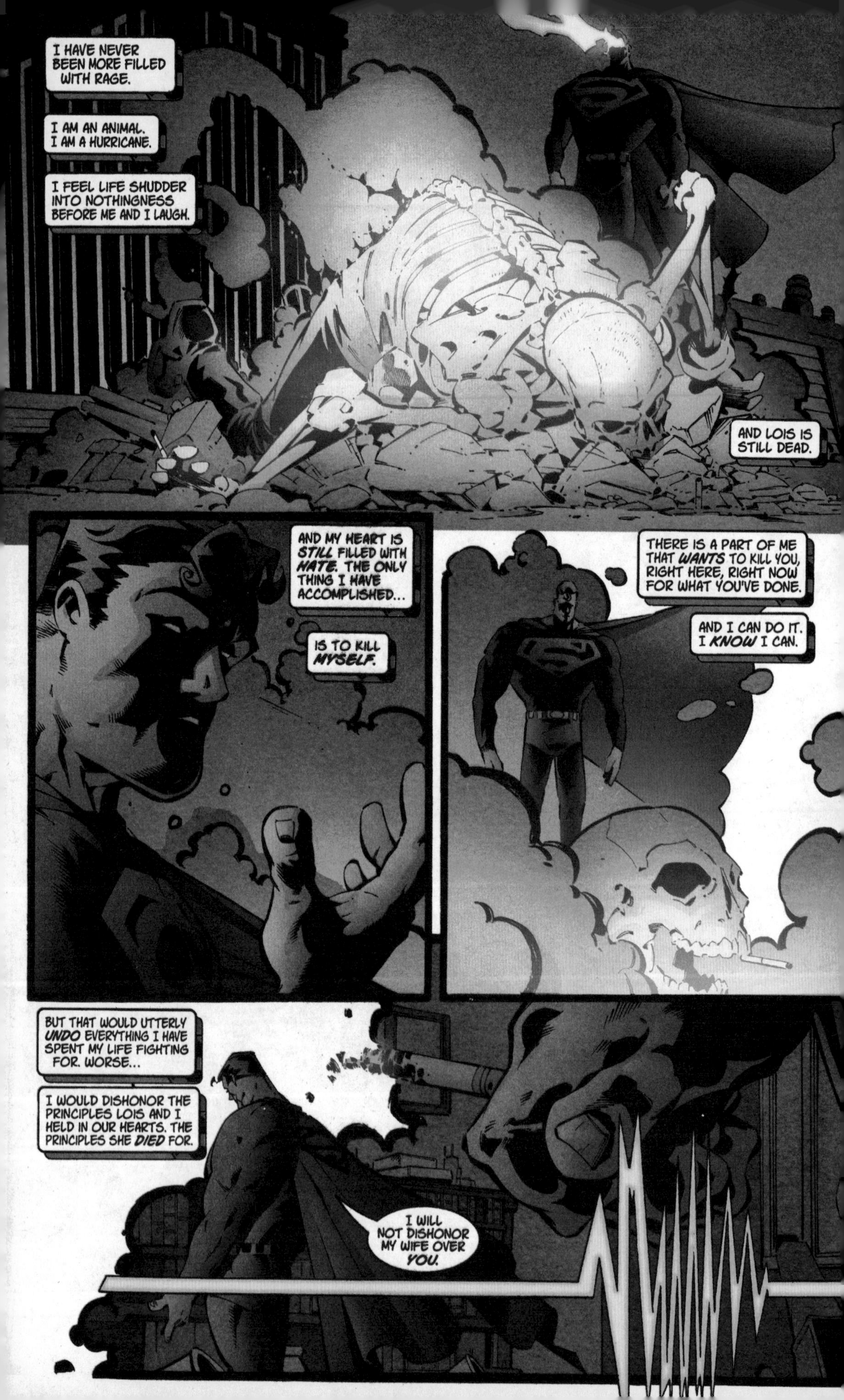
I HAVE NEVER BEEN MORE FILLED WITH RAGE.
I AM AN ANIMAL. I AM A HURRICANE.
I FEEL LIFE SHUDDER INTO NOTHINGNESS BEFORE ME AND I LAUGH.
AND LOIS IS STILL DEAD.
AND MY HEART IS *STILL* FILLED WITH *HATE*. THE ONLY THING I HAVE ACCOMPLISHED...
IS TO KILL *MYSELF*.
THERE IS A PART OF ME THAT *WANTS* TO KILL YOU, RIGHT HERE, RIGHT NOW FOR WHAT YOU'VE DONE.
AND I CAN DO IT. I *KNOW* I CAN.
BUT THAT WOULD UTTERLY *UNDO* EVERYTHING I HAVE SPENT MY LIFE FIGHTING FOR. WORSE...
I WOULD DISHONOR THE PRINCIPLES LOIS AND I HELD IN OUR HEARTS. THE PRINCIPLES SHE *DIED* FOR.
I WILL NOT DISHONOR MY WIFE OVER *YOU*.

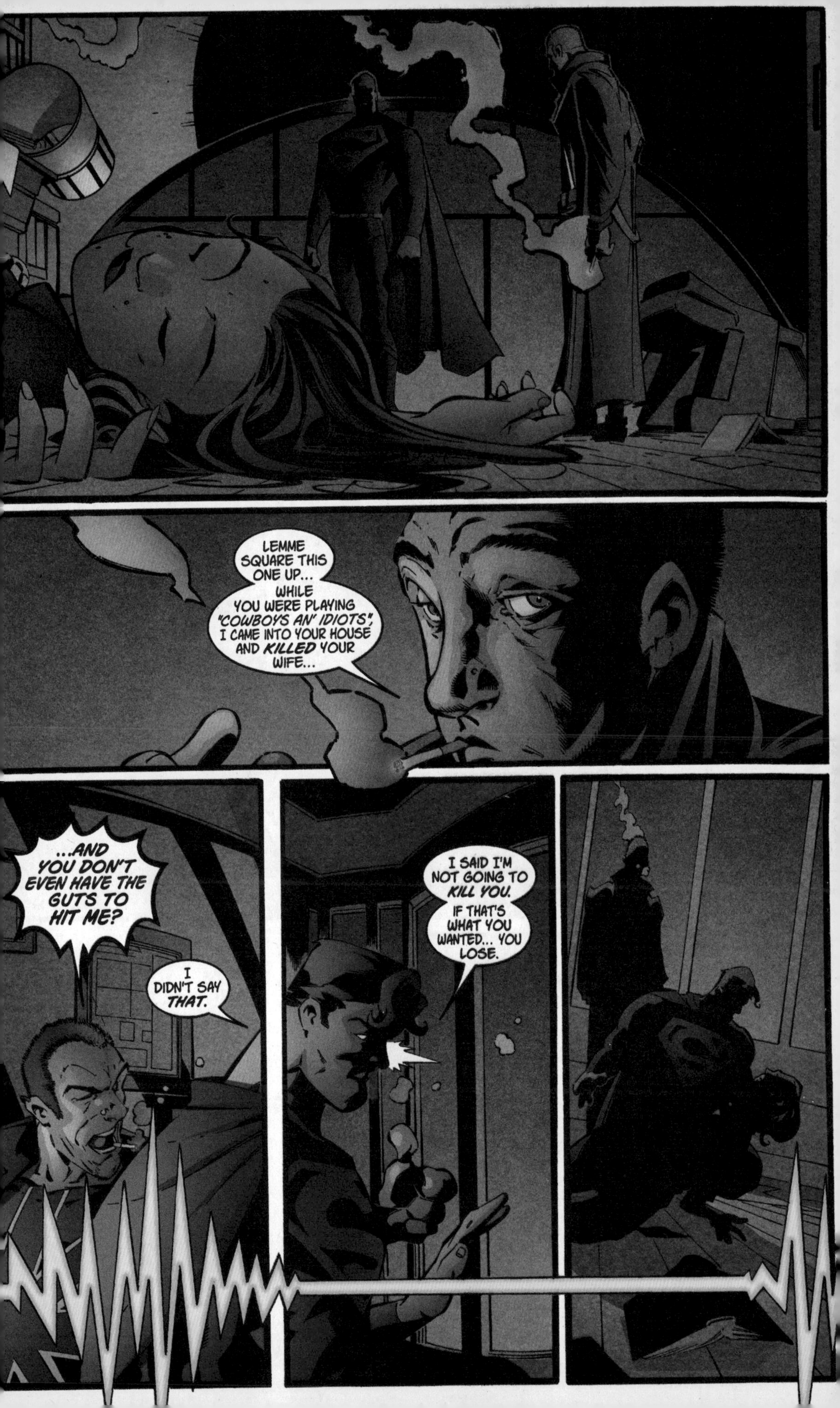
LEMME SQUARE THIS ONE UP... WHILE YOU WERE PLAYING "COWBOYS AN' IDIOTS", I CAME INTO YOUR HOUSE AND KILLED YOUR WIFE...
...AND YOU DON'T EVEN HAVE THE GUTS TO HIT ME?
I DIDN'T SAY THAT.
I SAID I'M NOT GOING TO KILL YOU.
IF THAT'S WHAT YOU WANTED... YOU LOSE.

VENGEANCE IS NOT JUSTICE.

BUT THIS IS? WHAT I DID... WHAT YOU WON'T --?

IT DOESN'T MATTER IF YOU RUN. I'LL FIND YOU WITHIN THE HOUR...

SOON AS I PUT LOIS SOMEWHERE SAFE, IT WILL BECOME MY LIFE'S AMBITION TO ENSURE YOU NEVER TASTE FRESH AIR EVER AGAIN.

...

...YOU'RE THE REAL DEAL, AREN'T YOU? THIS ISN'T A WUSS THING. YOU'RE NOT AFRAID OF ME...

YOU STILL BELIEVE. EVEN AFTER EVERYTHING THAT HAPPENED, YOU'RE GONNA HUNT ME DOWN AN' TOSS ME IN THE CLINK...

BUT YOU WON'T KILL ME. EVER.

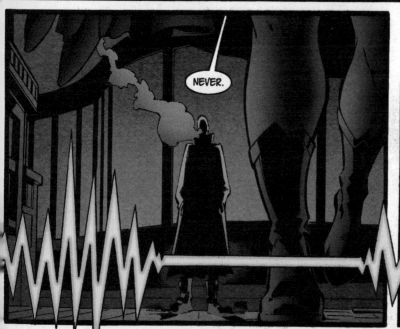

NEVER.

NEVER. THE END.

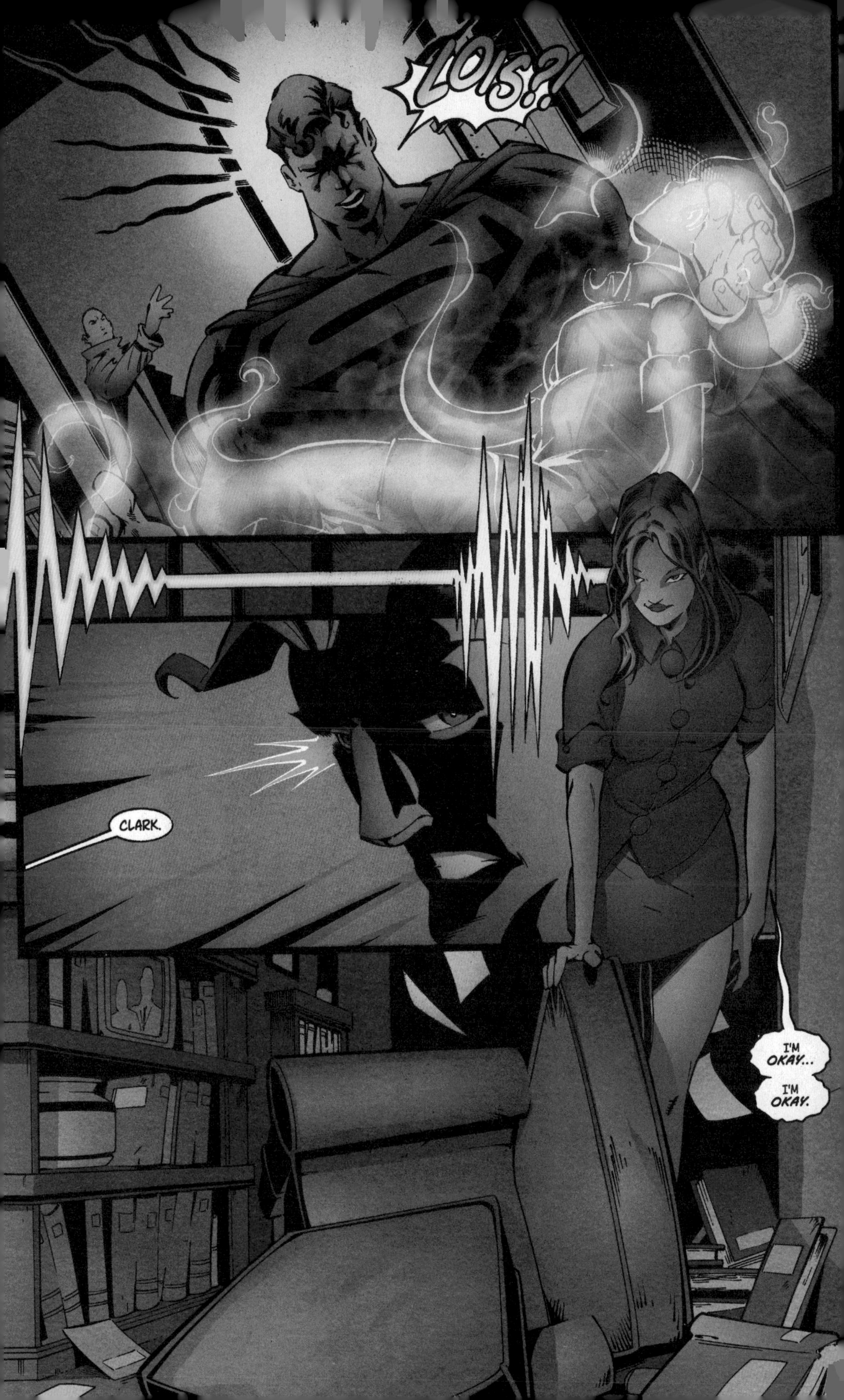
LOIS?!
CLARK.
I'M OKAY...
I'M OKAY.

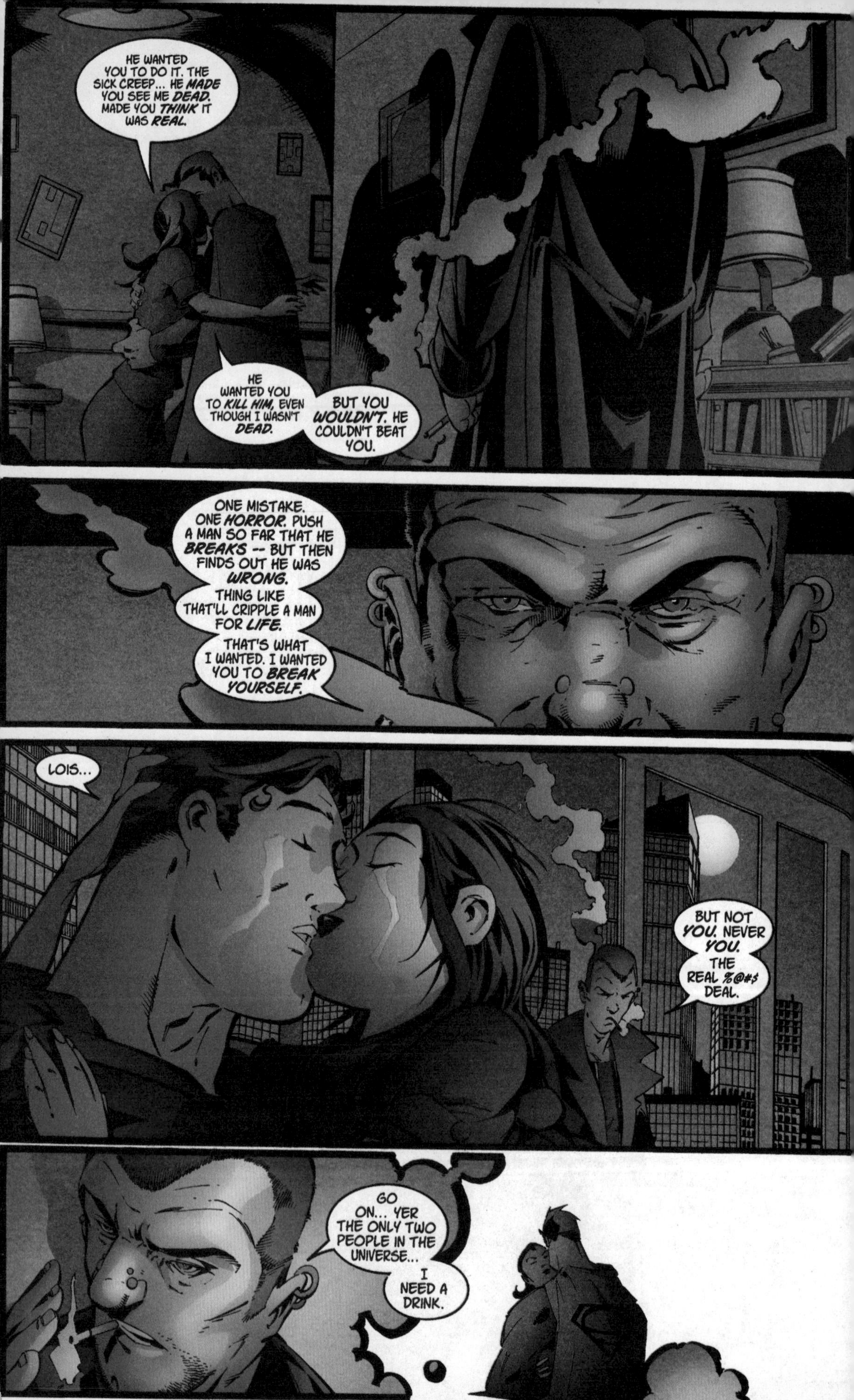
HE WANTED YOU TO DO IT. THE SICK CREEP... HE MADE YOU SEE ME DEAD. MADE YOU THINK IT WAS REAL.
HE WANTED YOU TO KILL HIM, EVEN THOUGH I WASN'T DEAD.
BUT YOU WOULDN'T. HE COULDN'T BEAT YOU.
ONE MISTAKE. ONE HORROR. PUSH A MAN SO FAR THAT HE BREAKS -- BUT THEN FINDS OUT HE WAS WRONG.
THING LIKE THAT'LL CRIPPLE A MAN FOR LIFE.
THAT'S WHAT I WANTED. I WANTED YOU TO BREAK YOURSELF.
LOIS...
BUT NOT YOU. NEVER YOU. THE REAL %@#$ DEAL.
GO ON... YER THE ONLY TWO PEOPLE IN THE UNIVERSE...
I NEED A DRINK.

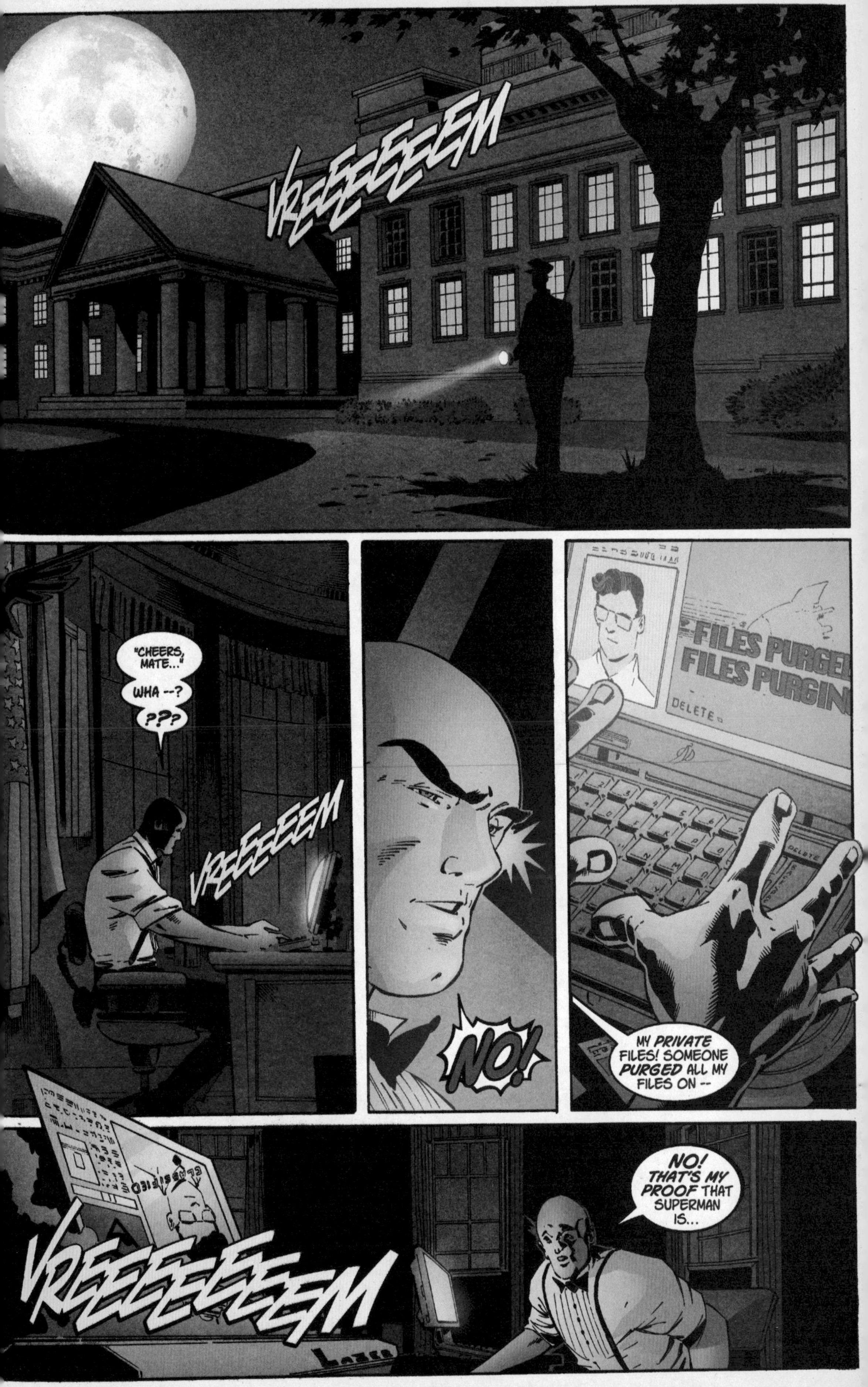
VREEEEEEEM
"CHEERS, MATE..."
WHA --?
???
VREEEEEM
NO!
FILES PURGED
FILES PURGING
DELETE
MY PRIVATE FILES! SOMEONE PURGED ALL MY FILES ON --
VREEEEEEEM
NO! THAT'S MY PROOF THAT SUPERMAN IS...

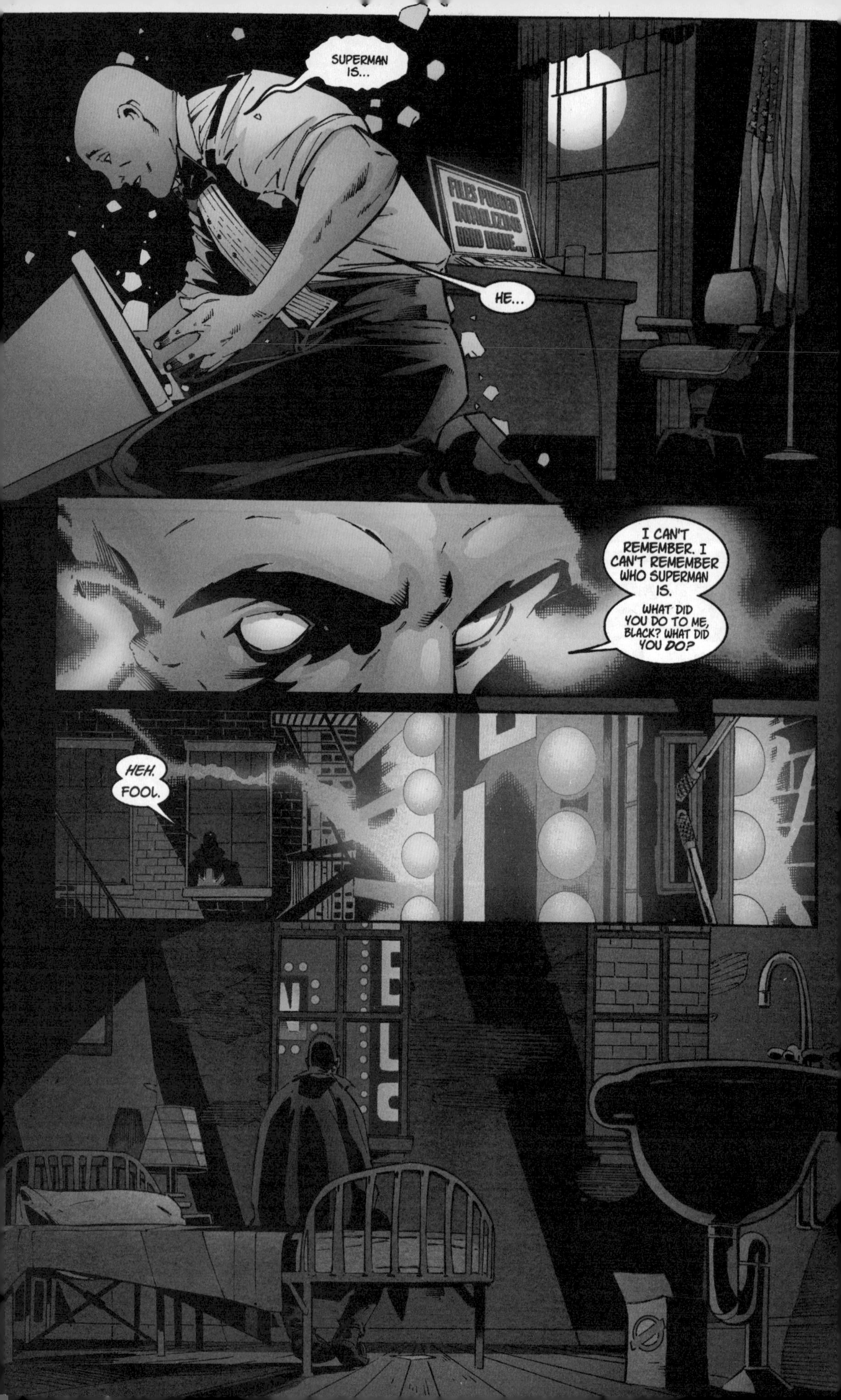
SUPERMAN IS...
FILES PURGED INITIALIZING HARD DRIVE...
HE...
I CAN'T REMEMBER. I CAN'T REMEMBER WHO SUPERMAN IS.
WHAT DID YOU DO TO ME, BLACK? WHAT DID YOU *DO*?
HEH. FOOL.

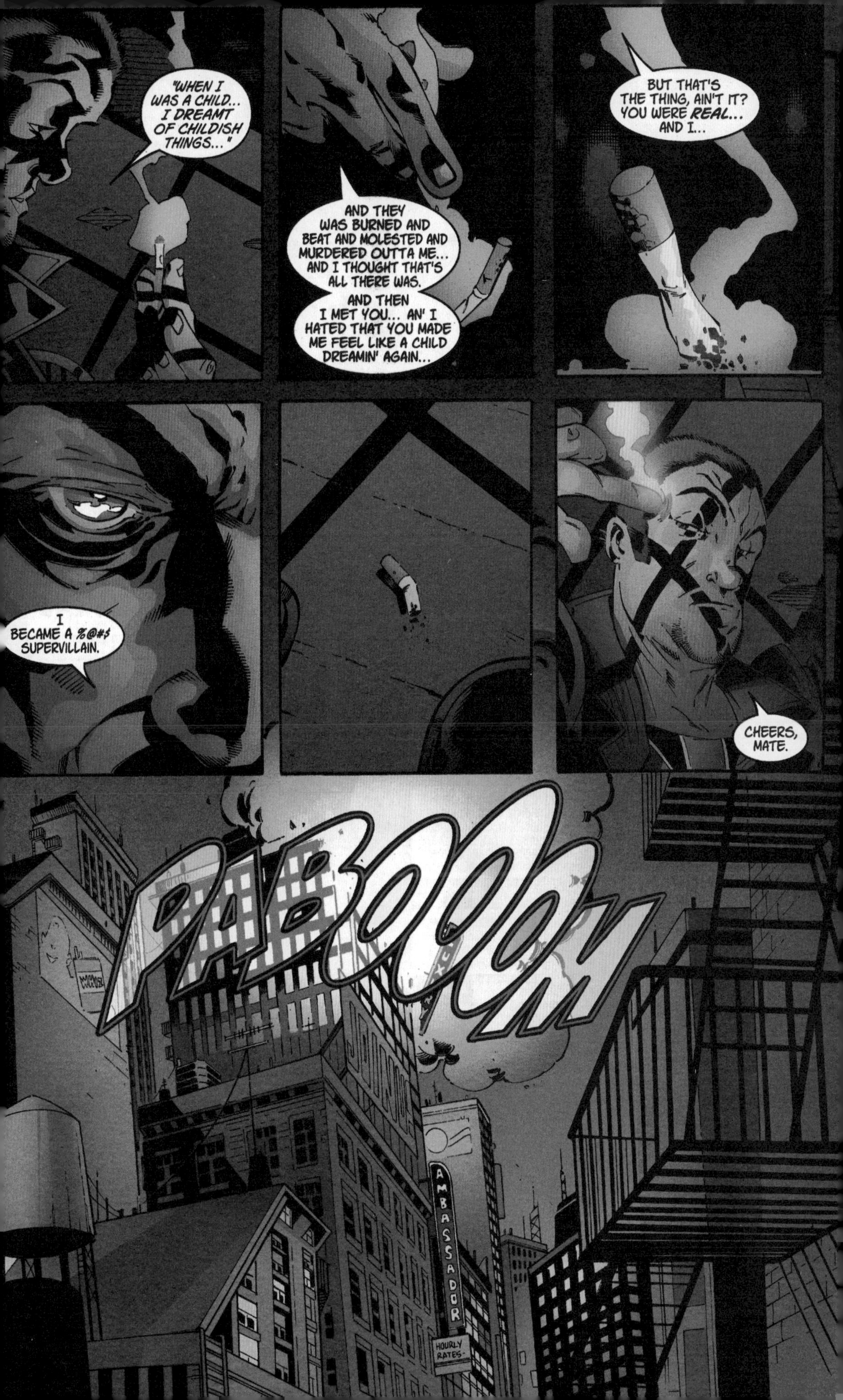
"WHEN I WAS A CHILD... I DREAMT OF CHILDISH THINGS..."
AND THEY WAS BURNED AND BEAT AND MOLESTED AND MURDERED OUTTA ME... AND I THOUGHT THAT'S ALL THERE WAS.
AND THEN I MET YOU... AN' I HATED THAT YOU MADE ME FEEL LIKE A CHILD DREAMIN' AGAIN...
BUT THAT'S THE THING, AIN'T IT? YOU WERE REAL... AND I...
I BECAME A %@#$ SUPERVILLAIN.
CHEERS, MATE.
PABOOOOM
AMBASSADOR
HOURLY RATES

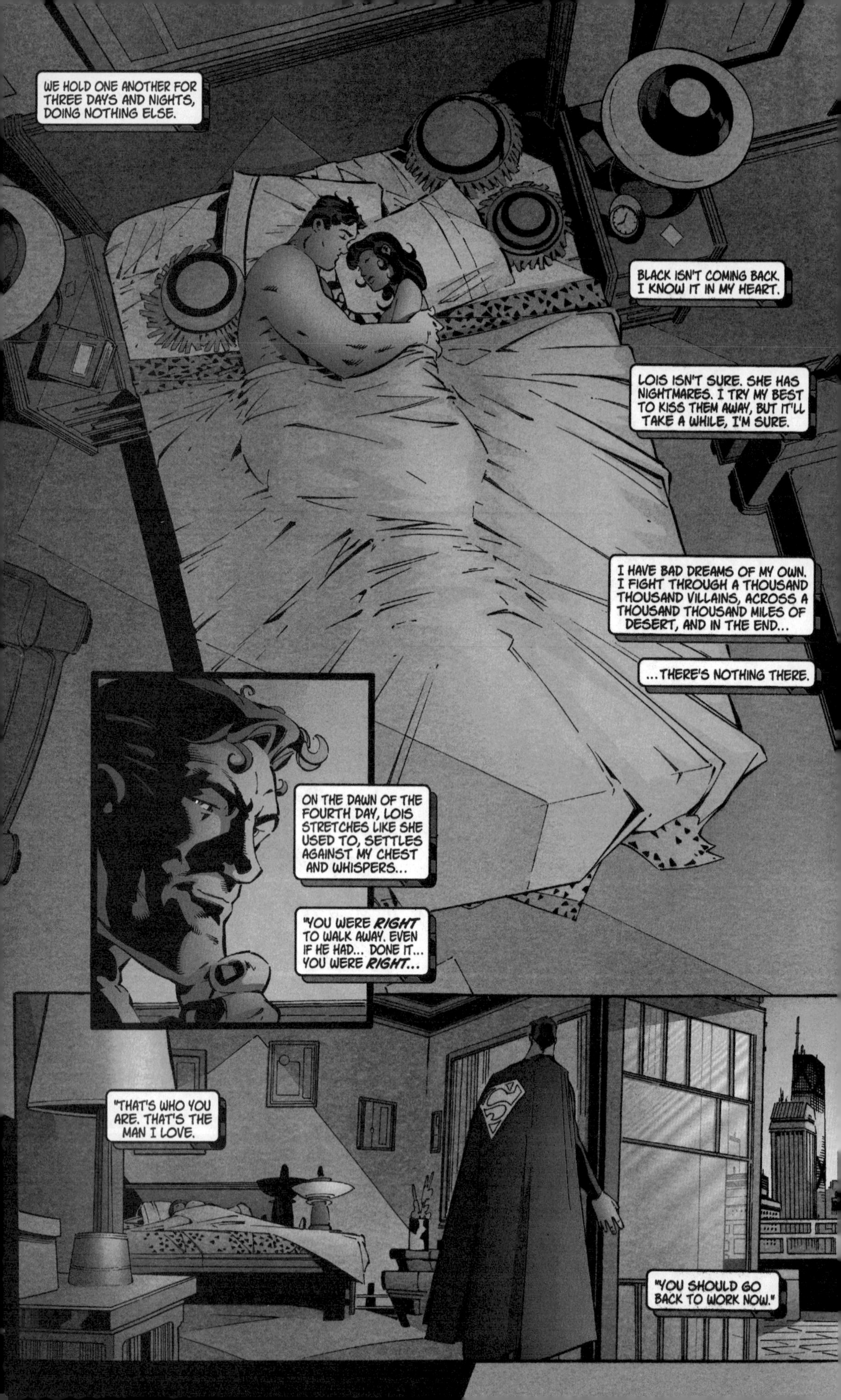
WE HOLD ONE ANOTHER FOR THREE DAYS AND NIGHTS, DOING NOTHING ELSE.
BLACK ISN'T COMING BACK. I KNOW IT IN MY HEART.
LOIS ISN'T SURE. SHE HAS NIGHTMARES. I TRY MY BEST TO KISS THEM AWAY, BUT IT'LL TAKE A WHILE, I'M SURE.
I HAVE BAD DREAMS OF MY OWN. I FIGHT THROUGH A THOUSAND THOUSAND VILLAINS, ACROSS A THOUSAND THOUSAND MILES OF DESERT, AND IN THE END...
...THERE'S NOTHING THERE.
ON THE DAWN OF THE FOURTH DAY, LOIS STRETCHES LIKE SHE USED TO, SETTLES AGAINST MY CHEST AND WHISPERS...
"YOU WERE *RIGHT* TO WALK AWAY. EVEN IF HE HAD... DONE IT... YOU WERE *RIGHT*...
"THAT'S WHO YOU ARE. THAT'S THE MAN I LOVE.
"YOU SHOULD GO BACK TO WORK NOW."

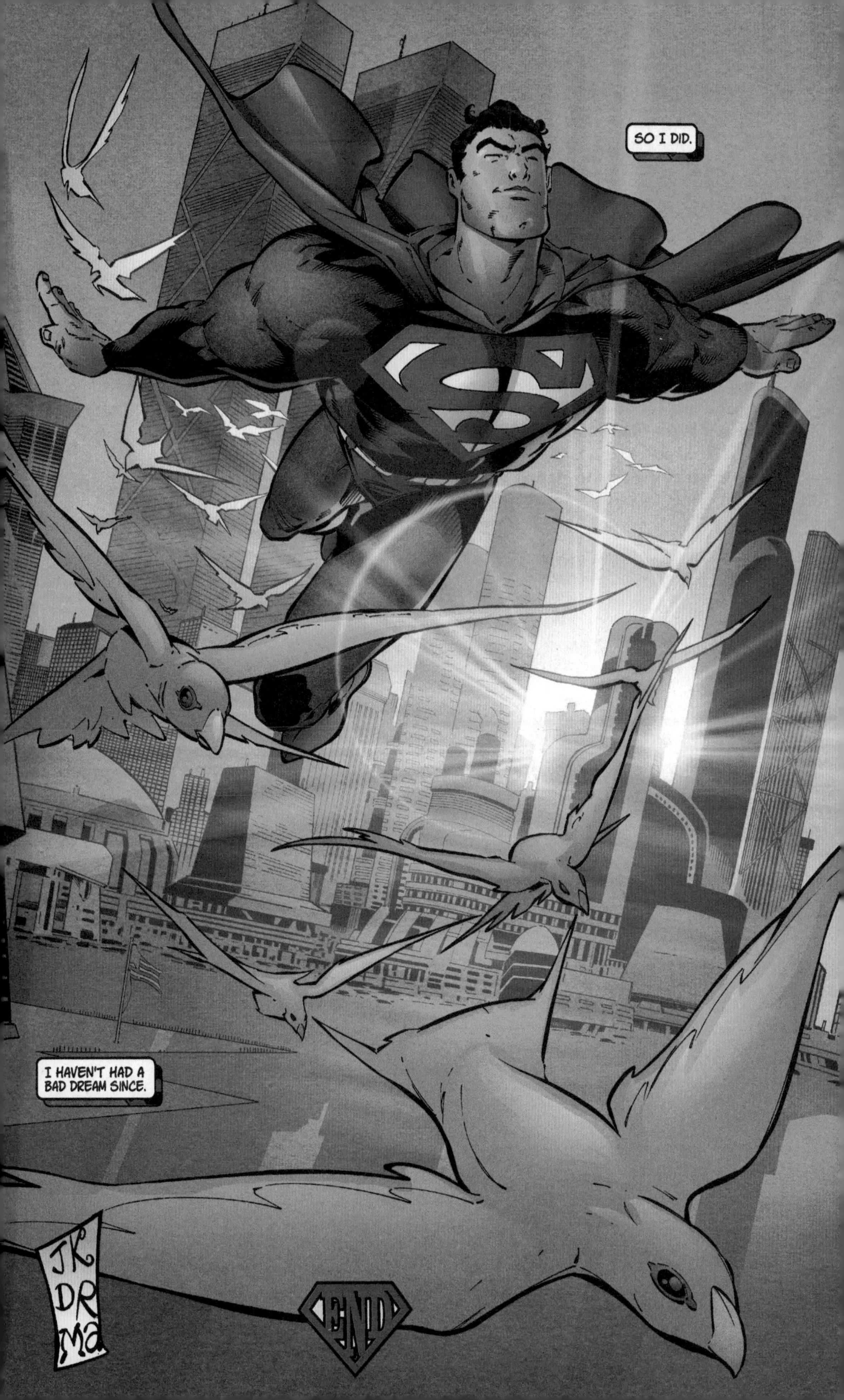
SO I DID.
I HAVEN'T HAD A BAD DREAM SINCE.
JK DR MA
END